Charles Cotesworth Pinckney

Founding Father

The Institute of Early American History and Culture is sponsored jointly by the College of William and Mary and Colonial Williamsburg, Incorporated.

Charles Cotesworth Pinckney

by James Earl. Courtesy of Carolina Art Association, Gibbes Art Gallery,
Charleston, South Carolina

Charles Cotesworth Pinckney

Founding Father

by
Marvin R. Zahniser

Published for the
Institute of Early American History and Culture
at Williamsburg, Virginia
By The University of North Carolina Press • Chapel Hill

To
ALEXANDER DeCONDE
Teacher, Friend

PREFACE

———◆●◆———

WHEN CHARLES COTESWORTH PINCKNEY DIED IN 1825 HIS COUNTRY-
men mourned the passing of another of the nation's founding fathers.
His contemporaries realized that Pinckney lacked Alexander Hamilton's brilliance and energy and that he had few of George Washington's charismatic qualities; yet Americans honored Pinckney as a
founding father because of his important services as a Revolutionary
soldier, constitution maker, diplomat, and statesman.

Historians have not been generous in their evaluation of Pinckney.
While many biographies of his friends Washington and Hamilton
have been written, little of a scholarly nature has been published on
Pinckney. Perhaps historians find it more absorbing to examine the
lives of strikingly successful people.

Even a brief résumé of Pinckney's life reveals that he was not (to
use the terminology of his day) a political character of the first importance. Yet to reconstruct his life gives interesting insights into
problems and events of our late colonial and early national history.
Through Pinckney's career one can follow the developing Revolutionary crisis in South Carolina. Through an examination of his later
role as a state politician it is possible to see why low-country South
Carolinians were anxious to secure a federal constitution that would
impose a system of greater order and unity upon the entire nation.
It is also possible to follow through Pinckney's career the development of the national party system in the south and to see the consequences of that development for the old regime of state politics in
South Carolina. Through Pinckney one can get a glimpse into the
nation's early diplomatic problems as well, and one can watch the
nation struggle to establish a national identity even as Great Britain
and France attempt to make the United States a virtual satellite. And
finally, because Pinckney was a leading member of the southern oligarchy, one can see through his career something of the composition
of that oligarchy, its assumptions about itself and about society, its

aspirations, and its standards of public and private conduct for its leaders.

In preparing the life of Pinckney, I have become a debtor to many people. My great debt to Professor Alexander DeConde of the University of California, Santa Barbara, is acknowledged in the dedication. I wish also to acknowledge the encouragement and helpful criticism given me by the following persons: Professors Wilbur R. Jacobs of the University of California, Santa Barbara, Max Savelle of the University of Washington, Harry L. Coles of Ohio State University, George C. Rogers, Jr., of the University of South Carolina, James Morton Smith of Cornell University, and Stephen G. Kurtz, Editor of Publications, and Miss Marise Rogge, Assistant Editor, of the Institute of Early American History and Culture. To Miss Sara Haden of Los Angeles, California, and Samuel G. Stoney and Mrs. Francis Stewart of Charleston, South Carolina, I am indebted for stimulating discussions about South Carolina society in the early national period.

Parts of Chapter VI were published as "The First Pinckney Mission to France," *South Carolina Historical Magazine*, 66 (1965), 205–17. The magazine's publication committee has kindly consented to use of the article here.

The following have been of great assistance in my search for pertinent materials: the staffs of the library of the University of California, Santa Barbara; The United States Archives; and the Southern Historical Collection of the University of North Carolina. Individual librarians who have shown an unusual appreciation for my problems are: Mrs. Granville T. Prior of the South Carolina Historical Society; Mr. Charles Lee, Director of the State Archives in Columbia, South Carolina; Mr. E. L. Inabinett and Mrs. Clara Mae Jacobs of the South Caroliniana Library, University of South Carolina; Miss Virginia Rugheimer and Mrs. Pringle Haigh of the Charleston Library Society; Miss Mary Isabel Fry of the Henry Huntington Library; and Miss Mattie Russell and Mrs. Virginia Gray of the Duke University Library.

Dr. and Mrs. C. H. Zahniser, my parents, have constantly encouraged me in preparing this study.

My greatest debt of gratitude is to my wife, Adrienne Allen Zahniser, critic, editor, and typist.

MARVIN R. ZAHNISER
The Ohio State University
Columbus, Ohio

CONTENTS

———◆●◆———

Charles Cotesworth Pinckney

Founding Father

I

THE EDUCATION OF A GENTLEMAN

And to the end that my beloved son Charles Cotesworth may the better be enabled to become the head of his family, and prove not only of service and advantage to his country, but also an honour to his stock and kindred, my order and direction is that my said son be virtuously, religiously and liberally brought up so . . . that he will employ all his future abilities in the service of God and his country, in the cause of virtuous liberty, as well religious as civil, and in support of private right and justice between man and man.

—From the will of Charles Pinckney, 1752.

THE SERGEANT AT ARMS OPENED THE DOOR OF THE SOUTH CAROLINA Commons House of Assembly and the newly elected members slowly came forward and arranged themselves before the speaker. According to custom and law, the speaker officially informed the representatives of their election and asked "if they were willing to qualify themselves as Members of the House." With the others, Charles Cotesworth Pinckney unhesitatingly answered that he was. The oath was administered. On December 5, 1769, at the age of twenty-four, Pinckney began his years of public service.[1]

There had evidently been no struggle on Pinckney's part to win his seat. Perhaps, as in George Washington's Virginia, it was necessary to humor some voters with toddy and meats, but Pinckney's

1. Dec. 5, 1769, South Carolina Commons House of Assembly Journals, South Carolina Archives Department, Columbia, S.C. (hereafter cited Commons Journals).

[3]

election so shortly after his arrival from England suggests that little intrigue was needed to carry his election. After all he was a barrister, a planter, a soldier, and more important, a Pinckney. Wealth, education, and social standing were his birthright. People took the participation of the Pinckneys in South Carolina's public affairs for granted. Why should it be different for this particular Pinckney?

For the Pinckneys in South Carolina the tradition of public service was not, in fact, really old. Thomas Pinckney, the first of that name in South Carolina, had arrived only some seventy years before on the British privateer *Loyal Jamaica*. Originally a resident of Bishop Auckland, Durham County, England (just south of Newcastle), Pinckney had lived in the West Indies for a short time. His later entrance into the Charleston merchant class was financed by the profits he amassed as a West Indian privateer. In 1692, the year of his arrival in South Carolina, he courted and married a Charleston girl, Grace Bedon. Grace soon died, but the enterprising Thomas shortly found another maiden to take her place. While in England in 1697 he married Mary Cotesworth, a resident of Bishop Auckland, and returned with her to South Carolina. From this marriage two sons were born, William and Charles, the latter being the father of Charles Cotesworth Pinckney.[2]

The merchant's life was good to Thomas Pinckney. He was able to educate Charles in England for a career in the law. After completing his education, Charles returned to South Carolina to open a law practice which in time established his reputation for both integrity and learning. The legal profession also furnished him with a considerable income. The Pinckney family fortune increased in later years, but it was Charles Pinckney's investments that provided his descendants with plantation homes and wealth in real estate. Charles Pinckney established the Pinckney family in South Carolina, both financially and socially.

Pinckney's interests extended beyond his own professional and financial advancement. A devout Anglican, he was known for his generous gifts of time and money to the church. He was also known for his broad-mindedness and resolute defense of the right of dis-

2. Harriott H. Ravenel, *Eliza Pinckney* (New York, 1902), 71; Mabel L. Webber, comp., "The Thomas Pinckney Family of South Carolina," *South Carolina Historical and Genealogical Magazine*, 39 (1938), 15–16.

senters to be seated in the South Carolina Commons House without taking the prescribed oath on the New Testament. In addition, he supported the cause of Negro education and was a conspicuous contributor to the building of a schoolhouse where Negroes were taught reading and religion for several years.[3]

In the best tradition of the planter class Charles Pinckney freely gave his talents and time to public service. He became an active member of the Commons House and a spirited defender of its privileges. In 1735 he chaired the committee appointed by the Commons House to assert its exclusive right to draft money bills. The resolutions reported by Pinckney stoutly rejected any pretensions of the royal Council to alter or amend money measures and asserted that the powers of the Commons House were as great as those of Parliament. Pinckney's defense of the Commons' powers led to his election as speaker in 1736, a position he held intermittently for four years. In 1750 the Crown recognized Pinckney's talents and political stature by appointing him a member of the royal Council of South Carolina.[4] In this position he was an advisor to the governor, a legislator of the province, and a judge in the Court of Chancery.

An experience with the royal government tarnished the honor of this appointment and angered Pinckney and his friends. Governor James Glen appointed Pinckney interim chief justice of South Carolina in 1752 to replace the deceased James Graeme. The royal mandamus confirming Pinckney's appointment never came.

Instead, Peter Leigh, the former high bailiff of Westminster, who had come under fire for supposed electoral corruption, received the appointment. Leigh's enemies accused him of using his official position to falsify a hotly contested Westminster election in favor of the

3. David D. Wallace, *South Carolina: A Short History, 1520–1948* (Columbia, S.C., 1961), 120–21; Edward McCrady, *The History of South Carolina Under the Royal Government, 1719–1776* (N.Y., 1899), 245–47.

4. Ravenel, *Eliza Pinckney*, 87; Charleston *South-Carolina and American General Gazette*, July 14, 1768 (hereafter cited *S. C. Gazette*); McCrady, *History, 1719–1776*, 172–76, 802, 804. A good analysis of the procedures followed in selecting Council members is found in M. Eugene Sirmans, "The South Carolina Royal Council, 1720–1763," *William and Mary Quarterly*, 3rd Ser., 18 (1961), 373–92. Sirmans states that Charles Pinckney was a protégé of William Bull, Sr., a member of one of the colony's two power centers which largely controlled appointments to the Council, 388. Other aspects of Pinckney's political career are touched upon in M. Eugene Sirmans, *Colonial South Carolina: A Political History, 1663–1763* (Chapel Hill, N.C., 1966).

ministerial candidate. Although the election took place in 1749, the friends of the losing candidate continued to persecute Leigh, taking their case against him into the House of Commons. While the charges of corruption and dishonesty were never proved, the government thought it prudent to conciliate the opposition. The problem of doing justice to Leigh was solved when the ministry learned of the vacant chief justiceship in South Carolina. Leigh arrived in South Carolina with the mandamus and replaced Pinckney who had served only a few months.[5]

The stir this episode caused in the Pinckney household and among all ambitious colonial Carolinians can well be imagined. If Pinckney was unable to secure a high position from the government, they asked, what chance had other Carolinians to be honored by the Crown? Even English placemen with questionable records were evidently to be preferred before colonials of the highest character.[6] It was a hard blow to Pinckney. The highest office he could ever hope to attain had been snatched from him by an unsympathetic and poorly advised government.

The woman who shared Charles Pinckney's mortification was Elizabeth Lucas, his second wife and the mother of Charles Cotesworth. Called Eliza by her friends, she had come to South Carolina from the West Indian island of Antigua late in the 1730's with her father George Lucas, an officer in the English army. Intending to settle in South Carolina he bought a plantation there, but he was suddenly called back to duty and appointed governor of Antigua. Mrs. Lucas was in poor health, so young Eliza shouldered the responsibility of running her father's plantation.[7]

Eliza not only ran the plantation efficiently but found time to experiment with raising indigo as well. Earlier attempts to grow indigo

5. H. H. Bellot, "The Leighs in South Carolina," Royal Historical Society, *Transactions*, 5th Ser., 6 (1956), 166–70; Peter Manigault to Gabriel Manigault, Aug. 25, 1753, Mabel L. Webber, ed., "Peter Manigault's Letters," *S. C. Hist. and Gen. Mag.*, 32 (1931), 187–88.

6. Charles Cotesworth Pinckney was old enough to share his father's distress. The whole affair, he wrote in 1819, "carries me near to my first recollection." He was seven at the time. See Charles Cotesworth Pinckney to ?, Sept. 1819, in Harriott H. (Mrs. St. Julian) Ravenel, *Charleston: The Place and the People* (N.Y., 1925), 146.

7. Eliza Pinckney to Mrs. Boddicott, May 2, 1740, Eliza Pinckney to Lady [Mrs. Nicholas] Carew, Sept. 2, 1743, Harriott Pinckney Holbrook, ed., *The Journal and Letters of Eliza Lucas* (Wormsloe, Ga., 1850), 6, 24.

in South Carolina had failed, but the depressed rice prices of the early 1740's stimulated local interest in searching for another money crop which might grow easily on the Carolina land. Just at this time Colonel Lucas instructed Eliza to plant indigo he had forwarded from the West Indies. Frost and storms ruined her first two efforts, but she persisted and on the third attempt met with limited success. The community took a keen interest in the project, especially after Eliza's neighbor and fellow experimenter, Andrew De Veaux, successfully grew several crops. Other planters quickly followed the lead of De Veaux and Miss Lucas. Within ten years the province was exporting over 216,000 pounds of indigo annually, a figure that quadrupled in another twenty years.[8] This was Eliza's first contribution to her adopted South Carolina and in its own way was as important to that colony as the contributions of her future husband, Charles Pinckney.

Even before her indigo experiments, Eliza had become acquainted in the higher social circles in Charleston. She seemed particularly happy to form a close friendship with Elizabeth Pinckney, the wife of her future husband. Mrs. Pinckney, Eliza wrote to a friend in 1740, was "always pleased" to see her and insisted the Pinckney house was Eliza's "home when [she was] in town. . . ."[9] Eliza was glad to accept Mrs. Pinckney's invitations, and soon an active correspondence developed between Mrs. Pinckney and Eliza. Even Charles Pinckney took time from his private and official duties to exchange medical advice or community news with this witty and charming girl. Eliza, on her part, was solicitous of Pinckney's health and seemed eager to please him, reading books he suggested and taking medicines he recommended in preference to those prescribed by her doctor.[10]

This friendship did not go unnoticed. When Charles Pinckney's first wife died in January of 1744 and he married Eliza within four months, one suspicious woman hinted that the first Mrs. Pinckney had been deliberately denied necessary care on her deathbed. Eliza

8. Eliza Pinckney to [Charles Cotesworth Pinckney], Sept. 10, 1785, Pinckney Papers, Charleston Library Society; David Ramsay, *The History of South-Carolina, 1670–1808*, 2 vols. (Charleston, 1809), II, 119; Ravenel, *Eliza Pinckney*, 7–9.

9. Eliza Pinckney to Mrs. Boddicott, May 2, 1740, Holbrook, ed., *Journal of Eliza Lucas*, 6.

10. See Miss Lucas's letters to her friend Miss Bartlett, n.d., and to Mr. Pinckney, Feb. 6, 1741, Ravenel, *Eliza Pinckney*, 28–30.

was properly indignant when she heard the rumor. She denounced the gossip, a Mrs. Gregory, as one possessed of "an envious malicious temper or a tatling gossiping one[.] I would charitably hope the latter. . . ."[11] Mrs. Gregory was probably not the only woman who seemingly envied Eliza's good fortune.

Despite their age difference of twenty-four years, the Pinckneys' marriage was a happy one. They lived at Belmont, Pinckney's plantation home about five miles north of Charleston. While Pinckney attended to his legal practice and plantation duties, his wife passed her time by beautifying Belmont, looking after her father's plantation, and trying to please her husband "even in triffles."[12]

The Pinckneys' happiness deepened when a son, Charles Cotesworth, was born in his father's Charleston East Bay "Mansion House" on February 14, 1745. Eliza soon described him as "a fine little boy" with "black Eyes" and even though he was only three months old, was hopeful that she could detect "all his papas virtues already dawning on him. . . ."[13] While the infant was gaining strength at the breasts of domestic slaves, his father and mother were studying the most modern methods to help Charles Cotesworth "play himself into learning." Charles Pinckney also worked diligently to build a set of toys that could help teach Charles Cotesworth his letters by the time he could speak. Pinckney was successful; his son recognized letters before he could pronounce them and began to spell before he was two years old.[14] This boy was going to have every advantage devoted parents and a family fortune could give him.

The Pinckneys soon added two new members to their family,[15]

11. Eliza Pinckney to Miss Bartlett [ca. Mar. 1745], Elizabeth Pinckney Papers, Duke University Library, Durham, N.C.

12. Eliza Pinckney to Gov. George Lucas [ca. 1745], Ravenel, *Eliza Pinckney*, 100.

13. Alexander S. Salley, Jr., ed., *Register of St. Philips Parish, Charles Town, 1720–1758* (Charleston, 1904), 89; Eliza Pinckney to Miss Bartlett [ca. May 1746], Elizabeth Pinckney Papers, Duke Univ. Lib.

14. Ravenel, *Eliza Pinckney*, 113; William Gilmore Simms, "A Memoir of the Pinckney Family of South Carolina," in *Dawson's Historical Magazine*, 2nd Ser., 1 (1867), 135; Eliza Pinckney to Mary Lucas [ca. Oct. 1747], Elizabeth Pinckney Papers, Duke Univ. Lib.

15. One son died in 1747 after living only 15 days. His name was George Lucas. Eliza Pinckney to Miss Bartlett, Dec. 2, 1747, Eliza Pinckney Letters, Duke Univ. Lib.; Salley, ed., *Register of St. Philips Parish*, I, 92, 139, 206.

Harriott in 1748 and Thomas in 1750. Like their older brother, they were given many opportunities to develop rapidly, both intellectually and spiritually. Their parents were devout Christians and regular attendants at divine worship. Mrs. Pinckney, one granddaughter later recalled, although unable to carry a tune loved many hymns and was particularly fond of Joseph Addison's:

> When all thy mercies, O my God
> My rising soul surveys,
> Transported with the view, I'm lost
> In wonder, love and praise.

The children were required at an early age to listen for the sermon text and to find it in the Bible as soon as they returned home from service. They were also expected to memorize the collect for the day, a task that seemed truly formidable to them.[16] This early religious training had a profound impact on the Pinckney children, perhaps more on Charles Cotesworth than on his brother and sister. In later life his piety never seemed labored but arose spontaneously from a mind and heart trained from childhood to love Christ and the church.

While the Pinckneys could give their children religious instruction, Charles Pinckney decided that he could not provide his boys with the proper academic and professional training in the colonies. The boys must be taken to England. Pinckney knew his wife would be pleased by this plan. Eliza had been hoping for a trip to England for seven years; she liked Carolina, but England was still "home."[17] Shortly after his disappointment over the chief justiceship, Charles Pinckney decided there was now no reason why he could not leave Carolina at once. After packing and preparing for their financial support in England, the Pinckneys sailed early in April 1753 aboard

16. Maria Henrietta Pinckney, *A Notice of the Pinckneys* (Charleston, 1860), 7–8.

17. Shortly after she was married, Eliza wrote to a friend explaining her sudden marriage: "I flatter myself if you knew the Character and merrit of the gentleman I have made choice of . . . you would think it less strange especially as it was with the approbation of my friends. Mr. Pinckney intends to bring me to England in a year or two. . . ." To Lady Carew, Jan. 11, 1744 [1745, by internal evidence], Holbrook, ed., *Journal of Eliza Lucas*, 24.

the *Edinburgh*. With them were William Henry Drayton, a future Revolutionary firebrand, his brother Charles, and a lad named Stoutenbrugh, all to be placed in school.[18]

The Pinckneys settled first at Richmond but later bought a home near Ripley, in Surrey, so that Pinckney could be within commuting distance of London and still enjoy this garden spot of England. Pinckney became homesick for South Carolina almost at once and began to talk about returning. But two things kept him in England for nearly five years: his boys and the desire of his wife to remain.[19] When war with France seemed to threaten ruin for South Carolina, Pinckney decided to cut his ties with Carolina. He would return to Carolina, dispose of his investments, and then take up permanent residence in England.[20] Eliza must have been very pleased.

The elder Pinckneys and Harriott left England in March of 1758 and arrived in Charleston on May 19. Late in June, Pinckney was gripped with a fever, lingered for three weeks, and died on July 12.[21] Eliza was heartbroken. She wanted to rejoin her boys in England but found herself compelled to stay in Carolina to manage her late husband's investments.[22]

18. Mr. Pinckney carefully wrote out a "Rent Roll of the Estate of Charles Pinckney In South Carolina the 24th day of January-A.D. 1753. For raising Funds . . . for the Support of myself and my Family in England." This rent roll is in the Benjamin Huger Rutledge Papers, South Carolina Historical Society, Charleston. Mr. Pinckney believed his rents should total over £682 per year. The departure of the Pinckneys was noted in the Charleston *S. C. Gazette*, Apr. 11, 1753. See also Charles C. Pinckney to ?, Sept. 1819, Ravenel, *Charleston*, 148.

19. Peter Manigault to Mrs. [Gabriel] Manigault, June 24, 1753, Webber, ed., "Peter Manigault's Letters," *S. C. Hist. and Gen. Mag.*, 32 (1931), 179. Peter found Mrs. Pinckney "a mighty good Sort of a Lady, though with all her Virtues she is a little addicted to Scandal. . . ." To his mother, Mar. 29, 1753, *S. C. Hist. and Gen. Mag.*, 33 (1932), 57.

20. Eliza Pinckney to Lady Carew [*ca.* Mar. 1758], Letterbook of Eliza Pinckney, S.C. Hist. Soc.

21. Eliza Pinckney to Mrs. George Lucas, Sept. 25, 1758, Eliza Pinckney Letterbook, S.C. Hist. Soc. In the Charleston, *S. C. Gazette* of Friday, July 14, 1758, this item appeared: "On Wednesday morning died (lately returned from *England* in a bad State of Health) the Honourable CHARLES PINCKNEY, Esq: one of the Members of His Majesty's Council; a Gentleman so well known and esteemed in this Province, for his distinguished Abilities, Integrity, Benevolence, and Public Spirit, that we can truly say his Loss is universally regretted."

22. Charles Pinckney's will, "South Carolina Gleanings in England," *S. C. Hist. and Gen. Mag.*, 8 (1907), 217–19. Charles Cotesworth Pinckney was left two homes in Charleston, two plantations, and odd pieces of land. Mrs. Pinckney was instructed to give Charles Cotesworth the Pinckney home in Surrey when

Charles Cotesworth and Thomas were never allowed to forget the example of their father, his high hopes and love for them, and the conduct that he would now expect from them. When Eliza wrote them of their father's death, she exhorted them to remember:

He has set you a great and good example, may the Lord enable you both to follow it, and may God almighty fulfill all your pius father's prayers upon both your heads; they were almost incessant for blessings both spiritual and temporal upon you both. . . . His affection for you was as great as ever was upon Earth, and you were good children and deserved it; he thought you so, he blessed and thanked God for you and had most comfortable hopes of you— . . . God Almighty bless guide and protect you, make you his own children, and worthy such a father as yours was. . . .[23]

Gradually, the mantle of his father settled upon the shoulders of Charles Cotesworth. Four years after his father's death his mother reminded young Charles that "you must know the welfare of a whole family depends in a great measure on the progress you make in morral Virtue, Religion and Learning. . . ." She further urged him to fortify himself "against those Errors into which you are most easily led by propensity. What I most fear for you is heat of temper. . . ."[24]

Hopefully, Charles Cotesworth was learning both the academic disciplines and the discipline of himself at an academy in Camberwell, run by a Mr. Gerrard. Both Charles Cotesworth and Thomas had been placed in the academy when their parents left England. Charles Cotesworth liked the academy and became attached to Gerrard, but the boys had to move in 1760. Thomas seemed to be sickly at the school, and Mrs. Pinckney's friends advised her that the air at Camberwell was the cause.[25]

The boys then attended another private school in Kensington Borough, London, run by a Mr. Longmore. Charles Cotesworth seemed to sink no roots there; it was nearly time for him to enter a public school where he would prepare himself for the university. His first

he reached the age of 21. He was also to be given family land in Durham and York. Mrs. Pinckney's desire to return at once to England is seen in her letter to Mrs. [Wilhelmina] King, May [1759], Letterbook of Eliza Pinckney, S.C. Hist. Soc.

23. Eliza Pinckney "To my dear Children, Charles and Thomas Pinckney," Aug. 1758, quoted in Ravenel, *Eliza Pinckney*, 170–71.

24. Eliza Pinckney to Charles Cotesworth Pinckney, Apr. 1758, *ibid.*, 211.

25. Eliza Pinckney to "My dear Children" [*ca.* Aug. 1760], Eliza Pinckney Letterbook, S.C. Hist. Soc.

preference, he wrote his mother, was Warrington, where his friend Thomas Evance was going. Another school he suggested was Harrow. Eliza vetoed both. Warrington, she replied, was a school "to fitt young Gentlemen for the Ministry, and as you are not to be brought up to the Church, it will not do for you." As for Harrow, it could "hardly be called a publick school, and as Doctor Thackeray is dead I don't think of that. . . ." Her choice was Westminster School and despite her son's next letter suggesting the Charter House, an institution that claimed John Wesley and Sir William Blackstone among its alumni, young Charles went to Westminster.[26]

Before admission to Westminster, Pinckney was no doubt routinely interviewed by the headmaster, Dr. William Markham, and by two other doctors of divinity, a truly "awful meeting" if Jeremy Bentham is to be believed.[27] Bentham remembered as well that Westminster School was a "wretched place for instruction," where a "great reputation . . . was compatible with worthlessness." Teachers were often "perfect sinecurists," distinguished "for some one or other trifle which was valueless."[28]

Dr. Markham, Bentham recalled, was the school's "great glory." Tall, portly, and pretentious, Markham was a serious scholar of the classics. The boys stood "prodigiously in awe" of Markham, particularly when he "lifted his hand, waved it, and repeated his Latin verses." Bentham believed that Markham's major occupation was not teaching, however, but "courting the great. . . ." Markham too often abandoned his pedagogic duties to cultivate his talents as a sycophant.[29]

Pinckney was undoubtedly as much in awe of Dr. Markham as his fellow students were. Even though Pinckney did not board in the school, he quickly impressed Dr. Markham as a person of sterling

26. Eliza Pinckney to Mr. Longmore, Aug. 31, 1760, Eliza Pinckney Letterbook, S.C. Hist. Soc.; Eliza Pinckney to Charles Cotesworth Pinckney, Feb. 1761, Ravenel, *Eliza Pinckney*, 209–10.

27. John Bowring, ed., *The Works of Jeremy Bentham*, 11 vols. (Edinburgh, 1843), X, 27. The exact date of Pinckney's admission cannot be determined since the admissions book during Dr. Markham's head mastership is missing. See G. F. Barker and Alan H. Stenning, comps., *The Record of Old Westminsters . . .*, 2 vols. (London, 1928), I, v.

28. Bowring, ed., *Works of Bentham*, X, 30–31.

29. *Ibid.*, 30.

character. In a school dispute where contradictory evidence had been presented, Dr. Markham supposedly turned to Pinckney and said, "I know the strictness of your principles, and your attachment to *truth*. Speak, Pinckney. My decision shall be guided by your senti-ment."[30] Certainly Pinckney's character at a later time makes the story entirely believable.

Pinckney's reactions to Markham and to Westminster were gen-erally favorable. Of course, he entered school as a young man almost full grown, and therefore escaped the humiliations of the fagging system, a "horrid despotism," Bentham remembered, by which the small boys were bullied by their seniors.[31] Pinckney was impressed by the regularity and strenuousness of the routine. The boys spent between eight and nine hours in school; every day was a school day with Thursday and Saturday afternoons off. But even on Saturdays there were Bible lessons to be prepared and "exercises to be done out of school and shown up on Monday morning."

Each boy advanced through the various "forms" or grades accord-ing to maturity in translating the works of Phaedrus, Martial, Ovid, Homer, and Virgil, or as his skill improved in scanning and writing Latin verses. The higher the form, the more the student worked with Latin and Greek. In the highest form, the seventh, the students began to translate some of the Psalms and acquired the rudiments of Hebrew. Pinckney recalled that when in the "Shell," between the fifth and sixth forms, he translated what he described as the "Cas-tilinarian War" as part of his supplementary study program.

The educational curriculum at Westminster, then, was entirely a classical one. Pinckney later reminisced that he was educated in two areas, the classics and religion. One could not go through West-minster, he believed, "without being a fair Latin and Greek scholar and being able to assign a reason for the faith that is in you."[32]

But Pinckney was learning more than the prescribed skills of the curriculum. He was gaining insights into the tone of British society

30. Alexander Garden, *Eulogy on General C. C. Pinckney, President-General of the Society of the Cincinnati* (Charleston, 1825), 11. Garden also attended Westminster, though at a later date than Pinckney.

31. Bowring, ed., *Works of Bentham*, X, 31.

32. Pinckney to ?, Sept. 1819, Ravenel, *Charleston*, 149–51.

and the feelings of the British ruling classes toward America. After all, he was mixing with the sons of England's elite.[33] In public schools like Westminster, there was a mingling of the aristocracies of the Old and New Worlds. The sons of England's best families would easily reflect the attitudes of their parents that these colonial "aristocrats" were upstarts, mere *nouveaux riches*. Surely Pinckney was stung by the snubs or barbs reserved for "colonials" even from friends. Perhaps this would help to explain why Pinckney and nearly every other South Carolinian educated in England did not identify with England, why, despite a residence there of sixteen years, Pinckney still thought of himself as an American. To an intelligent and proud colonial like Pinckney, every slight from the English wellborn would have had a cutting edge.

Pinckney showed his continuing self-identification as an American when the Stamp Act was passed in 1765, levying a direct tax upon America, the first of its kind and one bitterly resented by many Americans. The fact that Pinckney had a portrait painted of himself vehemently declaiming against the act is evidence enough of his feelings. His brother Thomas had the same reaction to the British regulation. Thomas, five years younger than Charles, soon joined a group of Americans being drilled in military techniques by a sergeant of the Royal Guards and became known to his English friends as "the Little Rebel."[34] If one can judge by the reactions of the Pinckney brothers, Americans in England sensed their alienation from England even before Americans in the colonies. Certainly the longer Charles Cotesworth Pinckney stayed in England, the more attached he became to America. This might not have happened had he felt himself accepted among England's better families or had he found English life generally congenial.

33. Among Pinckney's schoolmates were Francis G. Osborne, later the 5th Duke of Leeds; Robert B. Smyth, later a banker and an ardent republican; Richard Nassau Molesworth, later 4th Viscount Molesworth; Paul Henry Maty, a scholar of some repute late in the 18th century; George Atwood, who made his reputation as a mathematician; John Crewe, later 1st Baron Crewe; and Charles Fearne, a noted lawyer very early in his career. See Barker and Stenning, comps., *Record of Old Westminsters*, I, 34, 232, 324; II, 632, 651, 706–07, 863–64.

34. Ravenel, *Eliza Pinckney*, 247; Thomas Pinckney to James Ladson, Jan. 4, 1824, Joseph Johnson, *Traditions and Reminiscences, Chiefly of the American Revolution in the South* . . . (Charleston, 1851), 88.

If Pinckney was unable to associate easily with the choice families, he could still attend the best schools as he prepared himself for
the legal profession. After completing public school, the accepted
place to go was either to Oxford or to Cambridge and from there
to one of the Inns of Court for the formal legal training. By enroll-
ing at Westminster School, Pinckney's university and college within
the university were almost automatically determined. Students of
Westminster were expected to attend Christ Church College, Oxford,
and it was there that Pinckney matriculated on January 19, 1764.[35]

English universities were not intellectually stimulating in the eighteenth century. Oxford, at the time Pinckney matriculated, was going
through a difficult period. Tutors were generally indifferent, students
lackadaisical or worse, and academic standards nominal or nonex-
istent.[36] Oxford students, according to the paper *North Briton*, were
known as:

> Fellows! who've soak'd away their knowledge
> In sleepy residence at College;
>
> .   .   .
>
> Mere drinking, eating; eating, drinking;
> With no impertinence of thinking.

If one can judge from the use of the Christ Church library, intellectual stimulus was at a low point, the average withdrawal per year
being only 150 books.[37] Fortunately for Pinckney, his college was
considered the best of a bad lot, the "show College of the Century."
And Pinckney was also fortunate in the tutor assigned him, Cyril
Jackson, a former fellow student under Dr. Markham. Jackson had
been a brilliant student at Westminster and a favorite of Dr. Markham. Later Jackson became the sub-preceptor of the royal family
and eventually dean of Christ Church College itself. One might

---

35. Henry L. Thompson, *Christ Church* (London, 1900), 26; Joseph Foster, ed.,
Alumni Oxonienses: The Members of the University of Oxford, 1715–1886,
4 vols. (London, 1891), III, 1118. Mrs. Pinckney hoped to join her boys sometime in 1764 and take them to Geneva to finish their education. See Eliza Pinckney to Mr. Keate, Feb. 1762, Ravenel, *Eliza Pinckney,* 224–25.

36. A. D. Godley, *Oxford in the Eighteenth Century* (London, 1908), ch. 3.

37. William R. Ward, *Georgian Oxford: University Politics in the Eighteenth
Century* (Oxford, 1958), 218. See also Walter G. Hiscock, *A Christ Church
Miscellany . . .* (London, 1946), 90.

wonder how well Pinckney and his tutor got along, for Jackson did not always treat his students with the greatest kindness.[38] Jackson was also a year younger than Pinckney, a factor that would not have made the situation easier.

Since the academic standards were not rigid, it seems likely that Pinckney took time to drink his beer with the other students and to engage in the political discussions that are always a part of university life. In Christ Church he was surrounded by Whig influences. Christ Church, in fact, was a lonely academic outpost of ministerial Whiggism in a predominantly Tory Oxford.[39] Yet there was a strong undercurrent of anti-Hanover feeling among the undergraduates. In 1747 a group of Christ Church students paraded through the streets cursing the House of Hanover and mobbed a canon of Windsor, Richard Blacow, who dared to reprove them for their disloyalty.[40] How strong this anti-Hanover feeling was while Pinckney attended Christ Church is difficult to estimate, but he was no doubt fully acquainted with the shortcomings of the ruling family.

It is also possible that Pinckney adopted the prejudice of his fellow Oxonians toward men whose wealth was based on commerce rather than land. The *Oxford Magazine* of 1769 mentioned this aversion for the merchant in a piece of doggerel:

> But when become a son of Isis,
> He justly all the world despises,
> Soon clearly taught to understand
> The dignity of gown and band,
> Nor would his gownship e'er degrade
> To walk with wealthiest son of trade.[41]

Pinckney, at a later time, avoided investing his capital in commercial projects. Perhaps like his fellow Oxonians he thought it beneath his station to associate with wealthiest sons of trade.

While at Christ Church, Pinckney received training that complemented his advanced professional studies at the Middle Temple. Wil-

---

38. Godley, *Oxford*, 61; Thompson, *Christ Church*, 170; see W. P. Courtney in *DNB* s.v. "Jackson, Cyril"; Hiscock, *Christ Church Miscellany*, 90.
39. Godley, *Oxford*, 253; Ward, *Georgian Oxford*, 141.
40. Godley, *Oxford*, 253–56.
41. Quoted in *ibid.*, 121.

liam Blackstone, the eminent legal historian, gave a series of private lectures on the development of the English legal system that Pinckney made a point to audit. Blackstone's lectures were learned and gracefully written, forming the basis for his famous *Commentaries*. Some scholars have been sparing in their praise of Blackstone's scholarship, but aspiring lawyers like Pinckney learned many basic concepts about the growth and development of the English law by attending Blackstone's lectures. His arguments on the cumulative character of rights and liberties for men and society, and on the necessity to protect these freedoms collectively, appeared sound to his audience. Americans found these arguments exceedingly useful in a very few years. Pinckney attended the lectures and diligently jotted down four volumes of notes. Blackstone had gained another disciple.[42]

While studying at Oxford, Pinckney also began his work at the Middle Temple, matriculating there on January 24, 1764. At the Inns of Court the students joined one of the temples, where prospective chancery clerks, solicitors, or attorneys gathered to audit lectures, discuss legal questions, and dine with eminent jurists who had been elected benchers. Students were expected to capitalize upon their opportunities by visiting court sessions, attending Parliament, discussing legal problems with their learned superiors, and by reading widely in disquisitions on the law.[43]

Unfortunately, the system of training had broken down. The temples were no more academically demanding than were the universities. As Sir William Holdsworth has commented, legal education in the eighteenth century "is a very melancholy topic. Neither at

42. James Herring, ed., *National Portrait Gallery of Distinguished Americans*, 4 vols. (Phila., 1865), I, 2. Herring may have received this information from Harriott Pinckney, daughter of Charles Cotesworth Pinckney, who lived until 1866. Pinckney may easily have been in the group of auditors that included Jeremy Bentham. See Bowring, ed., *Works of Bentham*, X, 45. For a concise summary of Blackstone's career, see G. P. Macdonell in *DNB* s.v. "Blackstone, William."

43. Henry F. MacGeagh, comp., *Register of Admissions to the Honourable Society of the Middle Temple*, 2 vols. (London, 1949), I, 361. Pinckney matriculated at the Middle Temple just five days after he had enrolled at Christ Church. Obviously he was trying to meet the Middle Temple residence requirement of five years even as he was being tutored at Oxford. For a detailed discussion of the Inns of Court, see Dunbar P. Barton, *The Story of Our Inns of Court* (London, 1925); H. H. Bellot, *The Inner and Middle Temple: Legal, Literary, and Historic Associations* (London, 1902); and George Godwin, *The Middle Temple; The Society and Fellowship* (London, 1954).

the Inns of Court nor in the Universities was there any effective teaching of law. . . ." At the Middle Temple, the student's ancient obligation to "perform legal exercises" and to remain in residence for a period of time could often be commuted for a money payment. Exercises consisted of little more than reading a few lines written on a piece of paper, and a student called to the bar for his final performance merely swore some oaths against Popery and went through the form of a legal argument.[44] The only obstacles that prevented one from being called to the bar were prescribed in 1762: no person was to be called to the bar sooner than five years after his admission, even if he had practiced in the colonies or in Ireland; no person under twenty-one years of age could be called; and each candidate was to "keep commons in ye [dining] Hall twelve terms before he be called to the Bar. . . ."[45]

It was not a rigorous system. Each candidate could get as much or as little out of the five-year program as he wished. There is every reason to believe that Pinckney used his time conscientiously, reading widely, attending the courts of law, and observing parliamentary debates even as he continued his studies at Oxford. In fact, his mother received word from friends in London that her elder son was working harder than he should. Writing to Charles Cotesworth, Eliza lamented that he was "extremely thin, it is said owing to intense study. . . ." Eliza blamed herself, recalling that she had urged him to disciplined study since he had been a child. "Should I by my over solicitude for your passing thro' life with every advantage, be a means of injuring your constitution," she continued, "how shall I answer to myself, the hurting of a child so truly dear to me, and deservedly so; who has lived to near twenty-three years of age without once offending me."[46]

This letter indicates that Pinckney was applying himself; moreover, it gives some insight into Pinckney's values and character as a young man. He was obviously anxious to honor the family name and to please his mother. Not many parents can say of a youth of twenty-

44. William S. Holdsworth, *A History of English Law*, 12 vols. (London, 1938), XII, 77–79.
45. *Ibid.*, 23–24.
46. This letter, printed in Ravenel, *Eliza Pinckney*, 246, was probably written late in 1767.

two that he has never once offended them. His strong sense of duty and his determination to do what his family expected of him professionally suggest a socially sensitive individual, one who did not have a bent to nonconformity. There is no record to indicate that he ever challenged his parents' determination that he become a lawyer. Pinckney seemed to be well aware of the place he would fill in his own South Carolina society. He prepared himself to fill it well.

In order to complete his education and restore his impaired health, Pinckney abandoned his studies at the temple in 1768 for a tour of the Continent. But he did not go to the Continent merely to travel; instead of touring extensively, he attended the Royal Military Academy at Caen, France, to study military science. With her port and borders to protect and her slaves to control, South Carolina put a high value on martial skills. Pinckney wanted to be the complete man, ready to serve his country and his family in both peace and war.

Eliza worried, however, that her son was wasting his time. Although she assured Charles that his excursion to France had her approval, she warned that "six months loss of application now must be of consequence. As you are in France you may perhaps be inclined to see more of the Continent; but I hope you will not think of gratifying that inclination at present. I therefore beg of you my dear child, to return to Oxford as soon as your health will permit, and apply closely to your studies."[47] Eliza never allowed Charles Cotesworth to forget that responsibilities preceded pleasures.

Pinckney's formal schooling was completed in January of 1769 when he was called to the bar. After riding one circuit, an experience valuable in itself and certain to add to a young lawyer's prestige in the colonies, Pinckney was prepared to assume his twofold duties as a lawyer and as head of the Pinckney family.[48]

Surely Pinckney had regrets as he prepared to leave for South Carolina. England had been his home for sixteen years. His life had centered around English friends and schools. With his educational training, considered the best possible in his day, he could have prac-

47. This undated letter is printed in Simms, "Memoir of the Pinckney Family," *Dawson's Hist. Mag.*, 2nd Ser., 1 (1867), 137.
48. Ravenel, *Eliza Pinckney*, 246–47.

ticed law in England and would have been assured of standing in the community. His profession would also have guaranteed him a comfortable income. For one like Pinckney, who loved to read and investigate different fields of knowledge, the advantages of London were legion. Libraries, lectures, and museums were easily accessible. Royal pageantry and parliamentary sessions would have provided diversion and stimulation.

Yet, like most young men from the colonies trained in law, Pinckney chose to abandon London for a parochial American town. He was drawn to his boyhood home for a variety of reasons. His mother and sister Harriott were there. Most of his financial inheritance was in Carolina properties. But these were hardly insurmountable obstacles to staying in England; he and his family could have made the necessary adjustments. The one part of Pinckney's inheritance that could not be transferred to England was his social position. In England, Pinckney would have been an educated and cultured colonial but a colonial nevertheless. In Charleston he would quickly become a member of the established oligarchy. As a planter and a lawyer he would have influence and standing with two politically and socially prominent groups. If he played the role expected of him by the community—and Pinckney usually did—he might have to make occasional sacrifices, but the hardships of public service would be eased by his enhanced position within the circles of the low-country aristocracy.

It is possible that even before Pinckney returned to South Carolina provision had been made by family friends to launch his public career. Whatever planning was necessary, it appears that no more than six or seven months elapsed between his return to Charleston and his election as representative to the Commons House from St. John's Parish, Colleton County.[49]

As Pinckney stood before the speaker on December 5, 1769, and took the oath required of all new Commons House members, he was aware of the political deadlock and crisis that had developed between the royal government and the Commons House of Assembly. Did

49. The time necessary to ride the circuit, to pack, and to complete the journey from England would indicate that Pinckney could not have arrived in Charleston much before July 1, 1769. He was elected to the Commons House on Sept. 20, 1769, according to the Charleston S. C. Gazette, Sept. 21, 1769.

he recall, one wonders, that his father had urged him to "employ all his . . . abilities in the service of God and his country" and "in the cause of virtuous liberty . . ."? Certainly Charles Cotesworth's character and principles were already established. Nearly every conflict in the next six years between the royal government and the South Carolina citizenry would find Pinckney defending "virtuous liberty."

II

A GENTLEMAN BECOMES A REBEL

———— ◆•◆ ————

*I entered into this Cause after much reflection, and through principle,
[and] my heart is altogether American.*

—Charles Cotesworth Pinckney, 1780.

*He [Pinckney] was an early, decided and devoted promoter of the
revolution.*

—Christopher Gadsden, 1825.

———— ◆•◆ ————

SOUTH CAROLINIANS WERE CERTAIN THEIR LIBERTIES WERE IN DANGER.
They must act decisively, they counseled one another, or corrupt and
tyrannical royal ministers would destroy their liberties. Three days
after Pinckney entered the Commons House the members voted overwhelmingly to send £10,500 currency to England "for the Support
of the just and constitutional Rights and Liberties" of Englishmen.[1]
Everyone knew the money would be sent to London to help pay the
legal fees and election expenses of John Wilkes.

A daring politician and seasoned profligate, Wilkes had crudely
attacked George III's speech from the throne in the *North Briton*
(No. 45) in April 1763, bringing both royal and ministerial wrath
upon his head. Fearful that a suit against him for seditious libel would
result in a prison sentence, Wilkes fled to France but came back in
1768. His friends thereupon enthusiastically and repeatedly returned
him to Parliament, only to have him systematically expelled by a
scandalized and indignant House. Wilkes's supporters also founded

1. Dec. 8, 1769, Commons Journal, S.C. Archives.

the Society of the Gentleman Supporters of the Bill of Rights, which promptly solicited funds from interested parties and organizations to assist the debt-ridden martyr.

London rabble and South Carolina gentry rallied to Wilkes's support. While the Middlesex mechanics expressed their support of Wilkes by rioting and burning ministerial effigies, Charleston gentlemen helpfully proffered funds from the public purse. Of course the governor and Council refused to approve the Wilkes fund bill; money bills were supposed to support the royal government, not undermine it. Besides, how dare the Commons House presume to allocate public funds without consent of the governor and Council? To the governor, to the Council, and to the ministerial attorney-general, the Commons' action seemed a clear violation of the colony's constitution.

For its part, the Commons House sturdily maintained that its action was not illegal, that it was following the long-established practice of borrowing funds from the treasury and pledging to repay them through the next annual tax bill.[2] Determined to override the Crown on this crucial constitutional issue, the Commons House refused to approve any money bills acceptable to the governor and Council. South Carolina now entered a period of protracted constitutional deadlock. The Wilkesite planks in South Carolina's "Bridge to Revolution" were firmly in place by the end of 1769.

Bickering between the governor and the Commons House was not a new condition in South Carolina.[3] Nor was it unusual for disputes between governor and legislature to involve the appropriation of money. In the 1760's, however, the struggle for power between the Crown and Commons House became more intense. Passage of the Stamp Act in 1765 hardened the Assembly's determination to defy or evade assertions of prerogative that it thought were illegal or novel.

2. For a discussion of the Wilkes case see George F. Rudé, *Wilkes and Liberty: a Social Study of 1763 to 1774* (N.Y., 1962); Charles Chenevix Trench, *Portrait of a Patriot: A Biography of John Wilkes* (Edinburgh, 1962). Jack P. Greene has explored the significance of the Wilkes case for South Carolina in his "Bridge to Revolution: The Wilkes Fund Controversy in South Carolina, 1769–1775," *Journal of Southern History*, 29 (1963), 19–52.

3. Jack P. Greene, in *The Quest for Power: The Lower Houses of Assembly in the Southern Royal Colonies, 1689–1776* (Chapel Hill, 1963), argues that throughout the colonial period it became almost habitual for the southern assemblies to disobey Crown instructions. In the Revolutionary era, therefore, it was an easy transition to open opposition against the Parliament and Crown.

When the British government levied taxes on tea and other commodities the following year and when corrupt customs officials harassed the wealthy Carolina merchant Henry Laurens in 1767, both events seemed to confirm the suspicions of many Charlestonians that a concerted ministerial program to subvert South Carolina's liberties was under way. The sharp cries of Massachusetts and Virginia against Great Britain's new taxation and administrative policies encouraged Charleston to adopt a nonimportation agreement in June 1769. This nonimportation agreement and the attempt to support John Wilkes were related parts of South Carolina's expanding protest against measures of the royal government.[4]

Pinckney had come home to a turbulent and divided colony. Since South Carolina's prosperity had not really been affected by Great Britain's novel administrative and taxing policies in the 1760's, even many who considered themselves good Whigs were hesitant to antagonize Britain or to make it appear that South Carolina was in a state of limited rebellion. Reason, petition, and patience, they believed, would serve to erase unsound measures and steady the course of an erratic and ill-advised ministry.

While Pinckney had many friends in this conservative group, he thought them overly optimistic, if not naïve. Perhaps he had seen too much of the venality and corruption of official London life to believe in the essential benevolence and reasonableness of the government. At any rate, Pinckney immediately threw in his lot with the colony's more assertive Whigs. From his vote in the Commons House to support the Wilkes fund bill, Pinckney aligned himself with the bolder Whig spirits and continued this association throughout the Revolutionary era.

Historians have generally thought of Pinckney as a moderate in the period from 1769 to 1775. For example General McCrady, South Carolina historian, believed that as late as 1776 Pinckney "had as yet taken no decided position with either party," but McCrady made the mistake of watching Pinckney's mouth rather than his feet.[5] Pinckney was never a public firebrand. There is no record that he ha-

4. Wallace, *South Carolina*, 231–41.
5. Edward McCrady, *The History of South Carolina in the Revolution, 1775–1780* (N.Y., 1902), 110.

rangued public meetings of the citizenry as did his friend Edward Rutledge or the radical merchant Christopher Gadsden. Yet Pinckney was repeatedly placed on committees that took provocative stands against the government; moreover, his closest friends or relatives, men like William Henry Drayton or Arthur Middleton, were his associates on those committees. Although retiring in public debates, Pinckney was always to be found in the ranks of the more forward party.

Certainly Pinckney never thought that his Revolutionary career was opening as he voted for the Wilkes fund bill. This first step had no revolutionary overtones. Nor did his next when he joined a Commons House committee in replying to a Council message that the Wilkes fund bill was illegal. The Council sternly maintained that all money bills must have its approval. Pinckney and his House colleagues indignantly replied that the Council's contentions were "altogether unparliamentary and unprecedented . . . altogether Groundless, and unsupported by truth or Justice. . . ."[6] Four months later the Council's coordinate authority to amend and to pass money bills was upheld from London. The Commons' leaders were thunderstruck.[7]

Pinckney and other prominent House members composed a series of resolutions on this royal instruction, claiming that it was founded upon "false, partial and insidious" information. Whoever had furnished the information on which it was based was "guilty of high misdemeanors and Enemies to his Majesty and the Province."[8] The instruction must be revoked. In an angry mood the House appointed a Committee of Correspondence to contact the ministry through the colony's agent in London, Charles Garth. Pinckney, perhaps because he knew Garth, was placed on this committee. He also wrote to his brother Thomas about the controversy; from London, Thomas sent him the welcome news that the instruction would be withdrawn.[9] But Thomas' information was incorrect and the constitutional impasse continued.

6. Apr. 9, 10, 1770, Commons Journal, S.C. Archives.
7. A copy of the royal instruction dealing with this controversy is in *ibid.*, Aug. 16, 1770.
8. *Ibid.*, Aug. 29, 1770.
9. Committee of Correspondence to Charles Garth, Charleston, Apr. 10, 1772, in Theodore D. Jervey, ed., "Garth Correspondence," *S. C. Hist. and Gen. Mag.*, 33 (1932), 136–38. Garth, like Pinckney, was a graduate of Westminster School. See also Thomas Pinckney to Charles Cotesworth Pinckney, Apr. 16, [1772], Pinckney Family Papers, Library of Congress, Washington, D. C.

One casualty of this political quarrel was an educational bill that Pinckney had some part in sponsoring. Throughout the 1760's and even earlier, Charlestonians had been aware that South Carolina's educational system did not meet the province's needs. Each year the state's most promising young men were forced to go north or to England in order to get a sound education. Lieutenant-Governor William Bull recognized the need for schools and in January 1770 asked the legislature to take some action. Pinckney served on the larger committee appointed to consider the Governor's request and later on the select committee of five which wrote the education bill. The committee's efforts were largely wasted. Alarmed over the Wilkes fund dispute, Bull prorogued the Commons House before the bill was reported from committee. Yet the committee did have some value, for South Carolina had publicly admitted its educational needs. Not until 1801, however, did Pinckney have the satisfaction of helping to found South Carolina College, the type of institution he and his colleagues had envisioned in 1770.[10]

In these early years Pinckney did not usually receive such important committee assignments. In fact, he may have wondered in 1771 whether he was a deliberative member of the Commons House or merely its messenger. He repeatedly had the duty of carrying House messages to the Council or to the governor. Still he found himself placed on committees where his legal training was useful, and he could console himself that while serving his legislative apprenticeship he was gaining experience in preparing and reporting bills to the House.[11]

A sign that his apprenticeship had ended after only three years came in 1772 when Pinckney was appointed to an important Committee on Grievances. House members buzzed angrily when Governor Charles Greville Montague, hoping to discourage the attendance of obstreperous Commons House members, announced that all September election writs should be returned at the distant town of Beaufort instead of Charleston. On October 8, the day set for the

10. Jan. 30, Mar. 1, 3, 31, 1770, Commons Journal, S.C. Archives; James H. Easterby, "The South Carolina Education Bill of 1770," *S. C. Hist. and Gen. Mag.*, 48 (1947), 96–100; Daniel W. Hollis, *The University of South Carolina*, 2 vols. (Columbia, S.C., 1951), I, 10–11; Henry W. De Saussure to Charles Cotesworth Pinckney, May 17, 1824, Pinckney Family Papers, Lib. Cong.
11. Jan. 20, Sept. 10, Oct. 11, 1771, Commons Journal, S.C. Archives.

return, Governor Montague (to his consternation) learned that a quorum had formed in the Beaufort courthouse and was ready to receive his messages, with the intransigents once again in charge. Clearly beaten, Montague then ordered the House to reconvene in Charleston. By the time Pinckney and other House members had retraced the seventy-five miles to the seat of government, their tempers were understandably short. It was then that Pinckney, together with nine other representatives, was appointed to a Committee on Grievances. The committee accused Montague of acting in bad faith, of indulging his ill feelings toward the House, and of evading, if not violating, the election law by refusing to conduct business at Beaufort.[12] Pinckney had once again joined those persons harassing the governor and trying to limit royal prerogative.

Pinckney's rise in the Commons House was unusually rapid. While he could not have advanced so quickly had his work in the House not been commendable and his politics pro-American, there were other reasons for his advance. Of course he was a Pinckney, a man of talents and training, and was entitled to a place in his province's political life. But he consolidated his position in other areas, making a name as a philanthropist, soldier, musician, and scientist. It was also soon apparent to his friends and fellow townsmen that he was a sterling Christian and that he intended to support his parish church. Pinckney, then, did the things one would expect of an educated leader of the social community.

Just after returning from England in 1769, Pinckney became a member and a constant supporter of the Charleston Library Society. This gave him numerous opportunities to associate with some of the colony's most distinguished citizens, including Lieutenant-Governor Bull and the library's faithful sponsor, Gabriel Manigault.[13] Also, the press noticed Pinckney favorably when he received an ensign's commission in the Charles-Town Militia Regiment in June 1772.[14] Threatened by Indian attacks, Spanish coastal raids, or slave insurrections, South Carolinians were highly conscious of their need to develop

12. *Ibid.*, Oct. 8, 22, 23, 1772; McCrady, *History, 1719–1776*, 696–700. Among the committee members were John Rutledge, Thomas Lynch, Colonel Charles Pinckney, and Thomas Bee.

13. Charleston *S. C. Gazette*, Oct. 5, 1769. Pinckney's certificate of membership, dated Oct. 4, 1769, is in the Charleston Library Society.

14. Charleston *S. C. Gazette*, June 4, 1772.

an effective militia and were happy to honor those supporting the program. From 1772 Pinckney worked regularly on House committees to regulate the provincial militia.[15] It was only natural to place this up-and-coming militia officer on the important defense committees.

Young Pinckney also developed his budding interest in botany, becoming known to his contemporaries as one of the south's most prominent scientific botanists. In 1773 he was one of the founders of the Charleston Museum—still in existence—and was among its first curators and officers.[16] Pinckney was enthusiastic in encouraging the theater arts and musical productions as well. In these early years he was an accomplished violoncello player and is said to have performed as a young man for the celebrated annual St. Cecilia Society Ball.[17]

His interests were obviously broad and his avocations both numerous and time-consuming. Yet Pinckney did not neglect the law and professional advancement. He received his commission to practice law at the South Carolina bar on January 19, 1770. Nine months later he became a solicitor of the Court of Chancery.[18] The surviving Chancery records are brief and it is often impossible to determine the nature of the cases; but it is clear that Pinckney won his first case in Chancery against the formidable opposition of James Parsons and John Rutledge, two of the colony's eminent lawyers.[19] Every lawyer wanted to do his best in Chancery where the governor and his Council were the judges.

In his second year of practice Pinckney handled a spectacular case that put him before the public eye. Dr. John Haley, an ardent American, and Peter DeLancey, an equally ardent Anglophile, started an

15. Oct. 29, 1772, Aug. 14, 1773, Mar. 1, 3, 1774, Commons Journal, S.C. Archives; Charleston *S. C. Gazette*, May 17, 1773.

16. Laura M. Bragg, "The Birth of the Museum Idea in America," *Charleston Museum Quarterly*, 1 (1923), 3–13.

17. Ravenel, *Charleston*, 426.

18. McCrady, *History, 1719–1776*, 481. Pinckney's petition to practice in the Court of Chancery was received by the Court and granted Oct. 12, 1770. Anne K. Gregorie, ed., *Records of the Court of Chancery of South Carolina, 1671–1779* (Washington, D.C., 1950), 579.

19. Gregorie, *Records of Court of Chancery*, 585–86, 593, 600, 603, 611. The case came into Chancery in May 1771, and the judgment was handed down Mar. 27, 1773. Other cases which Pinckney argued in Chancery are included in this volume.

argument "at a genteel house of entertainment in St. Michael's Alley."
Tempers flared when DeLancey called Haley a liar. Haley challenged
DeLancey to a duel at once. They went upstairs, faced each other
across a table, and fired at the same moment; DeLancey slumped over
dead. The Crown decided to prosecute Haley for murder. Haley
despaired for his life but hired Pinckney, James Parsons, Thomas
Heyward, and Alexander Harvey to defend him. Pinckney and his
colleagues argued the case before a packed courtroom pleading for
acquittal on grounds that Haley had not killed DeLancey with malice
aforethought. At worst Haley was guilty of manslaughter, they said,
not murder. Their argument was so convincing that the jury brought
in a verdict of manslaughter. Pinckney and his colleagues, the press
reported, "acquired no small degree of Applause" for the ingenuity
of their argument and presentation of their client's case.[20] There is a
touch of irony in the Haley case. Pinckney later became an active
sponsor of legislation to outlaw dueling. How many times, one wonders, did he recall that he had helped to establish one of the precedents
by which surviving duelists escaped severe punishments, precedents
that he later denounced as a mockery of justice.

The royal government recognized Pinckney's abilities as a barrister
by appointing him acting attorney-general in 1773 for the judicial
districts of Camden, Georgetown, and Cheraws. His supervisor, Attorney-General Sir Egerton Leigh, was the son of the man who was
appointed chief justice in the place of Pinckney's father in 1752.
Memories alone might have chilled the sons' relationship. Pinckney
would have been cool toward Leigh in any case, for Leigh was generally detested for the supposed seduction of his own sister-in-law, a
niece of Henry Laurens. If the Crown hoped to attach Charles Cotesworth Pinckney to the royal interest through an official appointment,
the office should have been regulated by some person other than Sir
Egerton. The offer may have been prompted by Lieutenant-Governor Bull, a judicious servant of the government. Bull knew Pinckney
socially and through their associations in the Library Society. Bull
may have even anticipated a family tie as well since Pinckney was
courting a daughter of Henry Middleton, Bull's son-in-law. No doubt

20. Charleston S. C. Gazette, Nov. 7, 1771; Ravenel, Charleston, 182–83.

Bull marked Pinckney as an outstanding young man and perhaps hoped to bring him into the circle of principled Tories. Whatever the reason for his appointment, whether Crown politics or family interest, Pinckney filled the position capably and seemed to thrive on the physical hardships he encountered while riding the back-country circuit.[21] This experience also broadened his contacts in the back country and spread his reputation as an honest and principled lawyer.

Faithful service to his parish was also a portion of the Pinckney legacy. Pinckney was active in the affairs of St. Philip's Parish, holding parish offices soon after he returned from England. He served as church warden for two years and then as vestryman in 1774, a position he held intermittently for many years.[22] While piety was not necessarily the hallmark of most vestrymen, no man would repeatedly be elected if his character and judgment were not generally well regarded.

Pinckney was surely considered an excellent marital prospect by the young ladies of Charleston and by their anxious parents as well. He was obviously a lawyer with a future, a man of the best family, and good company too. Josiah Quincy, a traveler from Massachusetts who visited Charleston in 1773, noted in his diary that he "was much entertained with Mr. Pinckney's conversation, who appeared a man of brilliant natural powers" complemented by the polish he had acquired through his education. Among his friends and family Pinckney loved to tell anecdotes and was always ready for a hearty laugh, even at the wrong time, if he saw a ludicrous situation. There was nothing stuffy about Pinckney,[23] although he was properly dignified.

Pinckney could scarcely be called handsome; perhaps "masculine"

21. Webber, comp., "Thomas Pinckney Family," *S. C. Hist. and Gen. Mag.*, 39 (1938), 22; Eliza Pinckney to Thomas Pinckney, Apr. 8, 1773, in Eliza Pinckney Letterbook, S.C. Hist. Soc.; Bellot, "The Leighs in South Carolina," Royal Hist. Soc., *Transactions*, 5th. Ser., 6 (1956), 175–76.

22. Charleston *S. C. Gazette*, Apr. 12, 1772, Apr. 12, 1773, Apr. 11, 1774. McCrady states, *History, 1719–1776*, 457, that Pinckney was a parishioner of St. Michael's Church. Pinckney is buried in St. Michael's churchyard, and a plaque in his honor was hung within that church, but he was never an official in St. Michael's parish as he often was in St. Philip's.

23. Josiah Quincy, *Memoir of the Life of Josiah Quincy, Jun. . . .* (Boston, 1825), 103.

would be a better word. He was big-boned, broad-shouldered, and inclined to stoutness. His eyes were dark and expressive, his nose Roman shaped, and his mouth wide, seemingly ready to laugh. Although his face was very round and heavy, it was not totally unattractive.

At least Sally Middleton did not find it unattractive. It is uncertain how long the Pinckney-Middleton courtship continued but one may assume that it was a proper time. The public announcement of the wedding, appearing in the *South Carolina Gazette* of October 4, 1773, noted that through this marriage "an Alliance was completed, between two as respectable Families as any in the province. . . ." The "Alliance" of Charles Cotesworth Pinckney and Sally Middleton was indeed a social triumph for the two families, for both sides brought wealth and prestige to the marital altar.

That the marriage enhanced Pinckney's social and political influence is obvious. Sally's father Henry, owner of nearly twenty plantations and eight hundred slaves, was one of South Carolina's most affluent and influential citizens.[24] Arthur Middleton, Sally's brother, was also a man of importance in South Carolina, particularly during the Revolutionary era. When Arthur returned from his education at the Middle Temple in 1763, he married Mary Izard, a member of another rising South Carolina family. Early in the 1770's Arthur was elected to the Commons House and was later appointed to committees which were controlled by the aggressive Whigs and on which Pinckney sat.[25] The Pinckney-Middleton connection took on an added significance in 1774 when Edward Rutledge, Pinckney's close friend and future business partner, married Henrietta Middleton, Henry's second daughter. Rutledge, by 1775 an influential figure in the politics of South Carolina, was the younger brother of John Rutledge, the governor of South Carolina during the darkest days of the Revolutionary War.[26]

With this educational and family background and with these

24. See John G. Van Deusen in *DAB* s.v. "Middleton, Henry, 1717–1784."
25. See Katharine E. Crane in *DAB* s.v. "Middleton, Arthur, 1742–1787."
26. John Rutledge's biographer, Alexander Barry, has not done justice to his subject in *Mr. Rutledge of South Carolina* (N.Y., 1942). For a more reliable brief life see Robert L. Meriwether in *DAB* s.v. "Rutledge, John."

powerful family connections, a man of reasonable talent and ambition could scarcely fail to gain some prominence in public life. Pinckney built his political career in South Carolina upon a solid social foundation. If not greatness, at least opportunities for service would be thrust upon him.

The opportunities for service began to increase rapidly as South Carolina drifted into the Revolutionary crisis. Pinckney and his fellow South Carolinians were probably not as surprised by the development of a crisis atmosphere in the colonies in the 1770's as were New Yorkers or Pennsylvanians. Each time the legislature met after 1769, South Carolinians were impressed with the government's iron determination to rebuild its authority in areas long since encroached upon by wily and assertive legislatures. Each prorogued assembly reminded Carolinians of the ministry's larger program, evident since 1763, to reorganize the Empire for the purposes of sounder administration and tighter central control.

The other colonies were lulled by a partial repeal of the hated Townshend duties in 1770. Although the government retained the tax on tea, relinquishing the tax on paper, paint, lead, and glass, most colonists were little inclined to challenge the government's theoretical right to tax the colonies when the economic yoke was so light and the principle obscured by healthy prosperity.

But when Parliament passed the Tea Act in 1773 to alleviate the financial distress of the East India Company, the colonies were provoked once again to consider the principle of colonial subordination explicit in such a measure. The Tea Act was designed to price the tea of the East India Company below that of the commonly used, smuggled Dutch tea. Counting on the Franklinian frugality of the Yankees, the government was confident that Americans would purchase the cheaper legal tea, thus saving a near-bankrupt East India Company, and in the process of purchase would admit the government's right to levy an excise tax. Americans saw the trap. By the time the first consignments arrived, reception committees had been organized to prevent landing of the tea. In most cases this method proved successful and the ships returned to England still loaded with tea. In Massachusetts, however, Governor Thomas Hutchinson tried to outwit the Americans by refusing to allow the loaded ships to leave the harbor. His challenge was accepted and the tea simply dumped into the harbor.

The British government was stunned and outraged by Bostonian audacity. Believing that retreat under this extreme provocation would mean the virtual surrender of British authority in America, the government in 1774 guided coercive measures through Parliament that seemed tyrannically harsh both to Bostonians and to their fellow Americans. The "Intolerable Acts," as the Americans called them, brought Massachusetts government firmly under royal control, closed the port of Boston until the East India Company had been compensated for its losses, and attempted to encourage Crown officials in Massachusetts in their duty by protecting them from suits in hostile provincial courts. In the Quartering Act of June 1774, applicable to all the colonies, the government was authorized to quarter troops not only in deserted buildings and taverns but in occupied dwellings as well.[27]

These assertions of parliamentary authority made clear the nature of the crisis facing the Americans. No longer were their victories over governmental authority to be won by chipping away at prerogative, usually exercised through the person of the colonial governor. Now the challenge was coming directly from an aroused Parliament as it reclaimed powers the colonial legislatures long ago assumed they had won.

In order to cope with this powerful parliamentary challenge, the colonies were forced to unite in their protest efforts. The Stamp Act Congress of 1765, the nonimportation agreements of the late 1760's, and the establishment of Committees of Correspondence in 1772 and 1773 were evidence of past American awareness of the need for a united opposition to parliamentary measures. Passage of the Intolerable Acts was certain, therefore, to provoke vigorous colonial protests. Petition, mob violence, and the cowing of colonial governors

27. Useful accounts of the background to the Revolution are John C. Miller, *Origins of the American Revolution* (Boston, 1943); John R. Alden, *The American Revolution, 1775–1783* (N.Y., 1954), chs. 1–3; Bernhard Knollenberg, *Origin of the American Revolution: 1759–1766* (N.Y., 1960); Benjamin W. Labaree, *The Boston Tea Party* (N.Y., 1964).

had formed part of previous programs of protest; and while everyone assumed the use of similar techniques in 1774, a favorable outcome was not taken for granted. This time, Parliament might not be prepared to compromise its authority in the name of imperial unity.

In retrospect, there was no broad concerted movement toward independence in South Carolina until war broke out, and even then many prominent Carolinians were reluctant rebels. South Carolina moved toward revolution by fits and starts, hesitant to take steps that might sever the ties of sentiment or commerce that bound the province so tightly to England; choosing principles over heart and purse is rarely an easy decision. The real political divisions in South Carolina in the prewar period appeared as men answered the question: how far should the province go to impress the ministry that its recent administrative measures were objectionable and dangerous to the liberties of Englishmen overseas? While it is customary to speak of conservatives, moderates, or radicals, it is exceedingly difficult to categorize many prominent Carolinians. Men changed their views with changing circumstances. But almost everyone agreed that some action should be taken, however mild; almost everyone was a Whig of one stripe or another. The more aggressive leaders favored taking collective action with the other colonies, challenging the Crown through the legislature and extralegal committees, even depriving the Crown of the power to enforce laws that colonists thought were unconstitutional. Pinckney was a staunch member of this group.

Pinckney, however, is more a shadow than a central figure during 1773 and 1774, though usually in the House voting with the progressives and attending the town meetings that debated possible courses of action. Perhaps he was preoccupied with his new wife and with establishing his legal practice. It is also likely that he hesitated to take a bold public stand when his relatives and best friends were in sharp disagreement over how far to pressure Great Britain. When the province decided to send five delegates to the Continental Congress in July 1774, Pinckney's father-in-law, Henry Middleton, was elected by the more conservative faction, while Edward Rutledge was elected by those favoring a vigorous protest program. Although Pinckney largely agreed with Rutledge on the course to pursue, he was more reluctant than Rutledge to challenge the conservative position of Middleton.[28]

Pinckney revealed his political orientation more by his actions than through public speeches, his opportunities for expression coming chiefly through the extralegal organizations of the province. South Carolina, like the other American provinces, was forced to construct extralegal committees because the governor or acting governor had the power to disrupt systematic colonial protests through the regular provincial assembly. If protest was to be carried forward, therefore, it was necessary for Carolinians to sanction committees that could express the public will and that could be convened to debate public policy. Over a period of two years in South Carolina, these groups expanded in number and in self-constituted power. From January 1774 until January 1775, the General Meeting and its agent, the ninety-nine-member General Committee, were the instruments of policy. In January 1775, a General Provincial Congress met in Charleston to determine larger policy, its executive agent also being called a General Committee. Under the authority of this General Committee, *ad hoc* committees were appointed to fill the needs of the hour. It was the General Committee that served as the focus of policy debate and decision-making until South Carolinians reluctantly composed a constitution, adopted on March 26, 1776, just five days after news arrived in Charleston that Parliament had declared the Americans in rebellion.[29]

Pinckney seems to have begun his active cooperation with these extralegal organizations shortly after the Provincial Congress was constituted, when Charleston learned in April 1775 that the King had requested increased forces for better execution of the coercive laws against which the Continental Congress had protested. Within a few days the General Committee determined that prudence demanded the seizure of supplies stored in Charleston's royal arsenals. The Special

---

28. Wallace, *South Carolina*, 252–54; John Drayton, *Memoirs of the American Revolution* . . . , 2 vols. (Charleston, 1821), I, 129–30. Edward Rutledge's shifts in position illustrate the difficulties in categorizing men as conservative, moderate, or radical in this dynamic period. Rutledge might be considered a radical in the early phase of the Revolutionary crisis and a conservative as the Continental Congress moved toward adoption of a Declaration of Independence.

29. Wallace, *South Carolina*, 253–56.

Committee chosen for this purpose was appointed by Colonel Charles Pinckney, a Charleston lawyer, president of the Provincial Congress, and a close friend and cousin of Charles Cotesworth Pinckney. Colonel Pinckney appointed William Henry Drayton, leader of the forward faction, to head the committee. Since Colonel Pinckney told Drayton to choose whomever he wanted for his colleagues, Drayton named extremist Arthur Middleton, Charles Cotesworth Pinckney, and two other useful men.[30] It is unlikely that the ardent and often precipitate Drayton would have chosen Pinckney if he had been a trimmer in the conflicts between the aggressive and conservative patriot factions. Drayton, himself a recent convert to extreme measures, had only scorn for the faint-hearted. It is possible that Pinckney was appointed to appease the moderate faction, but if this is true, it was not long before he was acting in concert with Drayton and with his brother-in-law Arthur Middleton.

During the night of April 22, 1775, Pinckney and his accomplices simply walked into the government magazines at three different locations in and around Charleston, not even bothering to disguise themselves. Indeed, the major reason the raid was not staged during the day was to avoid embarrassing the highly respected Lieutenant-Governor William Bull. Drayton and Stephen Bull, who participated in the raid, were both nephews of the Lieutenant-Governor.[31] By this burglary Pinckney and his friends left the government temporarily powerless to arm native Tories.

Three days after this provocative episode Pinckney was appointed to a Committee of Intelligence. This committee also included his friends Drayton and Arthur Middleton. Their task was not easy; it was to persuade up-country leaders that they should make common cause with the low country, presenting a united front to Great Britain. Despite skillful propaganda, the best that lawyers and gentle-

30. Drayton, *Memoirs*, I, 175, 221; Wallace, *South Carolina*, 256–58. Colonel Charles Pinckney appointed these men on Jan. 16, 1775. The other men were William Gibbes, a merchant, and Edward Weyman, known to be astute in matters of intrigue.

31. Drayton, *Memoirs*, I, 222; Ravenel, *Charleston*, 199; Wallace, *South Carolina*, 257–58. Professor Wallace states that the raid took place on the night of Apr. 21, but Lieutenant-Governor Bull, in his message to the Commons House on Apr. 25 (Tuesday) said that the arms had been taken "last Saturday." This indicates that the raid was carried out very early Saturday morning, or Saturday evening. In either case, the correct date would seem to be April 22.

men could devise, many up-country leaders remained more fearful of the Charleston oligarchy's power than they were of royal despotism, a residue of the bitter sectional struggle of the 1760's.[32]

Early in May 1775, while the Second Continental Congress was debating a resolution to put the colonies in a state of defense, news arrived in Charleston that the royal government had decided to arm Negroes and Indians for an attack upon South Carolina. This report, sent from London by the paranoiac Arthur Lee, was utterly without foundation, but many alarmists in Charleston were ready to believe the worst. To meet "whatever events might arise," the Special Committee, of which Pinckney was still a member, was enlarged and instructed to "form such plans as they should think immediately necessary to be carried into execution. . . ."[33] This was a broad grant of power and the Special Committee used it to hasten the construction of Charleston's defenses.

The Special Committee misused its power in at least one disgraceful episode. Two Charleston workers, Laughlin Martin and James Dealy, were accused of drinking a seditious toast: "Damnation to the [General] Committee and their proceedings." They were also accused of planning to cooperate with Indians and Negroes in the rumored attack on Charleston. Whether or not Pinckney, Middleton, and Drayton believed this unproven story, the Committee decided to make Martin and Dealy examples of what might happen to other non-cooperators. An order was given to tar and feather the two men, an order that was promptly executed.[34] Pinckney and his lawyer friends such as Drayton evidently believed that the fight for community rights justified destroying the rights of individuals.

The Secret Committee showed its more constructive side by au-

32. Robert W. Gibbes, ed., *Documentary History of the American Revolution*, 3 vols. (N.Y., 1853–57), I, 107; Richard M. Brown, *The South Carolina Regulators* (Cambridge, Mass., 1963). Brown makes it clear that the Regulator movement of the late 60's was not as much a sectional conflict as it was an effort by back-country settlers to control lawlessness within their region.

33. Wallace, *South Carolina*, 258; Drayton, *Memoirs*, I, 231. Five days later the news of Lexington arrived.

34. Drayton, *Memoirs*, I, 273–74; McCrady, *History, 1775–1780*, 23–24. Pinckney was not responsible for another incident of this nature ordered by the Secret Committee in mid-August. See Arthur Middleton to William Henry Drayton, Aug. 12, 1775, Joseph W. Barnwell, ed., "Correspondence of Hon. Arthur Middleton," *S. C. Hist. and Gen. Mag.*, 27 (1926), 126; William Moultrie, *Memoirs of the American Revolution . . .* , 2 vols. (N.Y., 1802), I, 80.

thorizing a clandestine expedition to seize gunpowder from a schooner expected to sail into Savannah. When the schooner fell into the trap, delighted Georgians and South Carolinians divided nearly seventeen thousand pounds of powder between them. The windfall came just in time. Pinckney, Drayton, and Arthur Middleton received a letter from the South Carolina delegates in the Continental Congress telling of the newly authorized Continental Army's desperate need of powder. The Secret Committee at once began to solicit powder both in Georgia and in South Carolina and was soon able to forward over five thousand pounds late in July to the Continental Congress in Philadelphia and to its recently appointed army commander, George Washington.[35]

Drayton and Middleton took genuine delight in hatching plots and directing secret expeditions, but Pinckney was happiest in the more regulated life of the soldier. He had already developed an exceedingly exalted idea of a soldier's value to society. Perhaps his imagination had been fired as a boy as he translated Caesar's *Gallic Wars* or as he discovered the thrilling exploits of great Spartan and Athenian soldiers. Also, Pinckney had been in England during the exciting days of the Seven Years' War when the forces of General James Wolfe defeated Montcalm's army on Quebec's Plains of Abraham, and when Robert Clive was winning stunning victories over the French in India. Pinckney's own experiences as a young man thus reinforced his boyhood impressions of a soldier's importance to the community. Age did not tarnish his romantic notions. In one order for the day he urged his men to "procure . . . the most glorious of all characters— that of being esteemed good soldiers."[36] Duty, honor, service—all were sacred words to Pinckney in every area of his life, and in the role of the soldier he found them most meaningful. His highest ambition was to be a worthy soldier.

By 1774 Pinckney had already gotten some limited military experience. After his short period of service as an ensign in the Charles-

35. Drayton, *Memoirs*, I, 269–73. This letter, dated July 1, 1775, was signed by Henry Middleton, John Rutledge, Thomas Lynch, and Christopher Gadsden. This request followed shortly after the battle at Breeds Hill, Boston. Edward Rutledge gave Pinckney early notice of this battle. Edward Rutledge to Pinckney, June 22, 1775, Miscellaneous Manuscripts, Charleston Lib. Soc.

36. Orders by Major Pinckney, Dec. 28, 1775, Gibbes, ed., *Documentary History*, I, 244.

ton militia regiment, Lieutenant-Governor Bull promoted him to lieutenant in a new company of light infantry, supposedly the elite corps of an army serving as scouts, flank guards, and skirmishers within the larger standard infantry battalion.[37] Because of his early study at Caen and his more recent military training, Pinckney was ready for an important post when the Provincial Congress decided in June 1775 that three regiments of regulars should be raised to protect the province. Since the Provincial Congress decided to select the officers of each regiment by ballot, the number of votes a man received determined his seniority within his rank. Pinckney received 140 votes for captain, becoming the ranking captain of the South Carolina regiments.[38]

The newly elected officers had no army, but they were authorized to recruit in parts of North Carolina and Virginia as well as in South Carolina. Pinckney and Thomas Lynch, Jr., also a captain in Pinckney's regiment, were assigned to recruit in New Bern, North Carolina.[39] While in New Bern, Pinckney alertly spotted two disguised British officers who he had learned (through an intercepted letter) would soon arrive in order to arouse lethargic Loyalists. The officers were undoubtedly General Donald McDonald and Colonel Alexander McLeod. Pinckney rushed to the local Council of Safety to urge arrest of the two men. The Council refused, pedantically insisting that Pinckney's purloined letter mentioned only one officer being sent, yet Pinckney was asking the Council to arrest two men. How could

37. Charleston *S. C. Gazette*, May 17, 1773; Walter Millis, *Arms and Men: A Study in American Military History* (N.Y., 1956), 22.

38. "Miscellaneous Papers of the General Committee, Secret Committee and Provincial Congress," *S. C. Hist. and Gen. Mag.*, 8 (1907), 190.

39. Thomas Lynch, Jr., one of the South Carolina signers of the Declaration of Independence, had been a fellow student of Pinckney's at the Middle Temple. Lynch returned to South Carolina in 1772 and soon entered the colony's political life. He was elected a member of the First and Second Provincial Congresses, 1774–1776, and was also a member of the Second Continental Congress, 1776–1777. During his recruiting mission in North Carolina with Pinckney, Lynch contracted a fever which left him a partial invalid the remainder of his life. Lynch disappeared at sea in 1779 while in passage to the West Indies to recover his health.

His father, Thomas Lynch, was also active in the cause of resistance. Lynch, Sr., represented South Carolina in the Stamp Act Congress, 1765, was a member of the General Committee, 1769–1774, and was elected delegate to the First and Second Continental Congresses. Lynch suffered a paralytic stroke early in 1776 and died soon after in Annapolis, Md. For sketches of the lives of the two Lynches see John G. Van Deusen in *DAB* s.v. "Lynch, Thomas, 1727–1776," and "Lynch, Thomas, 1749–1779."

Pinckney ask the Council to arrest every suspicious-looking person that came into New Bern? This was a weak argument, Pinckney countered. Obviously the older man was an advisor or superior while the younger man was the field officer. In the heat of argument Pinckney must have overstepped the bounds of propriety, for the Council curtly told him to be satisfied that it had allowed him to recruit in New Bern. In time Pinckney's anger with the temporizing Council of Safety was vindicated. McLeod and McDonald led a Loyalist Scots emigrant force at the skirmish of Moore's Creek Bridge in February 1776.[40]

Pinckney recruited only about six weeks in North Carolina. By early September he was back in Charleston drilling his recently re-cruited men, holding courts-martial, and trying to give his men more polish by chiding them on their personal habits. He deplored their repeated "drunkenness and rioting," pointing out that the "very ample pay the Colony allows" was not given to buy liquor but to "enable the men to procure such conveniences as were proper for their comfortable subsistence while in its service. . . ." Pinckney was particularly incensed when he learned that his soldiers were stealing civilian property. To steal, he scolded, was an "infamous breach of the trust reposed in them" as protectors of South Carolina property.[41]

Pinckney's admonitions brought some response, for his regiment was soon known by its smart appearance and orderly conduct. Yet Pinckney was always dissatisfied, always fearful that the regiment would somehow disgrace itself and him. When the first regiment was ordered into Charleston for duty after a period of eighteen months at Fort Moultrie, Pinckney lamented that his men might be "Infallibly Ruined," and that they would become a "Nucence and Burthen to the Country." He cautioned against the "Disappation and Seduction of the Town" and urged his men for the "Love of Military Glory, which should Swell the Soldiers breast and Lead him to Renown, to Exert every Endeavour to preserve and Increase the Discipline of the

---

40. Garden, *Eulogy on Pinckney*, 14–16; McCrady, *History, 1775–1780*, 126; Samuel A'Court Ashe, *History of North Carolina*, 2 vols. (Greensboro, N.C., 1908–25), I, 497–504; John Sanderson, *Biography of the Signers to the Declaration of Independence*, 2nd ed., 5 vols. (Phila., 1828), V, 221.

41. Orders by Major Pinckney, Dec. 28, 1775, "An Order Book of the 1st Regt., S.C. Line, Continental Establishment," *S. C. Hist. and Gen. Mag.*, 7 (1906), 79.

Regiment. . . ." Pinckney's orders for the day had two themes: all violators of regulations could count on swift and certain punishment, and soldiers should regulate their lives by the worthiest standards. While he was a strict disciplinarian, Pinckney always tried to see that his men were well provisioned. His men appreciated Pinckney's efforts to provide for their comfort, and though few loved him, he was respected.[42]

As Pinckney recruited and drilled his men in 1775, Lord William Campbell, the royal governor, was taking some weak steps to counteract the increasingly recalcitrant attitude of Charleston. Alarm spread throughout the city when insurgent leaders learned in mid-September that Lord William was attempting to recruit up-country Loyalists and that the Crown was planning to send troops into the Carolinas.[43] Actions taken by the Continental Congress in July had already indicated the crisis was deepening; of particular importance was the Congress's rejection of Lord North's plan of reconciliation. The Drayton faction therefore urged that Fort Johnson, the traditional southeastern guardian of the harbor, must be occupied before British men-of-war arrived to strengthen Lord William's hand.

The General Committee agreed. Acting through the Council of Safety, it instructed Colonel William Moultrie to seize the fort. On September 14, 1775, Moultrie ordered Captains Charles Cotesworth Pinckney, Barnard Elliott, and Francis Marion to prepare their companies to march in three hours.[44] At eleven o'clock that evening the detachment of 150 men stole from their barracks and marched in silence to Gadsden's Wharf on the eastern end of Charleston. The men quickly boarded two small packets. As the packets got under way, Colonel Isaac Motte called the officers into his cabin to discuss strategy. A detachment of Pinckney's grenadiers was to play the key role by scaling the walls on the south side of the bastion.

42. Orders by Colonel Pinckney, Jan. 6, 1777, *ibid.*, 133–34; Garden, *Eulogy on Pinckney*, 13–14; Charleston *S. C. Gazette*, Jan. 8, 1778. Pinckney wrote to General Lincoln in 1780: ". . . as all Physicians agree that the animal qualifications of Man are best invigorated by good wholesome food, I hold it to be an undoubted truth and an undeniable maxim in War that Soldiers should have their Bellies full." Fort Moultrie, Feb. 25, 1780, Ford Collection, Historical Society of Pennsylvania, Phila.
43. Drayton, *Memoirs*, II, 30–34.
44. *Ibid.*, II, 35; Moultrie, *Memoirs*, I, 88.

By the time about ninety of the men had landed on James Island it was nearly dawn. The decision was made to proceed toward the fort without Marion's company—still on board ship—in order to insure surprise. Pinckney's and Elliott's companies raced double time toward the fort expecting action at any moment. Much to their surprise the gates were open. The soldiers rushed in. To their consternation the cannon had all been dismounted and the fort largely abandoned. Alexander Innes, Lord William's secretary, and a detachment from a British ship had left the fort only two hours before. Lord William had evidently learned of the plan of seizure and had ordered a hasty withdrawal.[45]

Governor Campbell, justifiably alarmed by the colonials' seizure of Fort Johnson, concluded that royal authority had ended in Charleston and therefore fled to the *Tamar*, a British warship anchored in the harbor. From the ship Campbell could see rebellious Charleston busily preparing its defenses and military companies fortifying strategic points around the harbor. Pinckney made his contribution at Fort Johnson by remounting the cannon, fortifying the approaches to James Island, and drilling his inexperienced men. Under Moultrie's orders Pinckney also selected two hundred men for a mission that required speed, secrecy, and the cover of night: the erection of a battery at Haddrell's Point. With British ships at anchor in the harbor, Pinckney, now a major, and a motley crew of soldiers, laborers, and gentlemen volunteers quietly passed from Charleston to the landing at Haddrell's Point. The men fell to work with such enthusiasm that by dawn they were protected from the shots of the British ships. Within a few hours they had mounted the cannon, opened the embrasures, and fired warning shots at the ships from their eighteen-pounders, shots that drove the ships back toward Sullivan's Island.[46] Since the ships did not return the fire, Major Pinckney was denied his first taste of combat.

Pinckney did not confine himself entirely to nocturnal military

45. Accounts of this episode can be found in Drayton, *Memoirs*, II, 36–38; Moultrie, *Memoirs*, I, 86–88; "Diary of Captain Barnard Elliott," *Charleston Year Book, 1889* (Charleston, 1889), 159–60; Isaac Motte to [Council of Safety], Fort Johnston, Sept. 15, 1775, South Carolina Official box, Ford Collection, New York Public Library, N.Y.C.

46. Harriott Horry to Miss Trapier, Nov. 28, 1775, Ravenel, *Eliza Pinckney*, 268; Drayton, *Memoirs*, II, 163–64. Pinckney was promoted to major in Nov. 1775. The James Island battery was erected on Dec. 19–20, 1775.

adventures or to preparing his recruits for combat. In 1775 and 1776 he was also active in the legislatures of both the Commons House and its emerging Revolutionary counterpart, the Provincial Congress. With his military knowledge and legislative experience it was reasonable that he should become increasingly prominent in the legislative proceedings.

A measure of Pinckney's stature is seen in his selection as chairman of the committee to prepare a constitution for South Carolina. The logic of events in South Carolina and throughout the colonies called for establishing governments that could function independently of the Crown, temporarily at least. South Carolina was reluctant to take such a provocative step but finally the pressure became irresistible. The Battle of Bunker Hill was eight months past and the Battle of Moore's Creek Bridge just fifteen days in the future when on Sunday, February 11, 1776, the House elected an eleven-member committee to consider a new plan of government. The committee included the cream of South Carolina's oligarchy: John Rutledge, Colonel Charles Pinckney, Henry Laurens, Christopher Gadsden, Rawlins Lowndes, Henry and Arthur Middleton, Thomas Bee, Thomas Lynch, Jr., and Thomas Heyward, Jr.[47] Historian Edward McCrady believed Charles Cotesworth Pinckney was appointed chairman because he "had as yet taken no decided position with either party"; that is, Pinckney was neither an independence man nor an open advocate of reconciliation.[48]

Perhaps General McCrady was partially right, but if Pinckney was not yet publicly urging independence, as was Christopher Gadsden, he was very close to doing so. His feelings toward Great Britain were well known and his actions in the previous two years made Pinckney a likely target for royal reprisals if the Crown authority were reestablished. Certainly Pinckney's military activities marked him as one who favored a program of preparing for the worst. It is possible that in this crucial moment Pinckney seemed all things to all men, the progressives remembering his many services in the past two years, the moderates and conservatives that he had not been a public agitator. Pinckney, then, was possibly in a unique position to help bridge

47. The resolutions on the need for a constitution and the subsequent debates can be found in William E. Hemphill and Wylma A. Wates, eds., *Extracts from the Journals of the Provincial Congresses of South Carolina, 1775–1776* (Columbia, S.C., 1960), 181–263, *passim*.
48. McCrady, *History, 1775–1780*, 110.

the gap between the views of the radicals and conservatives. From conviction he favored radical measures, while by temperament he wanted to use moderate means to achieve them. Radicals such as Arthur Middleton and Pinckney's moderate kinfolk such as Colonel Charles Pinckney and Henry Middleton could all have confidence in Charles Cotesworth Pinckney.

It is unlikely, however, that Pinckney dominated this constitutional committee. With such a distinguished group, no man with the possible exception of John Rutledge was likely to overshadow the others. Pinckney continued his normal military and professional duties, and he was therefore unable to give his undivided attention to the committee work. Still, during the weeks of debate, Pinckney, along with John Rutledge and Major William Cattell (who evidently was added to the committee sometime after February 11) reported at different times on the committee's progress. On March 24, 1776, John Rutledge made the final report and the plan was ordered engrossed. Two days later the constitution, conservative in nature and with provision made for Charleston to be amply represented in the General Assembly, was officially adopted.[49]

Pinckney and his fellow South Carolinians hardly had opportunity to reflect on the gravity of this step. Rumors of British invasion or of Loyalist up-country plots kept Charleston in a state of excitement. In a matter of weeks Fort Sullivan would be under attack by the fleet of Sir Peter Parker and the troops of General Henry Clinton. Thomas Paine's *Common Sense*, appearing in January 1776, had not persuaded all Carolinians that the road to independence was the only course open to thinking patriots. Those who were undecided as to which way to turn—toward resistance or reconciliation—were deeply disturbed by the trend of events.

Pinckney was not among this number. When he wrote in 1780 that he had "entered into this Cause after much reflection and through principle"[50] he was surely referring to the evolution of his thinking early in the 1770's. From his first days in the Commons

---

49. Hemphill and Wates, eds., *Journals of Provincial Congresses*, vii, 254–55, 263–65.

50. Pinckney to Major Money, June 30, 1780, Pinckney Family Papers, Lib. Cong.

House, Pinckney had allied himself with the faction adamantly defending the prerogatives of the House or the liberties of South Carolina. He had repeatedly sought to reduce the power of the governor and Council. More than once he had been placed on the Committee on Grievances by the House, an indication that he was firmly committed to defending its interests. There is a consistency in his opposition to the measures of the royal government, a consistency that was founded upon principle.

Pinckney did not drift into the antigovernment camp because Crown policies had damaged his financial interests, as might be said of the merchant Christopher Gadsden. Pinckney, in fact, had little to gain personally by opposing the Crown. Nor was he a disappointed office-seeker. There is no evidence that the government angered Pinckney (as it had his father) by refusing him an appointment. Financially or politically, he had much to lose if a revolution were ignited but subsequently crushed. As Pinckney insisted, he had joined the Revolutionary cause on principle.

One wonders whether friendship also played a part in orienting Pinckney's thinking during the Revolutionary crisis. Several of his closest friends were the dynamic element within the insurgent group: Thomas Lynch, Jr., Arthur Middleton, and especially William Henry Drayton, called by Alexander Innes "one of the most virulent Incendarys in the Province. . . ."[51] Moreover, Pinckney's brother Thomas hoped at an early date that South Carolina would strike for its independence.[52] Innes probably had the Drayton-Pinckney-Middleton circle in mind when he wrote that the province was being urged to adopt "desperate measures" by "some hot headed Young Men of fortune. . . ."[53] Drayton and Arthur Middleton were both older than Pinckney and probably exercised considerable influence over him.

51. Alexander Innes to Lord Dartmouth, May 16, 1775, in B. D. Bargar, ed., "Charles Town Loyalism in 1775: The Secret Reports of Alexander Innes," *S. C. Hist. Mag.*, 63 (1962), 128. William M. Dabney and Marion Dargan, *William Henry Drayton and the American Revolution* (Albuquerque, N.M., 1962), 71, point out that Drayton became the leader of the revolutionary faction in the spring of 1775.

52. Thomas Pinckney to Harriott Horry, May 9, 1776, Pinckney Family Papers, Lib. Cong.

53. Innes to Dartmouth, June 3, 1775, Bargar, ed., "Charles Town Loyalism," *S. C. Hist. Mag.*, 63 (1962), 132.

So not only his own principles but also the views of his best friends and relatives encouraged Charles Cotesworth to support more forward measures.

By 1776 the time for debate had largely ended. Pinckney was ready to pledge his life and fortune to defend the cause of "virtuous liberty." Protests, mob violence, and even the genesis of armed insurrection had failed to move the ministry from its course. More forceful measures were now necessary. Animated by a "Love of Military Glory, which should Swell the Soldiers breast and Lead him to Renown," Pinckney was willing, perhaps eager, to defend by arms the cause of liberty he had supported peacefully for six years.

III

A PASSION FOR GLORY

———————

Death is the inevitable lott of all, and to make that lott useful to one's Country is the greatest felicity a patriotic soldier can hope for.

—Charles Cotesworth Pinckney, 1789.

At the commencement of the present war, he [Pinckney] entered into the service with the rank of Captain, and has since to the satisfaction of every real friend of American liberty in this State, been advanced by various promotions to that of Colonel. His family being as respectable as any amongst us, and his fortune abundantly competent, nothing but a passion for glory and a zeal for the cause of his country could have led him into this measure.

—Thomas Lynch, Jr., 1777.

———————

THE SPRING OF 1776 FOUND CHARLESTON ALIVE WITH ALARMING RUMORS. It was certain that the British were mounting a southern expedition, but how and when and in what force was not known. There were reports that Boston had been evacuated by the British and that the forces of Sir Henry Clinton had sailed into New York Harbor early in February. And it was definitely known that Lord William Campbell, South Carolina's last royal governor, was in New York City. Lord William was understandably anxious for revenge on those insubordinate South Carolinians who had defied his authority. Surely he had talked with Clinton and urged him to humble Charleston, that hotbed of southern intransigence.

Charleston continued steadily with defense preparations. Charles Cotesworth Pinckney, when not attending to his plantation and professional duties, was usually at Fort Johnson. Morale there was high. If the British came by sea, the defenders of Fort Johnson were hopeful they would bear the brunt of the British attack. The soldiers at Fort Sullivan on the eastern side of the harbor might fire a few rounds as the British passed by, but surely it was at Fort Johnson that the military reputations would be won—or perhaps lost. Pinckney and his men waited with anticipation but also with a sense of dread.[1]

Charleston did not have long to wait. By June 1 the British fleet, under the command of Sir Peter Parker, had anchored within a few miles of Charleston. Sir Peter and his fellow commander Sir Henry Clinton were not happy over the circumstances that brought them to Charleston. The original plan of the first campaign to the south had been shaped to stimulate the activity of Loyalists in the King's cause. By establishing a base from which Loyalists could operate militarily and politically, the royal government hoped to re-establish loyal governments in the south. British strategists had agreed that Cape Fear would be an advantageous area in which to establish a Loyalist headquarters. But when Sir Henry Clinton arrived at Cape Fear on March 12, 1776, he learned the disquieting news that a Loyalist force had been put to flight at Moore's Creek Bridge two weeks earlier with 850 Loyalists taken prisoner. Loyalists would probably not rally in North Carolina even if Clinton's troops landed and began operations. How then could he salvage some advantage from this expedition? Clinton, soon joined by the forces of Sir Peter Parker, decided to proceed to Charleston, take Sullivan's Island only, and use it as a base for Loyalist operations until a southern expedition could be mounted that had more promise of success than his own.[2]

Not knowing of Sir Henry Clinton's limited plans, Charleston was

1. McCrady, *History, 1775–1780*, 130–33. Pinckney's regiment was stationed at Fort Johnson in Jan. 1776. See "Return of Troops in Camp and Garrison at Fort Johnson, 13 January 1776," in "Papers of the Second Council of Safety of the Revolutionary Party in South Carolina, November 1775—March 1776," *S. C. Hist. and Gen. Mag.*, 4 (1903), 8.

2. Paul H. Smith, *Loyalists and Redcoats: A Study in British Revolutionary Policy* (Chapel Hill, 1964), 18–29; McCrady, *History, 1775–1780*, 130–33. Useful accounts of this brief campaign are Eric Robson, "The Expedition to the Southern Colonies, 1775–1776," *English Historical Review*, 66 (1951), 538–48; William T. Bulger, Jr., The British Expedition to Charleston, 1779–1780 (unpubl. Ph.D. diss., University of Michigan, 1957), ch. 1.

in a fever of excitement. Thomas Pinckney, a captain in his brother's regiment, wrote to his sister Harriott that Fort Johnson's 650 defenders were "very Cheerful" and hoped "to give a very good account" of themselves when the British fleet crossed the bar and entered the harbor. In the midst of great excitement Charles Cotesworth took time to relieve his mother's anxiety for the safety of her sons. It is doubtful that Eliza was comforted by her son's report that there were "not more than fifty-two vessels altogether, many of which are very small. . . . They can not get over the bar with this wind, so that we shall have no fighting to-day."[3]

Nor were the troops in Fort Johnson given the opportunity to fight at all during this first British attack on Charleston in June 1776. General Charles Lee, described by Pinckney as "very clever but . . . a strange animal," arrived in Charleston by June 4 and assumed command of the patriot forces.[4] If Lee's strategy had been adopted, the forces under Colonel William Moultrie at Fort Sullivan would have been withdrawn, leaving the brunt of a possible general attack to fall upon Fort Johnson and the defenses of the Charleston mainland. Lee believed that Fort Sullivan could not be successfully defended, that the fort would become a death trap, and that those who survived the British attack would probably be captured since there was no safe way to retreat.

Governor John Rutledge and Colonel Moultrie sharply disagreed with Lee, and Rutledge decided to defend Fort Sullivan. Because of a combination of circumstances—an unfavorable wind, the failure of Negro pilots to navigate the narrow channel skillfully, the palmetto wood defenses of Fort Sullivan which unexpectedly absorbed the pounding of the British guns—the British ships that attacked on June 28 were unable to subdue Fort Sullivan. Pinckney and his men watched idly from Fort Johnson as Colonel Moultrie's men methodically and successfully engaged the British ships. Pinckney lamented to his mother that he "was only a spectator" of the battle "though I and every man here declared they longed earnestly to have been there,

---

3. Thomas Pinckney to Harriott Horry, June 5, 1776, in Jack L. Cross, ed., "Letters of Thomas Pinckney, 1775–1780," *S. C. Hist. Mag.*, 58 (1957), 67; C. C. Pinckney to Eliza Pinckney, June 5, 1776, in Gibbes, ed., *Documentary History*, II, 1.

4. Pinckney to Eliza Pinckney, June 15, 1776, in Gibbes, ed., *Documentary History*, II, 4; John R. Alden, *General Charles Lee: Traitor or Patriot?* (Baton Rouge, 1951), 120; Moultrie, *Memoirs*, I, 141.

to have partaken the honor and danger with their fellow soldiers."[5]

As South Carolinians were celebrating this surprising defeat of the British, word arrived that Congress had proclaimed the colonies free and independent of Great Britain. For some this added an even more festive note to the occasion, but to most the Declaration of Independence was a sobering fact.

After the battle South Carolina had a new hero. Fort Sullivan was renamed Fort Moultrie and Colonel Moultrie was promoted to general a short time later. When Moultrie joined General Lee in an abortive campaign to capture St. Augustine, Pinckney's troops were transferred early in August to Fort Moultrie, now considered the new first line of defense. This assignment lasted eighteen months. Shortly after this transfer Pinckney became a colonel, the rank he retained until near the end of the war.[6]

The economic and strategic importance of Charleston seemed likely to make that city a prime target of future British attacks. For three years, however, British reverses in the north acted as a lightning rod for the south, diverting British energies outside the southern theater. As news drifted into Charleston about the battles of Long Island, White Plains, Trenton, and Princeton, most South Carolinians were content to continue their normal duties and to wonder when their turn for sacrifice would come.

Pinckney grew increasingly restless. Life at the fort was monotonous and his professional legal duties did not seem very rewarding when other Americans were fighting and dying for their country. Yet in this period of general inactivity, Pinckney did make one contribution to the cause of a widening American liberty. When the state legislature decided to revise the constitution of 1776, dissenters

5. McCrady, *History, 1775–1780*, 150–59; Thomas Pinckney to Harriott Horry, June 29, 1779, in [Rev.] Charles Cotesworth Pinckney, *The Life of General Thomas Pinckney* (N.Y., 1895), 46; Charles Cotesworth Pinckney to Eliza Pinckney, June 29, 1776, in Gibbes, ed., *Documentary History*, II, 7. Christopher Gadsden, the commander at Fort Johnson, said the fort was "just without gun shot, we fired only three shot at them just to let them see we were not asleep." Gadsden to Thomas Mumford, Feb. 19, 1777, Ford Coll., N.Y. Pub. Lib.

6. Drayton, *Memoirs*, II, 334–35; Pinckney, *Life of Thomas Pinckney*, 47. The first regiment was transferred to Fort Moultrie sometime between Aug. 4–20, as the letters of Thomas Pinckney to Harriott Horry indicate in Cross, ed., "Letters of Thomas Pinckney," *S. C. Hist. Mag.*, 58 (1957), 72–74. C. C. Pinckney became a colonel on Sept. 16, 1776, according to the "Order Book of John Faucheraud Grimké, August 1778 to May 1780," *S. C. Hist. and Gen. Mag.*, 13 (1912), 89.

stepped up their demands that the state government no longer support the established church. Dissenters felt it was unreasonable to ask them to take up arms for the liberties of America while they were being taxed against their will to support a state church. The principle of no taxation without representation should be valid in domestic questions too. Many of the oligarchy were indignant with this leveling suggestion. But when the Reverend William Tennant rose in the House and moved that the church be disestablished, Charles Cotesworth Pinckney was immediately on his feet supporting the motion. It was both right in principle and expedient as a war measure that the motion be approved, Pinckney argued. This was a war for the liberty of all Americans; it was nonsensical to fight for political liberty with one hand and to deny it with the other. Pinckney was no democrat but he saw the justice of the dissenters' argument and had the courage to defy many of his narrower Anglican friends. With Pinckney ardently supporting disestablishment, the low-country aristocrats began to join the dissenting cause one by one. The support for disestablishment gradually broadened to include a legislative majority. In the constitution adopted in 1778 all religious bodies were declared legally equal before the state.[7]

Pinckney was determined to abandon the legislative hall for the battlefield; there were no laurels in supporting even the most enlightened bills. Since the British would not come to Charleston, Pinckney decided to seek out the British by joining General Washington's army in New Jersey.

Before setting out early in July 1777, Pinckney solicited letters of introduction to Washington. Christopher Gadsden, his commanding officer, wrote one of the letters. Henry Middleton also wrote one for his son-in-law in which he told Washington that Pinckney wished to visit the army "in order to improve himself in military knowledge." Thomas Lynch, Jr., who was acquainted with Washington, flatteringly introduced Pinckney by swearing that "no man living had a

7. Anne King Gregorie, *Thomas Sumter* (Columbia, S.C., 1931), 63; D. Huger Bacot, "Constitutional Progress and the Struggle for Democracy in South Carolina Following the Revolution," *South Atlantic Quarterly*, 24 (1925), 61–72; Wallace, *South Carolina*, 280. A good account of Pinckney's support for disestablishment is found in a letter of his Baptist minister friend, Richard Furman, printed in [Wood Furman], *A Biography of Richard Furman*, ed. Harvey T. Cook (Greenville, S.C., 1913), 59–60.

higher spirit, a nicer sense of Honour or a more incorruptible Heart than he has." Lynch was confident that Washington could use a man of high principles and military skills and added that "I will willingly engage my life that the friend I now venture to recommend to your favor, is such an one."[8]

Tradition has it that Washington welcomed Pinckney into his official family as an aide-de-camp and that Pinckney participated in the battles of Brandywine and Germantown. No doubt Pinckney was with the army during these battles but the evidence to support the claim that he was a military confidant of Washington is meager. Washington mentioned Pinckney only once during the time he was with the army. "Colo. Pinkney of South Carolina paid me a visit two days ago," Washington wrote late in August. During their conference the two men discussed the readiness of Charleston to withstand a surprise attack. Pinckney, Washington observed, seemed apprehensive that Charleston had been "lulled into security" and that it would be "quite unprepared for an attack."[9]

On the day that Washington noted his interview with Pinckney, the general staff had held a council of war. The officers decided that a fleet carrying the army of Sir William Howe was on its way to attack Charleston.[10] Though Pinckney must have wished to return home immediately, he stayed with Washington's army for several more weeks. It was during these weeks in September and October 1777 that the army fought the unsuccessful battles of Brandywine Creek and Germantown. Pinckney may have had his first combat experience here.[11] If he distinguished himself in any way, however, Washington did not hear of it. Years later when Washington was evaluating candidates to command the United States Army, he informed the cabinet that "what [Pinckney's] spirit for enterprise is, whether inactive or

8. John C. Fitzpatrick, comp., *Calendar of the Correspondence of George Washington*, 4 vols. (Washington, D.C., 1915), I, 358; Henry Middleton to George Washington, July 5, 1777, Gratz Collection, Hist. Soc. of Pa.; Thomas Lynch to Washington, July 5, 1777, in *Charleston Year Book—1886* (Charleston, n.d.), 337–38.

9. Washington to the President of Congress, Aug. 21, 1777, in John C. Fitzpatrick, ed., *The Writings of George Washington*, 39 vols. (Washington, D.C., 1931–44), IX, 111.

10. William S. Baker, *Itinerary of General Washington from June 15, 1775, to December 23, 1783* (Phila., 1892), 84.

11. The evidence that Pinckney was with Washington's army during these battles is indirect or hearsay, but there is little reason to doubt it. The engagements at Brandywine Creek and Germantown occurred on Sept. 11 and Oct. 4,

indolent I am unable to say, never having had any opportunity to form a judgment of his talents as a Military character."[12] This comment hardly indicates that Pinckney was among Washington's inner circle of advisers or that he bore any significant responsibilities at Brandywine Creek and Germantown.

Having won no honors with Washington's army, Pinckney set out for Charleston where the next British blows were expected to fall. By early December 1777, he was with his troops at Fort Moultrie. A month later his regiment was ordered back into Charleston.[13]

News from Georgia made it appear that Pinckney's regiment must forego the debilitating joys of town life. Late in 1777 Governor John Rutledge received a call for reinforcements from General Robert Howe, who wanted to destroy the British post at St. Augustine. St. Augustine was not only a haven for Tories but also a supply base for the Florida Rangers, a raiding band that was terrorizing Georgia below the Savannah River. But Pinckney and the other South Carolina officers balked at Howe's request, arguing that Charleston could not be defended if stripped of its present garrison. And after all, they contended, Charleston was the vital center of southern resistance. It would not be wise to take chances with Charleston's safety. Howe could not be put off so easily. When Georgia was unable to raise sufficient troops for the campaign, Howe ordered General Moultrie to send 250 men from the South Carolina continental line to bolster his contingent.[14]

After informing Howe that a detachment under Pinckney was on

1777. On Oct. 5, Thomas Pinckney wrote a letter to Charles Cotesworth, an indication that he was not expected in Charleston for several weeks. This letter is in Cross, ed., "Letters of Thomas Pinckney," *S. C. Hist. Mag.*, 58 (1957), 145. Alexander Garden, Pinckney's friend and eulogist, stated that Pinckney was at Brandywine and Germantown, *Anecdotes of the American Revolution*, 3rd ed., 3 vols. (N.Y., 1865), I, 92.

12. Washington's evaluation of Pinckney, written in March 1792, is in Fitzpatrick, ed., *Writings of Washington*, XXXI, 512. Washington's knowledge of Pinckney in 1792 was based on hearsay, the contacts he and Pinckney had had at the federal Constitutional Convention, and visits at Mount Vernon. At best Pinckney was with Washington's army only four and a half months, for he was back in Charleston no later than Dec. 4, 1777.

13. Charleston *S. C. Gazette*, Jan. 8, 1778. The regiment returned on the seventh. See "Order Book of the 1st. Regt.," *S. C. Hist. and Gen. Mag.*, 7 (1906), 79, 106, and 8 (1907), 85.

14. Moultrie, *Memoirs*, I, 195; Kenneth Coleman, *The American Revolution in Georgia, 1763–1789* (Athens, Ga., 1958), 106–7; William Moultrie to Henry Laurens, Apr. 19, 1778, in Moultrie, *Memoirs*, II, 367.

its way, Moultrie added: "I think you will be glad to see [Pinckney] with the regiment." Pinckney left Charleston on April 24, 1778, not suspecting that the campaign he was beginning would be ruined by dissension among the commanders and sickness or death among the soldiers.[15] There would be no glory in Georgia.

Pinckney was optimistic upon reaching Savannah. He believed that the expedition was moving forward in a promising way although the needed supplies had not yet arrived from Charleston. By May 9 his troops had marched to Fort Howe on the Altamaha River. They stayed close to Fort Howe until June 14, together with the continental troops commanded by Colonel Samuel Elbert of Georgia. Sickness soon broke out in the camp, only adding to the troubles and irritations caused by the "exceedingly Sultry" weather.[16]

The troops grew restless as they waited well over two weeks for the promised supply galley from Charleston. Even the basic equipment they had brought was inadequate; there were too few canteens, camp kettles, and tents. Somewhere the requisition system had broken down and someone was to blame. Pinckney, a firm believer that military morale depended upon the creature comforts being generously supplied, decided that General Moultrie was responsible for their wretched situation. "I owe it to candor and to our friendship to tell you," Pinckney wrote Moultrie in an accusing tone, that "you have been much too parsimonious in your fitting us out for this expedition." However, Pinckney added, when the supplies from Charleston do arrive the troops will shake off their troubles and have "some amusement by the attack on Fort Tonyn."[17]

Thomas Pinckney in a witty letter to his sister sarcastically described the faltering Georgia expedition as a "glorious Campaign." Unfavorable weather conditions, spreading sickness, mounting deaths, and lack of supplies were not the only limiting factors. There was a complete lack of coordination—to state it mildly—between the commanders of the continental and militia troops. In Thomas Pinckney's

15. Moultrie to Howe, Apr. 18, 24, 1778, in Moultrie, *Memoirs*, II, 371, 377. A good account of the Florida expedition is found in Gregorie, *Thomas Sumter*, 64–69.

16. Pinckney to Moultrie, May 4, 1778, Moultrie, *Memoirs*, II, 380; John F. Grimké, "Journal of the Campaign to the Southward, May 9th to July 14th, 1778," *S. C. Hist. and Gen. Mag.*, 12 (1911), 61.

17. Pinckney to Moultrie, May 24, 1778, Moultrie, *Memoirs*, I, 212.

words, there was a "Chaos of Command." Colonel Andrew Williamson, commanding the South Carolina militia, refused to take orders
from General Howe who had a continental commission. Commodore
Bowlan insisted that he was completely free to use his ships as he
pleased. Governor John Houston of Georgia was particularly ob-
structive, even refusing to divide his ample rice supply with needy
continental troops.[18] Jealousy and pettiness were the "generals" who
decided the outcome of this expedition.

The problems generated by the lack of cooperation became more
serious as the troops approached and then occupied the abandoned
Fort Tonyn in East Florida. In order to drive farther into East Florida and to defeat General Augustine Prévost, the Americans needed
to pool their resources and to unify their command. But it was too
late to smooth over the childish bickering. With Colonel Williamson,
Governor Houston, and Commodore Bowlan insisting that each of
their commands be independent of the others, Pinckney despaired for
the expedition even if every other condition were favorable.[19]

The other requirements, of course, were not favorable. Pinckney
described their deplorable condition to General Moultrie on July 6:
". . . our number are now only half less than what they were when
we joined at Fort Howe: our horses, too, having no grain to support
them die daily." Sickness and lack of supplies brought the expedition
to a standstill. By July 10 Pinckney felt the troops must begin to retreat at once or they would not be able to retreat at all. This expedition, he feared, could possibly be crowned "another Saratoga, in
reverse. . . ."[20] The other officers agreed. In a council of war held on
July 11 the continental officers tried to find justification for the lives
that had been lost, claiming that the purpose of the mission had been
achieved since the enemy had been driven out of Georgia and Fort
Tonyn destroyed. General Howe and the army left Fort Tonyn three
days later, but not before Howe praised the "readiness with which
the Officers received orders, and the punctuality with which they

18. Thomas Pinckney to Harriott Horry, May 23, 1778, in Cross, ed., "Letters
of Thomas Pinckney," S. C. Hist. Mag., 58 (1957), 150; Charles Cotesworth
Pinckney to General Moultrie, July 10, 1778, Moultrie, Memoirs, I, 230; Thomas
Pinckney to Harriott Horry, July 11, 1778, Pinckney Family Papers, Lib. Cong.
19. Grimké, "Journal," S. C. Hist. and Gen. Mag., 12 (1911), 190–91; Pinckney
to Moultrie, July 10, 1778, Moultrie, Memoirs, I, 231.
20. Pinckney to Moultrie, July 6, 10, 1778, Moultrie, Memoirs, I, 229–31.

executed them." Howe seemingly was referring primarily to Pinckney, Colonel Elbert, and their regimental officers. With these words
of praise to sweeten an otherwise disagreeable mission, Pinckney
loaded the sick troops aboard ships for the trip back to Charleston
and was himself back in town by the end of July.[21]

The survivors returned weary and dispirited. Pinckney was certain
that one "campaign to the southward is more fatiguing than five to
the northward," particularly unsuccessful ones. Pinckney did learn
one lesson in this expedition: when an army is facing the enemy, all
jealousy about rank and position should be put aside. While Pinckney
felt abused when others were promoted over him, he did not become
surly and uncooperative. This generosity was characteristic of him,
but it was also founded upon his experiences in the Florida campaign
of 1778.[22]

After the Florida expedition it was apparent that Britain had taken
the offensive in the south. Charleston was redoubling efforts to
strengthen its approaches, Pinckney wrote to Henry Laurens, so that
"we may receive with due respect and military honours the British
Fleet and army." Pinckney assured Laurens, then in Philadelphia,
that he would "have no reason to blush for us in the hour of trial,"
for all their efforts would be inspired by "an utter detestation of the
British Tyranny. . . ." The enemy, he felt confident, would receive
a "more serious drubbing than we had the honour of giving them
June Seventy Six."[23] Occasional British reverses in the north were
making Pinckney unwisely overconfident.

The logical place for South Carolinians to give the enemy a "serious

21. The discussion in the council of war, the officers present, and the resolves
passed are in Moultrie, *Memoirs*, I, 232–36. Another account of the council meeting can be found in Grimké, "Journal," *S. C. Hist. and Gen. Mag.*, 12 (1911),
200–03. Howe's statement is in Charles C. Jones, Jr., "The Life and Services of
the Honorable Major Gen. Samuel Elbert of Georgia," *The Magazine of History*, Extra-Number, No. 13 (N.Y., 1911), 19. Pinckney's return to Charleston
was noted in the Charleston *S. C. Gazette*, July 30, 1778.

22. General Gadsden, Pinckney's old commanding officer, was not as generous
as Pinckney. Gadsden was indignant when General Howe was selected to command in the southern theater. Gadsden's slurring remarks about Howe became
cause for a duel between Howe and Gadsden shortly after the Florida expedition. Pinckney served as Howe's second, Barnard Elliott serving Gadsden as
second. Neither Howe nor Gadsden was injured. McCrady, *History, 1775–1780*,
305–08; Charleston *S. C. Gazette*, Sept. 3, 1778. In Johnson, *Traditions of the
Revolution*, 204–06, is a poem celebrating this duel.

23. Pinckney to Laurens, Oct. 13, 1778, Henry Laurens Papers, South Caroliniana Library, University of South Carolina, Columbia, S.C.

drubbing" late in 1778 was in Georgia. As part of their general strategy to subdue the south, the British planned first to invade and conquer Georgia. South Carolina became justifiably concerned when General Prévost launched one prong of the British attack from St. Augustine in November 1778.[24] It was better to meet the enemy in the buffer state of Georgia now, South Carolinians reasoned, than to have their own lands eventually suffer from certain military occupation.

Pinckney, Moultrie, and Barnard Elliott met with President Rawlins Lowndes in council late in November and evidently decided to send immediate aid to Georgia. They moved too slowly. By the time the troops of South Carolina had begun to march toward Georgia, the British were approaching Savannah by sea. On December 29, 1778, the British took the city after a short struggle. Georgia was now largely secured to the British armies for the duration of the war.[25]

At the time this fact was not clear to General Benjamin Lincoln who had replaced Howe as commander of the southern department. Lincoln wanted to defend Georgia vigorously or at least keep the British forces off balance by probing attacks. But Lincoln soon encountered the same discouraging pettiness in commanders that Howe had experienced in the Florida campaign. The South Carolina militia troops came and left the army as they pleased. They also claimed exemption from courts-martial for disobeying orders. In desperation Lincoln asked Pinckney and Moultrie to return to the legislature in Charleston and explain how difficult it was to plan strategy when the state militia would not take orders from Lincoln. Pinckney and Moultrie were to press for legislation subjecting the militia to courts-martial for disobeying orders. There had been determined resistance to this idea by Colonel Charles Pinckney and other prominent legislators, but when Charles Cotesworth Pinckney and Moultrie, who were "exceedingly warm," roused "the spirit as well as the indignation of the House . . . at the conduct of their fellow citizens," the House responded by passing a bill subjecting the militia to the rigors of martial law.[26]

---

24. Coleman, *American Revolution in Georgia*, 116–19.
25. Moultrie, *Memoirs*, I, 246–47; Coleman, *American Revolution in Georgia*, 120–21.
26. Charles Pinckney, Jr., to Mrs. Charles [Eliza] Pinckney, Feb. 24, 1779, Gibbes, ed., *Documentary History*, II, 106.

Pinckney returned at once to his troops stationed at Purrysburg, on the Great Yemassee Bluff overlooking the Savannah, where he remained as one of Lincoln's "mere Parade soldiers" until mid-April. But everything changed on April 19 when Lincoln called a council of war. Lincoln had decided to cross the Savannah River in order to cut the enemy's supply lines and to prevent the British from joining their Indian allies. Pinckney accompanied Lincoln on this expedition while General Moultrie remained to defend South Carolina with about twelve hundred troops.[27]

Contrary to Lincoln's and Pinckney's expectations, it was Moultrie's force that saw most of the action. On April 29 General Prévost crossed the Savannah River to procure provisions in South Carolina but decided to advance toward Charleston when only Moultrie's small force was deployed to counter him. Lincoln believed Prévost's thrust was entirely a diversionary action, intended to draw the American army back into South Carolina. Pinckney accepted Lincoln's reasoning, for at a council of war he joined other officers of Lincoln's army in refusing Moultrie's urgent pleas for substantial reinforcements.[28]

General Prévost saw that he had a chance to capture Charleston and therefore spurred his men on. By May 11 he was at the city gates. Because of Lincoln's incredible slowness in bringing his army back to Charleston and the belief of the newly re-elected Governor Rutledge that Prévost commanded an overwhelming force, Charleston almost capitulated in May 1779 rather than in 1780.[29]

Prévost's army brought the first severe financial reverses of the war to the Pinckney family. Thomas Pinckney's plantation at Ashepoo was burned by British marauders as part of their campaign to devastate the area between Savannah and Charleston. Everything in the home was lost, including the personal papers of Chief Justice Pinckney. The slaves were carried away as well. Eliza's home, Belmont,

27. Thomas Pinckney to Harriott Horry, Feb. 22, 1779, Cross, ed., "Letters of Thomas Pinckney," S. C. Hist. Mag., 58 (1957), 227; Moultrie, Memoirs, I, 374–75; McCrady, History, 1775–1780, 349–50.

28. Minutes of a Council of War, Silver Bluff, May 2, 1779, Miscellaneous Manuscripts, Henry Huntington Library, San Marino, Cal.; Bulger, The British Expedition to South Carolina (U. of Mich.), 46–47.

29. McCrady, History, 1775–1780, 364–66, 370–71, 376–77; Smith, Loyalists and Redcoats, 104.

was not burned nor were the Negroes taken, but nearly everything in the house was smashed. Charles Cotesworth immediately offered to divide his own estate three ways with his mother and brother, a "truly generous offer," Eliza wrote to Thomas, an offer which "greatly affected" her. But, she added, "I am . . . not surprised at his liberality."[30]

To Thomas Pinckney the financial hardships were not as important as the fact that he had yet seen no real action, a sentiment shared by his brother. Thomas expressed his feeling of lucklessness in a clever letter to his sister Harriott: "You may depend upon there being no action wherever I am," he complained. "It is now four Years since I began to strut under a Cap and Feather and have been running all about this and the Neighbouring States in pursuit of broken Bones" but without success.[31]

Charles Cotesworth had luck strikingly similar to his brother's. A series of unfortunate circumstances had frustrated his growing "passion for glory." When the British fleet had tried to destroy Fort Sullivan in June 1776, he was hurrahing from the sidelines of Fort Johnson. He had won no laurels at Brandywine and Germantown. The disastrous campaign to East Florida in 1778 was hardly the kind from which heroes are made. And early in 1779 he was tramping through Georgia with Lincoln while Moultrie was defending a besieged Charleston. Surely his fortunes would change.

The British conquest of Georgia in 1779 marked the beginning of the battle for South Carolina, for the state was no longer protected by the Georgia buffer. Yet immediately after Prévost's daring stroke, South Carolina did not appear seriously threatened. Lincoln's forces were defeated late in June as they attempted to cut down part of Prévost's retreating troops, but no new attack was launched by the British. Carolinians breathed easier when Prévost's men camped at Beaufort on Port Royal Island. Early in July Pinckney took up an

30. Eliza Pinckney to Thomas Pinckney, May [17], 1779, Ravenel, *Eliza Pinckney*, 275–76.

31. Thomas Pinckney to Harriott Horry, May 22, 1779, in Cross, ed., "Letters of Thomas Pinckney," *S. C. Hist. Mag.*, 58 (1957), 233. Thomas mentioned in this letter that Charles Cotesworth had been thrown by his horse Caesar and had suffered a shoulder separation, the only time Pinckney was injured during the war.

advanced position in the Port Royal area to observe the movements of these nine hundred British troops.[32]

This routine intelligence mission ended suddenly when the French admiral Charles-Hector, Comte d'Estaing, appeared unexpectedly off the coast of Georgia on September 8, 1779, with what seemed an armada to delighted Americans: twenty-two sail of the line, ten frigates and other ships, plus four thousand troops. Flushed with recent victories at St. Vincent and Grenada, d'Estaing announced that he would now drive the British army from its Savannah stronghold. South Carolinians were eager to assist d'Estaing, hoping their state could be secured for another campaign season.[33]

South Carolina rushed a sizable force to strengthen d'Estaing's contingent, much to his annoyance; the Comte saw no reason to share his certain victory with the American "insurgents." South Carolina's efforts were largely wasted. Against the advice of the continental officers, including his liaison officer Thomas Pinckney, d'Estaing foolishly procrastinated until Prévost had been reinforced by the picked Scottish troops at Beaufort, almost insuring failure of the siege. When finally launched on October 9, the attack was a miserable and disheartening failure. Charles Cotesworth Pinckney had no doubt that Savannah could have been taken if properly besieged. His only comfort in the costly operation was that his regiment preserved its "order inviolate," holding steady under severe fire.[34]

With the British established in Georgia and preparing to move north, South Carolinians realized their time for preparation was short. They erected additional batteries on the Charleston mainland and reinforced the defensive works around the harbor which they had allowed to fall into disrepair. Pinckney, who was stationed at Fort Moultrie, doubtless entertained hopes of repeating Moultrie's success

32. Moultrie to General Lincoln, July 5, 7, 1779, Moultrie, *Memoirs*, II, 10, 15–16.

33. McCrady, *History, 1775–1780*, 400–07; David Ramsay, *The History of the American Revolution*, 2 vols. (London, 1793), II, 122.

34. McCrady, *History, 1775–1780*, 409–10; Pinckney to Eliza Pinckney, Oct. 15, 1779, Pinckney Family Papers, Lib. Cong.; Thomas Pinckney to ? [*ca.* Oct. 10, 1779], quoted in Pinckney, *Life of Thomas Pinckney*, 62. A brief discussion of the Savannah siege is found in Christopher Ward, *The War of the Revolution*, ed. John R. Alden, 2 vols. (N.Y., 1952), I, 688–94. Alexander A. Lawrence, *Storm over Savannah: The Story of Count d'Estaing and the Siege of the Town in 1779* (Athens, Ga., 1951), gives the most complete account of the operation.

of June 1776. It was generally anticipated that there would be a major engagement between the defenders of Fort Moultrie and the now approaching British fleet as it attempted to sail past the fort. February or March of 1780 seemed to promise much for Charles Cotesworth Pinckney, long denied his meed of glory.

The strategy to hold Charleston by making the harbor its first line of defense was gradually abandoned by General Lincoln. He was perhaps overly sensitive to the fears of his naval officers that their ships would be destroyed if they tried to prevent the British fleet from sailing into the harbor. By withdrawing his small yet potentially useful navy (152 guns) from the harbor entrance, Lincoln allowed the British ships to sail over the bar and into the harbor unchallenged. Once there, they needed only a good southerly breeze at flood tide to sail past Fort Moultrie.[35]

Lincoln and Pinckney did not agree on the need to hold Fort Moultrie whatever the cost. Pinckney contended that the fort should be held to the last possible moment, even against siege tactics. He requested siege supplies from General Lincoln late in February but apparently did not receive them.[36] After the British fleet crossed the bar and entered the harbor on March 20, Lincoln seriously began to consider evacuating Fort Moultrie. In a long and persuasively written letter to Lincoln, Pinckney stated why he believed the fort should not be abandoned. First, it would be a serious blow to public morale since most Carolinians supposed the fort necessary to a successful defense of the city. Second, if the British were compelled to besiege the fort, it would give the town additional time to prepare for an attack. To abandon Fort Moultrie, Pinckney argued, would be to give up the harbor completely. Further, if the British attacked Charleston and were defeated, they could effectively stop any American harassment by retreating to Fort Moultrie. If the Americans re-

35. McCrady, *History, 1775–1780*, 438–41, 459. The best detailed account of the Charleston campaign is Bulger's British Expedition to Charleston (U. of Mich.). Bulger indicates that the arguments of the naval commanders justifying a retreat from the harbor entrance were sound, 99–101. McCrady disagrees with this position.

36. Pinckney to [Lincoln], Feb. 25, 1780, Gratz Coll., Hist. Soc. of Pa. Pinckney said that he had heard "abstinence much commended for quickening the mental Qualifications, and therefore held it to be truly philosophical that a General should fast. . . ." Lincoln could have interpreted this witticism as a criticism of his strategy.

tained the fort, however, and the British were defeated in the direct assault upon the town, the guns of the fort could then sweep them during the retreat. Finally, Pinckney believed that the guns and supplies of the fort could not be safely transported to friendly territory. If the guns at Fort Moultrie were to be used at all, it would be at the fort.[37]

Pinckney naturally hoped that the British would try to silence the fort's guns before sailing past, as they had attempted to do in 1776, but he was severely disappointed. Admiral Marriot Arbuthnot wisely decided to sail past Fort Moultrie quickly, allowing Sir Henry Clinton's army to take it later. Pinckney's men raced to their stations when the British fleet weighed anchor and prepared to pass the fort on April 7, 1780. A thunderous cannonade ensued as the passing ships exchanged shots with the guns at the fort. The Americans cheered when one ship was grounded (and eventually destroyed by its crew) and another was damaged. Fourteen British sailors were killed and another fifteen wounded. The Americans did not lose a single man, but the British had won the battle. The fort was neutralized as a point of defense.[38] Another chance for glory had slipped from Pinckney's grasp.

The outlook for Charleston became increasingly grim. By a series of advances over the next seven weeks the British land forces gradually blocked the different routes of retreat. General Lincoln was no doubt at fault when he decided to mass several thousand men on the Charleston neck. General Washington and Henry Lee thought Lincoln's strategy was foolish and historians have since agreed with their judgment. Ironically, Lincoln was not willing to risk losing the continental navy to defend the harbor's entrance, but he was willing to jeopardize the cream of the southern army in a foolish defense of the town. Lincoln should have abandoned the town, preserving his army intact to fight another day.[39]

37. Pinckney to Lincoln, Mar. 23, 1780, Ford Coll., N.Y. Pub. Lib.
38. Garden, *Eulogy on Pinckney*, 17; Maurice A. Crouse, ed., "Papers of Gabriel Manigault, 1771–1784," *S. C. Hist. Mag.*, 64 (1963), 10; Edward M. Riley, "Historic Fort Moultrie in Charleston Harbor," *S. C. Hist. and Gen. Mag.*, 51 (1950), 66–67; Bulger, British Expedition to Charleston (U. of Mich.), 125–26.
39. Henry Lee, *Memoirs of the War in the Southern Department of the United States*, 2 vols. (Phila., 1812), I, 125–26; Ward, *War of the Revolution*, ed. Alden, II, 697; Alden, *American Revolution*, 231.

Pinckney must assume a share of the responsibility for Lincoln's costly error, for he put extreme pressure on Lincoln to defend Charleston. For a man who had studied military tactics at a professional school and who considered himself a quasi-professional soldier, Pinckney showed exceedingly poor judgment in 1780. When the British clearly had the town at their mercy, General Lincoln called a council of war on April 19 to consider whether the town should be surrendered and the troops evacuated. Christopher Gadsden, the acting lieutenant-governor, was violently opposed to capitulation and even boldly brought the civilian council into the military meeting to challenge Lincoln and those officers who thought capitulation prudent. It was a stormy session with Gadsden clearly out of order. Lincoln, however, was too timid to object. Just after Gadsden and the council had left, Pinckney burst into the room obviously excited and rudely determined to have his say. He had heard, he said, that the town might be surrendered and had raced over from Fort Moultrie to object. After stating why the town should be defended, Pinckney turned on Colonel Laumoy, accusing him and his engineers of being defeatists and, by implication, cowards as well. Gadsden and Pinckney had their way; the council voted not to capitulate or evacuate.[40]

By May 7 the Charleston garrison was in a desperate situation. There was no escape route, the enemy had an overwhelming force, and the Americans were without any well-founded hope for major reinforcements. Lincoln called a council of war on May 8 to consider General Henry Clinton's terms of surrender. Sixty-one officers were there. As the presiding officer, Lincoln asked whether the terms of capitulation should be considered. Pinckney got the floor and in a heated speech declared that even though the town was doomed to fall, they should sell their lives dearly. Resistance to the "last extremity" would be both honorable and militarily valuable. A spirited resistance with the resources they had would cripple the British army. In this way they could contribute most to the cause of all America. But others arose and argued equally fervently for capitulation. When General Lincoln called for a vote, the capitulationists decisively defeated Pinckney's faction forty-nine to eleven. All the generals and

40. William Gilmore Simms, *South Carolina in the Revolutionary War* (Charleston, 1853), 128–29.

all the colonels but two favored receiving terms of capitulation. The overwhelming weight of talent believed that a desperate defense was a foolish measure.[41]

Why Pinckney advised holding out to the "last extremity" can only be surmised. He was undoubtedly chagrined over his earlier assertion that the British could not successfully besiege Charleston and perhaps hoped to compensate for his lack of judgment by bravery. Also, as he said, he was convinced that the British army could be badly mauled if it stormed the Charleston fortress. Many would be killed, perhaps even himself. But as he stated later, death inevitably came to every man. To make that death "useful to one's Country," he believed, was the "greatest felicity a patriotic soldier can hope for."[42] He might have seen that this could be his last chance for glory. All his failures to distinguish himself in the previous four years would be forgotten if he could play a conspicuous part in a heroic defense of his beloved Charleston.

Others were not so brave—or so foolish—as he, and the terms of capitulation were arranged. On May 12, 1780, the American continental troops marched out of town and stacked their arms. Pinckney's career as a Revolutionary soldier largely ended on that day. There would be no more engagements, no more marches through South Carolina and Georgia, no more chances for heroism. He had no more need for his horse Caesar. Pinckney's only suffering from 1780 to the end of the war would be mental. The frustration of being a captive while others were fighting and of being separated from his family and home were to be Pinckney's major trials during the next two years.

The captured officers were sent to Haddrell's Point near the present town of Mount Pleasant, South Carolina. Pinckney was fortunate that his cousin Colonel Charles Pinckney's plantation home, Snee Farm, was nearby. He was invited to stay there during his captivity. Pinckney was allowed some freedom, his friends and family were occasionally permitted to visit him, and he was permitted to keep a

41. One account of Pinckney's exhortation is in Ravenel, *Charleston*, 268. The record of the council of war held on May 8, 1780, is in *Charleston Year Book*, *1897* (Charleston, 1897), 349.

42. This statement is in an essay Pinckney prepared for delivery to the South Carolina State Society of the Cincinnati, July 4, 1789, and is in the Pinckney Family Papers, Lib. Cong.

Negro servant who carried his messages to town or brought him books, food, and newspapers.[43] He was bored but not especially uncomfortable.

Pinckney was angry, however, at being confined to Haddrell's Point. Writing to Major Money, a British officer, he complained that he had not given his parole for Haddrell's Point but for Charleston. He had brought his family to town, had had his children inoculated, and had arranged other affairs to suit his residence in Charleston.[44] The British tried to capitalize on his unhappiness; several British officers discreetly suggested that things could be very pleasant for him if he would consider a reconciliation with the Crown. These efforts did not go unnoticed. A rumor evidently circulated that Pinckney might be willing to compromise his position. Edward Rutledge was incredulous but nevertheless asked Pinckney if the rumor were founded in fact. "You, My dear Ned," Pinckney replied, "may be assured I will not do anything . . . at which my friends may blush. If I had a vein that did not beat with love for my country, I myself would open it. If I had a drop of blood that could flow dishonorably, I myself would let it out."[45] A reconciliation was impossible. Pinckney had grown to hate the British too much. The British took Pinckney at his word and acted accordingly. As a first step they compelled his wife Sally and his children to evacuate their town home. One month later the commissioner of sequestered estates seized nearly all his properties.[46]

A personal tragedy also plagued Pinckney during his confinement. His infant son, Charles Cotesworth, contracted smallpox and despite two inoculations did not survive the disease. Pinckney's letters to his mother from September through December 1780 are filled with concern for his stricken son. "Has my little Boy been yet inoculated? and is the pock of a favourable sort?" he wrote to Eliza when he first

43. General Moultrie also took up residence at Snee Farm according to his *Memoirs*, II, 116. For further details on Pinckney during his captivity, see Ravenel, *Charleston*, 279.

44. Pinckney to Major Money, June 30, 1780, Pinckney Family Papers, Lib. Cong. Pinckney assured Money that favors would not change his politics: "I entered into this Cause after much reflection, and through principle, my heart is altogether American, and neither severity, nor favour, nor poverty, nor affluence can ever induce me to swerve from it."

45. N.d., quoted in Ravenel, *Eliza Pinckney*, 297.

46. Pinckney to Harriott Horry, Oct. 8, 1782 [1780], Ravenel, *Charleston*, 280; Charleston S. C. *Gazette*, Nov. 22, 1780.

learned of his son's sickness. His expectations for a recovery fluctuated from day to day. By November Pinckney was resigned to losing his "little fellow" but was still ready to "hope for the best. . . ." Baby Charles Cotesworth evidently died in December of 1780 while his father was in town comforting him. Pinckney was not even allowed to stay in town for the boy's funeral but was curtly ordered back to Haddrell's Point. It was a sad Christmas season.[47]

Pinckney passed the wearisome hours at Snee Farm as best he could. He conversed with General Moultrie who was also confined there, with numerous other officers living nearby, or with Sally when she received permission to visit. Pinckney also played his cello to help pass the hours, at one point asking his mother to remind Sally to send "the musick Book I usually play from." In addition, he took an active interest in the education of his sister's son, Daniel Horry. Pinckney outlined a lengthy and difficult study program for Daniel, one that must have impressed his nephew with the disadvantages of having an educated but idle uncle.[48]

Pinckney's tedious situation changed in the summer of 1781 after the representatives of General Nathanael Greene and Lord Cornwallis concluded an agreement for the exchange of a limited number of prisoners. Those Americans not exchanged under the terms of the cartel were to be put on parole and sent to other places to await exchange. Pinckney, being one of those not immediately exchanged, was sent to Philadelphia in June 1781, perhaps sailing in the brig given to General Moultrie for the transportation of his family and friends.[49]

Philadelphia was kind to the exiled South Carolinians. Money was raised to tide over those who were utterly destitute. Charles Cotesworth, his wife, and his two girls, Maria and Harriott, were joined

47. Charles Cotesworth was born in the summer of 1780 according to a letter from Eliza Pinckney to Thomas Pinckney, Aug. 1780, Ravenel, *Eliza Pinckney*, 291. Colonel Pinckney's inquiries about his son can be found in his letters to Eliza Pinckney, Sept. 18, Nov. 10, 1780, Pinckney Papers, S.C. Hist. Soc. The last mention of young Charles was in a letter from Eliza Pinckney to [Thomas Pinckney], Dec. 4, 1780, Eliza Pinckney Letterbook, S.C. Hist. Soc. Eliza believed that "the poor little boy" would not recover, "though better today." See also Helen K. Hennig, *Great South Carolinians*, 2 vols. (Chapel Hill, 1940–49), I, 195.

48. Pinckney to Eliza Pinckney, Nov. 9, 1780, Pinckney Family Papers, Lib. Cong.; Pinckney to Harriott Horry, Oct. 8, 1782 [1780], Ravenel, *Charleston*, 280.

49. Moultrie, *Memoirs*, II, 200.

by Thomas Pinckney with his wife Elizabeth and infant son. Thomas was nursing a severe wound he had received at the Battle of Camden in August 1780. Although Thomas was permitted to return to Charleston for a time, the British commander there insisted that Thomas join the other captured American officers in Philadelphia. When Edward Rutledge with his wife and son reached Philadelphia, there was a small but happy family reunion. Rutledge had been exiled to St. Augustine after the fall of Charleston but was released on parole, like the Pinckneys, until an exchange could be arranged. Dr. George Logan, a prominent Philadelphia physician, kindly offered the three families the use of his country home Stenton just outside Philadelphia. Although rather dilapidated, Stenton was able to accommodate the party of ten.[50]

The friends enjoyed sharing their experiences of recent months, but Pinckney did not allow the joys of the reunion to dull his desire to rejoin the army. He remained alert to any possibility of an exchange; there was still a war on. He had written to George Washington less than a month after his captivity began, reminding Washington that he was the senior colonel captured "and in case of an exchange being upon the carpet hopes that he will not be forgot." Two months after arriving in Philadelphia, Pinckney again wrote to Washington implying that he had been unfairly treated in the recent exchange. He hoped Washington would forgive his "importunity" but asked him to "consider how irksome my present situation is" and how much he longed "to join in revenging the cruel outrages committed on my Country." Washington assured Pinckney that he would be "particularly careful" that no injustice was done to Pinckney because of his "personal regard" for him.[51]

Still there was no action for months on his case. Pinckney's rising hopes were dashed early in 1782 when it was rumored that eligible American officers would not be exchanged because Congress did not want to release the captured Lord Cornwallis, the price Great Britain

50. Mabel L. Webber, ed., "Josiah Smith's Diary, 1780–1781," *S. C. Hist. and Gen. Mag.*, 34 (1933), 81–82; Frederick B. Tolles, *George Logan of Philadelphia* (N.Y., 1953), 46.

51. Pinckney to Washington, June 9, 1780, Pinckney, *Life of Thomas Pinckney*, 74; Pinckney to Washington, Sept. 11, 1782 [1781], Gratz Coll., Hist. Soc. of Pa.; Washington to Pinckney, Sept. 24, 1781, Fitzpatrick, ed., *Writings of Washington*, XXIII, 133.

demanded for any meaningful exchange. Angry at this news, Pinckney went to the secretary of war's office and inquired if Congress had formally expressed itself on Cornwallis's exchange. When the officials there professed to know nothing of the matter, Pinckney went to the office of the secretary of Congress and demanded to see the journal of Congress. The secretary turned him away.

Pinckney's temper flared. He immediately fired off an angry letter to the delegates of South Carolina in Congress. Among them was his brother-in-law Arthur Middleton.[52] Pinckney's indignation is apparent in every paragraph. As a citizen he had been denied his right to inspect the proceedings of his duly elected delegates. This procedure was dangerous to the liberties of free men. A precedent was being established by which dishonest men could hide their questionable acts. Secrecy was not justified in this case. If the resolution on Cornwallis had passed and was founded upon the abilities of Cornwallis, Pinckney would be astonished for Cornwallis "has given no proofs of either military or political skills sufficient to intimidate us." Pinckney concluded by practically demanding to see the proceedings of the Congress on the Cornwallis matter.[53]

The delegates of South Carolina waited ten long days to answer Pinckney. Their formal reply must have infuriated him. No, they said, the journal could not be inspected. If he objected to this rule, please let him consider that it had been established before they were sent to Congress. As for the matter of Cornwallis' exchange, they had indeed voted against exchanging him and would be ready "to answer for our conduct . . . whenever . . . called upon by the Legislature of our Country."[54] Pinckney had lost his only battle against the classification of government information, but he had still learned what he wished to know.

Unknown to Pinckney, action was already being taken which led

52. Pinckney had fallen out with Middleton sometime in 1778. See Pinckney's letter to Henry Laurens, Oct. 13, 1778, Henry Laurens Papers, S. Caroliniana Lib. "Arthur Middleton," Pinckney confided to Laurens, "has turned most insufferably." Pinckney seemed to believe Middleton was shirking his legislative duties. But the ill feeling had evidently evaporated by the winter of 1782, for Pinckney was writing Middleton in a congenial tone.

53. Pinckney to Thomas Bee, Arthur Middleton, Isaac Motte, and Nicholas Eveleigh, Jan. 5, 1782, Arthur Middleton Papers, S.C. Hist. Soc.

54. Middleton, Bee, Motte, and Eveleigh to Pinckney, Jan. 15, 1782, *ibid.* The letter in the Middleton Papers appears to be a draft.

to his exchange. When General John Burgoyne of Saratoga fame was officially released from parole, Pinckney and Moultrie were part of the package exchange. Early in March 1782 Moultrie sent Pinckney his certificate of exchange observing with some understatement that it "will give you great pleasure."[55] Pinckney wasted no time in Philadelphia; in just over a month he joined the forces of General Nathanael Greene which were in camp near Dorchester, about fifty-five miles northwest of Charleston. Hostilities had largely ended, however, and Pinckney visited often with his family who were living at Arthur Middleton's plantation home on the Ashley River.[56] Charles Cotesworth Pinckney, like other Charleston exiles, was waiting for the British to evacuate Charleston voluntarily. Early in December 1782, after an occupation of over two years and seven months, the last British forces boarded their ships and sailed away. Pinckney and his family returned at once to their Charleston home.

For South Carolina the war was over. Hundreds returned to depleted or ruined fortunes, their reward for years of service to the patriot cause. Yet many could take satisfaction in the course they had followed. Pinckney certainly did. His fortune, his name and prestige, and his physical strength had been given freely to the cause he had adopted.[57] All his hopes and wishes to the contrary, Pinckney had neither the military talent nor the good fortune which make heroes out of common mortals. In fact, if his fellow soldiers were superstitious, they might have seen his very presence as an omen of ill luck, for Pinckney was not actively involved in a successful battle during the entire war. Yet he was a well-disciplined soldier whose conscientious devotion to duty caused Generals Lincoln and Howe to think highly of him. Pinckney never won the honors of a hero,

---

55. Moultrie, *Memoirs*, II, 354; Moultrie to [Pinckney], Mar. 3, 1782, Pinckney Family Papers, Lib. Cong.; Gibbes, ed., *Documentary History*, II, 159.

56. Pinckney's movements from Apr.-Oct. 1782 can be partially traced through his letters in the Pinckney Family Papers, Lib. Cong.; Arthur Middleton Papers, S.C. Hist. Soc.; Nathanael Greene Papers, Duke Univ. Lib.; and in Barnwell, ed., "Correspondence of Arthur Middleton," *S. C. Hist. and Gen. Mag.*, 27 (1926).

57. The state financial records of South Carolina show that Pinckney loaned the state at least £21,500 during the war. The first loan of £13,500 was made on Sept. 7, 1779, the second on Feb. 17, 1780. Records of these loans are in the Audited Accounts of Charles Cotesworth Pinckney, S.C. Archives.

but he did earn the commendation and gratitude of his countrymen for faithful service. In recognition of this service, he was promoted to general as the war drew to a close.[58]

General Pinckney might have been excused if he had resolved to ignore politics in order to restore his damaged fortune. But Pinckneys were expected to answer the call to duty, and the call was still there. Before the Revolution, Pinckney had responded to the patriotic appeal. Now his own economic and social class needed his abilities. In chaotic South Carolina a responsible government had to be organized —responsible to the oligarchy, that is. Up-country demands for a greater share of political power in governing the state were becoming more insistent and were being pushed by patriots who had risen to positions of influence during the war. Experienced parliamentarians and skillful politicians were needed to blunt the thrust of the democratic impulse. For Pinckney there was a new cause to serve and a new battle to fight.

58. The exact date of Pinckney's promotion to brigadier general by brevet is unknown. Under both the American and British military systems a brevet could be conferred on an officer, giving him a higher rank in the army-at-large than he held in his own corps. This was occasionally done as a reward for outstanding service. See Fitzpatrick, ed., *Writings of Washington,* XXXI, 512. Pinckney did complain to General Greene in June 1782 when a junior officer was promoted over him. Pinckney wrote to Greene: "I acknowledge I am hurt at the placing of a Junior officer over my head; nor can I deem such treatment a proper reward for seven years faithful service; . . . But however I may be afflicted by this promotion, you shall find that in any Duty you may think proper to order me upon, I can never deem myself justifiable to my Country in withdrawing my Services from her . . . on account of any affront I may imagine I have received." To Greene, June 27, 1782, vol. 2, Nathanael Greene Papers, Lib. Cong.

IV

PROTECTOR OF THE LOW COUNTRY

The separate independence and individual sovereignty of the several states were never thought of by the enlightened band of patriots who framed this Declaration [of Independence]. Let us, then consider, all attempts to weaken this union, by maintaining that each state is separately and individually independent, as a species of political heresy, which can never benefit us, but may bring on us the most serious distresses.

—Charles Cotesworth Pinckney, 1788.

TO THE CRIES OF "A FAT SHEEP—A FAT SHEEP—PRICK HIM! PRICK HIM!" the members of the South Carolina legislature, temporarily meeting in Jacksonboro in 1782, began passing bills to punish those who had cooperated or were then cooperating with the British occupation forces. Those whose sins were particularly heinous had their estates confiscated. Others were burdened with a tax (amercement) heavy enough to remind them for years of their errors. It soon became noticeable—disturbingly noticeable to some—that most of the "fat sheep" were low-country planters with impressive assets in lands and securities. And it also was evident that up-country representatives joined enthusiastically in passing the confiscation and amercement bills, perhaps seeing them as a way to settle old political quarrels and to weaken the political power of the low country in future years.[1]

Although Pinckney had been elected to the Jacksonboro legislature, he never attended its sessions, choosing instead to remain near

1. Garden, *Anecdotes of the Revolution*, I, 179; Charles G. Singer, *South Carolina in the Confederation* (Phila., 1941), 105–06.

[71]

General Greene's army as long as the British were in South Carolina. Pinckney nevertheless let it be known that he absolutely opposed the confiscatory measures; not even giving comfort to the enemy, he felt, could justify the passage of ex post facto measures. In taking this position he differed with his friend Edward Rutledge who not only favored confiscation and amercement, but who had written the first draft of the amercement bill. To his credit Rutledge was distressed as he saw how the acts were used by crafty members of the legislature to take revenge on their personal or political enemies. "I wish to God you or the Pinckneys, or all were here," he wrote to Arthur Middleton, for their combined opposition to the acts, Rutledge felt, would help to reduce the number of confiscations springing from "private Resentment."[2]

Eliza Pinckney took a maternal pride in the "lenient and merciful" attitude of Charles Cotesworth and Thomas, seeing it as evidence of their humanitarianism and forgiving spirits. One might wonder if Charles Cotesworth Pinckney was acting entirely from such commendable motives. After all, members of his own family stood to lose many hundreds of pounds or their entire estates if punishment were ruthlessly and impartially applied. Henry Middleton, Colonel Charles Pinckney, and Daniel Horry, Charles Cotesworth Pinckney's brother-in-law, were all "fat sheep" whose estates were in danger; each had in some way indicated his lukewarm sentiments or even his disinterestedness in the patriot cause and was therefore considered fair game by the revenge-minded. Charles Cotesworth exerted himself to help the ailing Colonel Charles Pinckney in his fight against confiscation. The estate was not confiscated but it was amerced. Charles Cotesworth then generously offered to stand as security for the money Colonel Pinckney would have to borrow to pay the tax. Although Charles Cotesworth could not save Horry from amercement,

---

2. Edward McCrady, *History of South Carolina, 1780–1783* (N.Y., 1902), 557; Eliza Pinckney to Daniel Horry, n.d., in Ravenel, *Eliza Pinckney*, 310; Edward Rutledge to Arthur Middleton, Feb. 8, 26, 1782, Barnwell, ed., "Correspondence of Arthur Middleton," *S. C. Hist. and Gen. Mag.*, 27 (1926), 3, 7. For an analysis of loyalism in South Carolina, see Robert W. Barnwell, Jr., Loyalism in South Carolina, 1765–1785 (unpubl. Ph.D. diss., Duke Univ., 1941). Richard Morris has cautioned against presuming that the majority of southern Loyalists were found among the upper classes; "Class Struggle and the American Revolution," *Wm. and Mary Qtly.*, 3rd Ser., 19 (1962), 27.

Edward Rutledge believed that "had it not been for the many Virtues of the Pinckneys his Estate would have been confiscated."[3]

By all the standards of family and class interest, Pinckney's position was a logical one. Only a moment of reflection would indicate that many of those under attack for Loyalist sentiments would be staunch supporters of the planter-merchant oligarchy once the smoke of war had cleared. Pinckney saw no reason to advance the cause of demon democracy by permitting the legislature to banish or confiscate the property of the more substantial merchants and planters. Too, Pinckney's leniency may have been due to his own lack of personal suffering during the war. While the war was being waged with the greatest cruelty on both sides in the Carolina back country, Pinckney was enjoying the relative comfort of Snee Farm and Stenton. True, he had lost his slaves and his capital, but this was to be expected. At least no members of his immediate family had died because of the war. The war experience, then, had not been as bitter for Pinckney as it had for many of his low-country friends and up-country men as well.

Edward Rutledge was neither so rational nor so generous in his instincts. Perhaps Rutledge's suffering during his banishment to St. Augustine explains his more severe attitude. He returned to Charleston willing to see even his own father-in-law, Henry Middleton, be disciplined. In later years neither Charles Cotesworth Pinckney nor Edward Rutledge changed his opinion on this question despite their close personal and financial relationship. As late as 1787 they voted differently on a motion to bring in a bill to repeal the confiscation and amercement acts. This disagreement between these firm friends was symbolic of the general split in South Carolina over the wisdom of the confiscation and amercement measures.[4]

Of course the war had been a shattering experience for South

3. Ravenel, *Eliza Pinckney*, 310; Charles Cotesworth Pinckney to [Colonel Charles Pinckney], July 24, 1782, Pinckney Family Papers, Lib. Cong.; Edward Rutledge to Arthur Middleton, Feb. 26, 1782, Barnwell, ed., "Correspondence of Arthur Middleton," *S. C. Hist. and Gen. Mag.*, 27 (1926), 8.

4. McCrady, *History, 1780–1783*, 585; Feb. 21, 1787, Journals of the House of Representatives, S.C. Archives. An analysis of the vote shows that the up country voted eight to one against repeal. See Singer, *South Carolina in the Confederation*, 124. Merrill Jensen discusses the punishments meted out to Loyalists throughout the states in his *The New Nation: A History of the United States During the Confederation, 1781–1789* (N.Y., 1950), 265–81.

Carolina, economically and psychologically, and men do not react alike to suffering and catastrophe. Usually sensible men can become a bundle of neuroses and fears, quick to see mortal danger to themselves or to their position in society in incidents that would normally evoke only laughter or a minimum of concern. This can be seen in several incidents that aroused South Carolina shortly after the British evacuated Charleston on December 14, 1782.

The first incident involved, on the surface at least, the ownership of horses that Tadeusz Kosciuszko of the Continental Army had captured from the British in a raid. General Greene, according to law and usage, intended to sell the horses at auction and to use the funds to support the Continental Army. Difficulties arose when several citizens identified the horses as their own and demanded that they be returned; after all, they argued, one's army was supposed to protect citizen property in all circumstances. Greene's army had no right to support itself by confiscating the property of American patriots, even if found in enemy hands.

Greene believed this claim was totally unwarranted but called a council of officers to discuss what ought to be done. Only one man rose to support the citizens' claims. The owners were absolutely correct in demanding the return of their horses, Pinckney explained, for under the doctrine of the right of postliminium, armies are obliged to restore property to the original owners when it has been recovered from the enemy.[5] The plea was in vain. The continental officers voted that the army should use the horses as it wished.

When the decision of the officers became known, anguished cries went up throughout the low country. Greene was denounced in the legislature as a would-be dictator, a potential Cromwell, an agent of the Confederation Congress determined to crush the hard-won liberties of South Carolina.[6] This was hardly a rational reaction. But these were not normal times.

First, many planters faced the gloomy possibility of ruin, for the British soldiers had carried off their Negroes—estimated in the thou-

5. McCrady, *History, 1780–1783*, 663–66; William Johnson, *Sketches of the Life and Correspondence of Nathanael Greene* . . . , 2 vols. (Charleston, 1822), II, 345, suggested that by this stand Pinckney became the first man to argue the states rights position, "the protosire of South Carolina republicanism."

6. Johnson, *Life of Greene*, II, 387–89; Allan Nevins, *The American States During and After the Revolution, 1775–1789* (N.Y., 1927), 396–97. The out-

sands—and had destroyed considerable plantation property. Forced to purchase Negroes in order to begin production, the planters found themselves paying exorbitant prices in the immediate postwar period. Interest rates on credit ran as high as 50 per cent. Only under ideal conditions, lasting several years, could many planters hope to repay their loans. Second, the state government was heavily in debt and searching desperately for sources of revenue. This suggested either the necessity of heavy taxation or the repudiation of the state's debts —or both. And a third disturbing factor was the drive led by Commodore Alexander Gillon and Dr. James Fallon to assert the power of the lower classes against old Tories, British merchants coming back into Charleston, and the patriot low-country oligarchy. The lower classes, in fact, threatened to get out of hand. Mob action became common. The situation became so disturbing that the bells of St. Michael's Church were rung at any sign of mass disturbance, whereupon all the peace officers and "responsible" citizens were expected to rush into the street fully armed, ready to suppress rebellion.[7]

One incident particularly alarmed the comfortable and the established. After prompting by Dr. Fallon, a group of "mechanics" burst from the City Tavern, "formed in array in the street, and marched with colours flying towards the square of St. Michael." The "peaceable part of the citizens flew to their arms, and met in the square, some on foot, some on horseback, and all . . . in consternation, not knowing the nature or direction of this singular appearance. A small corps of horse was soon paraded: Major [Thomas] Pinckney, . . . Col. [William] Washington, with a few gentlemen on foot, charged them sabre in hand. . . ." The mob was quickly dispersed; some were wounded and several were hustled off to the jail. It was rumored that Dr. Fallon had planned a revolution, intending to seize the chief officials in the state and city government, the Pinckneys and Rut-

burst in the legislature against Greene was triggered when Greene intervened to prevent the legislature from repealing the impost grant, a major means of support of the weak national government. Greene's protest, addressed to the governor, was laid before the legislature.

7. Singer, *South Carolina in the Confederation*, 27–29; Berkeley Grimball, *Commodore Alexander Gillon of South Carolina, 1741–1794* (unpubl. M.A. thesis, Duke Univ., 1951), 90–91; Richard Walsh, *Charleston's Sons of Liberty: A Study of the Artisans, 1763–1789* (Columbia, S.C., 1959), 136; Jackson Turner Main, *The Antifederalists: Critics of the Constitution, 1781–1788* (Chapel Hill, 1961), 21–26.

ledges, and the British merchants and "to ship them off [out of] the state. . . . After this he was to reform the government, and share among his friends the emoluments of the enterprise."[8]

Notwithstanding these disturbing signs, there was a spirit of optimism in South Carolina following the war. Pierce Butler wrote to a friend in the spring of 1783 that Charleston was taking on a new appearance. Commercial ships were arriving in encouraging numbers, with the wharves "a scene of bustle and activity. . . ." And, Butler added, all "ranks of men think of little else than repairing their losses."[9]

Certainly this was the major concern of Charles Cotesworth Pinckney. No doubt Pinckney was more fortunate than most, for he had not only his lands but also his profession upon which to rebuild his fortunes. The future looked bright to Pinckney, so bright that he failed to calculate carefully the consequences of a heavy indebtedness. Pinckney was one of those who borrowed heavily on long-term credit, thinking that the profits from newly acquired lands and Negroes would repay his debts with ease. Despite his lucrative legal practice, however, Pinckney became so involved financially in trying to pay off his plantation purchases that he faced ruin for the next ten years.[10]

Pinckney and Edward Rutledge became business partners in several financial ventures following the war. Caught up in the fever of optimism and speculation, they purchased two plantations, Tippicutlaw and Charleywood, which had been confiscated by the legislature, and a trading sloop which they named *Charleywood*. From Henry Middleton they purchased a thousand acres of plantable swamp. In 1792 with his brother-in-law Charles Drayton, Pinckney purchased an additional twelve hundred acres of swampland.[11] Only

8. This incident is described in the Phila. *Aurora*, Apr. 2, 1796. Why it was not mentioned at the time [1782–1783] is impossible to say; perhaps there was a deliberate news blackout. But the story was not contradicted in any papers examined for this study.

9. Butler to Thomas Fitzsimmons, May 18, 1783, quoted in George C. Rogers, Jr., *Evolution of a Federalist: William Loughton Smith of Charleston (1758–1812)* (Columbia, S.C., 1962), 97.

10. Pinckney to George Washington, Feb. 24, 1794, Vol. 265, George Washington Papers, Lib. Cong.

11. Henry A. M. Smith, "The Baronies of South Carolina: Wadboo Barony," *S. C. Hist. and Gen. Mag.*, 12 (1911), 48–51. Information on Pinckney's and Rutledge's purchases in the 1780's is scattered throughout the Pinckney Family Papers, Lib. Cong. See Articles of Agreement between Pinckney, Rutledge, and

patience and good fortune, it seemed, were necessary to put Pinckney on the road to affluence and ease.

Pinckney shared the enthusiasm of many prominent South Carolinians who believed the state's financial horizons would be considerably widened if an efficient system of water traffic between the back country and Charleston could be engineered. When plans were laid to organize privately financed canal companies, Pinckney was eager to share in the risks and profits of ownership. He bought shares in the Santee and the Catawba canal companies and in fact was elected a director in both. Although the men who met to organize the Santee Canal Company in November 1785 had hopes for great profits, the project took so long to complete (1800) and proved so costly that it became a financial burden to its owners. Pinckney was careful to buy only twenty shares in the Catawba Canal Company, organized in 1787, and saw his caution justified as its chief stockholder, William Smith, struggled for many years merely to regain his initial investment. At best, Pinckney's canal investments were a dead weight during this difficult period.[12]

Because of these investments and debts in the years immediately following the war, Pinckney was a lawyer by necessity. He enjoyed very little of the leisure which is supposedly a prerogative of the great planter. Instead, his life was one of sustained if gentlemanly toil.

Elijah Brewer for the repair of the sloop *Charleywood*, Jan. 15, 1789, Box 13. Statements and documents about the land bought from Henry Middleton will be found in Boxes 9 and 10. This land proved to have much fewer than 1,000 plantable swamp acres and became a source of friction with the Middleton family. On Pinckney's and Rutledge's debts, an official note dated Feb. 2, 1786, Box 13, shows that the partners owed Christopher Willman of Charleston 1,250 guineas. The bill of sale for Pinckney's and Drayton's purchase on Aug. 27, 1792, is in Box 3. See also Edward Rutledge to Henry M. Rutledge, July 21, 1796, Rutledge Papers, Dreer Coll., Hist. Soc. of Pa.; Nalbro' Frazier to Pinckney and Rutledge, Aug. 15, 1791, quoted in Rogers, *Evolution of a Federalist*, 228. Frazier wrote: "I trust I am addressing Gentlemen who will feel for the very unpleasant situation in which I am placed by having so much property detained from me, and who having the ability will do all in their power, as far as it regards the payments they have to make, to grant that relief I so much stand in need of." Pinckney and Rutledge also became debtors to a Captain Bissel and Peter Taylor, according to Rutledge's will in the S. Caroliniana Lib. The amount of the debt was not specified.

12. Charleston *S. C. Gazette*, Oct. 29, Nov. 12, 1785; Mar. 9, 1786, House of Reps. Jour., S.C. Archives; Charleston *City Gazette and Daily Advertiser*, May 23, 1792. The Santee Canal project is discussed in Henry Savage, Jr., *River of the Carolinas: The Santee* (N.Y., 1956), 241–48. The Catawba Canal project is discussed in Rogers, *Evolution of a Federalist*, 133–34, 361–62.

The circumstances of the 1780's made it comparatively easy for experienced lawyers such as Pinckney to earn handsome incomes. There was a shortage of attorneys—an artificial one perhaps—in South Carolina while at the same time there was a remarkable growth in litigation. Collection of prewar debts, disputes arising out of wartime conditions, and the problems related to financial insolvency all called for the attention of knowledgeable lawyers. Barristers thoroughly familiar with the intricacies of the law were therefore in great demand. It is to Pinckney's credit that he did not take advantage of the situation by crushing the less experienced or inadequately trained lawyers. He and Edward Rutledge took the lead in making it easier for new lawyers to practice. Causes were argued on their merit, "strict pleadings were disregarded; . . . and justice was not entangled in a net of technical rules."[13]

Pinckney rose quickly to the top in his profession. This was reflected in his earnings. If the Duc de la Rochefoucauld-Liancourt can be believed, Pinckney made between £3,500 and £4,500 sterling a year, a handsome sum. Pinckney mentioned to Charles Fraser that while on circuit he once earned fifty guineas before he had eaten breakfast. Even while receiving these impressive fees Pinckney gained a reputation for liberality, for he made it a practice to charge nothing of needy widows or orphans.[14]

In court Pinckney was a formidable opponent for any lawyer. Not because he was an orator—Pinckney's contemporaries are almost unanimous in saying that he was not a fluent speaker. Pinckney's talent lay in his ability to see the strong points of his own case and develop them logically and methodically through an extended argument. His habit of reading widely was advantageous, for he was able to strengthen his arguments with numerous references to the major

13. Christopher Gadsden, *A Sermon Preached . . . On the Occasion of the Decease of . . . Pinckney* (Charleston, 1825), 27–28; William Harper, *Memoir of the Life . . . of . . . Henry William DeSaussure* (Charleston, 1841), 15. The standards for admitting attorneys to law were fairly rigid. In 1785, the legislature provided that a man must have studied law within the state for four years or three years abroad at a law college. Thomas Cooper and David J. McCord, eds., *Statutes at Large of South Carolina*, 10 vols. (Columbia, S.C., 1836–41), IV, 668–69. Pinckney was on the committee which drafted the bill, Feb. 1, 1785, House of Reps. Jour., S.C. Archives.

14. Duc de la Rochefoucauld-Liancourt, *Travels Through the United States of North America, 1795 . . . 1797*, 2 vols. (London, 1799), II, 389; Charles Fraser, *Reminiscences of Charleston* (Charleston, 1854), 71; Garden, *Eulogy on Pinckney*, 29.

precedents or historical incidents supporting his case. John Julius Pringle, a giant at the bar in Pinckney's day, recalled in later years that he considered Pinckney his most skillful adversary because of his ability to argue and amass the relevant precedents in compelling order. Francisco de Miranda, who visited Charleston in 1783, believed Pinckney had a "profound knowledge in his profession, and strength in his arguments, even though his eloquence is neither as brilliant nor as sonorous [as Edward Rutledge's]."[15]

It was natural that some persons took delight in deflating a man of Pinckney's stature at the bar by a quick retort. One such incident concerned Judge Aedanus Burke, a witty Irishman who disliked the Charleston oligarchy in general, and perhaps General Pinckney in particular. Judge Burke also disliked lengthy pleadings, evidently a Pinckney habit. One day after Pinckney had been arguing a case before him for an extended period, Judge Burke suddenly arose, "tucked up his robe, took his hat and left the bench." Pinckney naturally stopped his argument. " '*Go on General Pinckney, go on*,' the judge said with a twinkle in his eye: '. . . you love to hear yourself talk. Meanwhile, I'll go out, and take a ——— and a peep at the Camel.' (a camel was at that moment exhibiting for a show, in front of the Court House among the people)." Edward Hooker, who recorded this story while visiting Charleston in 1805, stated that "peeping at the camel" had become a "bye word among the Carolina lawyers for *going out on any occasion*."[16]

Professor Rogers, the biographer of William Loughton Smith, tells how Smith scored a point on Pinckney in court. Five musicians hired Smith to prosecute Milligan, master of the City Tavern, for giving them a beating. Defending Milligan, Pinckney argued that Milligan was justified since the musicians had abused him in his own home, which was his castle. Smith wittily retorted that General Pinckney was "the first person since Don Quixote to mistake an inn for a castle!"[17]

When it came time to calculate the year's fees, Pinckney had the

15. Fraser, *Reminiscences of Charleston*, 70–71; William S. Robertson, ed., *The Diary of Francisco de Miranda, Tour of the United States, 1783–1784* (N.Y., 1928), 22. The quote was translated by Dr. Manuel A. Machado, Department of History, State University College of New York, Plattsburg.

16. [J. Franklin Jameson, ed.], "Diary of Edward Hooker, 1805–1808," American Historical Association, *Annual Report* (1896), I, 885–86.

17. Rogers, *Evolution of a Federalist*, 123.

best rejoinder to the gibes of Burke and Smith. And Pinckney was doubtless gratified by the enviable reputation he had established for integrity and learning and for the high example all knew he set for the junior lawyers. In every way Charles Cotesworth Pinckney was a worthy successor to his father at the bar.

Life must have seemed good to Pinckney after the war. His immediate family was together once again; his legal practice was flourishing, his investments were promising, and few men in public life were more highly respected. But life is uncertain, and Pinckney was to suffer when his wife Sally, who had borne him four children, who had suffered with him through the war, who had agonized with him over their son's death, and who was now sharing his hopes for the future, died early in May 1784.[18]

Pinckney waited over two years before remarrying. He chose Mary Stead, the daughter of a former Charleston merchant, to be his wife and the stepmother of his three girls. Judging by her letters, Mary was an intensive reader, a charming conversationalist, a person with intellectual interests that would complement those of her husband. Pinckney worked diligently to please and flatter his wife. She returned his affection and tried also to become a second mother to Pinckney's girls. She succeeded remarkably well. From all outward appearances it proved to be an ideal marriage.

Mary Stead brought not only charm and intelligence to the marriage but also a fortune, estimated in 1786 at £14,000.[19] Handling his wife's investments demanded a significant share of Pinckney's time and helped account for his refusal to accept a national office until the mid-1790's. Pinckney explained to George Washington how Mrs. Pinckney's estate problems tied him to South Carolina: "Mrs. Pinckney and her Brother and Sister have large demands on some persons in Georgia who are endeavouring to use every subterfuge

18. Charleston *South-Carolina Weekly Gazette*, May 8, 1784. Sarah Pinckney died on May 8. The cause of Mrs. Pinckney's death was not specified, the paper mentioning only that she had died "after enduring a long and tedious illness with Christian patience and resignation. . . ." In a codicil to his will, dated May 12, 1784, Henry Middleton ordered: "my Son in Law Charles Cotesworth Pinckney Esquire do receive every Benefit and Advantage, to which his Wife would have been entitled, had she survived me; and for this Purpose I give and devise the same to him, his Heirs Executors Administrators and Assigns for ever." Benjamin H. Rutledge Papers, S.C. Hist. Soc.

19. According to a statement on the draft of an estimate of Mary Stead's fortune in 1786, she and Pinckney were married on Sunday, July 23, 1786. This draft is in the Pinckney Family Papers, Lib. Cong.

to secrete their property and to avoid paying what they owe; her Brother [Benjamin Stead] is in Europe, and her Sister's Husband, Mr. Ralph Izard Jun:, is of so indolent a temper that the attending to this business of necessity devolves on me, and was I not to go to Georgia sometimes, particularly in April and November to watch over her affairs, her property there would be lost, and instead of protecting I should in fact sacrifice her interest."[20]

Along with his financial responsibilities, Pinckney's legislative duties became increasingly heavy during the 1780's. Even a hasty reading of the journals of the legislature shows the importance Pinckney assumed in the postwar politics of South Carolina. He was involved in nearly every significant question brought before the legislature, either as a committee member or through the committee assignments of his relatives. His brother Thomas was becoming an important man in South Carolina in his own right. Edward Rutledge, of course, had been a major political figure almost from the time that he had returned from England in 1774. Edward's brother Hugh, although perhaps not of the same political caliber as Edward, was speaker of the House of Representatives from 1782 to 1785.

The Pinckney brothers and Edward Rutledge were as popular in Charleston as they were influential in the legislature, as the biennial elections indicate. In the election of 1784 these three friends were near the top of the ticket among thirty delegates elected from Charleston. In 1786 Rutledge won the highest total vote (426) with Charles Cotesworth and Thomas placing fourth and sixth respectively on the election ticket. By 1788 the friends were the first three members on the ticket; the Pinckney brothers tied for first place with 510 votes and Rutledge drew only 4 votes fewer.[21]

Yet the Pinckneys and Rutledges did not agree on every measure brought before the legislature despite their close personal and financial relationship. Throughout the 1780's Charles Cotesworth and Thomas differed with Edward Rutledge about the wisdom of amercement. Charles Cotesworth Pinckney and Rutledge also parted company when arguing the question of permitting unrestricted slave importation into the state. Rutledge, perhaps influenced by his friendship

20. Pinckney to Washington, Feb. 24, 1794, Vol. 265, Papers of George Washington, Lib. Cong.
21. Charleston S. C. Gazette, Dec. 4, 1784; Charleston State Gazette of South-Carolina, Dec. 7, 1786, Dec. 4, 1788.

with Thomas Jefferson, was a leader in demanding the end of slave importation. Pinckney strongly disagreed. It was a practical matter, he argued, not a moral one. The expansion of the South Carolina economy depended upon slave labor; therefore the African trade should be kept open as long as the state needed labor.[22] Despite different viewpoints on crucial issues, however, the Rutledges and Pinckneys used their individual strength to promote one another's careers. Edward Rutledge, for example, insisted that Thomas Pinckney become the governor of South Carolina in 1787 and successfully used his influence to put Thomas into the office.[23]

Charles Cotesworth Pinckney and Edward Rutledge often worked together in state affairs that did not touch their personal interests. They helped to negotiate a boundary dispute with Georgia, a question that had intermittently troubled the relations between South Carolina and Georgia since 1732. Pinckney was perhaps the most active member of the legislature in the negotiations with Georgia, serving on nearly every legislative committee which made procedural or substantive recommendations. In April of 1787, after years of haggling, Pinckney and the other commissioners from the two states signed the Convention of Beaufort which alleviated but did not settle the quarrel. At the same time that Pinckney was negotiating with Georgia, he was also involved in trying to resolve a boundary dispute with North Carolina that had persisted since 1729. All his efforts came to nothing since neither state wished to make meaningful concessions. The question was not settled until 1815.[24]

22. Rawlins Lowndes stated that Pinckney had once said that as long as there was a single acre of swampland in South Carolina, he would oppose restricting the importation of slaves. Jonathan Elliot, ed., *The Debates in the Several State Conventions on the Adoption of the Federal Constitution*, 2nd rev. ed., 5 vols. (Phila., 1836), IV, 272–73. Jefferson wrote to Edward Rutledge in 1787: "I congratulate you, my dear friend, on the laws of your state for suspending the importation of slaves, and for the glory you have justly acquired by endeavoring to prevent it for ever. This abomination must have an end, and there is a superior bench reserved in heaven for those who hasten it." July 14, 1787, in Paul L. Ford, ed., *The Writings of Thomas Jefferson*, 10 vols. (N.Y., 1892–99), IV, 410.

23. Thomas Pinckney to Edward Rutledge, Nov. 24, 1791, in Thomas Pinckney Letterbook, 1791–1798, S. Caroliniana Lib. Charles Cotesworth wrote his mother that Thomas was elected governor "with the greatest éclat," securing 163 out of 170 votes. Feb. 22, 1787, quoted in Pinckney, *Life of Thomas Pinckney*, 89.

24. The dispute between Georgia and South Carolina is discussed briefly in George Hillyer, "Boundary Between Georgia and South Carolina," *Georgia Historical Quarterly*, 1 (1917), 155–60. Further information will be found in

Pinckney likewise worked constantly within the legislature to promote education, a matter of much greater interest to him than the boundary disputes. Although the effort to liberalize the ties with Great Britain had taken priority over earlier attempts to establish a system of higher education in South Carolina, Pinckney believed that the privileged of the state should now redouble their efforts to widen educational opportunities, particularly in the up-country areas. Pinckney's motivation here is not clear. Doubtless he believed in the intrinsic merit of educating the young. But since Pinckney was a practical man it is probable that he already saw how education might be one bridge between the two great and antagonistic sections of the state. Through a common education and through contact with low-country boys, the up country might eventually acquire social and political values compatible to those of the low country. An up-country leadership weaned on low-country values would be less likely to take "radical" positions on public policy, positions that would undermine the low-country establishment.[25] Although the time did not seem ripe to establish a state college, one could at least encourage up-country boys to acquire a basic education; the polishing process could begin at the lower educational levels.

Whatever his motives, Pinckney and Richard Hutson, the intendant (mayor) of Charleston, helped to organize the Charleston chapter of the Mount Zion Society in 1785. Its purpose was to promote the founding of an educational institution in the state and had been originally organized in the Winnsboro area during the war. After months of planning and consultation, the members of the Winnsboro chapter decided to sponsor a college in their town. The Society began to direct the erection of buildings late in the summer

---

Robert S. Cotterill, "The South Carolina Land Cession," *Mississippi Valley Historical Review*, 12 (1924–25), 376–84. An overview of the boundary problem with North Carolina is in Alexander S. Salley, *The Boundary Line Between North Carolina and South Carolina* (Columbia, S.C., 1929). A general discussion of the negotiations during the 1780's is in Singer, *South Carolina in the Confederation*, 126–39. Pinckney's part in negotiating the disputes can be traced in House of Reps. Jour., Mar. 17, 1783; Jan. 24, 1785; Feb. 2, 17, 23, 1785; Mar. 16, 21, 1786; Feb. 28, 1788; Journals of the Senate, Dec. 19, 1792, S.C. Archives. Additional information is in the May 17, 1787, issue of the Charleston *State Gazette*.

25. On this point, see Hollis, *University of South Carolina*, I, 15–17; Rogers, *Evolution of a Federalist*, 133.

of 1784, a project which the Charleston chapter enthusiastically supported the following year.[26]

Pinckney carefully guarded the interests of the Society in the legislature. He guided a bill through the House of Representatives which granted the Society a charter to establish the school at Winnsboro. Furthermore, Pinckney served as an officer of the Mount Zion Society and helped to raise money for the support of the college. In 1786 he was elected president of the Charleston chapter of the Society and later served as a trustee of the school itself.

Pinckney's interest in education was also demonstrated by his continuing support of the Charleston Library Society. He was elected president of this society in 1786 and served intermittently as an officer or consultant of the library for the next forty years.[27]

It was pressing financial needs and not the lack of educational facilities that troubled most South Carolinians in the 1780's. South Carolina had largely met the monetary assessments of the Continental and Confederation Congresses during the war, but the effort had weakened the state's ability to recover once the war had ended. The policies of inflation pursued by the state during the war precipitated a postwar conflict between creditors and debtors, aggravating an already unstable political situation. It was the old planter oligarchy who were in the most straitened circumstances. British confiscation of their property, mainly thousands of slaves, had forced many, including Pinckney, to borrow heavily in order to restock stripped plantations. An unprecedented failure of three successive crops early in the 1780's compounded their debts. A return to a "sound" currency and an insistence by the creditors on the prompt payment of

26. Singer, *South Carolina in the Confederation*, 26; Francis W. Bradley, *A Brief History of the Mount Zion Society* (South Carolina Pamphlets, Miscellaneous, Vol. 16, 1948). The incomplete minutes of the Mount Zion Society, Winnsboro Chapter, are in the S. Caroliniana Lib.

27. Feb. 25, Mar. 15, 1785, House of Reps. Jour., S.C. Archives; Charleston *State Gazette*, Feb. 27, 1786, Aug. 14, 1788; Charleston *City Gazette, or the Daily Advertiser*, Aug. 29, 1791. Pinckney's connection with the Library Society over many years can be briefly traced in Charleston *State Gazette*, Jan. 16, 1786; Charleston *City Gazette*, Jan. 22, 1796; *Charleston Courier*, Jan. 20, 1825. Pinckney also served on the first board of trustees for Charleston College. J. H. Easterby, *History of the College of Charleston, Founded 1770* (Charleston, 1935), 20.

debts would have meant ruin for hundreds of planters. There was a lack of specie in the state which likewise contributed to the desperation of the debtor elements.[28] With heavy debts, dear money, and pressing creditors, it was little wonder that even conservative planters had "radical" second thoughts on monetary policy.

The state itself was heavily in debt when the war ended. Since an immediate payment of state debts was impossible, promissory certificates called indents were issued to those persons able to prove their claims against the state. These indents earned an interest rate of 7 per cent per annum until the day of redemption. The state's postwar revenues were so inadequate that it was unable to pay even the annual interest rate on the indents and was forced to issue special indents to carry the debt.[29]

It is not surprising that some hard-pressed debtors proposed paper money schemes that would give them personal relief and provide the state a means to lighten its debt through inflation. At first glance, it might seem logical that the planters, including Pinckney, would support inflationary proposals. But Pinckney and many other planters regarded these inflationary plans as irresponsible, likely to damage the credit of the state and the planters as well. And planters wished to do nothing that would undermine the very source of plantation financing, the credit system. Pinckney and many of his fellow planters therefore found themselves standing with the creditors, often British merchants, in opposing any radical measures which would tarnish the fiscal reputation of South Carolina and dry up the stream of credit. Pinckney was indignant with the sponsors of inflationary schemes and believed that they lacked "some sense of character."[30]

Pinckney certainly had a personal interest in re-establishing the fiscal soundness of the state treasury. His indents might be of little value if the state virtually repudiated them through further inflation or paid them off on a pro rata basis. In addition to the loans that Pinckney had made to the state in 1779 and 1780, totaling £21,500,

28. Singer, *South Carolina in the Confederation*, 14–16; Rogers, *Evolution of a Federalist*, 135–37.
29. Wallace, *South Carolina*, 334.
30. Max Farrand, ed., *Records of the Federal Convention of 1787*, 4 vols. (New Haven, Conn., 1911–37), I, 137. Merrill Jensen discusses the general reactions to the problems of state indebtedness in *The New Nation*, 303–12.

the state also owed him £1,950 as payment for his services during the Revolutionary War.[31] Although Pinckney received adequate interest rates—10 per cent on the two loans and 7 per cent on the indents—he still had every right to expect the state to redeem the principal amount in sound currency. Why should those who sacrificed heavily during the war continue to finance an unfair share of the state's indebtedness? There was no satisfactory answer to this question from the repudiators and the cheap money men. In this fight Pinckney's self-interest coincided with what he sincerely felt was the best interest of the state.

In the legislature Pinckney not only helped to fight down the fiscal radicals' suggestions but also supported measures which he believed would promote the general prosperity and physical security of South Carolina. In particular he favored taking steps to strengthen the national Articles of Confederation government. Launched in 1781, that government was charged with many important responsibilities but lacked the constitutional authority to levy a tax directly upon the people. This appeared to be a fatal weakness to those desiring a powerful national government, a weakness the government itself tried to overcome by asking the states to grant it power to levy an impost. Although the government's request made in 1781 was rejected, a similar proposal was again submitted to the states in 1783. To grant the request would assuredly involve surrendering part of a state's control over foreign trade, but Pinckney and his political allies in South Carolina showed little concern about this issue. Pinckney, Edward and John Rutledge, and three other House members brought in a committee report in 1786 strongly recommending ceding control of all foreign trade to the Confederation government for a period of fifteen years.[32]

This recommendation was in keeping with Pinckney's general attitude that strong centralized government was necessary to insure the welfare of his own state. South Carolina's exposed position during the Revolutionary War had shown that the state could be effectively defended only in concert with the other states, and Pinckney

---

31. The indented certificate for £1950.8.2 1/4, dated Aug. 3, 1784, is in the Audited Accounts of Charles Cotesworth Pinckney, S.C. Archives.

32. Singer, *South Carolina in the Confederation*, 97; Feb. 8, 1786, House of Reps. Jour., S.C. Archives; Main, *Antifederalists*, ch. 4.

knew this better than most. Pinckney was likewise convinced that the state's mercantile needs and the burden of state debts could be met only if the central government pooled the resources of all the states and directed foreign trade policy.[33]

When the Confederation legislature issued the call for a convention to revise the Articles of Confederation, South Carolina was willing, even eager, to respond. The legislature was careful to choose five of the state's distinguished citizens.[34] It seemed natural that Charles Cotesworth Pinckney should be selected to represent his state. Even a casual perusal of the legislature's records in the 1780's indicates his commanding position within the South Carolina House of Representatives. His committee duties involved him in almost every facet of South Carolina's government—militia regulation, tax measures, boundary disputes, education promotion, and revision of the court system. No other person, with perhaps the exception of Edward Rutledge, was given as many important and time-consuming duties. Pierce Butler, John Rutledge, Henry Laurens, and the youthful Charles Pinckney were Pinckney's colleagues. It was an exceptionally capable delegation, but, the up-country people complained, one that represented primarily the low-country interests.[35]

Unlike his energetic cousin Charles, General Pinckney seems to have made no particular preparation for the work of the Constitutional Convention. He evidently regarded the trip to Philadelphia partly as a delayed honeymoon, for he took along his bride of ten months, leaving his children behind. The honeymoon, if it was that, had a bad start, for the couple were "horribly sea sick" on the jour-

33. Singer, *South Carolina in the Confederation*, 163–64; Rogers, *Evolution of a Federalist*, 146–47.

34. The election of the delegates took place at a joint sitting of both houses of the legislature, Mar. 8, 1787.

35. John Rutledge's stature in South Carolina has been indicated earlier. Charles Pinckney, son of Colonel Charles Pinckney (d. 1782), was both capable and highly ambitious. He was later governor of South Carolina four times, leader of the state's Republican party, and a foreign minister in Jefferson's first administration. Pierce Butler, an ex-officer in the British army, only came to real prominence in the legislature in the mid-1780's, and was not known extensively outside of South Carolina. Henry Laurens declined to serve. See Ernest M. Lander, Jr., "The South Carolinians at the Philadelphia Convention, 1787," *S. C. Hist. Mag.*, 57 (1956), 134–35.

ney. Yet there was one satisfaction. Pinckney wrote to his sister that he had been greeted by General George Washington in Philadelphia in "a very civil and frien[dly] manner. . . ." Pinckney was pleased as well by the "respectability" of the delegates he met and seemed confident that any plan adopted by the convention would be favorably received by the states.[36]

Pinckney entered into the work of the convention of May 25 with ambivalent attitudes. He wished to construct an energetic government, an aristocratic republic, yet he firmly believed that the "great art of government is not to govern too much."[37] His suspicion that New England planned to regulate the commerce of all the states to its own advantage under any new roof was balanced by his conviction that South Carolina's future commercial prosperity depended upon strong direction from a central government. And while the new government must have an effective regulative power over commerce, it must not be allowed to interfere with the south's peculiar local institution, slavery. Pinckney felt strongly that the federal government should assume debts contracted by the states during the war, and he hoped as well that the government would discriminate in favor of original creditors rather than the speculators who had bought up many of the loan certificates at drastically reduced prices.[38]

Despite his hope for a powerful centralized government, Pinckney took a position early in the convention that if adopted would have prevented the writing of a new constitution. In the debate over the powers of the convention Pinckney expressed doubt that the delegates had been granted the authority to do anything other than revise the Articles of Confederation. Technically, Pinckney's position was correct. His credential to the convention, signed by his brother the governor, authorized him to consider additional "clauses, articles and provisions" to the federal constitution but nowhere mentioned devising "a System founded on different principles" than the Articles of

36. Pinckney to Harriott Horry, May 14, 1787, Pinckney Papers, Charleston Lib. Soc.; Harriott Pinckney Horry to Charles Cotesworth Pinckney, June 6, 1787, C. C. Pinckney Papers, S. Caroliniana Lib.; Pinckney to Harriott Horry, May 30, 1787, Pinckney Family Papers, Lib. Cong.

37. Pinckney to General [Pickens?], Mar. 31, 1790, C. C. Pinckney Papers, S. Caroliniana Lib.

38. Farrand, ed., *Records of Federal Convention*, II, 400.

Confederation.[39] Perhaps in his reaction at this historic moment it is possible to see one reason why Pinckney never attained greatness. There was a lack of broad vision, a willingness to sacrifice great plans for technicalities, the absence of a statesman's view. Once the point had been settled otherwise, though, Pinckney cheerfully participated in the proceedings of the convention, doing what he could to make the new system acceptable to the people of South Carolina. At least he could be flexible.

Making the new constitution acceptable to his constituency was certainly Pinckney's major contribution in the convention. Pinckney was seldom an original thinker. There were few flashes of insight in his speeches before the delegates. His arguments were founded neither upon philosophical speculations nor upon a profound knowledge of comparative government, which is surprising for one with his classical education and wide reading habits. Experience was his guide, experience with the royal government and with the political institutions of South Carolina. He knew what would be acceptable to the important people, the Charleston oligarchy of South Carolina. He knew too what they would not tolerate.

The one thing they would not tolerate, Pinckney warned, was any plan to emancipate the Negroes or to prohibit immediately the importation of slaves; if either of these measures were adopted, it would be tantamount to rejection of the constitution by his state. Indeed, he would not be able to support a constitution which placed severe restrictions on slavery or the slave trade. Slavery was an area of vital interest which should be regulated only by the state legislatures.

Pinckney never attempted to defend slavery on moral grounds in the convention. To him it was strictly an economic question, a practical matter. Slavery was a fact, a condition. To Pinckney the emotional attack on slavery by Gouverneur Morris of Pennsylvania must have seemed both foolish and irrelevant. The delegates were there to write a new constitution which would promote the welfare of all the states. An attack on the most vital concern of the southern states would certainly mean that there would be no union. Why then bring forward moral issues? Nothing was to be gained.

39. *Ibid.*, I, 34; Elliot, ed., *Debates in the State Conventions*, I, 137.

In an effort to cool the hostility against slavery, Pinckney pointed out that the importation of slaves was an economic benefit to the north as well as to the south. The more slaves that were imported, the greater the volume of southern produce there would be. With perhaps a glance at the New England representatives, he then added that this would assure increased revenue to those engaged in the carrying trade; the shipping interests would make enviable profits by transporting the produce.[40] Pinckney did not need to add that the merchants of New England might also find it remunerative to transport slaves from Africa. No doubt he did not wish to offend the delicate sensibilities of his conscience-stricken northern colleagues.

Most of the delegates were agreed that the federal government should at some time be authorized to stop the importation of slaves. Pinckney seemed to believe that Virginia slave traders had cunningly encouraged this stand. He complained that if the direct supply of South Carolina's slaves were cut off, the value of the surplus slaves of the Virginia slave traders would naturally rise. By artificially increasing the price of Negroes, breeders in Virginia would prosper while Carolina and Georgia planters would suffer. Was the price of union to be an economic reverse for the south? Pinckney asked.[41]

The issue was not whether the government would have the authority to prohibit the importation of slaves, but rather at what time it would be given this power. Southern delegates saw that they could not obtain an unlimited importation clause in the new constitution and therefore worked to get the most generous stipulation possible. A compromise was evidently reached outside the convention. Although 1800 had been suggested as the year when Congress might stop the importation of slaves, the delegates quickly agreed to Pinckney's motion to substitute the year 1808.[42] It was fitting that Pinckney, who had consistently fought to protect the interests of the slave-owners, introduced this particular resolution.

Pinckney insisted that the slaves should be counted in determining

40. Farrand, ed., *Records of Federal Convention*, II, 371–73.

41. *Ibid.*, 371; Gaillard Hunt, ed., *The Writings of James Madison*, 9 vols. (N.Y., 1900–10), V, 209–10.

42. Farrand, ed., *Records of Federal Convention*, II, 415; A. W. Clason, "The South Carolina Convention in 1788," *Magazine of American History*, 15 (1886), 159.

the national political representation of each state. This issue would largely decide the political importance of South Carolina in the national legislature. Pinckney's belief that the slaves should be fully counted rested upon his assumption that wealth as well as population should be represented in the government, and slaves were wealth. Representation based on the total value of a state's exports would have been quite as acceptable to him. By either means some fair way had to be devised to protect wealth through the national government.[43] He considered as specious the objection that slaves had no political representation in South Carolina and therefore should have none in the national government. Universal liberties and political rights were not the issues involved, he assured carping northerners. Finding a just method to represent and to protect both wealth and population was the convention's task.

Pinckney's attempt to have each slave counted as one person in apportioning representation to the national legislature was no cynical scheme on his part to take political advantage of slavery.[44] It was a question of interest. Southern institutions simply had to be protected. The northern delegates were not as generous as Pinckney wished, and despite his efforts the convention decided to follow the three-fifths rule in counting the slaves. Pinckney was not satisfied with this settlement, but he accepted it in the spirit of compromise.[45]

At one point Pinckney did threaten to repudiate the work of the convention. There was a strong feeling in the convention that the national legislature should be given the power to tax exports. If granted and if the proposed government did pass an exports tax, it would be a serious blow to the economy of South Carolina, for almost its entire revenue was derived from the exportation of plantation products. It would be a severe temptation, he knew, for numerically predominant northern states to run the federal government on south-

43. Farrand, ed., *Records of Federal Convention*, I, 592–94.
44. Professor Dwight L. Dumond would not agree. In his *Antislavery; The Crusade for Freedom in America* (Ann Arbor, Mich., 1961), 38, Dumond maintains that Pinckney was one of the delegates who were "either blind to the truths of the Declaration [of Independence], or quite willing to explain them away, and more interested in protecting . . . [their] area than in promoting the national interest."
45. Max Farrand, *The Framing of the Constitution of the United States* (New Haven, Conn., 1913), 107.

ern revenue. Pinckney believed that if South Carolina were not to be given representation in the national government on the basis of its exportable wealth, then that wealth should not be taxed. The convention agreed that this reasoning was sound as well as politic and voted against empowering the legislature to tax exports.[46]

Pinckney's insistence that the economic welfare of the south be protected was certainly one of his most substantial contributions to the work of the convention. In taking his position he did not speak as a states rights man, but as one favoring a strong national government. He understood that the south would only approve a centralizing constitution when it was satisfied that its native interests were protected. Pinckney's frank warnings on the maximum concessions the south would make for the cause of a stronger union were a real service to the founding fathers as they shaped the new constitution.

Aside from the problems related directly to slavery, Pinckney spoke most often in the debates on the creation of the national legislature. He was particularly interested in the method of electing the lower house. No argument could convince him that its members should be elected by the people. The experience of South Carolina, he held, had shown that the people could be led to support demagogic measures. Most of them, for example, had "notoriously" favored issuing paper money as legal tender. This reckless proposal had been rejected by the legislature, proving that it was a more responsible body. It was the state legislatures, he insisted, that should elect delegates to the lower house. In them would be found the repositories of political wisdom in most states.[47]

This proposal would have worked nicely to the advantage of the low-country aristocracy, for in 1787 the conservatives were still firmly in power. Pinckney's plan would have had the effect of representing the wealth of South Carolina in both houses of the proposed national legislature. When it became obvious that his proposal would be rejected, Pinckney then suggested that representatives to the lower house be elected in a manner directed by the individual state legislatures. Alexander Hamilton of New York immediately saw the purpose of this proposal. It should be rejected, Hamilton emphasized, for it would certainly lead to the state legislatures' electing the repre-

46. Farrand, ed., *Records of Federal Convention*, I, 95.
47. *Ibid.*, I, 137.

sentatives. If this were done, the powers of the states over the central government would be too great.[48]

Unlike Hamilton, Pinckney was genuinely concerned lest the central government become too powerful. As part of his idea to preserve a proper balance between state and federal government, Pinckney advocated shortening the proposed terms for senators from six to four years. A residence of six years in another state, he claimed, would tend to weaken the sense of responsibility a senator should have to his own state; he would become the creature of the state in which he resided. Pinckney also believed that members of the upper house should serve without compensation. Since they were to represent the wealth of each state, they would be men who did not need salaries. The venerable Benjamin Franklin seconded Pinckney's idea, but it did not receive general support. Once it was settled that senators would receive "fixed stipends," Pinckney argued that it should be the states which paid them. Since senators were the agents of the state legislatures, their salaries should be paid from state funds. He was determined that the states should have some significant checks upon the shaping of national policies.[49]

In the heated debates on the distribution of representation to the national legislature, one of Pinckney's suggestions was adopted. It proved at the time to be the salvation of the convention. A deadlock had developed between the large and small states. The small states believed that each state should have equal representation in the upper house; their representatives feared the larger states might ignore their interests and therefore wanted a practical veto within the legislature. James Madison of Virginia and Rufus King of New York, among others, spoke strongly and sometimes bitterly against this small state plan. Delegates from the small states replied in equally vehement tones. When the issue came to a vote, there was a tie. This was the great crisis of the convention. Unless the delegates could reach some agreement which would compromise the two positions, the convention seemed likely to adjourn in failure.[50]

Charles Pinckney was on his feet immediately after the vote. He believed that the principle of equality in the second branch was in-

48. *Ibid.*, I, 358–59, 364.
49. *Ibid.*, I, 85–86, 429–30.
50. *Ibid.*, I, 494–97, 510.

admissible. But, he suggested, could not the states be divided into more than two classes and the senators apportioned among them? Charles Cotesworth rose to say that he did not favor his cousin's plan. He personally liked Franklin's idea of equal state representation in the second branch; he really sympathized with small state fears. In any case, a compromise seemed necessary. Pinckney then moved that a committee of one member from each state be appointed to devise and report a compromise. Gouverneur Morris and Elbridge Gerry of Massachusetts supported Pinckney's motion, but James Madison fiercely opposed it. Committees of this kind, Madison objected, were designed for nothing except delay.[51]

Delay was just what was needed at this point. Pinckney's motion was carried. Even though Pinckney was not elected to the committee which reported the "Great Compromise" on representation, his calm and sensible appoach had helped the convention through one of its most difficult moments. His experience in the South Carolina legislature had made Pinckney a believer in timely compromise; his statesmanship was founded upon achieving the possible. No one could describe Pinckney as a "visionary."

Pinckney spoke to the convention on other matters, mostly those in which he had had some personal experience. He opposed the suggestion that the federal treasurer be appointed by the legislature, assuring the gentlemen that South Carolina had tried such a plan and found it to have serious disadvantages. When the regulation of the militia was under consideration, Pinckney argued that the power to control the militia should reside in the federal government. He founded his argument, Madison recorded, upon "a case during the war in which a dissimilarity in the militia of different States had produced the most serious mischiefs." The members of the convention probably relived with Pinckney his trying experiences in Georgia during the summer of 1778.[52]

Pinckney's work was not limited to debate, for he was a member of several committees, the most important of which dealt with the problem of state debts. Whether the new government should assume the debts incurred by each state during the Revolutionary War was an open question, some states (with large debts) favoring it but

51. *Ibid.*, I, 510–15.
52. *Ibid.*, II, 330, 614.

others stoutly opposing it. Pinckney, like most South Carolinians, was in favor of assumption, but the committee returned with an ambiguous report that reflected the varying views of the committee members. In the committee appointed to consider the expediency of permitting the national legislature to pass a navigation act, Pinckney at first used all his influence to oppose any such power. When the north agreed to compromise on the Negro issue, however, Pinckney retreated from his earlier adamant opposition.[53]

As the work of the convention proceeded and finally drew to a close, Pinckney became increasingly pleased with the new plan of government. A nice balance between federal and state power had been arranged; the new government would be vigorous without being despotic. While he was not satisfied with the clause on the regulation of slave importation, still it was the best that the south had been able to obtain. It was a reasonable compromise and reasonable men should accept it. The national legislature would have extensive power over commerce, a measure that the mercantile community of South Carolina had favored for several years.

In his enthusiasm for the Constitution, Pinckney forgot his earlier doubts that the convention lacked authority to write a new constitution. When Elbridge Gerry arose and dramatically announced that he for one would be unable to sign the Constitution, Pinckney countered that he would not only sign the document but would "support it with all his influence."[54] This would not be the last time that Pinckney and Gerry disagreed.

On Monday, September 17, the delegates met to sign the Constitution. After concluding their business, the convention adjourned and the members went en masse to the City Tavern where they "took a cordial leave of each other."[55] The delegates were relieved that the sessions were over and that they were able to escape the terrible heat of late-summer Philadelphia. Most of the delegates were satisfied with the work they had accomplished and were anxious to report on the proposed constitution to their colleagues and constituents.

If Pinckney evaluated his efforts at Philadelphia objectively, he

53. *Ibid.*, II, 322, 375, 449–50; Farrand, *Framing of the Constitution*, 176–77.
54. Farrand, ed., *Records of Federal Convention*, II, 646–47.
55. John C. Fitzpatrick, ed., *The Diaries of George Washington, 1748–1799,* 4 vols. (Boston, 1925), III, 237.

should have realized that many delegates had outshone him in debate and in original thinking on the major issues before the convention.[56] Pinckney was no Hamilton, Madison, or James Wilson. His own younger cousin, Charles, had taken the initiative and prepared a plan of government. John Rutledge, if his committee assignments were an accurate gauge, was believed to be the senior and most able member of the southern delegation by representatives from the other states. A candid analysis of the convention's records indicates that Charles Cotesworth Pinckney made fewer significant contributions to the convention than did either Charles Pinckney or John Rutledge.

Yet Charles Cotesworth's work in Philadelphia was important. He had helped to create "a good national Govt. and at the same time to leave a considerable share of power in the States."[57] A government of balanced powers was Pinckney's ideal, with the ultimate aim of each level the protection of property. In this attitude he reflected the views of his low-country friends. Pinckney's presence at the convention was itself a contribution, for his friends knew him to be a sound and sensible man who would protect the interests of his constituents. An endorsement from Pinckney was certainly a weighty recommendation for the new plan of government.

There was work now to be done at home, personal as well as legislative. Because of their earlier rough voyage to Philadelphia, Pinckney and his wife Mary returned to Charleston by coach. On the way they stopped at Mount Vernon to visit with the Washingtons, remaining there overnight. Pinckney had developed an intense admiration for his old commander and indicated his respect by addressing Washington as "Your Excellency" in their private correspondence.[58] Pinckney no doubt discussed with Washington the prospects for ratification of the Constitution in South Carolina, assuring him that

56. William Pierce, a delegate from Georgia, noted that Pinckney, when "warm in debate . . . sometimes speaks well,—but he is generally considered an indifferent Orator." Farrand, ed., *Records of Federal Convention*, III, 96.

57. *Ibid.*, I, 137. Ulrich B. Phillips believed that the South Carolina conservatives wished the central government to have increased power throughout the 1780's as a safeguard to their property, in the event that the "radicals" of the up country gained control of the South Carolina legislature. Phillips, "The South Carolina Federalists," *American Historical Review*, 14 (1908–09), 542.

58. Oct. 11, 12, 1787, Fitzpatrick, ed., *Diaries of Washington*, III, 244. Pinckney's manner of addressing Washington is seen in his letter to Washington, Jan. 14, 1784, Gratz Coll., Hist. Soc. of Pa.

the low-country conservatives would do their best to control the state convention. He also promised to write Washington as soon as South Carolina had made its decision.

The major battle over the adoption of the Constitution was only partly fought in the state convention. The first test of strength between the Constitution men and the "anti's" came during the regular legislative session, beginning early in January 1788. Here, before the convention met, the representatives discussed the major issues and the up country expressed its dissatisfaction with the Constitution. It was quickly obvious that the pro-Constitution forces were led by the two Pinckneys, Charles Cotesworth and Charles, and by John and Edward Rutledge. Evidently according to strategy, Charles Pinckney laid the foundation for the subsequent discussions. He opened the debate by relating in detail the historical developments which had brought the delegates to Philadelphia, commenting favorably upon those parts of the Constitution most likely to relieve the national and state distresses experienced during the previous five years. It was an outstanding opening argument.

Those who were opposed to the Constitution, mostly up-country men, informally selected Rawlins Lowndes, a Charleston lawyer and former governor of South Carolina, to speak for them. Lowndes voiced the major objections of the reticent up-country members: the executive would be too powerful; southern states would be economically crushed by the larger eastern states; so much power at the seat of government could easily provide "great men" (a reference to Washington?) opportunities to subvert the liberties of the people; South Carolina would yield its sovereignty as a free and independent state; no man from the south could ever become president; the state could no longer freely print paper money; local institutions could not be protected; and the convention at Philadelphia had brazenly exceeded its powers by drawing up an entirely new plan of government. Lowndes was so convinced that his opposition to the Constitution was well founded that he closed one argument with the wish that the following epitaph would appear on his tombstone: "Here lies the man that opposed the Constitution, because it was ruinous to the liberty of America."[59]

59. Lowndes's arguments can be found in Elliot, ed., *Debates*, IV, 265–311, *passim*.

Lowndes's objections had to be met. Charles Cotesworth Pinckney largely assumed the task of rebuttal. In no other place can Pinckney's style of argument be seen so clearly. His comments were incisive, well arranged, and replete with precedents to justify certain clauses in the Constitution. He showed a surprising familiarity with international law and custom while discussing the provisions in the Constitution dealing with foreign affairs. He easily recalled arguments in the Constitutional Convention on diverse subjects and used them at the appropriate time; it was apparent that Pinckney had taken care to acquaint himself with the discussions in committees on which he had not sat.

The length of time Pinckney spoke and the persuasiveness of his arguments indicate that he had perhaps become the major spokesman for the Constitution forces in the House of Representatives. He spoke nearly twice as long as any other man during the debates and showed an acute grasp of the issues. Pinckney countered Lowndes's general lament that the south had yielded too much to the eastern states by showing that the south had bargained from a position of weakness. Militarily and economically, the south needed northern resources. And by yielding concessions to a national government, South Carolina was certainly not yielding her sovereignty, Pinckney protested, for neither South Carolina nor any other state ever had "individual sovereignty." This doctrine of state sovereignty, Pinckney maintained, was nothing but "a species of political heresy, which can never benefit us, but may bring on us the most serious distresses." Did Lowndes and others object to the clause on the importation of slavery? It was the best that could be gained from northern delegates with religious and political scruples against slavery. At least the southern states had assurances that there could be no emancipation. On the paper money issue, Pinckney rejoiced that the state could no longer print any. Printing paper money "had corrupted the morals of the people; it had diverted them from the paths of honest industry to the ways of ruinous speculation; it had destroyed both public and private credit and brought total ruin on numberless widows and orphans."[60]

Pinckney's rebuttal ranged over nearly every major objection to

60. *Ibid.,* 263–316, *passim*; quote on 306.

the Constitution brought before the legislature and clearly bested Lowndes. It is little wonder that Lowndes admitted he was "almost willing to give up his post. . . ." Pinckney likewise rose to satisfy an up-country delegate that Congress "had no power at all" to interfere in religious matters. Pinckney was brutally frank when another delegate questioned why the Constitution had no bill of rights. "Such bills," Pinckney replied, "generally begin with declaring that all men are by nature born free. Now, we should make that declaration with a very bad grace, when a large part of our property consists in men who are actually born slaves."[61] Pinckney obviously believed in preserving his reputation for candor.

It was not in the state legislature, however, that the issue would finally be decided. A state convention was necessary to vote on the question of ratification. Where it would be held was uncertain. Pro-Constitution men were eager to hold the convention in Charleston, where, as Judge Aedanus Burke complained, there were not fifty inhabitants who opposed the Constitution. The up-country delegates in the legislature were equally anxious that Federalist Charleston should not be the site of the convention. When the question came before the legislature, there was a narrow victory for those favoring Charleston, seventy-six to seventy-five.[62]

The closeness of the vote indicated that there might be an intense struggle in the state convention. The crucial question was how the middle-country parishes would vote; on the matter of the convention site, the eight transitional parishes had largely cast their forty-three votes against Charleston. Although this was a good omen for the up-country anti-Federalists, they were still unhappy, foreseeing a "fixed" convention. It was well known, Judge Burke wrote, that "four-fifths of the people [of the state] do, from their souls detest" the proposed Constitution. Federalists saw the importance of sending their strongest men to the convention. Charleston did its part. When the votes were cast in the middle of April, the two Pinckney

61. *Ibid.*, 287, 300, 315–16.
62. Burke to John Lamb, June 23, 1788, in George C. Rogers, Jr., "South Carolina Ratifies the Federal Constitution," in South Carolina Historical Association, *Proceedings* (1961), 50. Burke's letter, quoted in full, is an enlightening statement on the techniques used by the Constitution men to control the ratification convention. The vote on the convention site, Jan. 19, 1788, is in House of Reps. Jour., S.C. Archives.

brothers led the ticket, with Edward Rutledge and Christopher Gadsden receiving the next highest total votes.[63]

Delegates from the up country began to drift into Charleston the first week of May. They had probably never been so courteously received. Merchants and aristocrats kept open house. A heretofore unknown cordiality for many up-country delegates became commonplace. Once the convention organized, it was apparent that the pressure exerted on the delegates by pro-Constitution Charleston was having the desired effect. And when news arrived on the sixth day of the convention that Maryland had ratified the Constitution, a general defection began from the ranks of the anti-Constitution men. Even before May 23 the Federalists were clearly in charge of the proceedings and, although some delegates had not had their say, forced a vote on that day. Those favoring the adoption of the Constitution had a majority of seventy-six votes. Many delegates could not hide their joy and began to huzzah, to the considerable annoyance of the anti-Constitution men. It was a smashing victory for the low country, Judge Burke believed, against the will of the majority of South Carolinians.[64]

Pinckney was delighted and quickly sent the good news to George Washington. All Charleston was equally pleased. A great victory celebration was held. Bells rang, cannon boomed, and citizens paraded through the streets. A victory dinner was served at the "Federalgreen" where victory toasts were the order of the day.[65] There was

63. Rogers, "S.C. Ratifies," S.C. Hist. Assoc., *Proceedings* (1961), 59; Charleston *State Gazette*, Apr. 17, 1788. The sectional voting pattern within the South Carolina legislature is discussed in Main, *Antifederalists*, 23, 26–27. If the state were divided geographically into up-country and low-country parishes, the up country controlled about 93 votes, the low country perhaps 143. But the middle-country parishes often voted with the up country, considerably diminishing the normal voting strength of the low country.

64. Rogers, "S.C. Ratifies," S.C. Hist. Assoc., *Proceedings* (1961), 60; Elliot, ed., *Debates*, IV, 340; Ramsay, *History of South-Carolina*, II, 239n. The records of the debates in the convention are incomplete. Of limited value, therefore, is Alexander S. Salley, ed., *Journal of the Convention of South Carolina which Ratified the Constitution of the United States, May 23, 1788* (Atlanta, 1928). Orin G. Libby concluded that the low country voted a solid 88 per cent for the Constitution; the middle country split, 49 per cent for and 51 per cent against; and the up country cast only 20 per cent of its votes for the new constitution. *Geographical Distribution of the Vote of the Thirteen States on the Federal Convention, 1787–1788* (Madison, Wis., 1894), 43–44.

65. Pinckney to Washington, May 24, 1788, Vol. 240, Papers of George Washington, Lib. Cong.; Charleston *State Gazette*, May 29, 1788.

good cause to celebrate. Property was secure. Even if the up-country insurgents gained control of the state political machinery, a strong central government would protect the low country.

Pinckney could have had no regrets for his work in the 1780's. At the end of the war he had helped to moderate the temper of those South Carolinians determined to punish all who had cooperated with the British. In this, as in his argument with General Greene, he had tried to protect the property and position of his low-country friends. In the legislature he had unstintingly given his energies to reconstructing a war-shattered government and to placing it upon a sound financial footing. His contributions at the Constitutional Convention and his leadership of the ratification forces in South Carolina gave a fitting finish to his constructive work in the 1780's.

To a remarkable degree the low-country gentry retained control of the government in South Carolina after the Revolutionary War. In the political sphere, it sometimes seemed that the war had never taken place. To be sure, democratic agitation by low-country mechanics and up-country farmers greatly increased after the war, but the low country did not capitulate to their demands for a greater share of political power. The retention of political control by the low-country oligarchy can be explained partly in terms of the high caliber of men who were sent to the legislature from Charleston and from the other low-country parishes. Charles Cotesworth Pinckney was the prototype of the leaders produced in the Charleston area. Well-trained, conscientious and honorable, cultured, personable, with a deep sense of responsibility for the public welfare, he was well suited for leadership in South Carolina.

But he was fitted for leadership only as long as South Carolinians accepted the idea that men of talents and experience should lead and that the masses should remain content to follow. South Carolinians had also to accept the proposition that the greater part of the state was an appendage to Charleston if Pinckney's leadership was to continue to be effective. The time when these ideas were accepted was passing quickly. Yet while it lasted, Pinckney felt honored to represent the low country in the legislature and considered that his dutiful protection of its commercial and social interests was a contribution to the welfare of the entire state.

V

STEPS TO A LARGER STAGE

───────◆•◆───────

I am glad my nephew has been so long in France, as I trust he will
return a good Republican; at least he will find that the French have
been much mis-represented when viewed through a British medium,
and that they are not the People the British say they are.

—Charles Cotesworth Pinckney, 1793.

Charleston was the most aristocratic city in the Union notwithstand-
ing her Jacobin club, with her red liberty caps, and fraternal hugs.
There was a complete nobility in everything but the title, and a few
with that appendage. The political professions of her leading men of
those days were of the Jeffersonial school, but their practice was
aristocracy complete.

—Ebenezer S. Thomas, 1840.

───────◆•◆───────

THERE WAS NO DOUBT IN THE MINDS OF SOUTH CAROLINIANS AS TO WHO
would be chosen chief executive of the new federal government.
Only George Washington had the national prestige necessary to bind
the new Union together. The selection of South Carolina's seven
electors by the state legislature was merely a formality by which it
voted for the great Virginian. Pinckney had the pleasure of casting
one of South Carolina's ballots for his friend Washington.[1]

President Washington was quite aware, as was Secretary of the
Treasury Alexander Hamilton, that the new government would
gain considerable strength if the "loaves and fishes" were distributed

---

1. Jan. 7, 1789, House of Reps. Jour.; Pinckney and Edward Rutledge were
chosen presidential electors in 1792 as well; Dec. 4, 1792, Senate Jour., S.C.
Archives.

skillfully. Men of local importance must be encouraged to accept positions in the government or at least be given the opportunity to recommend suitable persons. In distributing southern patronage, Washington naturally turned to his friends the Pinckney and Rutledge brothers.

While Charles Cotesworth Pinckney and Edward Rutledge were financially unable to accept appointments themselves, they were keenly interested in patronage questions, particularly when their relatives or political friends desired open positions. Pinckney and Rutledge frequently wrote directly to Washington with recommendations, or they asked Senator Ralph Izard or Congressman William Smith to suggest certain names to Washington or to the cabinet member directly concerned with the appointment.[2] For their own families, the Rutledges and the Pinckneys were primarily interested in positions in the diplomatic corps and the judiciary, reflecting their cosmopolitanism and their occupations; later their sights were set upon cabinet positions and finally upon the presidency. In most cases of lesser patronage (the excise service, the post office, the mint, and the Bank of the United States) the Pinckneys and Rutledges asked mainly that they be consulted before appointments were made. They felt that their political enemies should not be strengthened by gaining government positions.

A recent study of patronage distribution in South Carolina in the 1790's concluded that four major factions sought to control patronage. Three of these, which were identified as the Izard-Manigault-Smith, the Read-Simons, and the Smith-De Saussure-Darrell factions, were closely linked with commercial and banking interests. Each had strong ties with the merchant community and was active in promoting closer relations with Great Britain. Behind each of these factions was seen the considerable, if often discreetly silent, power of the British merchants in Charleston.

The fourth patronage faction, the Pinckney and Rutledge brothers and their friends, were able to obtain the highest positions because of their friendship with Washington, but they were unable to control

2. George Washington to Charles Cotesworth Pinckney, May 5, 1789, Misc. Mss., Charleston Lib. Soc.; Washington to Edward Rutledge, May 5, 1789, George Washington Photostats, Lib. Cong.; Ralph Izard to [John] Owen, Aug. 11, 1794, John Owen to Ralph Izard, Aug. 13, 1794, Papers of Ralph Izard, Lib. Cong.; Ralph Izard to Charles Cotesworth Pinckney, Nov. 21, 1794, Ralph Izard Papers, S. Caroliniana Lib.; Rogers, *Evolution of a Federalist*, 180.

local patronage. Mainly because they refused to see all measures from the commercial point of view, they gradually lost the ear of Alexander Hamilton; and Hamilton had many jobs at his disposal. It would have been difficult for Charles Cotesworth Pinckney and Edward Rutledge to be commercially oriented in any case, but when the British and old Tory influence was so marked in the Charleston business community, good patriots such as they were unlikely to be narrowly concerned about protecting commercial interests.[3]

It is clear that the Pinckneys and the Rutledges represented no particular financial interest when they made patronage recommendations. Whom then did they represent? One might answer with some truth, the Pinckneys and the Rutledges! Perhaps a better question would be to ask how they analyzed their role, or whom they believed they represented. And one might ask as well what view the Pinckneys and Rutledges took of their relationship to the new national government.

It is first important to remember that the Pinckney and Rutledge brothers had their initial political training under the English parliamentary system. They had observed it firsthand from their years spent in England. As Sir Lewis Namier has shown, government in England of the 1760's and 1770's was not carried on by well-defined political parties, even though the names of Whig and Tory were often used, but by factions or interests led by great men or family chiefs. The followers of Pitt, Grenville, Rockingham, Bute, and Bedford were major factions. There were also independent politicians and a substantial group who supported the Court on most issues (called "King's Friends"), but the King's government was usually carried on by a coalition of sizable factions. When in the government the Pitt men were pro-ministry; when out, they were anti-ministry. The same change in terminology applied to the other groups. It was assumed that any faction could leave the government if the King refused to endorse its policies or if the other governmental factions refused to share the patronage and power in a mutually satisfactory manner. There were no binding party ties to silence the

3. Rogers, *Evolution of a Federalist*, 180–92. One reason Pinckney did not want William Smith returned to Congress in 1794 was that "the British merchants and old Tories are doing all they can to get him in once more." Pinckney to Thomas Pinckney, Oct. 5, 1794, Pinckney Family Papers, Lib. Cong. Edward Rutledge's feelings for these same groups were well known in South Carolina.

opposition of any governmental faction; policy was not set by a party but by the leaders of a faction. There was obviously a strong personal element in the political factions, where loyalty to leaders was at least as important as adherence to principle.[4]

The Pinckneys and the Rutledges drew on this experience as they defined their relationship to the new government. Certainly they considered themselves friendly to the federal government; they had helped to create it and their friend Washington headed it. Because patronage was given to their friends, they became an integral part of the government and felt obliged to use their influence to rally support for it. As was true in the English system, their family and friends were expected to be equally loyal to the new government. This was part of the price of sharing in patronage and policy making. Of course they were not bound to support the government if it followed policies which seemed dangerous or foolish or if the government ignored their patronage recommendations. While the Pinckneys and Rutledges were eager to support the government, they never felt honor bound to do so. They felt free to withdraw and take their "connections" with them whenever governmental policies displeased them. In this attitude they gave clear evidence of their British political roots.

Whom then did the Pinckneys and Rutledges represent? First, they represented men who were convinced that the wise and the virtuous should govern society—in the case of South Carolina, the Pinckneys, the Rutledges, and a few other choice families. Second, they represented those conscious of what the Revolution had cost, those who knew that Great Britain had been the enemy and France the friend, those who felt it was proper to reward such friends when possible. But the Pinckneys and the Rutledges were distinctly patriotic, ready to defend the national honor and the national interest against any other country, even if the cost be heavy. They were not faint-hearted, cash-register patriots. They represented those who felt

4. The literature on this subject is extensive. Sir Lewis Namier pioneered in an analysis of 18th-century politics with *The Structure of Politics at the Accession of George III*, 2 vols. (London, 1929), and *England in the Age of the American Revolution* (London, 1930). Also in harmony with the analysis of the "Namier School" is Richard Pares, *King George III and the Politicians* (Oxford, 1953); Keith G. Feiling, *The Second Tory Party, 1714–1832* (London, 1938); and John Steven Watson, *The Reign of George III, 1760–1815* (Oxford, 1960).

that old patriots who supported the Revolutionary War effort should have first claims on any national plan to reimburse holders of governmental securities, even if the old patriots no longer owned the securities.[5] They acted for those who felt it was dishonorable to use one's official position for personal gain. Politicians who became speculators in governmental securities because of their access to inside information were anathema to the Pinckney and Rutledge brothers. They represented men who saw themselves as enlightened public servants, devoted to the public good and guided by the most exalted standards of honor and patriotism.

These Charleston aristocrats astutely combined Republican principles with the traditional attitude of the privileged, *noblesse oblige*. They were a service gentry, self-appointed to guard both the local and the national interest. The Pinckneys and the Rutledges were the flower of the southern oligarchy, and it is difficult to deny that they were worthy of their heroic pretensions to leadership in South Carolina and the nation.

Whatever the different viewpoints on patronage and national policies among low-country factions, they all agreed that up-country demands for increased power in the state government ought to be resisted. Men of the up country were more determined than ever to increase their weight in the government of South Carolina. Their defeat at the state ratifying convention did not permanently discourage them. If anything, they were spurred to greater activity. And when the census of 1790 showed that approximately four-fifths of the state's white population lived in the up-country districts, the clamor for change became alarmingly loud.[6] It was time for some compromise, low-country men said, but compromise that yielded only the form and not the substance of up-country demands. A constitutional convention would appease the up country but if controlled

5. Farrand, ed., *Records of Federal Convention*, II, 400. Pinckney was also anxious for the national government to assume the state's debts. He complained to his sister in 1790 that the New York congressional delegates were "pointedly against it" and wished that New York "had remained a little longer out of the Confederation, and then the adoption of their debts would certainly have taken place." Pinckney to Harriott Horry, Apr. 17, 1790, C. C. Pinckney Papers, S. Caroliniana Lib. Pinckney had subscribed only $10,865.30 to the state debt and Edward Rutledge $1,331. A list of some of the subscribers to the state debt is printed in Rogers, *Evolution of a Federalist*, 202–03.

6. Wallace, *South Carolina*, 341–42.

by the low country could do little damage. Fabian tactics might yet win the day.

Charles Cotesworth Pinckney did not easily join with his colleagues in assenting to a state constitutional convention. This was consistent with his general position that the fewest possible political concessions should be made to the up country. He had strenuously opposed moving the state capital from Charleston late in the 1780's. On the floor of the legislature he regularly moved to commit or to postpone any bill or motion that called for a state constitutional convention.[7] Pinckney could not see why men of virtue, wealth, and education—he and his friends—should voluntarily relinquish control of the state government to up-country men of limited wealth, no family, and, presumably, little political acumen.

Others were more flexible and practical than he. The state legislature voted to hold a convention in Columbia in May of 1790, but it was careful to assign representation to the convention so that members from the dissident districts would be in a minority.[8] Nevertheless, the more enlightened leaders of the low country came to the convention certain that many concessions would have to be granted; the alternative might be up-country unrest similar to what the state had experienced in the 1760's. No one wanted a repetition of those disturbing years.

Pinckney, his brother Thomas, and Edward Rutledge were among the delegates from Charleston when the convention opened in the unfinished state house in Columbia. Charles Cotesworth was quickly placed on the two most important committees, the Committee of Elections and the Committee of Detail and Arrangement, the one ruling on delegates' credentials and the other composing the various drafts of the constitution.[9]

Many of the issues could not be settled in the committees but had to be fought out on the floor. Whether delegates to the legislature should be reimbursed for their service to the state was a subject for

7. Mar. 14, 15, 1787; Feb. 23, 1788; Mar. 4, 1789, House of Reps. Jour., S.C. Archives.

8. Mar. 4, 1789, *ibid.*

9. A list of the delegates elected from Charleston is in the Charleston *City Gazette*, Feb. 15, 1790. The proceedings of the convention can be followed in Francis M. Hutson, ed., *Journal of the Constitutional Convention of South Carolina, May 10, 1790–June 3, 1790* (Columbia, S.C., 1946); Wallace, *South Carolina*, 342–43.

lengthy debate. For many years Pinckney had opposed paying representatives, both in the state legislature and at the federal Constitutional Convention. His grounds were not novel. Men too poor to
pay their expenses as public servants could hardly be depended upon
to take responsible attitudes toward the protection of property; their
own stake in the status quo was still too small. Despite his strenuous
objections in 1790, it was decided that representatives to the legislature should receive a stipend.[10] The gates were now opened, he felt,
for up-country demagogues to flood the legislature and to be paid
for their disservices.

On May 18, the most explosive issue came before the convention,
one that found the delegates almost evenly divided. The up-country
delegates were determined to fix Columbia as the permanent site of
the state capital through a constitutional provision. Columbia was in
a central location, about equally accessible to both the eastern and
western extremes of the state, and thus it had the advantage of logic
as the capital site. But Charlestonians were still anxious to designate
Charleston the capital, or at least leave the door open for a return to
Charleston. This selfish attitude redoubled the determination of the
up country to make Columbia the constitutional capital, where the
"opulent at Charleston" could not exert such a powerful influence
upon legislative proceedings.[11]

Pinckney entered the fray, contending that to fix a constitutional
capital would "occasion feuds and animosities. . . ." It would be better, he believed, to allow each session of the legislature to govern its
own meeting place. The up country saw the purpose of this suggestion. Although the capital had already been moved to Columbia, at
some future time it could be moved back to Charleston by a majority
vote in the legislature. Perhaps the "opulent at Charleston" would
even stoop to corruption to obtain the necessary votes. At the first
test of strength on this issue, those favoring Columbia won by one
vote, 106 to 105. According to one observer, "all was violence and
confusion" during the vote.[12]

The low country was dismayed. Pinckney got the floor and in a
long harangue showed why no one place should be constitutionally
designated as the state capital. If Columbia were accepted, there

10. Charleston *City Gazette*, May 26, 1790.
11. *Ibid.*
12. *Ibid.*

would be great expense to finish the state house; the economic burden of this project would fall upon those very districts which opposed the move to Columbia; the lawlessness of the up country would make the state records subject to seizure since there was no force adequate to protect them. None of the points was very convincing, at least not to the sponsors of Columbia. When the issue was put to the final vote, the up country, supported by the middle-country parishes, won by four votes, 109 to 105.[13] Columbia would be the permanent capital of South Carolina.

This defeat redoubled the efforts of low-country politicians to salvage measures which they had felt confident of carrying before the convention began. To a large extent, the low country had its way. Yet when the final articles of the constitution were hammered out, both the "upper" and "lower" districts had some cause to be pleased. There was a general agreement that the fundamental law defining the organs of government, their functions, and their relationships was skillfully done. On the crucial issue of political representation the low country retained control of the Senate and of the lower house, although up-country representation increased in each house.[14] Various state officers were to have offices both in Charleston and in Columbia, and the sittings of the Court of Appeals were designed for the convenience of the upper and lower divisions equally. While James Madison thought the constitution something of a joke because of its provisions for a virtual double capital, the constitution reflected the growing strength of the up country in state affairs.[15] Provisions that on paper appeared ridiculous to outsiders made a great deal of sense to South Carolinians. At least the low country was satisfied. The constitution placed political control in the experienced hands of the slaveholding oligarchy, where it would remain until 1865.

One delegate believed that Charles Cotesworth Pinckney and Edward Rutledge were "undoubtedly the leading minds in the Convention."[16] If not the leading minds, at least they were part of the inner

13. *Ibid.*, May 31, June 1, 1790.
14. D. Huger Bacot, "Constitutional Progress in S.C.," *South Atlantic Qtly.*, 24 (1925), 65, estimated that the low country maintained a majority of 16 in the House of Representatives and of 1 in the Senate.
15. William Smith to Edward Rutledge, July 4, 1790, Smith Papers, S.C. Hist. Soc.
16. This statement appeared in the Columbia *State Gazette* and was quoted by Christopher Gadsden in *Sermon on the decease of Pinckney*, 28.

political circle that largely dominated the convention. Together Pinckney and Rutledge successfully worked to preserve the predominant political power of the wise and the good, and for this they earned the gratitude of their constituency.

Charlestonians expressed their appreciation of Pinckney by sending him to the state Senate as one of their two delegates, an office he held until the summer of 1796. Pinckney almost immediately achieved an ascendancy in the Senate which he had never had in the House. Perhaps this was because his associates were representatives of their local elite, and no one was better suited to lead them than General Pinckney. He was placed on nearly every important committee.[17] During the sitting of the legislature, he was probably the busiest member of the government.

The prominent position of the Pinckneys in South Carolina's politics did not escape the observant eye of President Washington when he made his tour through the south in 1791. Washington had been planning the trip for many months, hoping through personal contacts to strengthen loyalties to the federal government.[18] He was immensely gratified by the ostentatious welcome he received in Charleston. Together with a select group, Pinckney and Edward Rutledge met Washington at Haddrell's Point and accompanied him in a decorated boat to the shores of Charleston. The oarsmen for Washington's boat were twelve ships' captains who were, according to Washington, "most elegantly dressed." Many notable Charlestonians crowded into boats and came to Haddrell's Point to greet Washington. There were also musicians who serenaded the chief as he crossed the bay. The choir of St. Philip's Church had prepared a selection for the occasion and burst into a chorus that presumably stirred patriotic hearts:

> He comes! He comes! the hero comes
> Sound, Sound your trumpets, beat your drums
> From port to port let cannon roar
> His welcome to our friendly shore.[19]

17. For example, see Jan. 14, Feb. 11, Dec. 9, 1791, Senate Jour., S.C. Archives.
18. John A. Carroll and Mary W. Ashworth, *George Washington: A Biography*, VII (N.Y., 1957), 298. Douglas Southall Freeman wrote the first six volumes of this series.
19. The most complete account of Washington's visit to Charleston is in Alexander S. Salley, *President Washington's Tour Through South Carolina in*

There were other equally moving verses.

Pinckney neglected few opportunities to show his respect for Washington. He attended the banquet given in Washington's honor by the Society of the Cincinnati, visited an orphanage with the President, and even rode with Washington beyond the Ashley Bridge when Washington finally left the city. Pinckney accompanied Washington to the home of his kinsman Colonel William Washington, between Charleston and Jacksonboro, where they remained overnight. In the morning Pinckney and his cousin Charles Pinckney turned back toward Charleston after bidding Washington a warm farewell. At least it was warm on the part of Charles Cotesworth.[20]

As Washington continued his tour, his mind kept returning to Pinckney and his friend Edward Rutledge. There was a vacancy on the Supreme Court bench which needed to be filled. John Rutledge had left the bench to become the chief justice of South Carolina. Washington probably remembered the letter that he had received from Governor Charles Pinckney urging him to appoint another South Carolinian in Rutledge's place. If this were done, Governor Pinckney said, it would be "pleasing to . . . [South Carolinians] to

---

1791 (South Carolina Historical Commission, *Bulletin*, 12 [1932]). Also helpful is Archibald Henderson, *Washington's Southern Tour, 1791* (Boston, 1923). Robert Mills' account of the visit, dated May 2, 1791, is in the Misc. Mss., S.C. Hist. Soc. Washington's reaction to his festive reception is in Fitzpatrick, ed., *Diaries of Washington*, IV, 170–73.

20. Charleston *City Gazette*, May 10, 1791. Charles Pinckney, brilliant but enigmatic, began to move into the Jeffersonian camp early in the 1790's. At least he was not on good terms with his cousins, Charles Cotesworth and Thomas. Why this was so is difficult to determine. His father had died in 1782 in partial disgrace because he had hesitated to leave Charleston during the British occupation. Charles Cotesworth Pinckney was fond of the elder Pinckney, and even offered to stand security if his estate were amerced. He was genuinely grieved when Colonel Pinckney died in 1782. But Charles Cotesworth and young Charles never seemed close. Perhaps Charles was jealous because his cousins emerged from the war as heroes. It must have been difficult as well to see how close his cousins were to George Washington, to see them offered one position after another while Washington offered him nothing. And perhaps Charles Cotesworth and Thomas envied the mental agility of Charles or feared his ambition. See Pinckney to John Colcock, Apr. 20, 1782, to [Colonel Charles Pinckney], July 24, 1782, Pinckney Family Papers, Lib. Cong.; Pinckney to Arthur Middleton, June 24, 1782, Pinckney to Mrs. Daniel Horry, Sept. 22, 1782, Arthur Middleton Papers, S.C. Hist. Soc. In this last letter, Pinckney wrote to his sister: ". . . with the most heartfelt concern, I am obligated to acquaint you that our beloved kinsman died this day at three oclock—Give vent to your Tears, for he was a man of worth—We shall bury him early tomorrow morning." Charles Cotesworth Pinckney is of course referring to Colonel Charles Pinckney.

reflect that when their suits were taken from the tribunal and carried to another acting authority, that still a citizen of their own was one of the Judges."[21] Governor Pinckney was saying in essence that a South Carolinian on the Supreme Court bench would increase the confidence of his state in the federal government, something which was close to Washington's heart. Possibly Governor Pinckney was trying to suggest his own appointment, but if so, President Washington did not take the hint.

By the time Washington reached Columbia he had made his decision. There were two men who were capable of doing honor to the position of associate justice and who would rally exactly the same political interest to increased support of the federal government. Washington therefore decided to offer the position to both—in the same letter—and let them decide which one would accept. This was an unusual administrative procedure but it does give an insight into the intimate relationship between the Pinckneys and Rutledges. To Pinckney and Edward Rutledge, Washington wrote: "Will either of you two Gentlemen accept the office, and in that case, which of you?" Although the appointment would be temporary, Washington added, "there can be *no doubt*" that it would be confirmed by the Senate.[22] The tone of the letter makes it seem probable that Washington expected a double refusal.

Washington's fears were well founded, for both men declined the appointment. Rutledge's financial position was even more precarious than Pinckney's; Rutledge was notoriously generous with his friends, too often pledging himself as security for their debts. Rutledge had also bought considerable plantation property after the war, but he was not content with this. In a short time he would be speculating in Kentucky and Tennessee lands, hoping in vain for a quick profit through resale or settlement.[23] Rutledge was therefore forbidden by his financial situation from holding any public office that would cut him off from his law practice. But by offering a Supreme Court ap-

21. Henderson, *Washington's Southern Tour*, 147.
22. Washington to Pinckney and Rutledge, May 24, 1791, Fitzpatrick, ed., *Writings of Washington*, XXXI, 290.
23. John Rutledge, Jr., to Edward Rutledge, Dec. 15, 1797, Feb. 25, 1798, Rutledge Papers, Dreer Coll., Hist. Soc. of Pa. For an evaluation of Edward Rutledge's financial condition in 1794, see his letter to John Rutledge, Jr., Apr. 24, 1794, John Rutledge Papers, Duke Univ. Lib.

pointment to these powerful lawyer-politicians, Washington had nevertheless strengthened his administration in South Carolina. Washington's patronage inclinations were obviously well directed.

After visiting Charleston, Washington had a more accurate idea of the political situation there. The great families of the low country, he saw, were the ones that should be consulted and patronized; the right family, if well used, could be a lever to manipulate important connections. One indication of Washington's perception was that his secretary of the treasury, Alexander Hamilton, sent a letter to Pinckney asking his help in raising the tax on "distilled spirits." South Carolina had shown a reluctance to pay this tax, Hamilton complained, forcing the government to consider "the necessity of coercive expedients." Hamilton hoped that his instruction to the supervisor of the revenue to counsel either with Pinckney or Edward Rutledge before appointing inspectors of surveys and to consult their judgment periodically would help to relieve the distressing tax situation in Charleston. Hamilton assured Pinckney that the government was relying upon his "zeal for the Support of the national laws. . . ."[24]

Another politic move to tie the Pinckney-Rutledge interest to the national administration was the appointment of Thomas Pinckney as minister to Great Britain. Thomas, surprised by the appointment, apparently had no great desire to take the post. He was uncertain what his duties in England would be and turned to others for assistance. Writing to Edward ("Ned") Rutledge, Thomas requested: "as you made me a Governor and now insist upon my being a Minister, you must advise me in this situation, as you supported me in that former."[25]

Thomas also wrote to his brother asking him to recommend a reading program for novice ministers. Charles Cotesworth first assured Thomas that he was "exceedingly glad" and did "entirely approve" Thomas' resolution to accept the appointment. The older and better read brother then advised Thomas to consult Vattel's *The Law of Nations*, Wicquefort on *Ambassadors*, Grotius' *Questiones Publici Jures*, "and all Lord Chesterfield's works." In addition,

24. Hamilton to Pinckney, Aug. 3, 1791, C. C. Pinckney Papers, S. Caroliniana Lib.
25. Pinckney to Edward Rutledge, Nov. 24, 1791, Thomas Pinckney Letter Book, 1791–1798, S. Caroliniana Lib.

Thomas should read the works of Sir William Temple and in the papers of Lord Hendrickson, which, Charles Cotesworth added, are "in Ned Rutledge's study." To complete his reading, Thomas should see Sully's *Memoirs*, "several French works in this line which are excellent," and the *Droit d'Europe*. "The perusal of these works," Pinckney added perhaps facetiously, "will employ you till I see you."[26]

Charles Cotesworth helped his brother to prepare for the mission in every way that he could, and of course assumed direction of Thomas' financial interests. After Thomas left Charleston for London, his brother kept him informed of local news—the latest parties, the French émigrés who had fled revolt-torn Haiti and were now gracing Charleston society, news of the agricultural society and the progress on the Santee Canal, Ned Rutledge's courting of widow Eveleigh, their mother's worsening cancer—and even gave him some occasional advice. Pinckney reminded his brother to send "frequent and regular" dispatches to Secretary of State Thomas Jefferson.[27]

By the appointment of Thomas Pinckney to the Court of St. James, the Washington administration clearly consolidated its support among several of South Carolina's great families. At one stroke the administration had secured a competent minister and the good wishes of many important Charlestonians.

Alexander Hamilton, the dominant figure in the administration, took nothing for granted and was careful to continue cultivating Charles Cotesworth. Perhaps he knew that Pinckney and Edward Rutledge were correspondents of Thomas Jefferson[28] and realized how easily personal friendships could develop into a political alliance.

26. This letter is in Howard Swiggett, *The Forgotten Leaders of the Revolution* (Garden City, N.Y., 1955), 253.

27. Pinckney to Thomas Pinckney, July 1, 28, 1792, Feb. 4, 1794, Pinckney Family Papers, Lib. Cong.; same to same, Aug. 27, 1792, Gratz Coll., Hist. Soc. of Pa.; same to same, Nov. 13, 1792, Arthur Middleton Papers, S.C. Hist. Soc. Eliza Pinckney died in Philadelphia in 1793. She had gone there to consult with Dr. Tate, who supposedly had a cure for cancer. Earlier, Charles Cotesworth had assiduously collected leeches to place on his mother's cancer, but was disappointed with at least one shipment because "they were not of the right sort because they would not stick to the flesh." See Pinckney to Thomas Pinckney, Aug. 27, 1792, Frank H. Pinckney Collection, S.C. Hist. Soc.; same to same, May 21, 1793, C. C. Pinckney Papers, S. Caroliniana Lib.

28. Pinckney had not met Jefferson, but he had corresponded with him on agricultural subjects. As chairman of the Committee of Correspondence of the South Carolina Agricultural Society, Pinckney asked Jefferson's advice about

This Hamilton was determined to prevent. He tried to undermine Jefferson's political support in South Carolina as a vice-presidential prospect in 1792 by writing to Pinckney that though he once *"very much esteemed"* Jefferson, he had since found him "a man of sublimated and paradoxical imagination, entertaining and propagating opinions inconsistent with dignified and orderly government." John Adams, the incumbent, Hamilton described as a "firm, honest, and independent politician."[29]

Pinckney was probably puzzled by this letter. Did Hamilton represent the views of Washington toward Jefferson? Perhaps Pinckney believed that Hamilton's opinion had developed as a result of a mere personality clash. What Hamilton meant by accusing Jefferson of holding opinions "inconsistent with dignified and orderly government" must also have troubled Pinckney. Pinckney firmly believed that the "great art of government is not to govern too much," a position that would have been readily seconded by Jefferson.

Pinckney was largely satisfied with the policies of the new federal government. But he was unhappy because anti-slavery congressmen were presenting Quaker petitions to Congress. Congressional "intermeddling with our Negroes," he warned, was not to be allowed, for Negroes were "altogether a matter of domestic [i.e., local] regulation."[30] Pinckney was likewise unhappy because the government did not differentiate between original holders of public securities and speculators who had bought them up at bargain rates; Pinckney felt this was unfair to the patriots who had supported the Revolutionary cause with their purses during its darkest hours, had fallen on hard times, and had been forced to sell their securities at a fraction of their value. During the late 1780's and early 1790's, Pinckney had seen

---

procuring olive trees and caper plants for experimentation in South Carolina. Jefferson cooperated fully with Pinckney and the Society and arranged for 40 olive trees and 4 caper plants to be sent to South Carolina. Jefferson also forwarded a book to Pinckney on the proper methods for cultivating olive trees. See Charles Cotesworth Pinckney to Thomas Pinckney, July 1, 1793, Pinckney Family Papers, [Thomas Jefferson] to C. C. Pinckney, Oct. 8, 1792 (III–36–H), Personal Miscellaneous Manuscripts, Lib. Cong.; Charles Cotesworth Pinckney to Thomas Jefferson, Aug. 25, 1792, Gratz Coll., Hist. Soc. of Pa.

29. Hamilton to Pinckney, Oct. 10, 1792, in Henry C. Lodge, ed., *The Works of Alexander Hamilton*, 12 vols. (N.Y., 1904), X, 24.

30. Pinckney to General [Pickens?], Mar. 31, 1790, C. C. Pinckney Papers, S. Caroliniana Lib.

shrewd speculators swarming through the south, many of them agents of British merchant and banking houses or northern brokers who were later reported to have received advance information on the federal government's assumption policy.[31] And Hamilton, Pinckney could not forget, had been the person who had urged the administration to compensate these opportunistic holders of public securities. It was Hamilton also who was welcoming the British presence in the nation's major commercial towns.

Charleston was obviously one town that was feeling the influence of British merchants early in the 1790's. The merchants were entering the courts to collect their prewar debts, involving enormous sums and the financial welfare of several prominent merchant houses. Pinckney and Rutledge acted as lawyers for the defendants in a series of important cases to determine how much of the original debt should be paid and whether interest should be allowed on the debts during the Revolutionary years as well as during those since 1783.

One basic case provided the guidelines on the question of interest allowable on old debts. It involved William Higginson, the surviving partner of Greenwood and Higginson, against William Greenwood, the surviving partner of Leger and Greenwood. They claimed in 1790 that American citizens owed them £295,891 sterling. In suing Greenwood for his share of the joint claim, Higginson raised the question whether interest assessments against the original debt should be allowed in calculating the total sum owed. Pinckney opened the arguments for the defense in October 1791, soon bringing in Edward Rutledge and John Bee Holmes to assist him. In their defense of Greenwood against the claims of Higginson, the three attorneys presented the argument that interest on old debts should be disallowed from the time the Revolutionary War commenced. Once this question was introduced to the court, the case of Higginson versus Greenwood took on an importance beyond the immediate problem of claims allocation.

The court could make no decision for two years. Finally, in May 1793 a Charleston jury decided for Higginson. The jury also decided on the interest problem by disallowing interest during the war on the

31. Whitney K. Bates, "Northern Speculators and Southern State Debts: 1790," *Wm. and Mary Qtly.*, 3rd Ser., 19 (1962), 30–48. Professor Bates argues "that a small band of Northern merchants and brokers were most prominent among those who engrossed the major share of Southern state debts," 42.

debits and credits directly involved in this case. It claimed that five per cent interest since the peace was a just settlement that would not bankrupt the creditors or destroy the debtors.[32] Neither the creditor nor the debtor interests in the community were happy with the settlement. Pinckney and Rutledge took issue with the principle that old patriot debtors should have to pay any interest, and one suspects they believed these debts should have been lifted from patriot shoulders altogether.

Higginson pushed his claims as well against the estates of William Loocock and John Ward, winning substantial awards in both cases. During the Circuit Court's October term of 1793, Higginson won three more awards. In each of these cases Pinckney and Edward Rutledge represented clients opposing the claims of the British merchants.[33] It was bitter medicine for patriot-lawyers like Pinckney and Rutledge to lose these cases. Behind the British merchants towered the national government, or more accurately, the energetic figure of Alexander Hamilton.

Pinckney and Hamilton did not see eye to eye on another great issue of the day, the French Revolution. Pinckney sympathized with the cause of the French revolutionists when they established a republic in September of 1792. The bloody purges which followed the outbreak of revolution and the seemingly chaotic state of the republican government both alarmed and disgusted Hamilton. Pinckney took a more detached view, feeling that the "commotions which are the natural consequence of all great revolutions" would gradually subside.[34] This does not mean that Pinckney approved of the violence nor that he favored the equalitarian measures of the revolution. A low-country aristocrat who lightly waved aside the moderate political demands of the up country was not likely to be concerned for the welfare of the French peasant. Yet Pinckney was pleased that

32. Rogers, *Evolution of a Federalist*, 250–51. Pinckney believed that the case should be settled by a jury decision, but as Rogers has pointed out, the jury was composed of men active in the banking and mercantile community of Charleston. See also Pinckney to Thomas Pinckney, Oct. 28, 1793, Pinckney Family Papers, Lib. Cong.

33. Rogers, *Evolution of a Federalist*, 251–52.

34. Pinckney to Thomas Pinckney, Jan. 7, 1793, Pinckney Family Papers, Lib. Cong. Pinckney added, "I am glad my nephew [Daniel Horry] has been so long in France, as I trust he will return a good republican; at least he will find that the French have been much misrepresented when viewed through a British medium. . . ."

there was a movement toward republican government in France and on this basis considered himself a supporter of the revolution.

Pinckney's sympathy for the cause of republican France was quite evident in the personal reception he gave to Edmond Genêt, the youthful and indiscreet minister of France to the United States.[35] Some Americans did not wish to receive Genêt because he represented a government which had beheaded Louis XVI, America's ally in the Revolutionary War. Pinckney wished to suspend judgment until he knew the causes of the regicide. "We have heard," he wrote to Thomas, "of the decapitation of Louis, and altho every feeling must lament his death, . . . yet we are too far from the scene of action . . . to determine whether the measure was positively wrong, or excusable, or justifiable."[36]

Pinckney may have tried to glean some information about Louis' death from Genêt during the new envoy's triumphal visit to Charleston. His reception there was matched only by the one given Washington in 1791. During Genêt's stay in Charleston, Pinckney dined with him privately at least twice, once at his own home, the other time in the home of Ralph Izard. Genêt impressed Pinckney initially as being "a very sensible intelligent man." On another occasion Pinckney attended a banquet given by Monsieur Boutelle in Genêt's honor and at the conclusion of the banquet walked arm in arm with Boutelle to the theater to the accompaniment of band music and the cheers of bystanders. As a parting gesture, Pinckney provided horses for Genêt on his trip northward to Philadelphia.[37] Pinckney left no doubt in anyone's mind that he was a good republican, a staunch supporter of the French Revolution.

The impetuous Genêt was not content merely to receive the applause of the American people. Spurred by his government, he was

35. For the diplomatic background of Genêt's appointment and the effect his mission had upon American politics, see Alexander DeConde, *Entangling Alliance: Politics and Diplomacy Under George Washington* (Durham, N.C., 1958), 164–310.

36. Pinckney to Thomas Pinckney, Apr. 16, 1793, Pinckney Family Papers, Lib. Cong.

37. *Ibid.*, and Ralph Izard to   ?   , Apr. 17, 1793, Ralph Izard Papers, S. Caroliniana Lib. An account of the public procession to the theater is in Ebenezer S. Thomas, *Reminiscences of the Last Sixty-Five Years*, 2 vols. (Hartford, 1840), II, 32. Thomas observed that despite the liberty caps and fraternal hugs, Charleston was still the "most aristocratic city in the Union." See also Rogers, *Evolution of a Federalist*, 247.

determined to enlist American resources to defeat England in a war his nation had declared on that power in February 1793. President Washington decided that the United States would not allow itself to become a pawn of France and in April of 1793 issued a proclamation affirming American neutrality. Genêt was indignant and defiant. He continued to authorize the outfitting of privateers to prey on British shipping and over Washington's head boldly appealed to the American people for support. Washington and Hamilton were outraged, and even Jefferson felt that Genêt had grossly violated the standards of diplomatic propriety. When Genêt attacked Washington, Pinckney quickly turned on him and supported the efforts of the South Carolina legislature to end Genêt's project of raising a force to attack the Florida and Louisiana dominions of Spain, England's ally. Like Washington, Pinckney was convinced that America's best policy was neutrality in the wars of Europe, although he complained to his brother that America was not gaining sufficient benefits from her neutrality.[38]

The political temper of the south, despite South Carolina's general support of Washington's neutrality policy, was not pleasing to staunch administration supporters. There was a marked sympathy for the cause of France, a feeling that America should stand by its old ally even among those Charleston families who were later associated with the Federalist party. With perhaps a view to strengthening his administration politically in the south, Washington decided to offer Charles Cotesworth Pinckney the office of secretary of war.

Washington assured Pinckney that he was not needed in the administration to attend to "the mere details of the Office," for these could be done as well by a "character" much "less important" than Pinckney. The man wanted, Washington said, should not only be "competent . . . in the science of War" but should also possess "a

38. The essence of Genêt's instructions is in Meade Minnigerode, *Jefferson, Friend of France: The Career of Edmond Charles Genet . . .* (N.Y., 1928), 141–46. For the nature of Genêt's intrigue in South Carolina and Pinckney's reaction to it see Alexander Moultrie, *An Appeal to the People of South Carolina* (Charleston, 1794), 6–10; Dec. 7, 1793, Senate Jour., S.C. Archives; Pinckney to Thomas Pinckney, Aug. 12, 1793, Feb. 4, 1794, Pinckney Family Papers, Lib. Cong.; Rogers, *Evolution of a Federalist*, 253–57. Rogers points out that Genêt used a "number of malcontents, who were always ready to take advantage of a crisis to recover their lost prominence. Among these were army officers who had served within the militia during the Revolution" and who felt their services had not been properly recognized, 253.

general knowledge of political subjects, [be] of known attachment to the Government we have chosen, and of proved integrity." Washington tried to stress that the office was a political one. Pinckney admitted to Washington that of "all the public offices in our Country the one you mention to me is that which I should like best to fill; except in case of a general War, when if other matters would admit, I should prefer being in the field." Pinckney was still a soldier at heart, boyishly eager for a taste of combat and glory. But financial burdens, he lamented to Washington, absolutely forbade him to accept the office. "Inevitable ruin" would follow if he were to abandon his legal practice. And besides, since his children were all girls he felt compelled to leave his affairs "as little perplexed as possible." But he did close with a note that Washington kept in mind: "should you, when my affairs are in a more pleasant train, and I can with propriety dispense with an immediate attention to them, think fit to require my services in any way in which you judge me qualified, I will most chearfully serve; for tho I am very fond of and prefer private life, and shall be forty Eight years old tomorrow, I am too much flattered by your indulgent opinion not to wish to take a part in your administration."[39]

Moreover, Pinckney did not care to leave South Carolina when British depredations on American commerce made war between the two nations a possibility. Governor William Moultrie stressed this possibility in his message of April 1794 to the legislature, suggesting that the state move at once to a strong posture of defense. The legislature responded by authorizing the establishment of two divisions and by directing that the army have two major generals to command it, one for the lower and one for the upper military districts. Pinckney and Andrew Pickens were selected by the legislature as major generals. Charles Cotesworth wrote to his brother that he "had no idea of serving," but a fight was brewing in the legislature between the friends of Generals Thomas Sumter and Francis Marion. Deadlocked, friends of both men approached Pinckney and asked if he would be a compromise candidate for the position. Pinckney consented only after they promised to back him unanimously.[40]

39. Washington to Pinckney, Jan. 22, 1794, Fitzpatrick, ed., *Writings of Washington*, XXXIII, 294; Pinckney to Washington, Feb. 24, 1794, Vol. 265, Papers of George Washington, Lib. Cong.
40. May 10, 1794, Senate Jour., S.C. Archives; Pinckney to Thomas Pinckney, May 29, 1794, Pinckney Family Papers, Lib. Cong.

There was, of course, the question of which major general should be the ranking commander, a matter that was determined by having a child draw lots. Andrew Pickens' lot was chosen first, Pinckney wrote to Ralph Izard. Pinckney then asked Izard to assure Pickens that he would "with pleasure serve under him whenever our Divisions join, be so good as to make him my Congratulations on this event."[41] Pinckney was a generous man, one who did not need to prove his importance by seeking offices and grasping for power.

Pinckney plunged enthusiastically into the task of raising and training his division of twenty-one regiments. This was the kind of work he loved. Charleston strengthened its harbor defenses under his direction while its citizens made very brave, bombastic speeches against the policies of Great Britain. The British depredations, Pinckney wrote joyfully to Thomas, "have united all parties in this Country . . . [and] have thoroughly revived that military glow which fired our hearts in 1775." While they were making every preparation for war, they were still hopeful that peace "can be obtained salvo honore." Pinckney added that he wished the war between England and France could be concluded with the "Liberties of France fully established."[42]

Pinckney was careful to follow the progress of his brother's London mission even as he was helping prepare South Carolina to defend itself against coastal attacks by Great Britain. Thomas' position was delicate because of the mounting hostility between England and America over British violations of American neutral rights. His fellow South Carolinians joined with citizens from every state in denouncing the commercial measures of Great Britain. Congress began war preparations and announced an embargo on American seaports.[43]

Protests against British policies became so heated that Federalists saw a danger of being pushed into a war for which they had no stomach. Ardent Federalists were therefore not entirely displeased

41. Pinckney to Ralph Izard, Dec. 20, 1794, Pinckney Family Papers, Lib. Cong.
42. Pinckney to Thomas Pinckney, June 18, 1794, *ibid.* In 1794, Pinckney became virtually an executive agent of the federal government in Charleston. The governor, William Moultrie, had lost the confidence of the federal government, evidently because his brother was involved in the Genêt intrigue. Governor Moultrie was also less than enthusiastic in seizing French vessels violating American neutrality. Consequently, Pinckney was given power in at least one case by the secretary of war to seize a specific foreign vessel if the governor refused to take the proper action. See John Owen to Ralph Izard, Aug. 13, 1794, Papers of Ralph Izard, Lib. Cong.; Charles Cotesworth Pinckney to Ralph Izard, Nov. 5, 1794, Manigault Papers, S.C. Hist. Soc.
43. DeConde, *Entangling Alliance*, 95–98.

when French vessels began to capture American goods being carried to Great Britain or parts of her empire. Federalists seized this opportunity to denounce French actions vociferously, hoping to counter the mounting anti-British hysteria. During this period, when American commerce was being violated by both Great Britain and France, the administration decided to take the diplomatic initiative to ease the dangerous tensions between England and the United States. Self-interest clearly dictated that if only one power could be appeased, it was wise to appease one's best customer—and potentially most formidable enemy. At least this was the reasoning of the Washington administration. Accordingly, Chief Justice John Jay was nominated by President Washington as a special envoy to the Court of St. James. It was hoped that sending this conservative Federalist would impress Great Britain that the United States sincerely wanted peace, even at the price of French wrath.[44]

The appointment of Jay as envoy extraordinary left Thomas Pinckney in an awkward position. It appeared that either he had lost the confidence of his government or was not thought capable of conducting the crucial negotiations. Neither suggestion was especially flattering. One Charleston newspaper speculated that Jay had been sent because of Thomas Pinckney's "avowed republicanism, and attachment to the French and their cause. . . ."[45]

Charles Cotesworth Pinckney was embarrassed for his brother. He put the best face possible on Washington's action, assuring Thomas that he did not believe the administration lacked confidence in him but had appointed Jay because he was "acquainted with the present temper and disposition of the people. . . ." Five months later Charles Cotesworth admitted to Thomas that he "did not like the appointment" of Jay but "as the anti-federalists exclaimed against it, I held my tongue, saying nothing in its favour or against it." He was still certain, though, that "nothing personally disrespectful was meant" to Thomas by the appointment of Jay.[46]

The administration was able to assuage the Pinckneys' embarrass-

44. *Ibid.*, 102–03.
45. Charleston *City Gazette*, May 15, 1794. For the background of Jay's appointment see Carroll and Ashworth, *George Washington*, VII, 159–67. The standard account of the Jay mission is Samuel F. Bemis, *Jay's Treaty: A Study in Commerce and Diplomacy*, 2nd ed. (New Haven, 1962).
46. Pinckney to Thomas Pinckney, May 29, Oct. 5, 1794, Pinckney Family Papers, Lib. Cong.

ment by appointing Thomas envoy extraordinary to Spain. Charles Cotesworth was not certain that his brother would accept the appointment, but he felt that since Thomas' wife had recently died in London, a change of scene might comfort his "afflicted mind." Another complication, he wrote to Ralph Izard, was the expense involved. Thomas was spending £500 annually more than his plantation income, and with a recently ruined crop he was in no position financially to continue his work abroad. He accepted the post, however, and eventually negotiated the popular Treaty of San Lorenzo, usually called Pinckney's Treaty, which gave the United States an unrestricted use of the Mississippi River and a favorable boundary settlement in the southwest where American lands were adjacent to Spanish territory.[47]

While many of his friends were beginning to identify themselves with the developing national parties, Federalist and Republican, Pinckney steered a middle course in the politics of South Carolina. Candidates for Congress, he felt, should be identified with neither the pro-British nor the pro-French faction. He opposed, for example, the election of William Smith to Congress in 1794 because Smith had "shewn too great a bias to Britain and British politics. . . ." Smith, he believed, was tainted too much with the commercial spirit. Pinckney also believed that Smith had speculated in public securities early in the 1790's, using his position in government to gain useful advance information. As for other candidates in 1794, Pinckney felt they were not "sufficiently federal." The candidate he supported for Congress was John Rutledge, Jr., because "he prefers America to every foreign interest. . . ."[48] William Smith might have added that Rutledge had the weighty advantage of his name and Pinckney connection as well.

Another election struggle in 1794 revealed Pinckney's determination to avoid association with either national party. Within the legislature Pinckney and Edward Rutledge tried to have their friend David Ramsay elected as United States senator, but too many mem-

---

47. Pinckney to Ralph Izard, Dec. 20, 1794, C. C. Pinckney Papers, Duke Univ. Lib. The basic account of Thomas Pinckney's mission to Spain is Samuel F. Bemis, *Pinckney's Treaty: America's Advantage from Europe's Distress, 1783–1800*, rev. ed. (New Haven, 1960).

48. Pinckney to Thomas Pinckney, Oct. 5, 1794, Pinckney Family Papers, Lib. Cong.; Rogers, *Evolution of a Federalist*, 264.

bers distrusted Ramsay's unorthodox view that slavery was an evil that should be abolished. Ramsay's promise that he would support the southern position in Congress and the backing of Pinckney, a staunch advocate of slavery and slave importation, were not enough to secure Ramsay's election. As a result, Pinckney despondently advised Ralph Izard, he and Ned Rutledge were forced to vote for Jacob Read as senator "notwithstanding we greatly disapprove his antigallican prejudices. . . ."[49]

Pinckney's neutral stand was severely tested in the political eruption over the treaty concluded by John Jay in London. Probably no treaty in American history was ever so unpopular. Jay was vilified in almost every part of the Union as a traitor to his country and probably a secret pensioner of the British court.[50] No one, it seemed, was happy with the Jay Treaty but southerners were particularly angry. The British had carried away thousands of Negroes (just how many is uncertain) from South Carolina during the Revolutionary War, but the Jay Treaty was silent on the question of compensation for these confiscatory acts. Jay, in southern eyes, had obviously sold out the southern planters to fatten the pockets of greedy northern merchants.

In Philadelphia a mob was thrown a copy of the treaty and urged by one rabble rouser to "kick it to hell." The reaction in Charleston was just as violent. A belligerent crowd dragged the British flag through the street and burned it in a public demonstration before the doors of the British consulate.[51]

But the protest in Charleston was not confined to the mechanics. There was a general and anguished outcry from the disappointed noncommercial oligarchy as well, which was joined, if not led, by the Rutledge brothers, John and Edward. The Jay Treaty helped to inflame Edward's violent hatred of Great Britain. In 1782 Edward had declared that he would "as soon have an Alliance with a Band of Robbers as with the people of Great Britain." He described the

49. Pinckney to Ralph Izard, Dec. 20, 1794, John Brown Cutting to Thomas Pinckney, Dec. 19, 1794, Pinckney Family Papers, Lib. Cong.

50. Frank Monaghan, *John Jay, Defender of Liberty* . . . (N.Y., 1935), 388–90; Bemis, *Jay's Treaty*, 271.

51. Oliver Wolcott to Mrs. Wolcott, July 26, 1795; Wolcott to Alexander Hamilton, July 30, 1795, George Gibbs, *Memoirs of the Administrations of Washington and John Adams, edited from the Papers of Oliver Wolcott*, 2 vols. (N.Y., 1846), I, 218, 220.

British as the "Natural Enemies of this Country" and vowed that as "far as I have anything to do in Public Affairs, I will always mistrust them. Nor indeed will I trust them when I can avoid it."[52] Rutledge's Revolutionary passion had cooled in the years of peace, but British depredations upon American commerce quickly revived it. British refusal to yield any substantial concessions to Jay reaffirmed Rutledge's belief that the British people were indeed the "Natural Enemies" of America.

A committee of indignant citizens met at the Exchange on July 16 to discuss the treaty and to decide on a course of protest. At this first meeting John Rutledge expressed the indignation of the group in an outburst that was remarkable for its lack of restraint, particularly for one who professed to be a friend of Washington. The group then decided to ask the people of Charleston to elect a committee of fifteen who would frame proper resolutions on the treaty and present them to a town meeting. Pinckney, Christopher Gadsden, the two Rutledge brothers, David Ramsay, Aedanus Burke, General William Washington, and eight others were elected.[53] Pinckney was angry when he learned that he had been elected, for he had posted a notice on St. Philip's Church door stating that he would not serve on the committee.[54]

Nevertheless, when the time came for the meeting, several of the committee members were determined that the absent Pinckney would attend. When he did not come, a delegation went to his home. According to a report that Thomas Jefferson received, Pinckney treated the delegation "with great hauteur and disapproved of their meddling." It must have been a stormy conference. Pinckney told the

---

52. Rutledge to Arthur Middleton, June 23, 1782, in Barnwell, ed., "Correspondence of Arthur Middleton," *S. C. Hist. and Gen. Mag.*, 27 (1926), 18.

53. Philadelphia *Aurora and General Advertiser*, June 29, 1795. The votes were as follows:

Christopher Gadsden	792	John Mathews	440
John Rutledge	792	Tho. Norris	429
David Ramsay	775	Tho. Jones	411
Edward Rutledge	757	William Johnson	379
C. C. Pinckney	571	John Bee Holmes	372
T. T. Tucker	566	John Rutledge, Jr.	345
Aedanus Burke	545	J. J. Pringle	295
William Washington	480		

The list was printed in the *Aurora*, Aug. 11, 1795.

54. Pinckney describes the position he took in the controversy in a letter to Jacob Read, Sept. 26, 1795, Emmet Collection, N.Y. Pub. Lib.

delegation that his brother "approved of every article of the treaty, under the existing circumstances. . . ." Did they doubt the judgment of Thomas, their former governor and their friend? And why did they not respect Charles Cotesworth's determination not to get involved in the uproar? The committee retreated as gracefully as it could. Since that conference at Pinckney's home, Jefferson wrote to James Madison, "the politics of Charleston have been assuming a different hue."[55]

Jefferson's informant was certainly correct in reporting why Pinckney refused to attend the meeting. His brother had indicated to Secretary of State Edmund Randolph that, "all Circumstances considered," Jay had gained as much for the United States as could reasonably be expected.[56] As a matter of family loyalty, therefore, Charles Cotesworth could say nothing against the treaty or against the government that his brother was representing. Pinckney also believed that if he criticized the treaty, many would say that he was angry because Jay had replaced Thomas in the London negotiations. To neutralize himself completely, Pinckney refused even to read a copy of the treaty so that if an opinion escaped from him, it would carry no weight. He was unhappy about the treaty though and complained to Senator Jacob Read that many who were ordinarily "warmly attached" to the government wholeheartedly disapproved of the treaty.[57]

Pinckney was no doubt thinking primarily of his friends the Rutledges when he wrote to Read. John Rutledge's attack on the treaty was printed and circulated throughout the Union. Rutledge had just been appointed chief justice of the Supreme Court ad interim, but this in no way checked his outburst against the treaty. William Smith believed that John later regretted the speech he made, but

55. Jefferson to James Madison, June 1, 1797, Henry A. Washington, ed., *The Writings of Thomas Jefferson*, 9 vols. (N.Y., 1854–56), IV, 180. The resolutions of the select committee were printed in the Phila. *Aurora*, Aug. 1, 1795. At the meeting where these resolutions were approved, Charles Pinckney seized the opportunity to denounce the treaty. He attacked Washington for appointing an anti-western man like Jay to negotiate and even hinted that Washington was under British influence. Phila. *Aurora*, Aug. 7, 15, 1795. An extract of Thomas Pinckney's letter to the secretary of state, giving cautious approval to the treaty, is in *Aurora*, Aug. 17, 1795. The letter is dated Nov. 16, 1794.

56. Thomas Pinckney to secretary of state, Nov. 16, 1794, Thomas Pinckney Letter Book, January 1794–April 1795, S.C. Hist. Soc.

57. Pinckney to Jacob Read, Sept. 26, 1795, Emmet Coll., N.Y. Pub. Lib.

his "brother E. R., still remains violent . . . ; he has a most uncon-
querable aversion to the British nation. . . ."[58]

John Rutledge had better reason to moderate his feelings than did
Edward, for John's appointment as chief justice was still to be confirmed by a Federalist-controlled Senate. Federalists began to wonder
whether one who acted "like the *devil*" should be confirmed as chief
justice. Influential northern Federalists began to undermine Rutledge
by whispering that he was mentally deranged, a fact that would explain, they said, his violent opposition to the Jay Treaty.[59] No sane
man, particularly no sane bona fide Federalist, could rant as had John
Rutledge against a treaty so essential to commercial prosperity and
the national welfare!

When Thomas Pinckney's letter to Edmund Randolph was published, in which Pinckney expressed his general approval of the Jay
Treaty, the Rutledges greatly modified their anti-treaty stand, more
out of friendship for the Pinckneys than because they believed
Thomas' evaluation was sound. Edward Rutledge was particularly
anxious not to strain his friendship with Thomas Pinckney, a friendship that had "been warmed and cemented by a thousand affectionate Actions," one so close that their "Children have grown up
together as if they were the Children of the same Parents, and no
one act has ever been omitted on his [Thomas'] part, to give con-
stance to our friendship." With the Pinckneys moderately supporting
the treaty and the Rutledges modifying their opposition, the politics
of Charleston did indeed, as Jefferson noted, begin to take on a "different hue."[60]

Yet the Washington administration had cause to be alarmed for

58. Rutledge's speech is abstracted in Henry Flanders, *The Lives and Times of
the Chief Justices of the Supreme Court of the United States*, 2 vols. (Phila.,
1858), I, 633–36. Edward Rutledge's position is described in a letter from William Smith to Oliver Wolcott, Sept. 8, 1797, Gibbs, *Administrations of Washington and Adams*, I, 231.

59. Oliver Ellsworth to Oliver Wolcott, Aug. 15, 1795, in Gibbs, *Administrations of Washington and Adams*, I, 225. The rumors of Rutledge's mental in-
stability were not without some foundation in fact. See William Read to Jacob
Read, Dec. 29, 1795, Jacob Read Papers, S. Caroliniana Lib. William Read described how John Rutledge tried to commit suicide in the Ashley River but was
dragged out against his will by several Negroes and John Blake.

60. Edward Rutledge to Mrs. John Rutledge, Jr., Mar. 8, 1798, John Rutledge
Papers, Duke Univ. Lib.; William Read to Jacob Read, Dec. 16, 1795, Jacob
Read Papers, S. Caroliniana Lib. Read believed that "E. R. is sorry for the part

its political support in South Carolina. True, the Charleston merchants and bankers, the faction represented by William Smith, would continue to throw their considerable weight behind Federalist policies. But what of the faction represented by the Pinckneys and Rutledges, old patriots and planters who sympathized with France and the French Revolution? Obviously the Pinckneys and Rutledges were not Federalists in the Hamiltonian or party sense; rather, they were "federals," supporting the Washington administration because they recognized the need for a properly energetic government and because of their personal affection for Washington. But they would not blindly support a government following an "unpatriotic" foreign policy or one that lightly waved aside the just demands of an injured south. The roots of the Pinckney-Rutledge faction had not sunk deep into Federalist soil; when the roots were no longer nourished by confidence in Washington and in his desire to pursue genuinely national policies, they would seek more rewarding soil— perhaps Jeffersonian soil.

The Jay Treaty severely shook confidence in Washington's judgment and in his administration. Even the moderate Federalism of South Carolina's great low-country families began to dim and to be replaced by a Republican glow. The probable rejection of John Rutledge as chief justice might send the ruling families of Charleston en masse into the Republican camp. Partly in an effort to bolster his sagging southern support, Washington decided to offer Charles Cotesworth Pinckney the office of secretary of state. Having such a prominent southerner in charge of foreign affairs might help to quiet the restiveness of that section.

In his letter to Pinckney, Washington described the nation as gripped by a "violent paroxysm," and urged Pinckney to accept the office vacated by the disgraced Edmund Randolph. Randolph was disgraced in Washington's eyes because Washington believed Randolph had passed confidential governmental information to the receptive French minister, Joseph Fauchet. With the Jay Treaty and

---

he took and . . . he was hedging about some time before he left This City. . . ." In Dec. 1795 Edward Rutledge helped to suppress resolutions hostile to the administration proposed in the South Carolina House of Representatives on the Jay Treaty. Rutledge moved to postpone indefinitely considering those resolutions. Phila. *Aurora*, Dec. 28, 1795, Jan. 1, 1796.

Randolph crises in mind, Washington pleaded that it was time for old friends of government "to assist in piloting the Vessel" of state between the "rocks of Sylla and Charibdas." Washington assured Pinckney that this was one of the young nation's great crises, for diabolical efforts were being made "to embroil us in the disputes of Europe." If Pinckney would accept the post, Washington asked that he occupy it immediately. If not, "the less . . . there is said of the offer, the better."[61]

Pinckney's reluctance to accept the office is understandable. He would be called upon to defend the Jay Treaty and to join an administration that seemed to have lost its political momentum. Also, with his brother still abroad negotiating with Spain, circumstances could arise that might embarrass the administration. It might feel compelled against its will to support a treaty negotiated by Thomas, out of respect for the new secretary of state. Pinckney excused himself on the ground that his finances needed his continued attention, but these other factors probably influenced his decision.[62]

Two months after Pinckney declined the secretaryship of state, the Senate refused to confirm Washington's interim appointment of John Rutledge as chief justice. This was a blow to administration supporters in South Carolina and an insult to the Rutledge family. Rutledge's rejection may have given satisfaction to northern Federalists intent on petty revenge, but it was politically foolish. The prestige and powerful family connections of the Rutledges might easily have been placed entirely at the service of the Federalist party;

61. Washington to Pinckney, Aug. 24, 1795, Fitzpatrick, ed., *Writings of Washington*, XXXIV, 285. The Randolph affair is discussed in DeConde, *Entangling Alliance*, 121–26. Irving Brant has declared "Edmund Randolph, Not Guilty!" *Wm. and Mary Qtly.*, 3rd Ser., 7 (1950), 179–98.

62. Pinckney's letter of refusal, Sept. 16, 1795, is in Vol. 275, Washington Papers, Lib. Cong. He mentioned his letter of Feb. 1794 in which he had described his uneasy financial situation and then added: "The term which I had hoped would have been adequate to their final arrangement is not so near as I was fondly led to suppose, and I must appropriate a much longer time to their completion and the pursuits of my profession than I had then too sanguinely calculated would be necessary. Under these circumstances it is not in my power to accept the elevated station in which you have so obligingly offered to place me; and while I decline this reiterated instance of your friendship and partiality, I confess I do it with regret; for stormy Clouds o'er hanging the political Horizon, so far from preventing me from coming forward in public affairs, would rather induce me to accept one, did not the reasons mentioned in the Letter I have above referred to, still operate."

at least John's appointment would have silenced an erratic Edward much as Thomas Pinckney's appointment had silenced Charles Cotesworth. Old John was almost through as a state politician, but the support of his brothers Edward and Hugh in the cause of the Federalist party might have helped to prevent South Carolina from becoming a political question mark by the end of 1795. Political revenge is often sweet. In this case, though, it came at too high a price for the Federalist party.

Washington was understandably perplexed by the political situation in the south, although he realized that the major irritant there was his administration's foreign policy. To many South Carolinians who had experienced such severe suffering at British hands during the Revolutionary War, it made little sense to favor Great Britain over France. It was France that had helped America to defeat the British, and it was France that had now established a republic deserving American support.

To Washington and his advisers the issue was not that simple. The true interest of America, they believed, was to follow a policy of neutrality in Europe's disputes. Maintaining neutrality was not easy, however, when both England and France were anxious to use the resources of America in their contest. Washington's task was complicated by a tug-of-war between Hamiltonians and Jeffersonians, one group favoring the cause of England, the other that of France. Both factions hoped the administration would follow policies that were ostensibly neutral but in fact favored one power over the other.[63]

The Washington administration had made its peace with England, at least temporarily, through the Jay Treaty but at a political price it did not wish to pay again. Part of the criticism directed against the treaty had been motivated by a dislike of its negotiator, John Jay. Republicans believed Jay had been an unfortunate choice as a negotiator because of his well-known Anglophile sentiments. Sending Jay to treat with England, Republicans insisted, was like sending a sinner to dicker with the Devil; no substantial concessions could be

63. For a brief discussion of the divisive effect of the French Revolution upon American politics, see John C. Miller, *The Federalist Era, 1789–1801* (N.Y., 1960), 126–31. A more detailed development of this theme can be found in DeConde, *Entangling Alliance*; Nathan Schachner, *The Founding Fathers* (N. Y., 1954); and Paul Varg, *Foreign Policies of the Founding Fathers* (East Lansing, Mich., 1963), chs. 5, 6.

expected since both parties had similar interests, and both enjoyed their present relationship.

Washington wished to avoid repeating this mistake and determined not to send an ardent partisan of France to negotiate American disputes with that republic. His administration was already under heavy fire from Federalists who objected to the conduct of the American minister to France, James Monroe, a Republican senator from Virginia. In the first days of his mission, Monroe let his enthusiasm get the better of his judgment. Shortly after arriving in Paris in August 1794, Monroe received a cordial welcome from the French National Convention. Monroe responded to the Convention's hospitality by extolling the ties of friendship and principle that bound republican America and France. The president of the Convention enthusiastically embraced Monroe. It was a high moment in Monroe's life but infuriating to Federalists.[64]

Despite this beginning, Monroe's life in Paris was not a happy one, particularly after the Jay Treaty was published. During the Jay negotiations Secretary of State Timothy Pickering, John Jay, and even Thomas Pinckney had repeatedly assured Monroe that nothing in the treaty would anger France or give her cause for feeling ill treated. Monroe faithfully passed along these assurances to the French government. When the terms of the Jay Treaty became known, the French government was angry not only with the American government but also with Monroe. It initially concluded that Monroe had deliberately misled it or that Monroe's superiors had deceived him; either Monroe was a dishonest man or he lacked the confidence of his government. For his part, Monroe saw that he had been used as a decoy to distract France while the Jay negotiations were in progress.[65]

Monroe became nearly as anxious to resign as ardent Federalists

64. Monroe's speech and the reply of the president of the convention are in *American State Papers: Class I, Foreign Relations*, 6 vols. (Washington, D.C., 1833–59), I, 672–74. See also William P. Cresson, *James Monroe* (Chapel Hill, 1946), 130–31.

65. Cresson, *James Monroe*, 137–47; Thomas Pinckney to James Monroe, Feb. 18, Mar. 6, 1795, Monroe Papers, N.Y. Pub. Lib. In the latter letter, Thomas Pinckney assured Monroe: "The French government may I think rely with Confidence on ours for a strick performance of our engagements with their nation and a cordial Reciprocation of the friendly conduct and good Offices which it is our mutual Interest to cultivate." Monroe's sense of having been used is expressed in his letter to James Madison, July 5, 1796, in Stanislaus M. Hamilton, ed., *The Writings of James Monroe*, 7 vols., N.Y. (1898–1903), III, 21–22.

were to have him recalled. By the beginning of 1796 Washington realized that American relations with France were at the point of rupture. Negotiations through Monroe were all but impossible since neither Washington nor Secretary of State Pickering trusted Monroe to put his own nation's interests first. Washington made the decision to replace Monroe. James Monroe learned of his recall from the vinegar-tipped pen of Secretary Pickering, a firm if not fanatical Federalist. Pickering unfairly accused Monroe of being almost solely responsible for the deteriorating state of Franco-American relations because he had not properly exerted himself to stress the friendly views of the Washington administration toward France.[66]

Discharging Monroe was an easier task than finding a man competent, politically acceptable, and willing to replace him. Besides, there was a national election pending and Federalists were naturally anxious to appoint a minister who would strengthen the administration by increasing confidence in its foreign policy. This was especially true in the southern states. Oliver Wolcott, Jr., a prominent New England Federalist, assured Alexander Hamilton that unless "a radical change of opinion can be effected in the southern states, the existing establishment will not last eighteen months." The federal government itself, Wolcott believed, was threatened by general dissatisfaction with the administration's policies.[67]

Hamilton saw that it would be wise to appoint a southerner to the post in France, although his suggestions to Washington included the names of men from the northern states. In mid-June Hamilton believed that Pinckney, Henry William De Saussure of South Carolina, John Marshall of Virginia, and Secretary of War James McHenry (Hamilton's willing tool) would all be acceptable appointees.[68] After carefully considering the possible appointees for another three weeks, Hamilton advised Washington that the minister to France ought to be "a friend to the government and understood to be not unfriendly to the French Revolution." Pinckney, he believed, was the only man

66. Pickering to Monroe, June 13, 1796, in *Amer. State Papers, Class I*, I, 737–38. President Washington had learned of Monroe's offer to supply the Republican *Aurora* with items damaging to his administration, undoubtedly another good reason to recall Monroe. Louis M. Sears, *George Washington and the French Revolution* (Detroit, 1960), 260.
67. Wolcott to Hamilton, Apr. 29, 1796, Gibbs, *Administrations of Washington and Adams*, I, 334.
68. Hamilton to Oliver Wolcott, June 15, 1796, *ibid.*, 359–60.

who "fully satisfied the idea," but "unfortunately every past experience forbids the hope that he will accept. . . ."[69]

Washington also believed that Pinckney would be a capable appointee, yet his first choice was his fellow Virginian, John Marshall. If Marshall refused, as Washington believed he would, then Pinckney would be asked to accept the position. Washington wrote to Marshall, enclosing the letter to Pinckney, and asked Marshall to send the letter of inquiry on to Pinckney only if he were unable to accept the appointment.[70]

As anticipated, Marshall declined the appointment and posted the letter to Pinckney. Washington's letter to Pinckney was shrewdly stated for it appealed to Pinckney in the way most likely to elicit a favorable response. Washington described the nation as torn by factions which were "more disposed to promote the views of another [power], than to establish a national character of their own." Furthermore, Washington warned, unless "virtuous and independent men of this Country" were to serve their government in this crisis, it would "not [be] difficult to predict the consequences." Pinckney, he felt, was a logical man for this diplomatic position because his "abilities and celebrity of character are well known to the country" and because he was "acceptable to all parties."[71] A bit flattering, perhaps, but Pinckney had confidence in Washington's evaluation of men.

Upon receiving the letter Pinckney took it to Edward Rutledge and together they discussed the problems involved in Pinckney's leaving South Carolina; young men who were studying for the bar in his law office would have to find new sponsors, Pinckney's financial interests would inevitably suffer by his absence, and the legal work of his permanent clients would necessarily be assigned to another lawyer. Pinckney realized, Rutledge wrote to his son Henry, that he would need to make a "considerable sacrifice of personal emolument" as well as "hazard the malice of his enemies" if he accepted the appointment. After considering all the complications, however, Rutledge believed that Pinckney was "without a reasonable excuse" for refusing to undertake the mission. This was the time, the friends

---

69. Hamilton to Washington, July 5, 1796, Lodge, ed., *Works of Hamilton*, X, 181.

70. Washington to Marshall, July 8, 1796, Fitzpatrick, ed., *Writings of Washington*, XXXV, 128.

71. Washington to Pinckney, July 8, 1796, *ibid.*, 130.

agreed, "in which all private considerations, were to yield to the public good. . . ." The country must be saved. This was the call of duty, which Pinckney could not ignore.[72]

Pinckney was not eager to accept the appointment, particularly now that his brother Thomas had resigned and was about to embark from London for South Carolina. But like all good Pinckneys, Charles Cotesworth believed that public service was a duty of the virtuous. He did not agree to go to France because the Federalist party needed him but because his country was in danger, threatened by France without and torn by intemperate factions within. As a man identified with neither party, he sincerely believed that he might help to alleviate the factional strife within his own country as he negotiated the disputes which were troubling the two countries he loved best.

If in his preparation for the mission to France Pinckney reflected on the years that had passed since the federal Constitutional Convention, he would have realized that he had been slowly drawn into the vortex of national politics. As Pinckney had become notably more influential in the politics of South Carolina, Washington grew increasingly anxious to bring him into the administration. Washington seems to have understood quite clearly the political situation in South Carolina; the low country controlled the legislature and a few great families exerted tremendous influence in that region. The choice political plums should therefore be given to these families. Thomas Pinckney's appointment as minister to Great Britain and John Rutledge's appointment as chief justice of the Supreme Court revealed that Washington appreciated the structure of politics in South Carolina.

Support for Washington's administration had faded in South Carolina despite the earlier appointment of Thomas Pinckney. Now Thomas had resigned, leaving South Carolina without a representative

---

72. Marvin R. Zahniser, ed., "Edward Rutledge to His Son, August 2, 1796," *S. C. Hist. Mag.*, 64 (1963), 65–72. Pinckney had evidently put his estate on a sound footing. A statement of his taxable property in 1801 shows how remarkably he had recovered from the Revolutionary War. He listed as taxable property 6,524 acres of land, 89 Negroes, and 3 homes. In partnership with (the then deceased) Edward Rutledge, he owned 5,720 acres of land and 230 Negroes. This statement is in Folio 40, Box 13, Pinckney Family Papers, Lib. Cong. Pinckney's nontaxable property, such as bank stock, may also have been considerable by this time.

in the administration's highest circles. Federalists believed that as a man of unimpeachable integrity, Charles Cotesworth Pinckney could strengthen the administration in parts of the Union other than South Carolina and the south generally. Although Pinckney accepted the appointment to France as a nonpartisan, he was in reality a political appointee who had been suggested by Hamilton to strengthen the Federalist party. Pinckney, who had studiously avoided associating himself with either party, was being used by the Federalists to consolidate their strength for the impending national elections. Even before he left Charleston, Pinckney was described by one Federalist newspaper as a "decided and unequivocal friend to the Constitution and Government of HIS OWN COUNTRY."[73] In Pinckney one could see the complementary virtues of Federalism and patriotism.

Aside from his political qualifications for the position of minister to France, there were other factors which recommended Pinckney. He was a distinguished lawyer who was competent in the field of international law. It was as a Revolutionary soldier that he had initially made his reputation, a fact that might recommend him to the French people who had also been fighting Great Britain. Pinckney was a man of discretion and honor who was at the same time thoroughly acquainted with the everyday business of political give-and-take. Well educated, fluent in French, polished, and with a wide knowledge of "those various branches of science, which please, instruct, and illumine society," Pinckney could be at home in the most exclusive salons of Paris.[74] Pinckney prepared for his mission with a cautious optimism, an optimism he soon found to be unwarranted.

73. Phila. *Gazette of the United States*, Aug. 20, 1796. The Phila. *Aurora*, Sept. 13, 1796, believed the fulsome praise of Pinckney a "dirty and malicious insinuation against Col. Monroe. . . ."
74. Zahniser, ed., "Edward Rutledge to His Son," *S. C. Hist. Mag.*, 64 (1963), 70.

VI

MISSION TO FRANCE

———————————

I most ardently wish that we would banish all party distinctions and foreign influence; and think and act only as Americans—for all parties in this country [France] unite in thinking that we ought to act as if we were altogether their dependents, and indebted to them solely, and not to our own exertions for our liberty and independence.

—Charles Cotesworth Pinckney, 1797.

———————————

WITH PRESIDENT WASHINGTON WAITING TO CONSULT HIM AT PHILADEL-phia, Pinckney hurriedly began to provide for his personal and business interests while he was gone. He appointed a young Charleston attorney, David Deas, to take care of his legal business. Together with Edward Rutledge, he hastened to conclude a purchase of Congaree land with Peter Smith and [John?] Drayton. A few hours before leaving, Pinckney forwarded to John Chesnut a portrait of himself painted by a "young painter who is a native of this state." Although the likeness was "not strong," Pinckney admitted, the portrait "may sometimes remind you of a friend who has long and sincerely esteemed you."[1] Perhaps Pinckney felt he might be seeing his Charleston friends for the last time.

The Pinckneys—Charles Cotesworth, Mary, and young Eliza—sailed for Philadelphia on September 2, 1796. Their ship, the *South Carolina*, reached Philadelphia quickly despite "disagreeable" winds;

1. Edward Rutledge to Peter Smith, Aug. 4, 1796, Frank M. Etting Collection, Hist. Soc. of Pa.; Charles Cotesworth Pinckney to John Chesnut, Aug. 31, 1796, John L. Manning Manuscripts, Duke University Library; Pinckney's instructions for his attorneys, Sept. 26, 1796, Pinckney Family Papers, Lib. Cong.

they landed on September 14. Washington immediately invited the Pinckneys to dinner, an invitation the homesick Mrs. Pinckney declined because, as she said, "I could not speak to the President for my tears." The President promised Pinckney that he would be given copies of instructions and dispatches relating to French affairs which he could study on the voyage to France. At a later appointment with Secretary of State Timothy Pickering, Pinckney reviewed his instructions for the mission to France. Pickering also probably asked Pinckney to keep a close watch over Fulwar Skipwith, chief of the American consulate in Paris, for Pickering was certain that Skipwith was mismanaging American interests. Despite their marked contrasts —Pickering the self-made man, thin, hawk-nosed, narrow-eyed and intense; Pinckney the man of family, stocky, frank, friendly and easy —they seemed to have established a cordial relationship.[2]

After his conference with Pickering, Pinckney made immediate preparations for the voyage. In the midst of his activities he wrote to the American minister in London, Rufus King, asking him to furnish Pinckney's secretary, Henry Rutledge, with the papers necessary "to expedite his meeting me in Paris, for which place I shall immediately set out by way of Bordeaux."[3] From his ship the *Liberty*, anchored in Delaware Bay, Pinckney asked Pickering to forward at regular intervals Fenno's Federalist paper, Bache's Republican gazette, and Noah Webster's New York *Herald* as well. "Fenno's and Webster's papers," he added, "I have long taken. . . ." Pinckney also requested Pickering to pay Gilbert Stuart when he completed a portrait of President Washington and to have it forwarded to Paris.[4]

Pinckney likewise carefully drew up instructions for his attorneys while he was on board ship: Mrs. Elizabeth Izard, his wife's sister, was granted power to handle "the whole of the Georgia affairs" of Mary Pinckney; Belmont and Beach Hill were to be leased once again; the expenses of his daughters Maria and Harriott were to be "*fully*" paid" out of the "net profits of my own negroes, interest of Bank stock, and indents"; none of the sea islands were "to be planted

2. Mary Pinckney to Mrs. Gabriel Manigault, Sept. 16, 1796, Manigault Family Papers, S. Caroliniana Lib.; Carroll and Ashworth, *George Washington*, VII, 402; Timothy Pickering to Alexander Hamilton, Sept. 24, 1796, Pickering Papers, Massachusetts Historical Society, Boston, Mass.
3. Pinckney to King, Sept. 25, 1796; Rufus King Papers, Huntington Lib.
4. Pinckney to Secretary of State, Sept. 26, 1796, State Dept. Diplomatic Despatches, France, 5 (unpaged), National Archives, Washington, D.C.

next year, or till my return—except what the Man and negroes who take care of my stock may plant for provisions"; legal fees collected for him by David Deas were to be applied toward Pinckney's taxes. As a gift to his returning brother "Tom," Pinckney directed that the new volumes of the *American Encyclopedia* were to be bought for him.[5] The instructions to his attorneys reveal a prosperous yet prudent man.

Late in September the Pinckneys set sail for France. The trip was a terrifying experience. Driven by "violent storms," the ship pitched and rolled so much that the Pinckneys found it all but impossible even to walk about in their cabin. No comfort either was the captain, a man with a "rough, violent, obstinate" temper. He became so obnoxious that General Pinckney, known to be a strict disciplinarian, all but authorized the mate to stage a mutiny by promising to testify in his behalf at a court hearing. The mate immediately led the mutiny and the Pinckneys completed their voyage under a new acting captain.[6]

At a later time Pinckney may well have viewed this nearly disastrous voyage as an omen of what awaited him in France. Certainly his mission of reconciliation had been undermined before it officially began. Pierre Auguste Adet, the French minister to the United States, had written to the minister of foreign relations, Charles Delacroix, denouncing Pinckney and the forces behind his mission. Adet warned Delacroix not to be deceived by Pinckney's republican posture, for he was "totally devoted" to the Washington administration and was its "deluded instrument." Adet hoped that the Executive Directory, France's governing body, would not fall into the "trap" which the Hamiltonians had baited with the republican Pinckney, but would reject him as the tool of the Hamiltonians whose "protestations of friendship are false" and whose flattery is "treacherous."[7]

Pinckney's instructions to "remove jealousies and to obviate complaints by showing that they are groundless" and "to restore that

5. Instructions for his attorneys, Sept. 26, 1796, Pinckney Family Papers, Lib. Cong.

6. Mary Pinckney to Mrs. Gabriel Manigault, Nov. 14, 1796, Manigault Family Papers, S. Caroliniana Lib.

7. Adet to Minister of Foreign Relations, 21 Vendémiaire, An 5 [Oct. 3, 1796], Frederick J. Turner, ed., *Correspondence of the French Ministers to the United States, 1791–1797* (American Historical Association, *Annual Report* [1903]), II, 951.

mutual confidence which has been so unfortunately and injuriously impaired" were therefore seen by the Directory as the work of the crafty and "treacherous" Federalists. Nor was Pinckney's mission strengthened after he had sailed by the claims of Republicans that his powers as minister were insufficient to negotiate outstanding differences with France; Pinckney, they said, had only been granted the ordinary powers of a minister, which were not sufficient to negotiate an extraordinary crisis. Republicans predicted that his rejection was all but certain.[8]

While Pinckney was at sea, Adet was issuing proclamations through the American press that were designed to influence the election of 1796. French sympathizers were encouraged to express their sentiments publicly. And Adet dramatically announced that because of the administration's unfriendly policy toward France, he was suspending his ministerial functions. The government of France had obviously determined to defeat the Federalist party and to have its supposed friend Thomas Jefferson elected to the presidency. Thus Pinckney was in the unenviable position of representing an administration which the French considered thoroughly discredited. In the view of the French government, Pinckney's identification with the Federalist party was probably proved conclusively when his brother Thomas became John Adams' running mate in 1796. The fact that Thomas Pinckney was nearly maneuvered into the presidency by the Hamiltonian Federalists did nothing to support Charles Cotesworth's claim that he was a political neutral and a friend of France.[9]

Minister Monroe, meanwhile, had received menacing news from the French foreign minister in Paris. After informing Monroe that Adet's functions had been suspended, Delacroix added that the Direc-

8. The Phila. *Aurora* of Jan. 27, 1797, asked: "But will Mr. Pinckney be received as our minister? It is reasonably to be supposed, that he will not. He left this country before the minister of the French Republic by order of his government suspended his functions here, he therefore cannot carry power to negociate an accommodation of that break. . . . The Federal executive, if they sincerely wish an accommodation of grievances, will then, certainly be ultimately under the necessity of sending an envoy extraordinary, or of transmitting to Mr. Pinckney extraordinary powers."

9. Stephen G. Kurtz, *The Presidency of John Adams; The Collapse of Federalism* (Phila., 1957), 125–32; DeConde, *Entangling Alliance*, 471–74. Good short accounts of the Hamiltonian intrigue to place Thomas Pinckney in the presidential chair can be found in Schachner, *Founding Fathers*, 406–11; John C. Miller, *Alexander Hamilton: Portrait in Paradox* (N.Y., 1959), 446–50. From his listening post at The Hague, John Quincy Adams later heard that the Direc-

tory had issued an *arrêt* instructing the French navy to treat American ships "as these suffer the English to treat them." Delacroix left little doubt in Monroe's mind that these actions were taken to express French displeasure over the Jay Treaty.[10] Even before Pinckney had landed at Bordeaux, then, the Directory had "suspended" diplomatic relations with the United States and was harassing American commerce. Clearly the Alliance of 1778 was dead in fact if not in form.[11] Adet officially informed Pickering of the new French naval policy on October 27, 1796. By November 15, 1796, when Pinckney landed at Bordeaux, Adet had made the French position clear: either the Federalists would be turned out of office and Pinckney replaced by a Jeffersonian, or France would continue, perhaps expand, its policy of virtual warfare against the American merchant marine.[12]

Unaware of all these developments, Pinckney learned at once from the American consul in Bordeaux that letters of recall had been sent to Adet. There was no doubt that he would be coolly received in Paris, Pinckney perceived, for it was common knowledge that the French "think we have slighted them and thrown ourselves into the arms of their Enemy." Nevertheless, the Pinckneys decided to enjoy themselves in Bordeaux while waiting for their baggage to land and for their carriage to be overhauled in preparation for the notoriously rutted roads. The city administration was cordial to the Pinckneys, even offering to reserve theater seats every evening for the family. The Pinckneys attended, but to Mrs. Pinckney's horror, she was

---

tory was angry with Thomas Pinckney because he had misled Monroe during the Jay negotiations and because through the Pinckney Treaty he had lessened American dependence upon France. Adams learned that the Directory transferred its hostility toward Thomas Pinckney to his brother. Adams to John Adams, Apr. 30, 1797, Worthington C. Ford, ed., *Writings of John Quincy Adams*, 7 vols. (N.Y., 1913–17), II, 161–62.

10. Minister of External Relations to the Minister Plenipotentiary of the United States, 16 Vendémiaire, An 5 [Oct. 7, 1796], *Amer. State Papers, Class I*, I, 745; Monroe to Minister of Foreign Affairs, Oct. 12, 1796, Archives des Affaires Étrangères, Correspondance Politique, États-Unis, Vol. XLVI, Part II, 7, reproductions in the Library of Congress. (Hereafter cited as U.S. Pol. Corr., Fr. Archives.) Adet officially informed Pickering of the new French naval policy on Oct. 27, 1796, Carroll and Ashworth, *George Washington*, VII, 413.

11. The French government had told Monroe in Feb. 1796 that it "considered the alliance between us as ceasing to exist from the moment the [Jay] treaty was ratified," Monroe to Secretary of State, Feb. 16, 1796, *Amer. State Papers, Class I*, I, 730.

12. Carroll and Ashworth, *George Washington*, VII, 413–14; DeConde, *Entangling Alliance*, 439–42.

seated beside "two ladies of pleasure." She seemed to take some comfort that "there were but few others present. . . ."[13]

After the weather had cleared and their carriage alterations had been finished, the Pinckneys set out for Paris on November 25. They did not escape the lower elements of society by leaving Bordeaux. A band of *poissardes*—fishwives—stopped Pinckney's carriage and forced the reluctant South Carolina aristocrat to descend, give them the fraternal embrace and, no doubt, the standard gift of money.[14]

After an exhausting trip of ten days, the Pinckneys reached Paris on the evening of December 5. It was cheering to find several friends there waiting for them, including Mr. and Mrs. Henry Middleton. Pinckney was especially happy to see his nephew and secretary, Henry Rutledge.[15]

Together Pinckney and young Rutledge began their duties the following morning when they gave James Monroe his letters of recall. Monroe told Pinckney of the Directory's hardening position toward America. Whether Monroe also told Pinckney of the anger his recall had caused in France is uncertain, but despite Monroe's personal bitterness over his abrupt recall by Washington, he was friendly to Pinckney and did his best to orient him to his new duties. Monroe was not certain that Pinckney would be received, but both men agreed that the attitude of the Directory toward America could be determined quickly by the way it treated the new American minister. On that same day, therefore, Monroe informed Delacroix by letter that Pinckney was ready to present his letters of credence to the Directory.[16]

Shortly after the Pinckneys moved into their five-room apartment

13. Pinckney to Secretary of State, Nov. 17, 1796, State Dept., Diplomatic Despatches, France, 5: 2–3, National Archives; Mary Pinckney to Mrs. Gabriel Manigault, Nov. 14, 1796, Manigault Family Papers, S. Caroliniana Lib.

14. Mary Pinckney to Mrs. Gabriel Manigault, Nov. 16, 1796, Manigault Family Papers, S. Caroliniana Lib.; Pinckney to Secretary of State, 30 Frimaire [Dec. 20, 1796], *Amer. State Papers, Class I*, II, 5; James Iredell to Mrs. Iredell, Feb. 9, 1797, Griffith J. McRee, *Life and Correspondence of James Iredell*, 2 vols. (N.Y., 1857–58), II, 490; Herring, ed., *National Portrait Gallery*, I, 8.

15. Pinckney to Secretary of State, 30 Frimaire, Dec. 20, 1796, State Dept., Diplomatic Despatches, France, 5: 6, National Archives; Mary Pinckney to Mrs. Ralph Izard, Jan. 6, 1797, Charles F. McCombs, ed., *Letter-book of Mary Stead Pinckney* . . . (N.Y., 1946), 44.

16. Pinckney to Secretary of State, 30 Frimaire, State Dept., Diplomatic Despatches, France, 5: 6, National Archives; Mary Pinckney, in writing to Mrs. Gabriel Manigault, Dec. 18, 1796, in McCombs, ed., *Letter-book*, 34, stated that

at the Hotel des Tuileries, Rue St. Honoré, an unexpected guest knocked on the door. Only Mary Pinckney was at home. It was "Mr. T. Payne," the controversial author of *Common Sense*. Paine asked Mrs. Pinckney if she had heard that the government of France had suspended the functions of its minister in America, Pierre Adet. Mary, probably untruthfully, answered no, but she was aware that "some coolness" existed between the two governments. Coolness, Paine burst out, "no, it is indignation, and indignation well founded." Mary, fearful that Paine might be under the influence of liquor, wisely said nothing more and the mercurial Paine soon left.[17] Paine, who was working behind the scenes to prevent an open rupture between the United States and France, urged the Directory to postpone action to reject Pinckney. Since Pinckney's appointment had not yet been confirmed by the recessed Senate, Paine argued, the government of France could consider Pinckney as in "suspension" or the office of American minister as in "*vacance.*"[18]

The Directory at first seemed unsure how to treat the "deluded instrument" of the Washington administration. On December 9, three days after receiving Monroe's note, Delacroix informed him that he would grant the two American ministers an audience that very afternoon if it were convenient for "citizen Pinckney." Delacroix greeted Pinckney, Monroe, and Henry Rutledge with "great stiffness," but after a few minutes of conversation the atmosphere became more friendly. Delacroix not only accepted Pinckney's letters of credence, but also promised to send cards of hospitality immediately to Pinckney and Rutledge; no stranger in Paris was immune from arrest without these permits. In reporting on his conversation with Pinckney to the Directory, Delacroix said that near the end of the interview Pinckney began to argue that he was now the American

---

Pinckney "thinks the behaviour of . . . [Monroe] to him has been very candid"; Monroe to Minister of Foreign Affairs, Dec. 6, 1796, in *Amer. State Papers, Class I*, I, 746. Delacroix had indicated to Monroe that he wanted an audience with Pinckney immediately upon his arrival. See Delacroix's note to Monroe, Dec. 2, 1796, Vol. XLVII, Part IV, U.S. Pol. Corr., Fr. Archives.

17. Mary Pinckney to Mrs. Gabriel Manigault, Dec. 13, 1796, Manigault Family Papers, S. Caroliniana Lib.

18. Moncure D. Conway, ed., *The Writings of Thomas Paine*, 4 vols. (N.Y., 1894–96), III, 368*n*. Paine's correspondence suggesting that Pinckney could legitimately be regarded as in suspension and the unenthusiastic reaction of Delacroix to Paine's reasoning will be found in Vol. XLVI, Part IV, U.S. Pol. Corr., Fr. Archives. Delacroix felt that France's substantial grievances made such subterfuges unnecessary.

minister by action of the French government, that the very act of accepting his letters of credence was a recognition of his official status. Delacroix firmly replied that the Directory decided who would be received. Recognition was a matter of substance, not of diplomatic niceties. Delacroix even hinted that Pinckney would not be received until the American government had satisfied French grievances. Despite these last remarks, Pinckney and Rutledge returned to their apartment encouraged.[19]

Evidently the Directory did not consider the interview with Pinckney satisfactory. Perhaps he had shown too much spirit and a disposition to defend the actions of his own country. Monroe at least admitted that President Washington had acted wrongly and encouraged the French government to believe that once in office the Jeffersonians would take a different tack in foreign policy.[20] Monroe's sympathy for France and his tendency to see his own country as acting treacherously probably made Pinckney in contrast seem a stiff-necked Federalist to Delacroix and to the Directory.

The first sign of trouble came the next day, for Delacroix failed to forward the cards of hospitality. Two days later, on December 12, Pinckney learned why the permits had not been sent. The Directory had decided "that it will no longer recognize nor receive a minister plenipotentiary from the United States, until after a reparation of the grievances demanded of the American government, and which the French republic has a right to expect."[21]

Pinckney was puzzled and did not know how to respond. Although

19. Delacroix to Monroe, 19 Frimaire, An 5 [Dec. 9, 1796], in *Amer. State Papers, Class I*, I, 746; Pinckney to Secretary of State, 30 Frimaire [Dec. 20, 1796], *ibid.*, II, 6; Rapport du Secretaire Général des Relations extérieures [on his conversation with Pinckney], 25 Frimaire, An 5, in Vol. XLVI, Part IV, U.S. Pol. Corr., Fr. Archives.

20. At one point Monroe unwisely wrote to the French government: "By patiently enduring . . . the wrongs of the present President, you will leave him without excuse, you will enlighten the Americans, and decide a contrary choice at the next election. All the wrongs of which France may have to complain will then be repaired," quoted in Adolphe Thiers, *The History of the French Revolution, 1789–1800*, trans. Frederick Shoberl, 5 vols. (Phila., 1894), V, 24. Unfortunately, Thiers does not give the location of this interesting letter nor does he indicate its date. The letter is not in Monroe's Presidential Papers, Lib. Cong., nor is it included in Hamilton, ed., *Writings of Monroe*.

21. Delacroix to Monroe, 21 Frimaire, An 5 [Dec. 11, 1796], in *Amer. State Papers, Class I*, I, 746. Delacroix explained to Adet that if France received Pinckney, it would have been supporting the maneuver by Washington to blame Monroe and Republicans for the "actual state of affairs." Delacroix to Adet, 14 Nivôse, An 5, Vol. XLVII, Part I, U.S. Pol. Corr., Fr. Archives.

the government of France claimed to have grievances against the United States, the Directory did not wish to negotiate them. Instead, it demanded capitulation on the outstanding issues before it would receive him. If this imperious policy were to be maintained, Pinckney realized that he could do little to relieve the strained situation. The decision of the Directory not to receive him, he informed Delacroix, "has filled me with real sorrow. . . ." Pinckney assured Delacroix that he had come to negotiate in good faith and felt certain that many points of difference could be resolved. Suspecting that the Directory was hostile because it believed him to be an ardent Federalist, Pinckney added that "devoted as I am, to the liberty, prosperity, and independence of my own country, the freedom, happiness, and perfect establishment of the French republic have always been dear to me. . . ."[22]

When Henry Rutledge delivered this note of December 13, Delacroix told Rutledge that he had no knowledge of an American minister to France since Monroe had presented his letters of recall. When Rutledge then asked if Pinckney would be allowed to remain in Paris, Delacroix coldly replied that he would need to consult the Directory for instructions. Two days later Rutledge's question was answered. Monsieur Giraudet, who identified himself as the chief secretary in the department of foreign affairs, called on Pinckney and inquired if Pinckney were "acquainted with the laws of France, as they applied to strangers." Pinckney did not miss the point. He then asked Giraudet whether the Directory actually intended that he leave Paris, to which Giraudet replied he was not certain but would ask persons in authority.

That evening Giraudet returned to assure Pinckney that the Directory wished him to leave not only Paris but France itself. Just when he must leave, Giraudet did not know, but he assured Pinckney that an extended stay would bring him into distasteful contact with the dreaded minister of the police générale. Pinckney, now angry as well as alarmed, protested that the police might throw him into jail as they would a common stranger. Remember, he told Giraudet, he had been received by Delacroix who had promised him and Rutledge cards of hospitality. Pinckney correctly saw that the Directory was trying to force him to leave France on his own responsibility, something

22. Pinckney to Minister of Foreign Affairs, Dec. 13, 1796, *Amer. State Papers, Class I*, II, 6–7.

which no prudent minister would do. Therefore he insisted that any communication Delacroix had to make on the expulsion of his mission should be in writing.

In describing the events of his first days in Paris to Timothy Pickering, Pinckney expressed indignation about the apparent relationship between the probable rejection of his mission and the presidential election in the United States. He believed the Directory was temporizing "until the event of the election of President is known; thinking that, if one public character [Adams] is chosen, he will be attached to the interest of Great Britain; and that, if another [Jefferson] is elected, he will . . . be devoted to the interest of France." Pinckney lamented that many members of the French government entertained the "humiliating idea" that Americans "are a people divided by party, the mere creatures of foreign influence. . . ." Pinckney hoped that Americans "will never suffer any foreign nations to interfere in her concerns; and that an attempt to divide her citizens will be the 'signe de ralliement' and render them more united."[23] Dispatches of this kind were a delight to Secretary of State Pickering; they were so readable, so publishable, and so irritating to Republicans.

While Pinckney was waiting for his written order to leave France, Monroe had his final interview with the French government. Following Monroe's conciliatory speech, Paul Barras, president-general of the Directory, ungraciously responded that Americans should remember they owed their liberty to France. The American people, Barras cautioned, should "weigh in their wisdom the magnanimous benevolence of the French People with the crafty carresses of certain perfidious persons [British?] who meditate bringing them back to their former slavery" under Great Britain. He urged Monroe to assure the American people that they would always have the blessings of the French citizenry and of the French government that "knows how to grant peace as it does to cause its sovereignty to be respected."[24] There was an ominous tone to the speech despite the cordial remarks made about Monroe's service as minister.

23. Pinckney to Secretary of State, 30 Frimaire [Dec. 20, 1796], *ibid.*, 6–8. Pinckney stated in this dispatch that he would have sailed immediately for Philadelphia if he had not believed fresh instructions were on the way to him at Paris.

24. Cresson, *James Monroe*, 153–54. The speech by Barras is in *Amer. State Papers, Class 1*, I, 747. Monroe made certain that he did not lose his favored position with the Directory by mentioning Pinckney in his reply.

Pinckney's temper rose as he read the speech of Barras. To one who had spent six years fighting the British, the claim of Barras that France had won the American Revolutionary War seemed pretentious. Pinckney noted that while Barras professed friendship with America in one breath, in the next he made a thinly veiled threat against her if she did not capitulate to the demands of France. In enclosing the Barras speech in a letter to Pickering, Pinckney noted that he "need not comment on so wild a composition," but he felt that it revealed "the disposition of the Directory . . . toward us, and the disorganizing and delusive system which they have adopted" to divide the American people.[25]

When Pinckney received a written order to leave France in the latter part of January 1797, the unabated anger of the Directory toward America was confirmed. In weighing the probable reasons for his expulsion, Pinckney initially believed that the government of France "may have intercepted some [instructions] for me, the tone of which I hope was firm; or they may perhaps be so elated with Buonaparte's late success in Italy that they are determined to keep no measures with any Nation that will not be implicitly submissive to them. . . ." It is also probable that the Directory had learned by fast ship that John Adams was likely to be elected president and had decided to take a drastic step to indicate its displeasure. Diplomatic intercourse on both sides of the Atlantic was now broken.[26]

As he reflected on the causes of his rejection, Pinckney began to believe that he would not have been expelled had there not been a Republican party encouraging French intransigence. The French

25. Pinckney to Secretary of State, 17 Nivôse, Jan. 16, 1797, State Dept. Diplomatic Despatches, France, 5: 28, National Archives. John Quincy Adams noted that the "language of Genet was decency and modesty" when compared to Barras' speech. Adams added: "I have not heard it mentioned by an individual but with disgust at its thrasonical bombast, and ridicule at its bullying menaces. This tone has been instigated by their American partisans, who have suggested to them that the American government and people must be frightened into a violation of their treaty with Britain and of their neutrality." Adams to John Adams, Jan. 14, 1797, Ford, ed., *Writings of John Quincy Adams*, II, 80.

26. Pinckney to Harriott Horry, Jan. 26, 1797, C. C. Pinckney Papers, S. Caroliniana Lib.; John Quincy Adams to Abigail Adams, Feb. 8, 1797, Ford, ed., *Writings of John Quincy Adams*, II, 110; on p. 66 John Quincy Adams noted in a letter to his father that the *Rédacteur*, a newspaper used by the government to announce its official publications, "explicitly denies . . . that the Directory have determined to suspend their intercourse with the government of the United States," Dec. 30, 1796.

were simply trying to destroy the Federalist administration by exploiting the disloyalty of deluded Americans. The anti-French missives that he was receiving from Secretary Pickering, reinforced by his own experience, were beginning to have an effect upon Pinckney. "I most ardently wish that we would banish all party distinctions and foreign influence," Pinckney wrote to Pickering when he learned of Adet's "disorganizing manoeuvres," and "think and act only as Americans. . . ."[27]

While Pinckney seemed to favor neither political party at this time, a new tone in his letters indicates that he was moving away from his earlier sympathy for France. The belligerent posture France had assumed toward the United States was certainly the major reason for his change in attitude but there could be a personal factor in this change also. Pinckney had come in good faith to negotiate but had found himself spurned as though he were an enemy. He had been officially ignored, socially ostracized,[28] and even threatened with arrest and imprisonment. These were novel experiences for a man of Pinckney's background, particularly when coming from a supposed friend, republican France. Although Pinckney tried to be patient, his temper, which was never far from the surface, began to rise. Scarcely realizing it, perhaps, Pinckney was beginning to acquire the hostile attitude toward France which was one mark of the confirmed Federalist.

Mrs. Pinckney was not sorry to leave Paris. Her letters to friends were full of complaints. "Nothing can be more unpleasant than our present situation," she wrote to her sister Elizabeth Izard, living "in the most uncomfortable manner, at great expense, in cold smoky apartments, and unable to entertain any of our country people, and the children losing their time." Even when she moved to new "lodgings" on January 5, Mrs. Pinckney was not happy: "these are rather more comfortable and quiet, but they are dark and the situation much less agreeable." But, she added, "we were on the Road to Ruin where we were, and lived in the most disagreeable manner. We paid 67 louis

27. Pinckney to Secretary of State, Feb. 1, 1797, *Amer. State Papers, Class I,* II, 18.

28. Mrs. Pinckney lamented that "a minister non recu is a kind of scarecrow in this city," to Mrs. Gabriel Manigault, Jan. 21, 1797, Manigault Family Papers, S. Caroliniana Lib.

d'ors for 21 dinners, without the satisfaction of seeing one friend, except on New Year's day, when Mr. and Mrs. Middleton (and Mr. Horry) dined with us."[29]

Even when they went shopping they were uncomfortable, for their dress and general appearance were "the objects of merriment to the gazing crowd. . . ." Nevertheless, Mrs. Pinckney and Mrs. Middleton "amused" themselves "with the shops ranged round the court of the palais égalité."[30]

Despite the tenuousness of their stay, General Pinckney sent Eliza to "Mrs. Campan's" at St. Germain to learn French fluently and to master the basic dance steps. Pinckney himself whirled away at least one evening at a "musical and dancing party at an american house." It was an intimate party, Mrs. Pinckney told Mrs. Manigault. Only seven or eight couples were invited, and the music was performed by amateurs who both played and sang. From ten until one, a fiddler performed and the party danced away the hours.[31] Life was not entirely unpleasant in Paris. The Pinckneys took great pleasure in attending the daily public lectures of the noted physicist Jacques Alexandre César Charles on "optics." Mrs. Pinckney marveled that "he gives his lectures with so much clearness" that he could be understood "without any knowledge of the mathematicks. . . ."[32]

It was just after one of Charles's lectures, on the morning of January 26, that the Pinckneys "found on the table the orders of the Directory that we must quit the territories of the french republic."[33] On that same day Pinckney wrote a letter to his sister denouncing the imperiousness of the French government. It was obviously determined to smash all governments unwilling to honor every French request. "I trust," Pinckney added, that "America values her inde-

29. Mary Pinckney to Mrs. Ralph Izard, Dec. 19, 1796, Jan. 6, 1797, McCombs, ed., *Letter-book*, 27, 44. The children to whom Mrs. Pinckney referred were her stepdaughter Eliza, and States Rutledge. States was the son of John Rutledge. Daniel Horry was Pinckney's sister's 27-year-old son. During the XYZ mission, Horry published a pamphlet attacking Thomas Paine, no doubt encouraged by his uncle, William Vans Murray to John Lusac, Apr. 7, 1798, William Vans Murray Papers, Lib. Cong.

30. Mary Pinckney to Mrs. Ralph Izard, Dec. 11, 1796, McCombs, ed., *Letter-book*, 25.

31. Mary Pinckney to Mrs. Gabriel Manigault, Jan. 11, 1797, Manigault Family Papers, S. Caroliniana Lib.

32. Same to same, Feb. 3, 1797, *ibid*.

33. *Ibid*.

pendence too highly ever to relinquish it."[34] In this angry mood the Pinckneys prepared to leave Paris, Mrs. Pinckney grieving to see her "respectable husband, beloved and esteemed by his country" being "driven from post to pillar" at "his time of life. . . ." On Sunday morning, February 5, the carriage was loaded and ready for the trip. At eleven o'clock it began to roll toward Amsterdam. They arrived twelve days later, "after an expensive and tedious journey. . . ."[35] In Amsterdam the Pinckneys would wait five months to learn what course their government intended to take.

The news of Pinckney's expulsion from France reached Charleston as early as February 22 and was officially known to the Adams administration on March 21.[36] John Adams, who had been president less than three weeks, was now faced with a crisis in foreign relations that threatened ruin to American commerce if not war itself. Adams immediately began to think of sending a new minister to France, almost a habitual response of the founding fathers in a foreign affairs crisis. Adams did not like or trust the Pinckneys because of their supposed electoral intrigues in 1796. He was ready to win the good will of France by superseding Charles Cotesworth with a Jeffersonian Republican. Adams was even willing to send Vice-President Jefferson himself, but Jefferson declined.[37]

The idea that at least one other person should join Pinckney had already been considered. Even before Washington left office, it had been suggested that another eminent citizen should be appointed a

34. Pinckney to Harriott Horry, Jan. 26, 1797, C. C. Pinckney Papers, S. Caroliniana Lib.

35. Mary Pinckney to Mrs. Gabriel Manigault, Feb. 13, 1797, Manigault Family Papers, S. Caroliniana Lib.; Pinckney to Secretary of State, Feb. 18, 1797, State Dept., Diplomatic Despatches, France, 5:41, National Archives.

36. John F. Grimké to Colonel [Jacob] Read, Feb. 23, 1797, Jacob Read Papers, S. Caroliniana Lib.; Edward Stanwood, A History of the Presidency, rev. ed., 2 vols. (Boston, 1921), I, 56.

37. Adams believed that Thomas Pinckney had intrigued to replace him as minister to England early in the 1790's. Adams was also acutely aware that Alexander Hamilton had tried to have Pinckney, Adams' supposed running mate, elected president in 1796. See Kurtz, Presidency of John Adams, 194, 228–29; John Adams to Elbridge Gerry, Apr. 6, 1797, in Charles F. Adams, ed., The Works of John Adams, 10 vols. (Boston, 1850–56), VIII, 538; Pinckney, Life of Thomas Pinckney, 158–66. Adams' policy alternatives at this critical moment are discussed in Alexander DeConde, The Quasi-War: The Politics and Diplomacy of the Undeclared War with France, 1797–1801 (N.Y., 1966), 17–18.

joint negotiator with Pinckney. Washington, with his usual good sense, judged that little would be accomplished by appointing another negotiator and furthermore hesitated from fear that he might offend Pinckney. "What would that Gentleman *think* of having a person treading on his heels by the time he arrived in Paris . . . ?" Washington asked Hamilton.[38]

Hamilton was not as concerned about Pinckney's sensitivity as he was that peace should be maintained with France. If it had been necessary or useful to send a five-man delegation to Paris, Hamilton would have been willing. Besides, Hamilton did not really trust Pinckney as a negotiator, for he had not yet identified himself with the Federalist party.[39] In any case, once Washington had retired without taking action to appoint an added envoy, Hamilton was in no position to repeat his suggestion directly to a hostile Adams. Hamilton's intrigue to place Thomas Pinckney in the presidential chair in 1796 was well known to Adams. Any advice that Hamilton had for Adams was therefore necessarily channeled through Hamilton's friends in the cabinet: Pickering, James McHenry, and Oliver Wolcott, Jr.[40]

The news forwarded by Pinckney to the secretary of state convinced both Adams and Hamilton that some action must immediately be taken to forestall war. On March 2, 1797 (12 Ventôse), the Directory issued a decree which enlarged the list of contraband, authorized French ships of war and privateers to bring neutral vessels carrying merchandise belonging to Britain or British subjects into French ports, and warned that every American ship which did not carry a bill of lading (*role d'equipage*) "in due form" would be a lawful prize.[41] The situation was becoming intolerable. Either American commerce would be ruined by France while the two nations were legally at peace, or the conduct of France might force the United

38. Washington to Hamilton, Jan. 22, 1797, in Fitzpatrick, ed., *Writings of Washington*, XXXV, 373.

39. Broadus Mitchell, *Alexander Hamilton*, 2 vols. (N.Y., 1962), II, 424. Hamilton believed that "Pinckney has had too much French learning to consider him . . . as perfectly safe. . . . I do consider him, as in some sort, a *middle* character." Hamilton to Pickering, May 11, 1797, Lodge, ed., *Works of Hamilton*, X, 262.

40. Miller, *Hamilton*, 451, 457.

41. Pinckney to Secretary of State, Mar. 8, 1797, *Amer. State Papers, Class I*, II, 10–12.

States to declare a war it could not prosecute successfully. The only alternative was negotiation.

This approach had been tried through Pinckney, however, with no success. Perhaps, Adams reasoned, if another attempt were made with additional negotiators, the government of France might at least receive the mission. Because it was negotiating from a position of weakness, the United States must swallow its national pride and openly become the supplicant. It was a difficult decision for crusty old John Adams, but it was necessary—and John Adams liked to think himself a realist.

Alexander Hamilton believed that the Directory had not closed the door to all negotiation, for it had not stated that it would refuse to receive a commission of ministers plenipotentiary whose only purpose was to preserve peace. If a prominent Republican were placed upon the commission, Hamilton suggested to William Smith of South Carolina, the French might receive the entire commission. Hamilton, of course, was ready to suggest acceptable commission appointees. He believed that James Madison would serve admirably to disarm the government of France, yet if united with Pinckney and a good Federalist like George Cabot of Massachusetts, Madison could do little harm.[42]

Secretaries Pickering, Wolcott, and McHenry were opposed to appointing a commission, for they believed that such action would only encourage their enemies in the Republican party. Once Hamilton explained to them that another mission would silence Republican criticism and thrust the responsibility for any hostilities upon France, their opposition began to melt.[43] Wolcott, however, protested Hamilton's suggestion that Madison be sent. "Can it be safe to appoint a man known to be of the French party . . . ?" he asked. Wolcott added

42. Miller, *Hamilton*, 454–55; Hamilton to George Washington, Jan. 22, 1797, Lodge, ed., *Works of Hamilton*, X, 234.

43. Hamilton to James McHenry, Mar. [22], 1797, Lodge, ed., *Works of Hamilton*, X, 242–43; Hamilton to Oliver Wolcott, Apr. 5, 1797, in Gibbs, *Administrations of Washington and Adams*, I, 490; Nathan Schachner, *Alexander Hamilton*, 2 vols. (N.Y., 1946), II, 362. James McHenry wanted to give Pinckney extraordinary powers and to let him resume the negotiations. McHenry was fearful of alienating the Rutledges "and generally to the Southward, where they have great influence" if Pinckney were asked to accept diplomatic colleagues. McHenry to Pickering, May 28, 1797, Bernard C. Steiner, *The Life and Correspondence of James McHenry* (Cleveland, 1907), 225.

that he had "no objection to sending a man of neutral politics, if he is a man of sincere firmness and integrity." Pinckney, he believed, was a man of "this description."[44]

Neither Federalists nor Republicans were entirely comfortable with the thought that Pinckney would hold the balance in any three-man commission. Leaders in both parties seemed to believe that he would support the policy of either party, depending upon the circumstances and the men sent to Paris to join him. This analysis was based upon Pinckney's political neutrality and friendly attitude toward France when he left the United States, not upon his new view of France. From his residence in the Batavian Republic, Pinckney was busily writing his friends letters that revealed his disgust with the conduct of France in Europe and with Adet's intrigue in the United States.[45] Pinckney soon believed that France was making an open "attack on our National independence"[46] and prayed, as he had earlier advised Pickering, that American policy toward France would be "firm." "Mean submissions," he counseled the receptive Pickering, "are generally returned with contempt and renewed oppression."[47]

Adet was aware that Pinckney's earlier friendly attitude toward France had changed. Pinckney had written to his southern friends about his experiences in France, Adet reported, and had told them that France had "insulted" his nation's honor. As a result, the whole southern political climate had changed. Former friends of France in the south, Adet believed, would now fight France "*avec plaisir.*" Adet received further evidence of the estrangement of the Pinckney connection when Jefferson forwarded to Adet a letter he had received

44. Wolcott to Hamilton, Mar. 31, 1797, in Gibbs, *Administrations of Washington and Adams*, I, 487.

45. Pinckney to Rufus King, Mar. 24, 1797, Rufus King Papers, Huntington Lib.; Pinckney to Secretary of State, Apr. 28, 1797, State Dept. Diplomatic Despatches, France, 5:72, National Archives. In the latter communication, Pinckney indignantly described the "tyrannic conduct" of France toward the United States.

46. Pinckney to Secretary of State, May 6, 1797, State Dept., Diplomatic Despatches, France, 5:102, National Archives.

47. Pinckney to Secretary of State, Mar. 8, 1797, in *Amer. State Papers, Class I*, II, 12. While Pinckney regretted the belligerent conduct of France, he believed that "all Europe united" against the United States should not cause alarm if every American were as attached to America as Frenchmen were to France. See Pinckney to William Smith, July 16, 1797, Rogers, *Evolution of a Federalist*, 315.

from Edward Rutledge, in which Rutledge "complained bitterly" of the way his friend Pinckney had been treated. Pinckney, Rutledge assured Jefferson, had been "attached to the interests of France for twenty years. . . ." Because of Pinckney's experiences, Adet stated, "our friends" in the south had become "very cool" toward France.[48]

The influence of Charles Cotesworth Pinckney in the south was also well known to Adams, and when he decided to appoint a three-man commission to negotiate with France, he felt bound to include Pinckney as the representative of the south. Yet despite Pinckney's influence in South Carolina, the wisdom of his reappointment was certainly debatable. The insult given to the American nation by Pinckney's forcible expulsion was kept before the public. It might have been wiser if the Adams administration had at least given the appearance of some change in policy. With Pinckney at the head of the commission, the continuity between the Washington and Adams policies toward France was clearly established. France was given little chance to save face by accepting an entirely new commission not identified with policies and incidents of the past.[49] Many Republicans objected to naming Pinckney to the commission, the senators from the states of Virginia and North Carolina even voting against his confirmation. Federalists responded to Republican objections to Pinckney by saying that any person who refused to toady to France and who was unwilling to subordinate his own country's interests to those of the "Great Nation" was unacceptable to Republicans.[50]

After considering various candidates for the mission, President Adams decided to put John Marshall of Virginia on the commission. Hamilton was pleased with this appointment, for Marshall was a man

48. Adet to Minister of Foreign Relations, 11 Germinal, An 5 [Mar. 31, 1797], 27 Floréal, An 5 [May 16, 1797], Turner, ed., *Correspondence of the French Ministers*, 1004, 1018.

49. Pickering withheld from publication certain parts of Pinckney's correspondence because it was so biting when discussing French policies. To release it, Pickering rightly believed, would "render him [Pinckney] personally objectionable" to the French government. Pickering to Thomas Pinckney, June 15, 1797, Pickering Papers, Mass. Hist. Soc.

50. John Rutledge, Jr., to Edward Rutledge, June 27, 1797, Rutledge Papers, Dreer Coll., Hist. Soc. of Pa. Young Rutledge bluntly told Jefferson that South Carolina was offended because the Virginia and North Carolina Republican senators voted against Pinckney's confirmation.

"on whom perfect reliance could be placed," one who could probably "secure Pinckney's cooperation."[51]

For the third commissioner, Adams wished to nominate his old friend from Massachusetts, Elbridge Gerry, but dropped the idea when Pickering and McHenry heatedly objected. They felt that Gerry would be eager to please France and not careful enough to defend his own nation's interests. After Chief Justice Charles Dana of Massachusetts refused the appointment, Adams decided that he would send Gerry whether the cabinet members favored it or not. Although Gerry was a quasi-Republican, he had atoned for this considerable sin by voting for Adams in 1796 and was therefore personally acceptable to Adams.[52]

Jefferson and other Republicans were pleased with Gerry's appointment. Jefferson wrote to Gerry that he believed the welfare of the United States and the preservation of peace were dependent upon "your acceptance of this mission." Jefferson's letter to Gerry indicates a lack of confidence in either Marshall or Pinckney, although Jefferson had earlier written to Thomas Pinckney that his brother's conduct "has met with universal approbation. It is marked with that coolness, dignity, and good sense we expected from him."[53] Whether or not Thomas Pinckney took Jefferson's flattering phrases about his brother seriously, it is certain that Gerry was pleased by Jefferson's confidential words to him.

The commission was an able one, distinguished by both talents and experience. It was also a geographically balanced delegation and promised to enlist the support of patriots throughout the Union. But a uniting of three capable men does not necessarily make a capable delegation, one able to negotiate and settle outstanding differences

51. Hamilton to Pickering, May 11, 1797, Lodge, ed., *Works of Hamilton*, X, 262.

52. James T. Austin, *The Life of Elbridge Gerry*, 2 vols. (Boston, 1828–29), II, 152–53; Theodore Sedgwick to Ephraim Williams, June 23, 1797, Papers of Theodore Sedgwick, Mass. Hist. Soc.; Manning J. Dauer, *The Adams Federalists* (Baltimore, 1953), 109. Gerry really was not free to vote as he wished in 1796, for when his brother was all but bankrupt in 1792, John Adams secured Samuel Gerry the position of federal collector of the port of Marblehead. See Eugene F. Kramer, The Public Career of Elbridge Gerry (unpubl. Ph.D. diss., Ohio State University, 1955), 119.

53. Jefferson to Gerry, June 21, 1797, Austin, *Life of Gerry*, II, 155; Jefferson to Thomas Pinckney, May 29, 1797, Henry A. Washington, ed., *The Writings of Thomas Jefferson*, 9 vols. (N.Y., 1854–56), IV, 177.

in the most expeditious manner. As an old diplomat himself, President Adams knew this. Adams feared that the commission would be torn by indecision or by petty feuds since no commissioner was likely to establish a clear intellectual predominance over the others. But Adams decided to use commission diplomacy because it suited the domestic political situation; it would rally more support for his administration's foreign policy than the appointment of any single person. And if the commission proved an awkward instrument for negotiation? There were risks of course, but if both France and the United States were properly conciliatory, the techniques of negotiation would not seriously impede a reconciliation.

Pinckney's life since leaving Paris had not been especially pleasant. To Rufus King, the American minister in London, Pinckney complained that his life was a dull one, filled with little but writing letters to contacts in France, analyzing the reports returned to him, and forwarding pertinent information to Secretary of State Pickering.[54]

The most disturbing news that Pinckney forwarded to Pickering concerned the decree of the Executive Directory of March 2, 1797.[55] Pinckney was disgusted and alarmed by this new evidence of French hostility. He wrote to Pickering that he was attempting to contact members of the French government to inform them "how strongly America feels and reprobates the hostile conduct of France in the capturing of our vessels" and to assure them "that if the present measures are persisted in, and our present grievances unredressed, that such an alienation in the sentiments of America will take place, that the name and character of a Frenchman will be as much and as generally hated in our Country, as it was formerly greatly and affectionately esteemed."[56]

Pinckney was certain that if the majority of fair-minded French-

---

54. Pinckney's major contact in Paris was Major James G. Mountflorence, in whom Pinckney developed considerable confidence. Mountflorence was attached to the American consulate. Pinckney also mentions corresponding with "a lady" in Paris who was supplying him information. Pinckney to Secretary of State, Apr. 30, June 28, 1797, State Dept., Diplomatic Despatches, France, 5: 96–98, 153–54, National Archives; Pinckney to Rufus King, June 27, 1797, Rufus King Papers, Huntington Lib.

55. The decree is printed in *Amer. State Papers, Class I*, II, 12–13.

56. Pinckney to Secretary of State, Apr. 5, 1797, State Dept. Diplomatic Despatches, France, 5:71, National Archives.

men understood the American position toward France and realized how reprehensible the Directory's measures appeared to Americans, there would be a popular demand to review the Directory's American policy. Therefore he assiduously forwarded papers and documents to politicians or persons of influence, justifying American conduct. He requested John Quincy Adams, then minister at The Hague, to draw up "some observations" on the *arrêt* of 12 Ventose, which Adams wrote and which Pinckney forwarded to members of the national assembly. Pinckney also had published one thousand copies of Secretary Pickering's letter to him of January 16, 1797, in which Pickering argued forcefully that France had treated America in an unjust if not tyrannical manner. Pinckney assured Pickering that everyone he had contacted "is struck with the sound arguments it contains, and the masterly manner in which the facts are displayed, . . . while at the same time lament the mistaken policy of their Government." Pinckney had a copy of Pickering's missive sent to every member of the French legislature.[57] France, it seems, was not the only nation capable of conducting diplomacy at the popular level suggested by Genêt and Adet! Undermining the policy established by a nation's executive was apparently acceptable to Americans so long as it was not their executive that was attacked.

Pinckney was grateful for the advice he received from John Quincy Adams, with whom he seemed to have established a friendly personal relationship. To his father, John Quincy Adams confided that he had "been much gratified" by Pinckney's frankness and by his staunch patriotism. John Quincy Adams was pleased to tell his father that he had formed "an high opinion of [Pinckney's] character and personal merit."[58] Adams was kind enough to introduce the Pinckneys to important persons in the Batavian Republic's government and to visit points of interest with them. The Pinckneys also enjoyed the company of Mr. and Mrs. William Vans Murray who

57. Pickering's letter, a real tour de force, is in the Diplomatic and Consular Instructions, State Dept., Vol. 3, 326–419, National Archives. Pickering attached 163 documents to the letter. See also Pinckney to Secretary of State, May 28, 1797, State Dept., Diplomatic Despatches, France, 5:113, National Archives; Pinckney to Secretary of State, June 5, 1797, Papers of George Washington, Lib. Cong. A copy of Pickering's letter is in Vol. XLVII, Part II, U.S. Pol. Corr., Fr. Archives.

58. John Quincy Adams to John Adams, May 11, 1797, Ford, ed., *Writings of John Quincy Adams*, II, 165–66.

arrived at The Hague in June 1797. Murray was the new American minister to the Batavian Republic, replacing John Quincy Adams who had been named American minister to Prussia. While the Pinckneys and the Murrays were congenial, Murray was disturbed to find Pinckney not "well made up" on "some points of federal doctrines." Pinckney, according to Murray, exhibited the "ways of thinking which might make a man a great favourite with a military regiment filled with local politics." Pinckney's political views were those of one who "had not been in Congress for some time, and in the federal party." Nevertheless, Murray concluded, Pinckney was an entertaining companion as well as "a very clever man, shrewd and vigilant—a good scholar and a good lawyer."[59]

The Pinckneys amused themselves by sightseeing and by attending lengthy evening dinners. Mrs. Pinckney was intrigued by the waltz which was then the rage in Amsterdam, although she and the General had some reservations about its decency. General Pinckney, she believed, "would not permit Eliza to be walsed, unless occasionally in a country dance," although Pinckney did not deny himself this pleasure and willingly "walsed" until two in the morning if the company was engaging.[60]

Because of their cramped quarters, the Pinckneys were unable to entertain friends in turn. This did not disturb Pinckney, for he was distressed at the sums they had spent during their two months in Paris. He insisted that his family would "live with all possible economy" at Amsterdam, to compensate for their "exceedings at Paris." Therefore they settled in a two-room apartment and rented a carriage only when the need arose.[61]

Pinckney's economies did not preclude occasional visits to places of scientific or cultural interest. The family visited Leyden and saw the botanical gardens there, the "salle d'anatomie," and the library,

59. Murray's less favorable opinion of Pinckney was given after Pinckney came out against the Alien and Sedition Laws. See Murray to John Quincy Adams, Mar. 22, 1797, in Worthington C. Ford, ed., "Letters of William Vans Murray to John Quincy Adams, 1797–1803," American Historical Association, Annual Report, 1912 (Washington, D.C., 1914), 530. His first and more favorable opinion was given in a letter to James McHenry, July 14, 1797, in Steiner, Life of James McHenry, 234.

60. Mary Pinckney to Mrs. Gabriel Manigault, Mar. 30, 1797, Manigault Family Papers, S. Caroliniana Lib.

61. Mary Pinckney to Mrs. Gabriel Manigault, Apr. 21, 1797, ibid.

"which is rich in botanical works." They also toured Rotterdam for a few days in May and dined with Mr. Beeldemaker, the American consular agent in that city.[62] But the Pinckneys found that the doors of most important people in the Netherlands were closed to them, for no one wished to offend France by appearing friendly to an agent of the United States, particularly one who had been unceremoniously expelled from France. Their social life was thus confined mainly to American families or to agents of the American government in the Batavian Republic, a lonesome life as Mary Pinckney reflected upon it.[63]

Pinckney naturally wondered what further part he would play in the continuing Franco-American crisis. Every week seemed to bring some new evidence of persistent French hostility toward the United States. Late in April 1797 Pinckney read in a Paris newspaper that he had been supplanted in his mission by James Madison; indeed, Madison was already in Paris negotiating. Pinckney's reaction to this startling news shows the caliber of the man and his thinking on French policy. To Secretary Pickering he wrote:

> If . . . it is thought the service I was sent to perform can be better executed by Mr. Maddison or any other gentleman, I earnestly request that no idea of delicacy with regard to me may prevent the nomination from immediately taking [place]. Perhaps political circumstances might render some other character a more acceptable Agent than myself. It is generally thought in France, and my heart swells proudly at the idea, that I am the friend of and beloved by our illustrious Washington. To men determined to see no neutrality, but a partiality in their favor; and to allow of no independence, but what is submissive to their will; the friend of Washington cannot be acceptable. Act therefore in this case as the honor and interest of our Country requires.[64]

The Paris account was soon proven to be inaccurate. Pinckney did not learn for nearly three months that he had been appointed head of a three-man commission to negotiate with France. Although Secre-

62. *Ibid.*

63. *Ibid.* Mrs. Pinckney mentioned to John Marshall that only one girl Eliza's age had visited her during their entire seven months in the Batavian Republic. Marshall to Polly Marshall, July 30, 1797, Albert J. Beveridge, *The Life of John Marshall*, 4 vols. (Boston, 1916–19), II, 231.

64. Pinckney to Secretary of State, Apr. 30, 1797, State Dept., Diplomatic Despatches, France, 5:97–98, National Archives.

tary Pickering wrote him about the proposed mission on May 27, Pinckney read about it first in a Baltimore paper published on June 2. His reaction was what one would have expected from Pinckney: "Pray present my respectful acknowledgments to the President," he wrote to Pickering, "for having given me Colleagues of such distinguished merit and ability and inform him, that tho' I have not the pleasure of being personally acquainted with either of these gentlemen [Dana and Marshall], I am no stranger to their high reputation and respectable character. . . ."[65]

When Pinckney learned that Gerry, rather than Dana, was to join Marshall, he was equally pleased. He and Gerry had known each other since the days of the federal Constitutional Convention and considered themselves friends. In fact, Pinckney and Gerry had been corresponding even before Gerry's appointment, Gerry asking Pinckney to secure some medicine for Mrs. Gerry's ailing eyes. Pinckney had purchased some *"Baume de Fioravcuti"* for Gerry, and in his letter to Gerry quoted from a book by George Adams on the best manner to apply the balm. Pinckney had also urged Gerry, his "dear friend," to use his "extensive influence and abilities . . . to unite all parties. Banish the degrading idea that America is either under the influence or dread of any foreign nation. . . ."[66] Pinckney, then, undoubtedly anticipated many pleasant moments with Gerry, his friend of ten years.

Pinckney had never met Marshall. Although Marshall was born into a farm family of back-country Virginians, he and Pinckney had enough in common to establish an instant rapport. Both were successful lawyers, had fought in the Revolutionary War, had served in their state legislatures, and had supported the adoption of the federal Constitution. More important, in 1797 both saw eye to eye on the problems of Franco-American relations.

Reflecting the views of her husband, Mary Pinckney wrote to her cousin that they were not returning to France under any illusion

65. Pickering to Pinckney, May 27, 1797, Diplomatic and Consular Instructions, Vol. IV, 63, Pinckney to Secretary of State, July 15, 1797, State Dept., Diplomatic Despatches, France, 5:160, National Archives.

66. Pinckney to Gerry, June 5, 1797, Elbridge Gerry Papers, Lib. Cong. John Adams had written to Pickering: "Mr. Pinckney has been well acquainted with Mr. Gerry. They have always been on terms of friendship, and I doubt not he will be as well pleased as if Mr. Dana had accepted," Oct. 26, 1797, Adams, ed., *Works of John Adams*, VIII, 556.

that "submission will . . . avail a nation with the french republic," for they had seen repeated examples where the French "take one state after another, enflame the minds of the people, render them discontented with their government, and use them as the tools to accomplish their ambitious projects."[67] This analysis of Mary Pinckney could just as easily have come from the pen of Timothy Pickering or perhaps John Marshall. Once Marshall had arrived at The Hague and had compared his views with those of Pinckney, he wrote to George Washington that he could not help but "be very much pleas'd" with General Pinckney. To Secretary Pickering, Marshall added that he had found Pinckney to be "indefatigable in collecting information material relevant to our country. . . ."[68]

Pinckney's firm attitude toward the government of France was no doubt strengthened by a letter from Washington which Marshall delivered personally when he arrived early in September. Washington assured Pinckney that his recent conduct was "universally approved: that it deserves to be so, is my decided opinion." Washington also recommended Marshall as a "firm friend, upon true principles to his Country, sensible and discreet," and was certain that Pinckney would find Marshall "well worthy of . . . friendship and confidence."[69]

While Pinckney and Marshall waited impatiently in Amsterdam for Gerry to arrive, Pinckney had an opportunity to study the instructions that were to guide the commission in its negotiations. Without looking at the specific objectives the envoys were to seek, Pinckney could have seen by perusing the general governing principles that there was little hope for an agreement without a radical change in the Directory's policy. Although the envoys were told to negotiate in the spirit of compromise, they were neither to grant aid to France "during the present war" nor to make commitments inconsistent with any prior treaty. Also, the envoys were not to acknowledge the validity of any French decrees that restricted American

67. Mary Pinckney to Mrs. Gabriel Manigault, July 13, 1797, Manigault Family Papers, S. Caroliniana Lib.
68. Marshall to Washington, Sept. 15, 1797, [J. Franklin Jameson, ed.], "Letters of John Marshall when Envoy to France, 1797–1798," *Amer. Hist. Rev.*, 2 (1896–97), 300; Marshall to Pickering, Sept. 9, 1797, State Dept., Diplomatic Despatches, France, 6 (unpaged), National Archives.
69. Washington to Pinckney, June 24, 1797, Fitzpatrick, ed., *Writings of Washington*, XXXV, 470–71.

commerce. In essence, the United States would maintain its neutrality, make no loans to France, and adhere to the Jay Treaty.[70]

As Pinckney and Marshall discussed the recent events in western Europe, neither saw much hope that the government of France would be willing to negotiate on the basis of Pickering's instructions. France was not in a conciliatory mood. The military victories of Napoleon Bonaparte at Millesimo, Mondovi, Lodi, and Mantua had cowed the Pope and frightened Austria. Shortly after Austria had been forced to recognize the creation of the Cisalpine Republic in northern Italy, France had arrogantly crushed Venice under the pretext of an outbreak at Verona. France had also established the Ligurian Republic of Genoa in May 1797, just two months before Pinckney and Marshall set out for Paris.[71]

Equally ominous for the United States were the changes in the government of France that resulted from the coup of 18 Fructidor (September 4, 1797). Murray lamented that this "dreadful convulsion" had eliminated every member in the government friendly to the United States. John Quincy Adams fully agreed. To his father he predicted that the new government would mete out nothing to the United States but "unqualified injustice, under the Machiavelian mockery with which they have so long duped the world. Everything that envy and malice, both against our country and against you personally, can suggest, they will attempt."[72]

70. Pickering's instructions, July 15, 1797, are in *Amer. State Papers, Class I,* II, 153–57. Henry J. Ford, in Samuel F. Bemis, ed., *The American Secretaries of State and Their Diplomacy,* rev. ed., 10 vols. (N.Y., 1958), I, 216, suggests that the instructions were written by Marshall.

71. Charles D. Hazen, *The French Revolution,* 2 vols. (N.Y., 1932), II, 890–910, 914.

72. William Vans Murray to James McHenry, Sept. 22, 1797, in Steiner, *Life of James McHenry,* 275; John Quincy Adams to John Adams, Sept. 21, 1797, Ford, ed., *Writings of John Quincy Adams,* II, 211. The implications of the coup for Franco-American relations is discussed in E. Wilson Lyon, "The Directory and the United States," *Amer. Hist. Rev.,* 43 (1937–38), 518–21. The 18 Fructidor successfully purged the more moderate members of the legislature, some being jailed and others banished. Liberty of worship and freedom of the press were checked by the new leadership, ex-terrorists who had called upon General Bonaparte for assistance in restoring themselves to power. Shailer Mathews, *The French Revolution 1789–1815,* new and rev. ed. (N.Y., 1923), 314–15; Albert Meynier, *Les coups d'état du Directoire,* 3 vols. (Paris, 1927–28), I, *Le dix huit fructidor an V*; Robert R. Palmer, *The Age of Democratic Revolution: A Political History of Europe and America, 1760–1800,* 2 vols. (Princeton, 1959–64), II, 255–57.

There was also a new minister of foreign relations, Charles Maurice de Talleyrand-Périgord. Talleyrand had escaped France during the turbulent summer days of 1792, eventually making his way to the United States where he remained for thirty months. During his residence in the United States he had formed strong opinions of Americans, few of them favorable. Mary Pinckney was indignant when she learned that Talleyrand was reporting in Paris "that the male part of the [American] community do nothing but drink Madeira wine, and the women are only employed in suckling their children. . . ." Talleyrand was particularly disgusted by the Americans' love of money which he felt they often "boorishly expressed."[73]

This was a strange comment from one of whom it was said: "When . . . not plotting, he's trafficking," and who followed a "lifelong rule that he would do nothing for nothing."[74] Yet Talleyrand's desire for the easy franc did not negate his substantial talents as a diplomat and a politician. He was a master not only of the art of extortion, but of intimation and intimidation as well. He also had an uncanny ability to find the weak point in his opponent's armor. Talleyrand no doubt looked forward to his encounter with the three Americans. Negotiation with them could provide a delightful situation to sharpen his varied techniques of diplomacy. Late in July, Talleyrand forwarded letters to several municipal administrators directing them to give the American envoys "all help possible" on their journey toward Paris.[75]

Pinckney and Marshall were anxious to proceed to Paris, but Gerry still had not landed fifteen days after Marshall arrived at The Hague. The news from Paris became increasingly grim as they waited for Gerry. "Things look black in France—in *Paris*," Mary Pinckney wrote to her cousin. It was rumored that 150 members of the Council of Five Hundred had been arrested and thrown into jail. On the day

73. Mary Pinckney to Alice Delancey Izard, Dec. 18, 1796, McCombs, ed., *Letter-book*, 40; Charles Maurice de Talleyrand-Périgord, *Memoires*, eds. Paul-Louis Couchaud and Jean-Paul Couchaud, 2 vols. (Paris, 1957), I, 239. See also Richard M. Brace, "Talleyrand in New England: Reality and Legend," *New England Quarterly*, 16 (1943), 397–406. Talleyrand's views toward America are summarized in DeConde, *Quasi-War*, 41–42. A more detailed analysis is found in George Lacour-Gayet, *Talleyrand, 1754–1838*, 4 vols. (Paris, 1928–34), I, 181–206.

74. Louis Madelin, *Talleyrand* (N.Y., 1948), 61.

75. See Talleyrand to Commissaire Du Directoire exécutif, 13 Thermidor, An 5 [July 31, 1797], in "Letters Communicated by Rev. H. F. Jenks," Mass. Hist. Soc., *Proceedings*, 2nd Ser., 15 (1901, 1902), 89.

Pinckney left for Paris, he confided to a friend that his expectations were "not at all sanguine" that the envoys had it in their power "to preserve peace consistently with the honour and interest" of the United States.[76]

Pinckney and Marshall had finally decided that they should wait no longer for Gerry. They had heard, Pinckney wrote to Secretary of War James McHenry, that their "presence at this junction at Paris might be important," but they would commence no "direct negotiations, before we are joined by Mr. Gerry, without circumstances, should indicate great possible advantages."[77]

Even as Marshall and Pinckney were starting their journey, Gerry arrived at Hellevoetsluis and was at The Hague two days later. When Pinckney learned that Gerry had landed, he immediately forwarded instructions advising him which roads to travel, the proper bribe that must be paid to get through French customs, and the most satisfactory inns on the route. Pinckney warned Gerry to "put a French coc[k]ade" into his hat before he reached Antwerp, or he would "meet with continual interruptions and be liable to have . . . [his] passport examined." Pinckney also mentioned that their "Suites in Paris" had already been rented and that the envoys would all be "under the same roof."[78]

As the Pinckneys and Marshall traveled toward Paris, Pinckney must have recalled his entrance into the city ten months earlier. Then he had treasured some hope that Franco-American relations could be repaired. Now his attitude was quite different. The way in which France had bullied or subjugated the smaller states of Europe made him suspect that France would treat the United States unfairly in any negotiation. The violence and disorder in Paris, where laws were flouted by the very ministers elected to uphold them, and the notorious dishonesty of public officials had turned him against the

76. Mary Pinckney to Mrs. Gabriel Manigault, Sept. 8, 1797, Manigault Family Papers, S. Caroliniana Lib.; Pinckney to [John] Luzac, Sept. 18, 1797, Pinckney Papers, Charleston Lib. Soc.

77. Pinckney to McHenry, Sept. 19, 1797, Misc. Mss., Huntington Lib.

78. Elbridge Gerry to Mrs. Gerry, Sept. 22, 1797, [Worthington C. Ford, ed.], "Letters of Elbridge Gerry, 1797–1814," Mass. Hist. Soc., *Proceedings*, 3rd Ser., 47 (1913–14), 481; Pinckney to Gerry, Sept. 22, 1797, in Carl L. Lokke, ed., "Three Letters of Charles Cotesworth Pinckney during the XYZ Mission," *S. C. Hist. and Gen. Mag.*, 35 (1934), 44–47.

French Revolution. By the time that Pinckney started for Paris late in September 1797, he was convinced that corrupt and power-mad men had betrayed the republican idealism of the early revolutionary days, the idealism that had won his loyalties. Pinckney's experiences and observations had forced him to accept the Federalist view of the French Revolution.[79] He was increasingly indignant with those Americans who encouraged France in her intransigence by attacking Federalist policies. Those deluded Americans, as Pinckney well knew, were all to be found in the Jeffersonian camp. It was not hard for Pinckney to equate the Jeffersonian party with a lack of patriotism or at least political realism. Between his expulsion from France in January 1797 and his return in September, Pinckney had become anti-French and a Federalist as well.

79. John Adams had no confidence in the French Republican experiment: "I don't know any antigallicans who believe the French to be Republicans or capable of a Republican Government—any more than a Snow ball can exist a whole week in the streets of Philadelphia under a burning sun of August or September. There are many who believe the French Republican System cannot endure and I am one of them." Adams to Elbridge Gerry, May 30, 1797, Gratz Coll., Hist. Soc. of Pa.

VII

NOT A SIXPENCE

———◆•◆———

The newspapers, which are under the regulation of the police, are filled with invectives against America. I am described as a wretch sold to Britain, and every means are used to prepare the public mind for hostilities against our country.

—Charles Cotesworth Pinckney, 1797.

Thanks be to God, that in the greatness of his goodness he has made our enemies instrumental in uniting the good people of these states, more than ever I expected to have seen them in my day.

—Rev. John Murray, 1798.

———◆•◆———

THE PINCKNEYS AND JOHN MARSHALL, RIDING IN SEPARATE CARRIAGES, did not wait for Elbridge Gerry at Antwerp, but went on toward Paris. By September 27 they were in Paris and had moved into their "ready furnished Hotel" in St. Germain, Rue de la Fontane Grenelle. The Pinckneys took the larger apartment on the second floor, leaving the two smaller ones below for Marshall and Gerry.

When the frugal Gerry arrived on October 4,[1] he must have squirmed when he learned of the "enormous rent" his colleague Pinckney had obligated him to pay.[2] Marshall could not have been

---

1. Oct. 4, 1797, John Marshall's Journal in Paris, Mass. Hist. Soc.
2. The rent for the three apartments was 70 louis d'or a month, of which Pinckney paid half. The louis d'or was the 20-franc gold piece issued after the French Revolution. Pinckney to Harriott Horry, Oct. 11, 1797, Pinckney Mss., Charleston Lib. Soc.

happy either, for he had accepted the mission to France as a financial godsend and hoped to save enough to alleviate his embarrassed financial condition. Being in the same apartment building had at least one advantage, for the commissioners were able to compare their views on the political situation in France and to decide on the proper tone to maintain in their negotiations. All were agreed that only an attitude of firmness would bring favorable action from the government of France. In mid-October Pinckney reported to his sister "that the most perfect harmony and cordiality subsists between my Colleagues and myself."[3]

That "most perfect harmony and cordiality" was strained on the very day Pinckney so enthusiastically described it. Marshall and Gerry had the first of their long series of disagreements. Three days before, the envoys had visited the home of Talleyrand, the minister of foreign relations, and had presented him with their letters of credence. Talleyrand was polite but promised them nothing more than cards of hospitality. When the envoys received a letter on October 11 from the meddlesome Thomas Paine in which he advised the envoys to accept the status of an unarmed neutral for the United States, Marshall believed that Talleyrand had prompted the letter and wished to ignore it. Gerry sharply dissented, arguing that no channel of communication should be closed nor any plan scorned. Pinckney favored sending neither the "cold and repulsive" answer advised by Marshall nor "such as Mr. Gerry advised." Instead, Pinckney wrote a cautious and noncommittal letter which they forwarded to Paine the next day.[4]

Almost without realizing it, Pinckney and Gerry had opened the door to Talleyrand to proceed on the basis of unofficial negotiations. Talleyrand followed up his initial unofficial approach through Paine by sending to Pinckney's apartment Jean Conrad Hottinguer, a Swiss

3. *Ibid.*; Beveridge, *Marshall*, II, 211.
4. Envoys to Secretary of State, Oct. 22, 1797, in *Amer. State Papers, Class I*, II, 158; Oct. 5–11, 1797, Marshall Journal, Mass. Hist. Soc. Paine evidently considered himself a close adviser to Talleyrand on American affairs. He wrote to Talleyrand: "In two or three days I will give you some thoughts upon American affairs. I presume you do not mean to assure the commissioners of anything at the first interview. . . . Mr. Pinckney has a good deal committed himself [to the Federalist viewpoint on France] in his correspondence with Pickering, which his last has been foolish enough to publish." 7 Vendémiaire, Vol. 48, Part IV, 268, U.S. Pol. Corr., Fr. Archives.

financier who was described by the envoys as "a gentleman of considerable credit and reputation." Hottinguer arrived as the Pinckneys and Marshall were dining together on the evening of October 18. At Hottinguer's request Pinckney excused himself to talk privately with the banker. Since Marshall did not understand French, the retreat for privacy was more a formality than a necessity. Pinckney let Hottinguer do the talking. After hearing what Hottinguer had to say, Pinckney immediately informed Marshall and Gerry that the Directory was angry because of President Adams' unfriendly remarks about France in his message to Congress of May 16, and demanded satisfactory explanations of those remarks. The Directory also wanted the United States to reimburse its citizens for any debts due them by France and to assume financial responsibility for French spoliations of American commerce. Furthermore, France expected a loan from the United States as well as a bribe (*douceur*) for the Directory, both of unspecified amounts.[5]

Pinckney and Marshall were dismayed by these terms and felt that their nation's honor would be sullied even by discussing them in a preliminary and informal way. Gerry was not as certain. War was a terrible thing, Gerry felt, and it was the responsibility of the envoys to avoid it. Reluctantly and as a concession to Gerry, Pinckney and Marshall agreed to ask Hottinguer for details on the original propositions. Pinckney contacted Hottinguer, and on the evening of October 19 he returned to Pinckney's apartment with the terms in writing. The size of the *douceur* immediately caught the eyes of the envoys. The Directory wanted a "sweetener" of 1,200,000 livres, about a quarter of a million dollars.[6]

Though other details of the proposed settlement were not given, the envoys now largely knew the terms upon which the Directory would continue the negotiations. Pinckney and Marshall quickly de-

5. Hottinguer was no stranger to Marshall, for Marshall's brother had negotiated a loan through Hottinguer at Amsterdam. Beveridge, *Marshall*, II, 259*n*. See also Envoys to Secretary of State, Oct. 22, 1797, *Amer. State Papers, Class I,* II, 158. Adams' speech to Congress which supposedly angered the government of France is in James D. Richardson, ed., *A Compilation of the Messages and Papers of the Presidents, 1789–1927*, 20 vols. (Washington, D.C., 1896–1927), I, 233–39.

6. Envoys to Secretary of State, Oct. 22, 1797, *Amer. State Papers, Class I,* II, 158; Oct. [19], 1797, Marshall Journal, Mass. Hist. Soc.; Beveridge, *Marshall*, II, 259.

cided that those terms were unreasonable and also that their informal negotiations must be discontinued. Again Gerry disagreed. Gerry thought that it would be wise to use the French demands as a starting point in the negotiations, hoping that in the bargaining process the Directory's terms would be moderated. Pinckney and Marshall were convinced that Gerry was naïve in thinking the Directory would soften its attitude toward the United States, particularly since Napoleon had just concluded a stunningly successful campaign against Austria. But in order to conciliate Gerry, Marshall finally tentatively offered to return to Philadelphia for fresh instructions.[7]

Talleyrand's agents were not slow to see which envoy might be the most receptive to flattery or threats. Although warned by President Adams to avoid division "like a rock or quicksand," Gerry was certain that preserving peace was more important than agreeing with his colleagues. Gerry was well satisfied that influential Federalists wanted war with France in order to discredit republican institutions in America and to pave the way for an alliance with monarchical England. For these reasons Gerry did not allow his natural indignation over French conduct to close his mind toward negotiations. Moreover, he was perfectly willing to negotiate on much less favorable terms from the beginning of the mission in order to preserve peace and to confound the enemies of republicanism in the United States.[8]

When Talleyrand again offered to meet the envoys unofficially, Pinckney and Marshall informed his second agent, Lucien Hauteval, an old business acquaintance of Gerry, that they would meet Talleyrand only after he gave them an official appointment. Gerry decided that he would accept the invitation, reasoning that a social call would be proper for he had known Talleyrand since the early 1790's. Gerry swore later that Pinckney and Marshall had encouraged him to visit

7. Oct. 20, 21, 1797, Marshall Journal, Mass. Hist. Soc.
8. Samuel E. Morison, "Elbridge Gerry, Gentleman Democrat," *New Eng. Qtly.*, 2 (1929), 23; Adams to Gerry, June 8, 1797, Adams, ed., *Works of John Adams*, VIII, 548; Adams had written to Gerry an opinion of his character that Adams' advisers held, an opinion that proved to have some foundation: "Some have expressed doubts of your orthodoxy in the Science of Government—others have expressed fears of an unaccommodating disposition and others of an obstinacy that will risque great Things to secure Small ones.—Some have observed that there is at present a happy and perfect harmony among all our Ministers abroad, and have expressed apprehensions of danger that your appointment might occasion an interruption of it," 549.

Talleyrand privately, a charge Pinckney hotly denied. Although Gerry was snubbed when he went to see Talleyrand and vowed that he would not go again, he had now made it clear to Talleyrand that he would negotiate independently of his colleagues.[9]

Talleyrand saw that Pinckney and Marshall must become more cooperative before he would work successfully through Gerry. Late in October the time to frighten the two former soldiers seemed at hand. News arrived that a triumphant peace had been forced upon Austria. Almost before the booming of the victory cannon had died away, Mr. Bellamy, a partner in a Hamburg commercial firm, was knocking at Pinckney's and Marshall's door. Finding only Marshall at home, Bellamy proceeded to recount the impressive military power of France and the state of near collapse in England. France, Bellamy reiterated at several points, was astride Europe and not to be trifled with, especially in her hour of triumph.

The following day, October 27, Hottinguer informed the envoys that the Directory was "becoming impatient and would take a decided course with regard to America" if its demands were not met. Pinckney quickly retorted that the *douceur* was a dead issue. Hottinguer reminded the envoys of French military power, adding that France had determined there would be no neutrals in her struggle with England; all nations must identify themselves either as friend or foe. An alarmed Gerry replied that if war were declared against the United States, the whole world would know that France had brought it on. Pinckney added that no one in the United States wished for war, but that it would be better to have open war than to allow France to destroy American commerce surreptitiously through enforcement of the Directory's hostile decrees.

Hottinguer expressed hope that the United States, for its own sake, would not be so foolish as to conclude an alliance with Great Britain. Pinckney retorted that he did not favor an alliance with England, but if France forced America to the wall, she would have to guard her own interests by whatever means possible. Hottinguer then returned to what had become the major issue, the *douceur*. Pinckney, who was finding it difficult to control his indignation, reminded Hottinguer that the envoys had said their last word on that humiliating topic.

9. Oct. 25, 1797, Apr. 3, 1798, Marshall Journal, Mass. Hist. Soc.; Gerry to John Adams, July 8, 1799, Elbridge Gerry Papers, Lib. Cong.

"No," Hottinguer said, "you have not." What was their final answer? In exasperation Pinckney cried that their answer was "no, no, not a sixpence."[10]

Hottinguer was not discouraged by Pinckney's petulant outburst and insisted that a *douceur* would be money wisely spent. The envoys rhetorically asked what guarantee there was that a bribe would alter the vicious anti-American policies of the Directory. Of course there was none and the shrewd Yankees would pledge no money without guaranteed results. Hottinguer asked if they did not realize that the wheels of French diplomacy rarely moved without the driving power of money. With tongue in cheek and a straight face, Pinckney answered that he understood France determined her policy toward the United States solely on principle and "disinterested affection." It was Hottinguer's turn to look surprised. He then shifted his ground and reminded the envoys of the generous assistance America had received from France during the Revolutionary War; America owed France a debt of gratitude which France now wanted to realize in a *douceur* and a loan. Pinckney and Marshall also shifted their ground, responding that the help of France had been extended only to serve its selfish national interests. America owed France nothing.[11]

In an attempt to break the impasse, Gerry continued his independent diplomacy by visiting Talleyrand and Hauteval. Talleyrand again pressed the issues of a loan and the necessity of explanations for the unfriendly references to France in President Adams' speech to Congress in mid-May. The loan, Talleyrand emphasized, was a *sine qua non* of any negotiation. If the envoys believed they had no power to grant a loan, then they should courageously assume the power. Were they not envoys extraordinary and ministers plenipotentiary? The welfare of their nation demanded that they use the powers and discretion granted them by their government. Gerry

10. Oct. 27, 1797, Marshall Journal, Mass. Hist. Soc.; Envoys to Secretary of State, Oct. 27, 1797, *Amer. State Papers, Class I*, II, 161. Many years later Pinckney told his friend Thomas S. Grimké that his answer had been "Not a sixpence, sir." Asked why he had not denied saying "Millions for Defense but Not One Cent for Tribute," a phrase credited to him by Robert G. Harper, Pinckney replied that the phrase had become part of the nation's patriotic folklore. To deny authorship, Pinckney felt, was unnecessary and would have been ostentatious. See Yates Snowden, "Millions for Defense," *S. C. Hist. and Gen. Mag.*, 1 (1900), 100–02.

11. Oct. 27, 1797, Marshall Journal, Mass. Hist. Soc.; Envoys to Secretary of State, Oct. 27, 1797, *Amer. State Papers, Class I*, II, 162.

reported to his colleagues that the Directory would take additional
hostile measures against the United States in one week if the envoys
were unable to soothe its irate temper. Pinckney and Marshall were
concerned but reminded the anxious Gerry that they were authorized
neither to pay a bribe to the Directory nor to make a loan to France.[12]

The threats and pressure tactics of Talleyrand were not totally
without effect even upon the stout hearts of Pinckney and Marshall.
When the Directory, through Hauteval, suggested that one envoy
return home to request authority to make France a loan and the
others remain to negotiate, they rejected the offer. The Directory
wanted the bribe immediately but would not promise to suspend
depredations on American commerce. Yet if the Directory had agreed
to suspend naval seizures of American vessels, the envoys were evidently prepared to promise the *douceur*. They told Hauteval that if
France were "disposed to do us justice . . . we might not so much
regard a little money as he [Hauteval] stated to be usual altho' we
should hazard ourselves by giving it."[13]

This new sign of flexibility by Pinckney and Marshall no doubt
encouraged Talleyrand, for he sent Bellamy the next morning to
continue the softening process. For an hour Bellamy reviewed the
political and military situation in Europe, laying particular stress
on disasters that had befallen nations opposing France. The United
States, he continued ominously, could expect a fate similar to that of
Venice if it continued on its obnoxious and uncompromising course.
Bellamy concluded by warning the envoys not to resort to open
diplomacy, for if they did France would encourage its followers in
America to place the blame for any deterioration in relations "on
the british party as France terms you. And you may assure your-
selves," Bellamy added, that "this will be done."[14]

The envoys were indignant with the insinuation that America was
nothing more than the tail on the French kite. They firmly resolved
once again to discontinue their secret negotiations on November 1

12. Oct. 28, 1797, Marshall Journal, Mass. Hist. Soc. For a discussion of 18th-
century attitudes toward loans of this nature, see Charles S. Hyneman, *The
First American Neutrality: A Study of the American Understanding of Neutral
Obligations during the Years 1792 to 1815* (Urbana, Ill., 1934), 40–41.
13. Oct. 29, 1797, Marshall Journal, Mass. Hist. Soc.; Envoys to Secretary of
State, Oct. 29, 1797, *Amer. State Papers, Class I*, II, 163.
14. Envoys to Secretary of State, Oct. 30, 1797, *Amer. State Papers, Class I*,
II, 163; Oct. 30, 1797, Marshall Journal, Mass. Hist. Soc.

but found that only the unofficial channels of communication were open to them.[15] The threats continued to come from Talleyrand's agents, three of whom became known to history as X, Y, and Z.[16]

On November 3, the envoys learned through Bellamy that the Directory was planning to complain to their government about the hostile disposition of Pinckney and Marshall toward France. The Directory had information, Bellamy continued, that if Aaron Burr and James Madison had been sent as the envoys, the differences between France and the United States would have been easily resolved. Pinckney and Marshall were angry over this attempt to intimidate them and determined to write directly to Talleyrand stating their position on the issues dividing France and America. Gerry balked, however, suggesting a delay until a copy of their letter was first approved in Philadelphia. Such a transaction would take at least two months![17]

Talleyrand saw that even Gerry's patience was wearing thin under the insults and pressures of his agents. As a conciliatory gesture, Talleyrand sent word that if the envoys really wanted an accommodation, they would pay him "regular visits" at his home. Gerry took the hint and accepted a dinner invitation at Talleyrand's home. At his arrival on the evening of December 2, Gerry found both Bellamy and Hottinguer already there. After a rather dull dinner (Gerry did not understand French) Hottinguer asked Gerry "in direct terms" whether the *douceur* was going to be paid. Gerry screwed up his courage and replied positively not. The matter was then dropped.[18]

Pinckney was finding it impossible to hide his resentment at Talleyrand's attempts to intimidate the envoys and at his acting more like an artful highwayman than the representative of a great power. When the newspapers began to pile abuse on Pinckney as a "wretch sold to Britain," he lost all patience with Talleyrand and the Directory. He warned Edward Rutledge that "every means are used to prepare the public mind for hostilities against our Country" and

15. Nov. 1, 1797, Marshall Journal, Mass. Hist. Soc.
16. When Adams submitted the correspondence of the envoys to Congress, he substituted the letters X, Y, and Z for the names of Hottinguer, Bellamy, and Hauteval when mentioned by the envoys.
17. Envoys to Secretary of State, Nov. 3, 1797, *Amer. State Papers, Class I*, II, 165; Nov. 4, 5, 1797, Marshall Journal, Mass. Hist. Soc.
18. Envoys to Minister of Foreign Affairs, Nov. 11, 1797, *Amer. State Papers, Class I*, II, 166; Nov. 7, 1797, Marshall Journal, Mass. Hist. Soc.

hoped that if war came "my Countrymen will act with coolness and heroism." Pinckney complained to Rufus King that despite their efforts to seek some middle ground with France, "the condemnation of our vessels is pressed forward with eagerness and rapacity."[19]

Pinckney and Marshall seemed to lose their perspective on the negotiations during November. Their feelings of resentment and indignation and the threats to the United States prompted them to overlook the true interests of the French government. France had very little to gain by a war with the United States. The cessation of trade with the United States would close a rich market for French silks, vinegars, wines, porcelains, and linens and would injure the prosperity of the French West Indies which was then dependent on American merchants. Louisiana, a colony of France's ally Spain, would be open to attack by American frontiersmen if war developed between France and the United States.[20] While Gerry was accused of timidity or cowardice, he saw more clearly than his colleagues that the true interest of France was peace.[21] But as Marshall's journal makes abundantly clear, he and Pinckney grew excited and began to take the French threats of war at face value. Therefore, as a matter of principle, they wanted to discontinue the covert negotiations; to negotiate secretly with a blustering and imperious enemy, they believed, was beneath the dignity of their country and unworthy of gentlemen diplomats.

Pinckney despised the secret negotiations. Temperamentally he was incapable of the intrigue which is sometimes one of the most useful arts of diplomacy. A gentleman of honor, he believed, was obliged to be candid and frank in his relations not only with his associates but with his enemies as well. Pinckney seemed to believe that this code of gentlemanly conduct which regulated his private life was also applicable to the relations between nations. Since the conduct of France toward the United States had been unfair, if not provocative, Pinckney was ready to resort to the sword. He valued national and personal honor more than a mean peace.

19. Pinckney to Rutledge, Nov. 16, 1797, Pickering Papers, Mass. Hist. Soc.; Pinckney to King, Nov. 26, 1797, Rufus King Papers, Huntington Lib.
20. E. Wilson Lyon, "The Directory and the United States," *Amer. Hist. Rev.*, 43 (1937–38), 525–26.
21. Gerry wrote to Murray that "nothing but madness could prompt her [France] to the measure [of war]," Apr. 23, 1798, Elbridge Gerry Letterbook, 1797–1800, Gerry Papers, Lib. Cong.

Every day that passed found Pinckney readier to leave Paris. Just five weeks after entering Paris, Pinckney despaired of the negotiations and began to seek information about arranging a homeward passage. To Captain Woodman of the ship *Aurora* he wrote on November 9:

As it is possible our negotiations with this republic may not have a favorable issue, and that my colleagues and myself may be ordered to leave France, . . . I should be glad to know if you take passengers and have accommodations for them. . . . This is not to be considered as an engagement to go in the Aurora, but merely as a letter requesting information. . . .[22]

The fact that this letter found its way into the public journals did not enhance Pinckney's standing in the Directory's eyes. But Pinckney was so disgusted that he cared very little for the Directory's favorable opinion. He was particularly dismayed as he watched the Directory work its craft upon his friend Gerry. After the envoys had specifically agreed on December 14 not to meet with Talleyrand's agents until those agents produced written authorization to negotiate, Marshall discovered Gerry talking with Bellamy three days later. Gerry then told Marshall that he intended to visit Talleyrand once again, this time with Bellamy. Marshall rushed to tell Pinckney of Gerry's duplicity and both deplored Gerry's resorting to the "old reprobated system of indirect unauthorized negotiation."[23]

In an effort to keep the wavering Gerry in line, the envoys held a joint conference the next day and made Gerry promise once again that he would neither negotiate with unauthorized agents nor pledge a loan to France. The envoys also decided to inform Talleyrand by letter that unless the negotiations were placed upon an official standing, they were ready to receive their passports. After numerous re-

22. This letter is printed in the Hartford *Connecticut Courant*, Jan. 22, 1798. The *Courant* editor dates the letter Oct. 9, but a letter of Mrs. Pinckney to Mrs. Gabriel Manigault of Nov. 5, 1797, Manigault Family Papers, S. Caroliniana Lib., mentions that "a fine ship now loading at Bordeaux for Charleston," named the *Aurora*, would be an ideal ship on which to book passage should the envoys be ordered out of France.

23. Dec. 17, 1797, Marshall Journal, Mass. Hist. Soc. Pinckney ruefully wrote to Rufus King that "The American Jacobins here pay him [Gerry] great Court," Dec. 14, 1797, cited in Beveridge, *Marshall*, II, 287. Just at this point in the negotiations, Gerry wrote a revealing letter to William Vans Murray which explains why he repeatedly broke his promises to his colleagues not to negotiate unofficially: "Any conflict with France would disgrace republicanism, and make

visions Gerry agreed to sign the letter. The envoys finally forwarded it to Talleyrand late in January.[24]

In the meantime, five days before Christmas Pinckney was approached by the later famous "lady" mentioned in the correspondence of the envoys to Secretary of State Pickering. This lady was Madame de Villette, the niece and adopted daughter—some said more —of Voltaire. Marshall and Gerry, in an attempt to economize, had vacated their first apartments in the latter part of November, taking rooms in the guest house run by Madame de Villette. Described by Mrs. Pinckney as "an agreeable pleasing woman, about 32 years of age," Madame de Villette quickly proved that she could be an "agreeable pleasing woman" to Gerry and Marshall as well.[25]

Marshall was visibly taken with this "lady," describing her to his wife as "a very accomplished, a very sensible, and I believe a very amiable lady whose temper, very contrary to the general character of her country women, is domestic and who generally sits with us two or three hours in the afternoon."[26] Marshall was so captivated by Madame de Villette that he completely forgot an appointment with Pinckney in order to accompany Madame to the theater. "What could I do," the flustered Marshall apologized to Pinckney, when Madame "invited me to accompany her?" Marshall asked Pinckney to "excuse my going but [you] will think I ought to have sent to stop you. I am sure I ought, but it did not occur to me." Madame de Villette had excellent opportunities to charm Gerry as well as

---

it the scoff of despots: and would likewise, unite us with G Britain, and thus produce an alliance which might bid defiance to Europe; for with the support which the british navy would have, by our commerce and seamen, it would be forever triumphant. God grant that none of these events may take place." Dec. 28, 1797, Gratz Coll., Hist. Soc. of Pa.

24. Dec. 18, 1797, Jan. 31, 1798, Marshall Journal, Mass. Hist. Soc. Pinckney wrote to Rufus King that the purpose of the letter to Talleyrand was to present a "statement of the claims of our country and declare our desire to enter into a discussion of their complaints and to do justice on all the points wherein we shall be convinced that justice is due. . . ." But if the Directory would not receive them, "it is my opinion and my colleagues tell me that it is theirs also, that we ought to request our passports and no longer exhibit to the world the . . . spectacle of three envoys extraordinary from a free and independent nation in vain soliciting to be heard." Dec. 27, 1797, Rufus King Papers, Lib. Cong.

25. Mary Pinckney to Mrs. Gabriel Manigault, Mar. 9, 1798, Manigault Family Papers, S. Caroliniana Lib.

26. John Marshall to Mrs. Marshall, Nov. 27, 1797, [E. G. Swem, ed.], "Letters from John Marshall to His Wife," *Wm. and Mary Qtly.*, 2nd Ser., 3 (1923), 81.

Marshall, for she always dined "with the two *batchelors*" and according to Mary Pinckney made "their situation very agreeable."[27]

Just how agreeable the situation was is not certain, but Madame de Villette, as an agent of Talleyrand, was probably as "pleasing" and "agreeable" as was necessary. Why Madame de Villette approached Pinckney and urged him to agree to a loan for France can only be surmised. Perhaps in the course of her afternoon conversations with Gerry and Marshall she had learned that Pinckney adamantly opposed the loan and had been sent by Talleyrand to moderate Pinckney's stand. She certainly was unsuccessful. Indeed, she only hardened Pinckney's attitude when she threatened that France would use the Republican party in the United States to discredit the envoys. Talleyrand, although a shrewd man, completely misjudged Pinckney and the politics of South Carolina when he used this tactic of intimidation. Pinckney knew that his family and friends in South Carolina would support him in his mission to France so long as he conducted himself with dignity and good sense. Few others mattered.[28]

Ten days after Pinckney's interview with Madame de Villette, Gerry received word that the Directory wished to send Pinckney home, but that it still desired to negotiate with Marshall and himself.[29] Perhaps Madame de Villette had found Marshall more pliable than his journal would indicate. It is also possible, indeed probable, that the government of France had intercepted Pinckney's mail to friends in South Carolina and had discovered how determined he was to refuse all of the Directory's unreasonable demands.

Marshall was by no means in the Directory's good graces, however, particularly after he wrote a brilliant and persuasive memorial defending the policy of American neutrality. In the course of the letter Marshall, and the other envoys by association, attacked France

27. Marshall to Pinckney, Tuesday evening [n.d.], Pinckney Papers, S.C. Hist. Soc.; Mrs. Pinckney to Mrs. Gabriel Manigault, Mar. 9, 1798, Manigault Family Papers, S. Caroliniana Lib.

28. Envoys to Secretary of State, Dec. 24, 1797, *Amer. State Papers, Class I*, II, 166. In a letter to Edward Rutledge, Jan. 25, 1798, John Rutledge Papers, Southern Historical Collection, University of North Carolina, Chapel Hill, N. C., Pinckney stated that he was ready to leave "deux fois vingt heures should we be ordered, and I hope in a fortnight if the same indignant conduct is still continued to us."

29. Gerry to John Adams, July 5, 1799, in Letter-Book of Elbridge Gerry, 1797–1801, Lib. Cong. (A reproduction from photostats in the New York Public Library.)

for unilaterally renouncing certain articles in the Treaty of Commerce of 1778 and defended the United States against French charges that the United States had virtually repudiated the Franco-American political alliance by signing the Jay Treaty with Great Britain. After procrastinating and agonizing for days, Gerry finally signed the memorial, called by Marshall's biographer "one of the ablest state papers ever produced by American diplomacy."[30]

It was also perhaps one of the longest papers of its kind. It is doubtful that either Talleyrand or the busy members of the Directory gave it more than a cursory reading. At least their attitude and tactics toward the American envoys and the nation they represented did not change. Even as Marshall was revising the memorial, the Directory published a new decree designed to strike at neutral shipping. A ship's cargo, the decree of January 18 stated, would now determine if a ship was to be treated as a neutral vessel, not the flag that it flew. Anything of English origin on board—goods, equipment, clothing—would subject the ship to seizure.

Pinckney and Marshall were dismayed by this new evidence of French hostility, and Gerry was alarmed. Pinckney watched with growing scorn Gerry's sensitivity both to the Directory's bullying tactics and to the flattering courtesies that he was receiving from Talleyrand and American "Jacobins" in Paris. There was reason to fear, Pinckney believed, that Gerry would make private promises to arrange the *douceur* or to negotiate a loan. When Pinckney learned that Gerry intended to have another private conversation with Talleyrand early in February 1798, he sent a note to Gerry's apartment stating that he still believed "a prompt, immediate, and decisive negative should be given to any proposition that may be made, or insinuation given to obtain money from us in any shape or under any pretence."[31]

Gerry was beginning to see new light on the loan question, however, particularly after Talleyrand helpfully analyzed the state department's instructions for him.[32] Talleyrand convinced Gerry that

30. Envoys to Minister of Foreign Affairs, Jan. 17, 1797 [transmitted the 31st], *Amer. State Papers, Class I*, II, 169–82; Beveridge, *Marshall*, II, 297.

31. Pinckney to Gerry, Feb. 2, 1798, Pinckney Family Papers, Lib. Cong. The decree is in *Amer. State Papers, Class I*, II, 182.

32. Talleyrand also doubtless prompted Nathaniel Cutting, the American consul at Havre, to address the envoys, begging them to reconsider their atti-

Pickering's instructions actually authorized the envoys to grant France a loan, a point that Gerry had positively denied several times. Talleyrand also persuaded Gerry to keep secret the subjects discussed in their conversations. Pinckney and Marshall were vexed as they saw Gerry flitting importantly from meeting to meeting with Talleyrand and his agents, but they held their tongues. Gerry finally dramatically announced to his colleagues on February 4 that although he could not tell them what he and Talleyrand were discussing, "he was to give an answer tomorrow or the day after, and that upon it probably depended peace or war."[33]

Gerry broke his mysterious silence on February 10. The Directory, Gerry explained, demanded a loan and would certainly order them out of France in twenty-four hours if it were not agreed to. Marshall replied that to promise a loan would destroy American neutrality and besides, that whole subject had been closed many weeks before. Gerry retorted that this was not true. The conversation degenerated to personal asides and, as Marshall remarked, soon became "rather unpleasant."[34]

Relations between the envoys were further strained when Gerry refused to sign a letter to Talleyrand protesting mounting French seizures of American vessels and requesting "in very explicit, at the

---

tudes. Cutting urged that an apology be given for anti-French sentiment in the United States, the United States defer pressing its monetary claims upon France, and "a loan of effective money" be made to France. Cutting reiterated Talleyrand's point that a loan would be cheaper than a war with France. Cutting to Envoys, Feb. 17, 1798, Gerry Papers, Lib. Cong.

33. Feb. 4, 1798, Marshall Journal, Mass. Hist. Soc. In a letter to his brother, Pinckney complained, "confidential communications and proposals are made to him [Gerry] by Mr. Talleyrand, under injunctions to conceal them from us, and he considers himself as pledged to comply with this request. . . . Money and the direction of American measures I am convinced is their object. To obtain these ends, they mean to exert themselves to keep up their party in America; and their attention and offers to Mr. Gerry are upon a supposition, that he belongs to that party. I am in hopes he will be firm; but he does not appear to me to be so decided for demanding our passports as he was before. I however still think he will act properly." Feb. 22, 1798, Pickering Papers, Mass. Hist. Soc.

34. Feb. 5, 10, 1798, Marshall Journal, Mass. Hist. Soc.; also Nov. 28, 1797, for an earlier suggestion of Mr. Pitcairn, an American living in Paris, that the American government purchase 32,000,000 Dutch florins from France at 20 shillings to the pound, twice their market value. Talleyrand's agents were certain the American government would not suffer by this "loan" to France, for the Dutch would doubtless redeem their florins at par when the war ended.

NOT A SIXPENCE 179

same time very respectful terms, our passports." Unknown to Pinckney and Marshall, Talleyrand had already decided to expel them and to persuade Gerry, whose "known attachment to France and conciliatory disposition," as he put it, would speed the negotiations, to remain.[35]

Gerry's urgent pleas to Pinckney and Marshall went unheeded. Pinckney repeatedly reminded Gerry that even if the loan were not made until the war was over, the French government could borrow immediately upon that promise and that any loan would therefore violate American neutrality and might possibly involve the United States in a war with England. Marshall added that he believed the government of France was pressing for a loan primarily in order to prolong the negotiations. Meantime, French ships rapaciously preyed upon American commerce. America would be better off in open warfare with France and the Directory knew it. Gerry became exasperated and retorted that Marshall was allowing his anti-French bias to warp his judgment.[36]

Marshall decided to see Talleyrand himself and hear from Talleyrand's own lips that there would be a war if a loan were not promised. Talleyrand haughtily told Marshall that he and Pinckney refused the loan because they "were English in [their] hearts" and because they were lackeys of the Adams administration which was also "entirely English."[37] When Marshall reported his conversation to Pinckney, adding that Talleyrand was threatening war, the envoys decided to hold a conference the next day to discuss the loan question once more.

Pinckney and Marshall then repeated why the loan could not be granted: their instructions specifically stated that no loan was to be made to France during the war and that to advance a loan would be to abandon neutrality, the cornerstone of American foreign policy. Gerry declared himself willing to chance the wrath of England, swearing that he would take no responsibility for a Franco-American war if a loan were refused, and argued that the clause in their instructions prohibiting a loan during the war implied that a loan could be

35. Feb. 18, 1798, *ibid.*; Pinckney to Rufus King, Feb. 18, 1798, Rufus King Papers, Huntington Lib.; Mémoire of Talleyrand, Feb. 15, 1798, quoted in Morison, "Elbridge Gerry," *New Eng. Qtly.*, 2 (1929), 25.
36. Feb. 26, 1798, Marshall Journal, Mass. Hist. Soc.
37. *Ibid.*

stipulated for the postwar period. Reaching no agreement, the envoys decided to seek an interview with Talleyrand and at that time allow him to mention first the absolute necessity of a loan as the price of peace. Pinckney, Marshall recorded in his journal, "desired it might be remembered that he protested against any treaty for a loan in any form. . . ."[38]

The day before the appointment with Talleyrand, Pinckney indignantly confronted Gerry with information that he had just received. It was true, was it not, Pinckney asked Gerry, that Talleyrand planned to keep Gerry in Paris and to send the other envoys home? Gerry was trapped and admitted that it was true. Pinckney retorted that "he knew it was true," for it came to him "through a channel he could not doubt."[39] Any confidence that Pinckney and Marshall might still have had in Gerry was now destroyed. Their colleague, who had been warned by President Adams to avoid divisions among the delegation like quicksand, had not only negotiated in secret but had virtually consented to their expulsion by his silence.

No new ground was covered in the interview with Talleyrand on March 2. The success or failure of the negotiations now seemed to depend upon the loan, while two months earlier it had been the *douceur*. Perhaps the difference was academic since either fund would be siphoned off into the Directory's hands. In order to break the deadlock, Gerry proposed to Marshall that the envoys write a letter to the Directory apologizing for statements made by Presidents Washington and Adams that had been offensive to France. Admit that their complaints "had been founded in mistake," Gerry urged, and the Directory might be more reasonable on the other issues that must be resolved. Marshall warmly replied that he was not convinced American policy or the statements of the presidents had been "founded in mistake" and would not say that they were. Exasperated, Gerry told Marshall "that he wished to God" Marshall "would propose something which was accommodating."[40]

When Talleyrand next saw them, he again suggested that the loan

38. Feb. 27, 1798, *ibid.*; Pinckney to Thomas Pinckney, Mar. 13, 1798, Pickering Papers, Mass. Hist. Soc.
39. Mar. 1, 1798, Marshall Journal, Mass. Hist. Soc.
40. Envoys to Secretary of State, Mar. 2, 1798, *Amer. State Papers, Class I*, II, 186; Mar. 6, 1798, Marshall Journal, Mass. Hist. Soc.

was the crucial issue. By making this rather than the bribe the *sine qua non* of any treaty, Talleyrand shrewdly widened the serious split among the envoys. Before the interview had ended, Gerry and Marshall offered to return to Philadelphia for new instructions, but Talleyrand showed no enthusiasm for this plan.[41] Talleyrand knew that nothing was to be gotten from Pinckney during his colleagues' absence. The angry South Carolinian would gladly have ended this diplomatic farce weeks before if he had been able to overcome Gerry's obstinate persistence.

Talleyrand now began to apply pressure to Pinckney and Marshall to leave France voluntarily and to allow their colleague Gerry to remain, because his "opinions, presumed to be more impartial, promise, in the course of the explanations, more of that reciprocal confidence which is indispensable." Talleyrand sent Pierre Beaumarchais, the noted French playwright, to impress Marshall with the distaste of the Directory for him and for Pinckney. They were considered by the Directory, Beaumarchais emphasized, "as being sold to the English." Beaumarchais hinted that unless Marshall cooperated with the wishes of the Directory, he would find himself with many powerful political enemies when he returned home.[42]

Marshall not only defended himself against the charge of being "sold to the English" but even tried to persuade Dutrimond, another agent of Talleyrand, that Pinckney should be acceptable to the Directory. When Dutrimond countered that it was Pinckney who was particularly offensive to the Directory, Marshall pointed out that while Pinckney "was a man of honor in whom his own government could confide, his politics had been of a complexion which ought to render him acceptable to France." Dutrimond remained unconvinced and warned Marshall that unless he and Pinckney

41. Envoys to Secretary of State, *Amer. State Papers, Class I*, II, 186; Mar. 6, 1798, Marshall Journal, Mass. Hist. Soc.

42. Talleyrand to Pinckney, Marshall, and Gerry, Mar. 18, 1798, *Amer. State Papers, Class I*, II, 191; Mar. 14, 1798, Marshall Journal, Mass. Hist. Soc. Beaumarchais, author of *The Barber of Seville* and the *Marriage of Figaro*, had played a significant part in securing aid for the rebellious American colonies. See Elizabeth S. Kite, *Beaumarchais and the War of American Independence*, 2 vols. (Boston, 1918). Beaumarchais was a logical person to approach Marshall, since Marshall was his attorney in a suit against the state of Virginia to recover a debt for supplies furnished the states during the Revolution. Beveridge, *Marshall*, II, 292*n*.

showed some willingness to accommodate the Directory, they would be expelled from France at the end of three days.[43]

When Marshall asked Gerry what he planned to do if his colleagues were expelled, Gerry replied that he would remain in Paris to prevent war, although he had vowed on March 20 and 21 that he "would certainly not stay" in Paris if his colleagues were ordered home.[44] Talleyrand surely had found one of Gerry's weaknesses—a genuine dread of war. Having seen how France had disposed of her enemies in Europe, Gerry could envision from Talleyrand's suggestions the coasts of New England in flames, soldiers in battle, and perhaps ultimately the triumph of militant Federalism.

Pinckney and Marshall began to pack their trunks. Eliza Pinckney, however, had become "most dangerously ill with a fever" and was not physically able to begin the long voyage to the United States.[45] Pinckney therefore requested the Directory to permit him and his family to remain in southern France until Eliza was well enough to travel.

As Pinckney awaited the decision of the Directory, he learned from Marshall that Talleyrand had advised Marshall not to return home by way of England. If he did, Talleyrand warned, every perceptive man would believe that Marshall had stopped to collect his well-deserved wages for disrupting Franco-American relations.[46] If Pinckney and Marshall thought Talleyrand's remark amusing, they saw nothing humorous in Gerry's determination to remain in Paris. They knew that by staying in Paris, Gerry might make them appear precipitate and eager for hostilities with France.

Gerry realized that his colleagues considered him naïve, if not a

43. Mar. 23, 1798, Marshall Journal, Mass. Hist. Soc. The Directory publicly accused Pinckney of having meddled in two previous general elections, the first time to aid Royalists running for office, the second to help anarchists. Pinckney denied the charge. William Vans Murray to John Quincy Adams, Apr. 13, 1798, Ford, ed., *Writings of John Quincy Adams*, II, 274n.

44. Mar. 20, 21, 26, 1798, Marshall Journal, Mass. Hist. Soc. Gerry evidently decided to stay in Paris between the 23rd and 26th, for on the 23rd Pinckney informed Murray that the envoys had determined not to negotiate separately with the Directory. Pinckney to William Vans Murray, Mar. 23, 1798, Pinckney Family Papers, Lib. Cong.

45. Pinckney to John Luzac, Apr. 6, 1798, Rufus King Papers, Huntington Lib.; Pinckney to Minister of Foreign Relations, Apr. 13, 1798, Vol. 49, Part V, U.S. Pol. Corr., Fr. Archives.

46. Mar. 29, 1798, Marshall Journal, Mass. Hist. Soc.

physical coward and—to use a favorite word of the day—a "dis-organizer" as well. But Gerry felt himself the injured party. To his wife he complained that his colleagues' "conduct to me has not been of that frank and friendly description which I expected."[47] When Gerry met with his fellow envoys on April 3 he found just how angry Pinckney had become with him. Pinckney, always frank, told Gerry that his decision to stay in Paris would embarrass his government and add to the danger of war. The indignation of patriotic Americans with Gerry for remaining under threats of the Directory would only increase friction between France and America. Pinckney made it plain that he believed Gerry had become a Gallican monkey, dancing to the tune of the Marseillaise rather than Yankee Doodle.

Gerry retorted that Pinckney and Marshall held personal grudges against him and had "views and objects [in the mission] which were not candidly communicated to him." Pinckney exploded at this veiled charge of deceitfulness and of playing party politics, crying "it is false sir" and in turn accusing Gerry of concealing information from them. Gerry foolishly challenged him to support this statement with one fact. Pinckney reminded Gerry of his "long and repeated conversations with Mr. Talleyrand and his agents on the subjects of our country, which were jointly entrusted to us, and which . . . [were] concealed from us." Gerry replied that he had promised Talleyrand to keep their conversations secret. This was exactly what he should not have done, Pinckney answered, for he had also been approached secretly but had refused to play the French game.

Pinckney, who was thoroughly aroused now, accused Gerry of duplicity and indecision, challenging him "to produce a single act on his [Pinckney's] part, which was not perfectly open and candid. . . ." Gerry evaded this challenge, instead asserting that Pinckney and Marshall were angry only because they had been slighted socially by Talleyrand, but he wished them to remember that he had first visited Talleyrand at their suggestion. That was untrue, Pinckney answered, a statement utterly without foundation. Gerry ended this tempestuous meeting on a conciliatory note by professing his respect and fondness for Pinckney "which he said could alone have prevailed on

47. Gerry to Mrs. Gerry, Mar. 26, 1798, p. 57, Elbridge Gerry Letter-Book, Lib. Cong.

him to have accepted the mission."[48] Pinckney made no such professions of good will. He later wrote to Rufus King that he had "never met with a man of less candor and so much duplicity as Mr. Gerry."[49]

This was evidently the last joint meeting of the envoys. There was really very little left to be said. Gerry, who William Vans Murray believed was being used as "an innocent baby-engine" against his government, felt that the burden of war or peace rested upon his slight shoulders; and he refused to lose the peace by appeasing his colleagues.[50] If Gerry was mistaken in his assumptions, his courage must be admired. He realized that he would face ridicule in the United States, but he was willing to risk his reputation for the cause of peace.

Marshall was ready to leave France forever, confirmed in his earlier belief that the French Revolution had betrayed the cause of republicanism. Of course he had enjoyed Paris and its many delights. To Fulwar Skipwith in Paris, Marshall wrote from Bordeaux asking that Skipwith present to Madame de Villette "everything which respectful friendship can dictate." And "when you have done," Marshall added, "you will have rendered not quite half justice to my sentiments."[51] On the same day Marshall penned a final and humorous note to Pinckney saying that he was happy to "bid I believe an eternal adieu to Europe (I wish to add) and to its crimes.—Mark I only mean its political crimes, for those of a private nature are really some of those so lovely that it required men of as much virtue and less good temper than you and myself to hate them." Marshall added that he was returning on the ship *Alexander Hamilton* which was "(a very excellent vessel but for the sin of the name which makes my return

48. Apr. 3, 1798, Marshall Journal, Mass. Hist. Soc.
49. Pinckney to King, Apr. 4, 1798, Ford, ed., *Writings of John Quincy Adams*, II, 277. Mary Pinckney reflected her husband's attitude. To Mrs. Gabriel Manigault she wrote: "Mr. Gerry they keep—He has been false to his colleagues, and wanting to his country. If he is not lost to all sense of feeling his duplicity must have planted a thorn in his breast, whilch the other gentlemen have a full reliance on the justice and approbation of their country," Apr. 15, 1798, Manigault Family Papers, S. Caroliniana Lib.
50. William Vans Murray to John Quincy Adams, June 8, 1798, Ford, ed., "Letters of William Vans Murray," Amer. Hist. Assoc., *Annual Report* (1912), 416.
51. Marshall to Skipwith, Apr. 21, 1798, Dreer Coll., American Lawyers, Hist. Soc. of Pa.

in her almost as criminal as if I had taken England in my way)...."[52]

Pinckney was also only too glad to leave Paris. He had not really wanted to join the second mission, suspecting the way he and his country would once again be treated. When his fears had been confirmed almost immediately upon his arrival in Paris, he was ready to curse France and take the consequences.[53] On April 15 Pinckney finally received his passports and permission to remain in southern France. He and his family left Paris within four days.[54]

While the Pinckneys were traveling the road to Lyons, politics were reaching the boiling point in the United States. On March 4, 1798, the administration had received dispatches and documents from the envoys in France that related the unsuccessful course of their negotiations. Although Adams did not reveal the contents of these documents, he nevertheless requested Congress in mid-March to adopt measures "for the protection of our seafaring and commercial citizens, for the defense of any exposed portions of our territory, for replenishing our arsenals, establishing founderies and military manufactories" and for revising the tax laws to provide needed additional revenue.[55]

Administration leaders found that Republicans, who controlled the House of Representatives, sat on their hands despite Adams'

52. Marshall to Pinckney, Apr. 21, 1798, Pinckney Family Papers, Lib. Cong. Marshall, while enjoying the freedom of Paris social life, was nevertheless shocked at a party when a "buffoon" imitated the sounds of a woman in childbirth, the cries of a newly born child, and "the noise of administering *un remede.*" Mary Pinckney to Mrs. Gabriel Manigault, Apr. 27, 1798, Manigault Family Papers, S. Caroliniana Lib.

53. Henry Rutledge, Pinckney's secretary, left Paris in the same provoked mood as his Uncle Pinckney. After a short tour in England, Rutledge wrote William Vans Murray that "Exercise and air have quite restored me, and I am now quite ready to fight the French." As for Gerry, Rutledge predicted that "Wherever he may direct his steps, disgrace and confusion will ever attend him." Rutledge to Murray, July 19, 1798, Gratz Coll., Hist. Soc. of Pa.

54. Mary Pinckney to Mrs. Gabriel Manigault, Apr. 15, 1798, Manigault Family Papers, S. Caroliniana Lib.; William Vans Murray to John Quincy Adams, Apr. 24, 1798, Ford, ed., "Letters of William Vans Murray," Amer. Hist. Assoc., *Annual Report* (1912), 399. Pinckney mentions Apr. 19 as the day he left Paris in his report to Pickering on the amount owed him for the two diplomatic missions. Pinckney's total expenses came to $28,875.93; his salary was $9,000 per annum. This report is in the Pinckney Family Papers, Lib. Cong.

55. Adams, ed., *Works of John Adams,* IX, 157.

urgent message. The administration hesitated to release the correspondence because of the possibility that the Directory would retaliate by harming the envoys; no one had yet forgotten the bloody days of the guillotine. There was also a feeling that publication of the correspondence would unnecessarily anger the Directory and make all attempts at further negotiation useless. Adams did not want to provoke war, even though he thought it likely to come.[56]

Thomas Jefferson, who found it difficult to believe that France would declare war on the United States, referred to Adams' resolute message of March 19 as "insane." Jefferson was convinced that Adams was willfully leading the nation into war by whipping up war hysteria. Other Republican leaders believed that Adams was at least overly belligerent. They demanded therefore to see the correspondence of the envoys. Most Republicans were certain that Adams was concealing it because it revealed the pacific temper of France. On March 30, William Branch Giles, a Republican congressman from Virginia, asked the President to release the correspondence, and three days later the House of Representatives officially made the request.[57]

When informed Federalists saw the eagerness of Republicans to read the correspondence, they joined with Republicans in asking for the documents. If Republicans wanted to commit suicide, they reasoned, Federalists were at least obliged to offer a helping hand. Adams almost immediately complied with Congress' request. Federalists were jubilant as they pored over the documents and read of the perfidy of Talleyrand and his three chief agents, X, Y, and Z. The hostility of France toward the United States seemed beyond doubt, and Federalists did not hesitate to capitalize politically on the situation. They denounced Republicans as the dupes of a monstrous military tyranny that was ready to crush any nation not completely subservient to it. Secretary of State Pickering joyfully informed John Jay that the Republicans were "thunderstruck" by the turn of events.[58]

56. Samuel E. Morison, *The Life and Letters of Harrison Gray Otis, Federalist, 1765–1848*, 2 vols. (Boston, 1913), I, 80–81; DeConde, *Quasi-War*, 68–69.

57. Dumas Malone, *Jefferson and His Time*, 3 vols. (Boston, 1948–60), III, 369–71; Dice R. Anderson, *William Branch Giles* . . . (Menasha, Wis., 1914), 59; Page Smith, *John Adams*, 2 vols. (Garden City, N.Y., 1962), II, 956–59; Kurtz, *Presidency of John Adams*, 298–99.

58. Pickering to Jay, Apr. 9, 1798, in Henry P. Johnston, ed., *The Correspondence and Public Papers of John Jay*, 4 vols. (N.Y., 1890–93), IV, 236. To

Federalists rushed the XYZ correspondence to the presses, publishing ten thousand copies. Eighteen hundred were distributed in Jefferson's Virginia alone. Federalists now shrewdly equated treason with the Republican party. The country went on a patriotic spree that was unprecedented in its short history, and Adams, who had only dreamed of such popularity, became the symbol of national dignity and independence. At banquets, in personal letters, and public addresses, he was praised for his wisdom and determination in the face of a powerful and hostile enemy. One New England minister praised God "that in the greatness of his goodness he has made our enemies instrumental in uniting the good people of these states. . . ."[59]

Despite this political windfall, ardent Federalists still had some cause for concern. Gerry was in Paris threatening America with peace. It was Pickering's prayer—hopefully an unusual one for a Secretary of State—that when the Directory learned the XYZ correspondence had been published, "it would then guillotine Mr. Gerry" and thereby "do a favor to this country. . . ." If Gerry forwarded news of peace, the opportunity to castigate and ruin the Republican party might slip from Federalist hands. It was only in an atmosphere of pending crisis that many Federalists believed they could lessen the influence of the Republicans.[60]

When John Marshall reached Philadelphia in mid-June, he was overwhelmed by the reception Federalists gave him. Enthusiastic congressmen rode out to meet him in their carriages. As he entered Philadelphia, church bells rang and cannon boomed. Never had an unsuccessful American minister received such a rousing welcome.

George Washington, Pickering wrote that "out of doors the French Devotees are rapidly quitting the worship of their idol," doubtless the "most corrupt government upon earth," Apr. 14, 1798, Pickering Papers, Mass. Hist. Soc.

59. Beveridge, *Marshall*, II, 477–78; Kurtz, *Presidency of John Adams*, 299–301; Rev. John Murray to John Adams, June 19, 1798, Morison, *Life of Otis*, I, 184n.

60. Pickering to Rufus King, June 12, 1798, Charles R. King, ed., *The Life and Correspondence of Rufus King*, 6 vols. (N.Y., 1894–1900), II, 347; Stephen Higginson to Oliver Wolcott, July 11, 1798, in Gibbs, *Administrations of Washington and Adams*, II, 71. As Wolcott put it: "If we pause now, the faction [Jeffersonians] will revive, and all the avenues for French poison and intrigue be again opened. . . . Nothing but an open war can save us, and the more inveterate and deadly it shall be, the better will be our chance for security in future." Fisher Ames agreed on the necessity of a war program: "My long letter amounts to this: we must make haste to *wage war*, or we shall be lost." Ames to Timothy Pickering, July 10, 1798, in Seth Ames, ed., *Works of Fisher Ames*, 2 vols. (N.Y., 1869), I, 234.

Ralph Izard of Charleston hoped that the enthusiasm would not wane before his friend Pinckney arrived.[61]

Pinckney of course had became a hero to Federalists throughout the country and was toasted at banquets in the same breath as Marshall and Adams. One observer believed that no "two men . . . can be more beloved and honored than Pinckney and Marshall."[62] It was unfortunate that Pinckney was unable to enjoy the highlight—in terms of popularity—of his political career. But his timing (or luck) had usually been poor.

While he was being feted in America, Pinckney, unaware of his new popularity, was in the city of Lyons. Arriving there about May 1, the Pinckneys were prevented from proceeding immediately to Bordeaux because Eliza was still very sick.[63] Their activities were therefore restricted, and they were without news from their friends in the Batavian Republic or the United States. Mrs. Pinckney complained that they led a "melancholy" life in Lyons, "unknowing and unknown." On May 24, Pinckney received the anticipated message from Secretary Pickering directing the envoys to return to the United States. In reporting this good news to Henry Rutledge, Pinckney noted that the messenger who had brought him Adams' notification of recall had first seen Gerry, "but Mr. G did not write to me." Pinckney believed "Mr: G's fears will get the better of his vanity, and he says (I am told) he will go [home]."[64]

With his recall in hand, Pinckney was anxious to proceed at once for Bordeaux, but he refused to leave Lyons before Eliza's fever was gone and she was strong enough to travel. He had already lost one child and did not want to experience that heartbreak again. By the latter part of June, Pinckney was convinced that Eliza could survive

61. Beveridge, *Marshall*, II, 344; Izard to Jacob Read, July [?], 1798, Ralph Izard Papers, S. Caroliniana Lib.

62. Robert Troup to Rufus King, July 10, 1798, in King, *Life of Rufus King*, II, 363.

63. Pinckney to Henry M. Rutledge, May 26, 1798, Dreer Coll., Hist. Soc. of Pa.

64. Mary Pinckney to Mrs. Gabriel Manigault, Apr. 27, May 28, 1798, Manigault Family Papers, S. Caroliniana Lib.; William Vans Murray to John Quincy Adams, June 8, 1798, in Ford, ed., "Letters of William Vans Murray," Amer. Hist. Assoc., *Annual Report* (1912), 416; Pinckney to Henry Rutledge, May 26, 1798, Dreer Coll., Hist. Soc. of Pa.

the rigors of a two-week carriage trip to Bordeaux; the Pinckneys left Lyons about June 20.[65]

On July 8 the Pinckneys arrived in Bordeaux. Only twenty months before, they had sailed up the Garonne River and anchored at Bordeaux. It must have seemed longer than that. Not only had Pinckney's missions been unsuccessful, but he and his family had been ostracized socially. Pinckney had been personally insulted, denounced as the pensioner of England, a power he had distrusted for years, and expelled from France under the threat of imprisonment. His country's commerce had been plundered, its citizens imprisoned, and its government calumniated. His Republican colleague Gerry had played the French game and deceived him and Marshall. Altogether, Pinckney's experiences had been enough to make him despise France and distrust Republicans who were seemingly blind to the rapacious conduct of France. Politically, Pinckney was now a far different man from the one who had sailed into Bordeaux in mid-November 1796.

The Pinckneys' plans to leave Bordeaux at once were changed when the French government unexpectedly laid a special embargo upon all American ships in French ports. Pinckney immediately wrote to Talleyrand and the minister of marine asking their assistance in booking passage home. While he waited for their replies, Pinckney visited the prisons of Bordeaux in order to compile a list of United States sailors being detained. Pinckney was horrified and angry when he discovered the treatment American sailors were receiving while in prison; he not only applied for their release but lodged a complaint through the American consulate about the "putrid and maggotty" food being served them and the lack of medical care for those in desperate need of it.

In writing to Secretary Pickering about these almost forgotten Americans, Pinckney added that he had heard Talleyrand was now in a more amicable mood. If this were true, Pinckney noted, it "can be only imputed to the spirit of unanimity which prevails, and to the preparations which are made and are making in America; but I shall think they are intended only to amuse us, till they are in a state of better preparation to attack us than they are at present, or as an

65. Pinckney to Minister of Foreign Affairs of the French Republic, July 11, 1798, Vol. 50, Part I, U.S. Pol. Corr., Fr. Archives.

insidious attempt again to divide us. . . ." Pinckney assured Pickering that a "spirit of determination and a state of actual preparation for war are the only measures to obtain an honourable peace and secure our independence."[66]

Talleyrand indicated to Pinckney that the Directory's attitude toward the United States was changing. In reply to Pinckney's inquiry about passage home, Talleyrand sent him a "polite letter" recommending that he take passage on the *Benjamin Franklin*. Pinckney was only too willing to comply until he discovered that the ship was already overly full. Eliza's health might be injured, he wrote Talleyrand, by sailing on a ship that was overcrowded. Therefore he would wait for another ship.[67]

Before he discovered an available ship, Pinckney made arrangements to help Americans stranded in Bordeaux. Pinckney authorized David Steinmetz, formerly of Philadelphia, to lend money to needy Americans, assuring Steinmetz that if his records were well kept and in order, he would be reimbursed and with interest by the United States government.[68]

This was probably Pinckney's last official act in France. By August 5 he was on board a Prussian ship, *The Hope of Emden*, which evidently sailed on the seventh, one day before Elbridge Gerry left Paris.[69] Pinckney and Gerry were returning to very different receptions, however. It was the warrior Pinckney, not the peacemaker Gerry, that Federalists were anxious to honor.

As the Pinckneys began their two-month voyage to America, they probably did not know the extent of military preparations in the United States or that Pinckney would be offered the position of major general in the army. Neither could Pinckney have known of the com-

66. Pinckney to Timothy Pickering, July 26, 1798, Pinckney Family Papers, Lib. Cong.; Pinckney to the Minister of Foreign Affairs of the French Republic, Aug. 3, 1798, Vol. 50, Part I, U.S. Pol. Corr., Fr. Archives; Pinckney to Rufus King, Aug. 5, 1798, Rufus King Papers, Huntington Lib.

67. Pinckney to Pickering, July 26, 1798, Pinckney to Minister of Foreign Affairs, July 31, 1798, Pinckney Family Papers, Lib. Cong.

68. Pinckney to Steinmetz, Aug. 3, 1798, Steinmetz to Pinckney, Aug. 8, 1798, *ibid.*

69. William Vans Murray to Timothy Pickering, Aug. 23, 1798, in Ford, ed., "Letters of William Vans Murray," Amer. Hist. Assoc., *Annual Report* (1912), 459; Morison, "Elbridge Gerry," *New Eng. Qtly.*, 2 (1929), 28.

plicated intrigue within the Adams administration that determined who the general officers would be. While Pinckney was resting in southern France and preparing to return home, John Adams was undergoing one of the most trying experiences of his exceedingly trying presidency.

Aroused by news of possible hostilities with France, Congress voted in May and June of 1798 to enlist a ten-thousand-man "Additional Army" for the duration of the crisis with France. This measure was followed in July by a law providing that twelve additional regiments of infantry and six troops of light dragoons be called if the crisis evolved into full-scale war. Adams' problems with the army began when Alexander Hamilton decided to seek the commanding position. Hamilton had long dreamed of winning military glory; he would gladly have been a New World Napoleon. Moreover, Hamilton saw that if France took the initiative and declared war on the United States, the American people would not only unite in fighting France but might also immunize themselves against the disease of "jacobinism." Hamilton naturally wished to share in any program that might weaken or destroy opposition to the Federalist program.[70]

Encouraged by his friends in the cabinet, Hamilton began to hope that he would be appointed commander in chief of the army. President Adams found such a thought revolting. When Adams asked Timothy Pickering who should receive the highest post in the army and Pickering replied "Colonel Hamilton," Adams reacted with shocked surprise. "Oh no," Adams exclaimed, "it is not his turn by a great deal. I would sooner appoint Gates, or Lincoln, or Morgan." Pickering protested that Morgan had a "broken constitution," Gates was an "old woman," and Lincoln was "always asleep," but Adams abruptly ended the conversation.[71]

Adams acted quickly to end Hamilton's intrigue for first place by appointing George Washington as commander in chief early in July

70. William A. Ganoe, *The History of the United States Army* (N.Y., 1928), 104–05; Miller, *Hamilton*, 468–70. The measures taken in preparation for war are described in DeConde, *Quasi-War*, 90–96, 101–02; Carlos E. Godfrey, "Organization of the Provisional Army of the United States in the Anticipated War with France, 1798–1800," *Pennsylvania Magazine of History and Biography*, 38 (1914), 129–32.

71. Miller, *Hamilton*, 475; Pickering to George Washington, Sept. 13, 1798, George Washington Papers, Lib. Cong.

1798. Since Washington stipulated that he would take the field only if the army clearly needed him, it became doubly important that the general officers be chosen with great care. As he had so often during his days as president, Washington turned to Hamilton for assistance, asking Hamilton if he would be willing to enter military service once again. Hamilton, determined to avoid any mere desk job, replied that indeed he would if he were "invited to *a station in which the service I may render may be proportionate to the sacrifice I am to make.*" Hamilton suggested that he would be "most useful" as inspector-general, the officer second in command.[72]

Washington was willing that Hamilton be appointed inspector-general, but he realized that political considerations as well as military ability must be weighed before appointing the second in command. On the same day that Washington received his official notification from Adams, he wrote to Pickering that several conditions seemed to suggest that Charles Cotesworth Pinckney should be given the post of inspector-general. If the French attacked, they would surely do so first in the south. The Negroes that could be armed and the known attachment of many southerners for France would almost force France to establish a beachhead in the south. Since this was true, it would follow that a man who knew the southern regions and who had powerful political support there should be the second in command of the army. Also, to place Colonel Hamilton over General Pinckney, Washington believed, would surely offend Pinckney's friends. "Disgust would follow," Washington added, "and its influence would spread where most to be deprecated, as his connections are numerous, powerful and more influential than any other in the three Southern States." Besides, Washington asserted that Pinckney was "an officer of high military reputation; fond of the Profession, spirited, active, and judicious. . . ."[73] The fact that Washington did *not* know all these things to be true suggests how anxious he was to name Pinckney inspector-general.

James McHenry, who carried Washington's commission to him on July 11, evidently persuaded him that he should reconsider the claims

---

72. Carroll and Ashworth, *George Washington*, VII, 519–21; Hamilton to Washington, June 2, 1798, in Lodge, ed., *Works of Hamilton*, X, 287.

73. Washington to Pickering, July 11, 1798, in Fitzpatrick, ed., *Writings of Washington*, XXXVI, 324–25.

of Hamilton to second place. Washington hesitated, however, and tossed the responsibility back to Adams. On the list of officers which Washington forwarded to Adams, he recommended that Hamilton be appointed major general, with Pinckney and Henry Knox to follow in that order. Washington also forwarded a duplicate list to Hamilton. From the accompanying letter that Washington sent to Hamilton, it appears that Washington wished Hamilton to withdraw his claims to second in command in favor of Pinckney. All of Pinckney's merits were paraded before Hamilton's eyes. Pinckney was described as a "brave, intelligent and enterprising Officer," one with "numerous and powerful connections. . . . Will he serve then under a junior Officer?" Washington asked.[74]

Hamilton did not take the hint. Instead he returned a vigorous defense of his own qualifications. Although Pinckney did indeed outrank him at the close of the Revolutionary War, Hamilton was certain that his own "military *service*" was far more significant than Pinckney's. "As to civil services since the war," Hamilton continued, "I am extremely mistaken if, in the minds of Federal men, there is any comparison between us. The circumstances of the moment, it is true, give him a certain *éclat*, but judicious men reduce . . . [Pinckney's] merit to the two points of judicious *forebearance* and the *firmness* not to sacrifice his country by base compliances." Hamilton added that he did not mean to "detract from General Pinckney" for he held him "in high estimation." But he felt that when all the circumstances had been considered, Pinckney "ought to be well satisfied" to serve under him.[75]

Hamilton made a convincing case for himself but neglected to counter Washington's argument that Pinckney's political supporters might be lost to the government if Pinckney were asked to serve under Hamilton. President Adams apparently believed that Pinckney's claims were superior to those of Hamilton, whom Adams had once called "a bastard brat of a Scotch peddlar," but Adams also felt that General Henry Knox should outrank them both; "no other arrangement will give satisfaction," Adams warned McHenry. With

---

74. Washington to Hamilton, July 14, 1798, in *ibid.*, 331; Steiner, *Life of James McHenry*, 311–12.

75. Hamilton to Washington, July 29, 1798, in Lodge, ed., *Works of Hamilton*, X, 300–01.

Hamilton as the fourth-ranking general officer, Adams evidently felt that the country need have little fear of Hamilton's vaulting ambition.[76]

Adams was unable to withstand the pressure when Washington sent him a virtual ultimatum that he would resign unless Hamilton were appointed inspector-general. Evidently Hamilton's defense of his claims and the earnest pleas of both Pickering and McHenry for Hamilton's appointment had convinced Washington that he could not deny Hamilton second place. Adams reluctantly capitulated and sadly found that his old friend Henry Knox must be ranked fourth among the general officers.[77]

Yet Adams was not nearly as unhappy as General Knox. In a bitter letter to Washington, Knox complained that he should have been "previously consulted on an arrangement in which my feelings and happiness have been so much wounded." Instead, he had "been dragged forth to public view" as militarily inferior to men his junior in rank, all in a "conspicuously odious" fashion. Knox declined any appointment if he were to be Hamilton's subordinate, declaring that General Pinckney too would not accept an appointment under Colonel Hamilton unless he had "mistaken his character greatly...."[78]

Washington was wounded by Knox's harsh words and apprehensive lest Knox's prediction about Pinckney prove true. As rumors of Pinckney's impending arrival reached Mount Vernon, Washington may well have wondered why he had permitted Hamilton to dissuade him from appointing Pinckney inspector-general. Pinckney would at least have had the confidence of many Republicans as well as Federalists in the south. Washington wrote nervously to Pickering that he had hoped Pinckney would "not play the second part of the difficulty created by General Knox." Other Federalists were equally on edge.[79]

76. Adams to James McHenry, Aug. 14, 1798, in Adams, ed., *Works of John Adams*, VIII, 580.

77. Washington to Adams, Sept. 25, 1798, in Fitzpatrick, ed., *Writings of Washington*, XXXVI, 460–61; Kurtz, *Presidency of John Adams*, 326.

78. Knox to Washington, July 29, 1798, in Fitzpatrick, ed., *Writings of Washington*, XXXVI, 347–48n.

79. Washington to Secretary of State, Oct. 18, 1798, *ibid.*, 334; George Cabot to Rufus King, Oct. 6, 1798, in King, *Life of Rufus King*, II, 439–40; Cabot to Oliver Wolcott, Oct. 6, 1798, in Henry Cabot Lodge, *Life and Letters of George Cabot* (Boston, 1877), 168.

As Pinckney completed the last hours of his journey from Bordeaux, he probably did not know that his reception by many Federalists depended upon his reaction to serving as Hamilton's subordinate rather than upon his late services as minister to France. Indeed, his public career as a national political figure was dependent upon his decision. Federalists waited hopefully, yet with considerable apprehension.

VIII

IN HAMILTON'S SHADOW

—————◆◆◆—————

General Pinckney is set up for President by Hamilton, and tis no more than fair to infer that the late, but few [peace] measures for which the public have applauded Mr. Adams, would be opposed by General Pinckney, and that in fact Hamilton would rule as effectually and fatally as if he himself were President.

—Philadelphia *Aurora*, August 28, 1800.

How has it happened that the men who have advocated all the measures of Mr. Adams, except that of pacification with France, have now fallen over to General Pinckney, behooves his friends to explain . . . [and] it presents the obvious idea, that General Pinckney's new friends have been detached from their first connection, because they have been disappointed in their wishes for a war with the French Republic.

—A Republican [Charles Pinckney], 1800.

—————◆◆◆—————

FEDERALIST HEARTS WERE SOON AGLOW WITH GOOD FEELING FOR CHARLES Cotesworth Pinckney. He quickly agreed to serve under Hamilton, accepting the inferior position with good grace. To James McHenry, Pinckney explained his ready assent: "I knew that his [Hamilton's] talents in war were great, that he is a genius capable of forming an extensive military plan, and a spirit courageous and enterprising, equal to the creation of it." Pinckney therefore sent Henry Rutledge to Hamilton with the word that he "rejoiced" at Hamilton's appointment and "would with pleasure serve under him."[1]

1. Pinckney to McHenry, Oct. 31, 1798, Papers of George Washington, Lib. Cong.

Pickering marveled at Pinckney's generosity. Here was a man with a "high sense of honor, of valuable military acquirements," and, Pickering added, one who "has made the military much his study, and is of great influence in the Southern States, on all which might be founded a claim to an elevated rank." And most astonishing of all, Pinckney even offered to serve under General Knox if it would soothe that gentleman's ruffled feelings. Pickering assured George Cabot that in Pinckney the Federalists had found "truly a patriot and an honest man."[2]

Although Republicans would not have equated willingness to serve under Hamilton with honesty and patriotism, yet most would have agreed that Hamilton's administrative and military abilities were superior to Pinckney's. Since such objectivity toward oneself is unusual among politicians and soldiers, it is easy to understand how Republicans and historians thought Pinckney's cooperative attitude indicated that he was weak-willed and ambitionless.

To interpret Pinckney's willingness to step down in favor of Hamilton as evidence either of weakness or laziness would be to misunderstand both his character and the situation in which he found himself. Pinckney coveted public honors, particularly military ones, but his ambition was usually governed by a high sense of patriotism, almost romantic in nature, which prompted him to place the welfare of the nation above his personal feelings. Hamilton, on the other hand, tended to confuse private ambition and the national interest. Perhaps Pinckney's and Hamilton's contrasting attitudes were formed as a result of different experiences. The doors to recognition, social position, and political power had opened for Pinckney as a matter of course, while Hamilton had advanced politically and socially through hard work and self-improvement. To Hamilton, power and place had always been objectives to fight for, while to Pinckney they had been tools and privileges to use responsibly.

Pinckney's generosity in the matters of rank and place was not unprecedented in his own life. His experiences in Georgia in 1778, when the expedition against East Florida had been plagued by petty differences over rank and command, had left Pinckney with a strong conviction that unanimity was the first consideration in a time of crisis. His generous attitude was clearly seen in 1794 when Andrew

2. Pickering to Cabot, Nov. 6, 1798, in Lodge, *Life of George Cabot*, 177.

Pickens was placed over him in the South Carolina state troops, and in 1797 when Pinckney believed James Madison had been sent to replace him in his mission to France. In each instance Pinckney put aside any twinges of envy or hurt in order to promote the common welfare. Finally, Pinckney no doubt realized that Hamilton had been Washington's choice to be inspector-general. To quarrel over rank might well ruin his friendship with Washington. For this reason alone Pinckney would not have disputed his rank.

Federalists were not concerned with Pinckney's reasons for agreeing to the third position but only with the fact that he had cooperated with Washington and Hamilton. It was feared that if Pinckney refused to serve under Hamilton and complained of being degraded before the nation, it would weaken the Federalist party in the south. With a sense of relief, therefore, the Federalists began to prepare a welcome for Pinckney that would please him and his southern friends.

Federalists in every major town through which Pinckney passed were urged to honor him with banquets and addresses complimenting him on his exemplary conduct while in France. Prominent citizens of Newark, New Jersey, presented an address to Pinckney congratulating him upon the "honorable discharge of the high and important trust confided in him." Pinckney responded that he was pleased to find the citizens of Newark "prepared to meet with firmness and resolution, every possible alternative of disastrous fortune"; he assured them that if they would unite and "act with decision and energy," they would have "nothing to fear from the hostility of France."[3] Going on to Trenton, where an honorary guard of government and military officers met him six miles outside town, Pinckney once again brought the message of preparedness. "*If we would have peace with France,*" he warned, "*it must be obtained, not by negociation, but by the sword.*" "I am convinced," he added, that to secure the independence of America "free from the ambition and intrigues of France, . . . we must fight for its preservation."[4] Pickering and other high Federalists were greatly pleased as they read Pinckney's speeches; truly Pinckney had returned from France, as Pickering had said earlier, "a patriot and an honest man." He was now openly in the Federalist camp.

3. Charleston *City Gazette*, Nov. 3, 1798.
4. Hartford *Connecticut Courant*, Nov. 5, 1798; Phila. *Gazette of the United States*, Nov. 3, 1798. Pinckney arrived in Trenton on Oct. 29.

Pinckney had been requested by Secretary of War McHenry to visit Philadelphia on his way to South Carolina, in order to discuss "some points" related to Pinckney's new military position. By the end of October, McHenry had decided that it would be wise to hold a joint conference that included Washington, Hamilton, Pinckney, and himself to decide upon appointments and strategy. Pinckney left Trenton for Philadelphia, stopping in Bristol for the evening. There he was embarrassed to find himself in the same tavern with Dr. George Logan, a Philadelphia physician who had taken it upon himself to preserve peace between France and the United States. Logan had quietly slipped out of Philadelphia in June and had boarded a ship for Europe. Federalists were enraged as they learned how Logan boldly made his way into Paris (about the time Gerry was leaving) and hobnobbed with Talleyrand and Merlin. And their anger knew no bounds when Logan began to write letters to his American friends describing the friendly disposition of France. Federalists denounced Logan as a "propagandist of sedition and philosophy," a "plaster of Paris propagandist" more worthy of hanging and public degradation than any man in the United States save Jefferson.[5]

Logan was on his way to Philadelphia with his unwanted assurances of peace when he met Pinckney, an apostle of preparedness. Pinckney was friendly to Logan, remembering Logan's kindness to him during the Revolutionary War when he, Thomas, and Edward Rutledge and their families had been exiled to Philadelphia. Pinckney ate breakfast with Logan to the background of murmurs and comments from surprised onlookers. Dr. Logan even offered Pinckney a seat in his carriage to Philadelphia. Naturally Pinckney declined.[6] The Federalist *Gazette of the United States* raged at the "effrontry" of Logan, "the late *illegitimate, spurious,* or *bastard* ENVOY to the French Republic," offering "the *General* a seat in HIS carriage."[7]

Pinckney was greeted in Philadelphia by an editorial from the Republican *Aurora* that must have angered him deeply. The *Aurora* deplored his belligerent speeches, assuring him that "peevish resentment" and "*hurt feelings*" were not cause enough for him to whip up a war spirit. After all, the *Aurora* shrewdly continued, the

5. Tolles, *George Logan*, 156–70.
6. *Ibid.*, 174–75.
7. Nov. 22, 1798.

"American *honor* is not a punctilio of chivalry" and for him to vent his private resentments by trying to promote a needless war only proved that he had become "an engine of party. . . ."[8]

Pinckney was happy to join Washington and Hamilton in discussions of military strategy and apportionment of responsibility for military districts; the generals also discussed the fittest candidates for officers' positions.[9] After their daily session of five hours, the generals would adjourn to keep their social engagements. Pinckney, Hamilton, and Washington dined together at least once in the home of Governor Thomas Mifflin. There Hamilton entered into a discussion of the political unrest in western Pennsylvania and Virginia, arguing that the situation in Pennsylvania was more serious than it had been during the Whiskey Rebellion in 1794. Now jacobinism was running rampant. Civil disturbances of this nature, Hamilton warned, should be met with crushing force.[10]

President Adams did not wish to use force, either in Pennsylvania or in the dispute with France. The three generals, seated together, heard Adams deliver his message of December 8 to the second session of Congress. Although Adams admitted that nothing was "discoverable in the conduct of France which ought to change or relax our measures of defense," the burden of his message was the need for good will and peace between nations.[11]

Adams' speech made it clear that he would make every effort to obtain an honorable peace, a fact which the three generals probably discussed at their meeting the next day. Perhaps their tedious task of selecting officers for the twelve paper regiments was all in vain. Hamilton, who had already formulated tentative plans for a joint Anglo-American land and naval force to strike at Spanish armies in

8. Nov. 13, 1798.

9. James McHenry to William [L.] Smith, Nov. 30, 1798, William L. Smith Papers, S. Caroliniana Lib. In Pinckney's and Hamilton's hands, in Vol. 293, George Washington Papers, Lib. Cong., are lists of persons who had applied or who had been recommended for various positions in the army. These lists were probably compiled during this meeting at Philadelphia. Two months after this meeting, Pinckney was assigned command of all troops and posts within the states of Virginia, North Carolina, South Carolina, Georgia, Kentucky, and Tennessee. James McHenry to Alexander Hamilton, Feb. 4, 1799, George Washington Papers, Lib. Cong.

10. Carroll and Ashworth, *George Washington*, VII, 553.

11. Richardson, ed., *Messages of the Presidents*, I, 271–75; Carroll and Ashworth, *George Washington*, VII, 554.

Central and South America, must have been depressed by the cold breath of peace.[12]

For Pinckney, the Philadelphia visit produced a welcome reunion with his brother Thomas, who had been elected to the House of Representatives when he had returned from England in 1796. There were also friends from South Carolina in Philadelphia with whom the Pinckneys dined and visited, a marked contrast to their months of social exile in France and the Batavian Republic.

But Pinckney had urgent military duties in the south. If France attacked, it would be in the south, and the first heavy blows would fall upon Pinckney's troops. Washington left Philadelphia for Mount Vernon on December 14, and the Pinckneys followed his route three days later. As the Washingtons and their few guests gathered around the Christmas table, they heard the sound of carriage wheels. The Pinckneys had arrived. After a delightful dinner, the conversation turned to politics with the Pinckneys relating their experiences in republican France. The Pinckneys' description of perfidious and corrupted France fell upon the sympathetic ears of the Washingtons and their guests.[13]

After a brief visit with John Marshall in Richmond, the Pinckneys resumed their journey toward South Carolina. Had things changed in South Carolina, they wondered, as their carriage rolled through the countryside of Virginia and North Carolina. Politically, the South Carolina they had left in 1796 had undergone a marked change. When Pinckney sailed from Charleston it had been a city noted for its friendly feelings toward France. The French cockade was almost a standard item of dress for hundreds of its citizens. True, French seizures of American vessels and the unlawful commissioning of privateers by Edmond Genêt, the French minister, had cooled Charleston's ardor somewhat, but in 1796 both Charleston and the

12. For the details of Hamilton's plan, see Schachner, *Hamilton*, II, 381–82; Hamilton to Rufus King, Aug. 22, 1798, and Hamilton to Francisco de Miranda, Aug. 22, 1798, in Lodge, ed., *Works of Hamilton*, X, 314–16. Pinckney, while still in France, had been informed of Hamilton's scheme by Rufus King. See Kurtz, *Presidency of John Adams*, 318. Pinckney evidently maintained a discreet silence on the plan although he did mention to James McHenry that he thought he would be wise to work for a cession of the Floridas, May 29, 1799, George Washington Papers, Lib. Cong.

13. Carroll and Ashworth, *George Washington*, VII, 559–60; Phila. *Gazette of the United States*, Jan. 14, 1799.

up country were still largely sympathetic to the French Revolution. This was one reason for Pinckney's appointment as minister to France; he came from a state friendly to France and was himself known to be sympathetic to its revolution.

With Thomas Pinckney and John Rutledge, Jr., in Congress and Edward Rutledge at the apex of his personal influence in South Carolina, the importance of the Pinckney-Rutledge coalition in determining the state's political leaning was obvious. Both Federalists and Republicans waited anxiously to see which way this family alliance would swing under the impact of Charles Cotesworth Pinckney's mission to France. Edward Rutledge of course considered Jefferson his friend and had headed the Jeffersonian presidential electoral ticket in 1796. John Rutledge, Jr., was also a Jeffersonian presidential elector in 1796. But the Pinckneys and Rutledges prided themselves on putting country above friendship. As the two family groups had been disappointed with Washington over the Jay Treaty and were tempted to repudiate his administration, so they would be prepared to divorce themselves from the Jeffersonians if that party were unwilling to follow "patriotic" policies.

Congressmen Thomas Pinckney and John Rutledge, Jr., almost at once found themselves in disagreement with Jefferson over foreign policy. To them, Jefferson was soft if not soft-headed on France. As the letters of Charles Cotesworth Pinckney began to arrive in the United States, Thomas Pinckney and the Rutledges swung behind a preparedness program, a program stoutly opposed by Jefferson.[14] Thomas Pinckney wrote to "my dear Ned" ridiculing the attitudes of "non resistance and passive obedience" held by Republicans. A *"friend of yours,"* Thomas added referring to Jefferson, "is of opinion that we have lost so much honor that what remains is not worth contending for! We do not however usually argue in this way on the loss of other possessions. Of these when but little is left, the reluctance to part with that little is augmented. Observe however that I do not subscribe to such supposed loss of honor—we may have lost advantages but I think not honor."[15] Edward Rutledge re-

14. See Thomas Pinckney's speech in Congress urging that preparedness measures be taken, *Debates and Proceedings in the Congress of the United States, 1789–1824*, 42 vols. (Washington, 1834-56), 5th Congress, Dec. 22, 1797, 774.
15. Thomas Pinckney to Edward Rutledge, Jan. 6, 1798, Washburn Manuscripts, 1796–1854, Mass. Hist. Soc. John Rutledge, Jr., wrote Edward on Mar.

sponded by lamenting the loss of spirit in Congress: "we are a much altered people," he believed. Twenty years had witnessed a remarkable and regrettable decay in the spirit of patriotism.[16] And the Republicans were obviously those who lacked the patriotic virtues.

John Rutledge, Jr., quickly went over to the Federalist party after Charles Cotesworth Pinckney's rejection by France and the insinuations made by Republicans that his conduct was not all that it should have been.[17] Once converted to Federalism, young Rutledge kept his Uncle Edward well informed of his changing opinions toward Jefferson and the Republicans. For example, he sent Edward a description of a dinner given in Monroe's honor, which Jefferson attended. Young Rutledge tried to give his Uncle Edward the impression that Jeffersonians had become levelers, associating with common scum. The dinner party, said John Rutledge, "was a complete medley. . . . Here you saw an american disorganizer, and there a blundering wild Irishman—in one corner a Banished Genevan . . . —on one side a greasy Butcher and on the other a dirty Cobler."[18] It was enough to make the aristocratic Edward shudder. His old friend Jefferson had indeed changed. He had unwittingly become a tool of France and was building his party partly on common mechanics. Together with Thomas Pinckney and John Rutledge, Jr., Edward Rutledge turned his back upon the Jeffersonian Republicans.

When news of the XYZ failure reached the United States, Thomas Pinckney and John Rutledge, Jr., supported in Congress a rapid buildup of the armed forces.[19] In South Carolina, Edward Rutledge pressed for state action to prepare Charleston for the probable on-

---

6, 1798, that "Mr. Jefferson told Major P and myself yesterday that we were much too weak to resist France, and that we ought to rub thro' our difficulties as well as we could preserving peace *in all events*." Rutledge Papers, Dreer Coll., Hist. Soc. of Pa.

16. Edward Rutledge to John Rutledge, Jr., Jan. 23, 1798, John Rutledge, Jr., Papers, Duke Univ. Lib.

17. Theodore Sedgwick to Ephraim Williams, May 20, 1798, Papers of Theodore Sedgwick, Mass. Hist. Soc. Sedgwick wrote: "Mr. Rutledge from S.C. who is the son of C[hief] J[ustice] Rutledge, has come out decidedly with us contrary to the calculations of every one. This is among the effects of the indignities which have been shewn to Genl. Pinckney."

18. Rutledge to Edward Rutledge, July 4, 1797, Rutledge Papers, Dreer Coll., Hist. Soc. of Pa.

19. *Annals*, 5th Congress, Mar. 28, 1798, 1334–38. Both Thomas Pinckney and John Rutledge, Jr., voted to suspend commercial intercourse with France. *Annals*, 5th Congress, Feb. 18, 1800, 530.

slaught. At a meeting of citizens in St. Michael's Church in May 1798, he warned that the "present situation of the United States was far more awful and critical, than it was at the beginning of our revolutionary war with Great-Britain; that nothing short of the patriotism which carried us thro' that revolution, could extricate us from our present dilemma; and that submission to the dictates of France now, would leave us in a much worse predicament, than a submission to Great Britain at that time would have done."[20]

Edward Rutledge further helped to stimulate the war spirit in South Carolina by joining many of his fellow citizens in raising a voluntary subscription to put Charleston's forts in fighting order, in mounting additional cannon around the harbor, and in financing the building of a sloop of war named the *John Adams*. The legislature, which was called into special session by Governor Charles Pinckney, voted additional money to help Charleston prepare for a French invasion.[21] A small fort was erected on Shute's Folly Island, near Charleston, and was named "*Fort Pinckney* as a tribute of respect for Major-General Pinckney, our late envoy to the Republic of France."[22] Charlestonians were in a belligerent and patriotic mood, and Charles Cotesworth Pinckney was their man of the hour.

The impact of the Pinckney and XYZ missions upon South Carolina politics was seen in the mid-term Congressional elections of 1798. Federalists replaced two of the three congressional delegates who had opposed the administration's preparedness measures. Thomas Pinckney approvingly reported to George Washington that South Carolina was determined to return men to Congress "who have no predilection for any foreign Country."[23] The election of

20. Charleston *City Gazette*, May 7, 1798.
21. Thomas Pinckney to John Rutledge, Jr., Aug. 1, 1798, John Rutledge Papers, Southern Hist. Coll., U. of N.C.; Charleston *City Gazette*, Sept. 28, 1798; John H. Wolfe, *Jeffersonian Democracy in South Carolina* (Chapel Hill, 1940), 121. Hartford *Connecticut Courant*, Aug. 13, 1798, reported that Governor Charles Pinckney had called a special meeting at his home of all legislature members in the Charleston vicinity late in July. Thirty members of the Senate and House attended. They "authorized an expenditure of a sum of money, equal to the providing tents and camp equipage for the quota of this state in the first requisition of 80,000, the repairing of Fort Mechanic and building a magazine there; mounting all the cannon in the state; [and] converting the present City Guardhouse into an armory. . . ."
22. Charleston *City Gazette*, Sept. 28, 1798.
23. Thomas Pinckney to George Washington, Oct. 23, 1798, George Washington Papers, Lib. Cong. Thomas Sumter, Lemuel Benton, and William Smith

Edward Rutledge to the governorship in December 1798 consolidated Federalist gains in South Carolina.[24]

Edward Rutledge has been an enigma to historians, a person difficult to analyze and place in any political camp. Historians have been especially puzzled by Rutledge's conduct in the late 1790's, for although he vehemently denounced France for measures it took against the United States, yet he was thought to hold Jefferson in high esteem. Perhaps it would be accurate to say that after the Pinckney missions to France, Edward Rutledge became a "foreign policy Federalist," one who believed that France had betrayed its revolutionary principles and was acting tyrannically toward the United States.[25] Rutledge did not support all Federalist measures; he was visibly alarmed by the Alien and Sedition Acts and strongly protested their passage to John Rutledge, Jr.[26] But Edward Rutledge considered himself a Federalist by late 1798. In a letter to Phineas

---

were the three men who opposed Adams' measures. Only Thomas Sumter was re-elected, Smith being succeeded by Abraham Nott and Benton by Benjamin Huger. Wolfe, *Jeffersonian Democracy*, 123. John Rutledge, Jr., had earlier complained to Edward Rutledge: "I have endeavoured to make Sumpter Smith and Benton [support preparedness measures], but it would be as difficult to make them jump into a fiery gulph as to get them, on any occasion, to vote differently from Monsieur [Albert] Gallatin," July 4, 1797, Rutledge Papers, Dreer Coll., Hist. Soc. of Pa.

24. Charleston *City Gazette*, Dec. 11, 1798.

25. Rutledge's speech at his inauguration as governor indicates his mood: "For more than two years, the hands of rapine have been filled with the spoils of our country: for more than two years, the remonstrances of our government have been neglected and despised and the nicest feelings of our nation insulted and abused. . . . The rulers of France are well read in the history of Mankind; they know that to conquer a brave nation, it is first necessary to divide it; and they have founded their hopes of success on the division of our fellow citizens. Let me conjure you then, gentlemen, by all the blessings which spring from social order, to give to the world the most decided proofs of our being inseparately united, and to dispense, if it should become necessary, with every local and temporary interest, for the permanent security of the country. . . . When we turn our eyes to the situation of Europe, and behold the nations whose independence has sunk beneath the usurpations of that power which now threatens to destroy our own; when we reflect that self-government is among the first of blessings, we must be persuaded that no sacrifice can be esteemed too great, to insure its maintenance and preservation." Rutledge's speech is printed in the Phila. *Gazette of the United States*, Jan. 15, 1799.

26. Edward Rutledge to John Rutledge, Jr., July 29, 1798, John Rutledge Papers, Southern Hist. Coll., U. of N.C. James M. Smith points out the general disillusionment with the Federalists over the Alien and Sedition legislation in his *Freedom's Fetters: The Alien and Sedition Laws and American Civil Liberties* (Ithaca, N.Y., 1956).

Miller describing the activities of the last state legislative session, Rutledge mentioned that the assembly "did not, all the good I wished them to perform. . . . However, I found them, and I left them perfectly Federal." He added, "I wish our own Government would repeal their Sedition Act, which is a good deal disapproved of, and has been made a handle of to lessen the confidence [in] the Administration."[27] Rutledge obviously wished to strengthen the Federalist administration.

Federalists in the north were pleased by this show of spirit in South Carolina and were happy when Edward Rutledge was elected governor. Their only concern about South Carolina was that Charles Pinckney had been chosen United States senator at the same time that Rutledge was elected governor. Was this a sign of reviving Republicanism? they asked. Edward Rutledge assured John Rutledge, Jr., that it was not. Charles Pinckney's election, he wrote to his nephew, "did not proceed from the principles of antifederalism. It arose from a combination of circumstances." Charles Pinckney had made many personal and political friends while he was governor. And he "was persecuted, and abused" by his enemies, endearing him even more to his friends, who made strenuous efforts to vindicate Pinckney by sending him to the Senate.[28] South Carolina had one foot in each national party camp early in 1799, but Federalist sentiment prevailed for the moment.

Through the newspapers Rutledge and his fellow South Carolinians followed the homeward route of Charles Cotesworth Pinckney. They read that he had exhorted the patriots of Petersburg, Virginia, to beware of the French, "a people artful and insidious in policy, bold and powerful in arms." Pinckney advised them to "be active in preparing for War" for only in this way could they "obtain such a peace as freemen need not blush to accept."[29]

Charleston prepared to give Pinckney a reception comparable to the one accorded John Marshall in Philadelphia. Citizens meeting at City Hall appointed a committee "to prepare an Entertainment" in

27. Jan. 1, 1799, Edward Rutledge Papers, S. Caroliniana Lib.
28. Dec. 28, 1798, John Rutledge, Jr., Papers, Duke Univ. Lib.
29. Charleston *City Gazette*, Jan. 26, 1799. Pinckney was at Petersburg on Jan. 11.

honor of Pinckney and assessed dues to pay for the festivities. As Pinckney approached Charleston early in February 1799, an escort of military men and civilian leaders met him three miles outside the town. Trumpets, horns, and the firing of cannon by the artillery and infantry announced his entrance into the city. Ships anchored in the harbor fired guns and the sexton rang the bells of St. Michael's Church. Pinckney, who entered town on horseback dressed in his military uniform, "appeared to be in perfect health."[30] It was a homecoming worthy of a hero. Proceeding toward Edward Rutledge's home, Pinckney must have been greatly moved by this demonstration and by the measure of affection his friends obviously held for him.

Pinckney saw that his neighbors and friends were now proudly displaying American cockades surmounted with a spread eagle, instead of the French cockades they had worn when he left in 1796. His friends accompanied him to the theater in great numbers to see a production in his honor, written ironically enough by a Frenchman. The theatrical festival, called "Charleston's Celebration, or the Happy Return," included the characters "Liberty," "Major General," "Maimed Soldier," and "Genius of Liberty" as well as a new musical composition entitled "General Pinckney's March." There was a rousing climax of songs and dances during which the "leading Patriots of America with their attributes" were displayed.[31]

The celebration culminated on the evening of February 8 at a banquet given in the City Hall. Nearly every important office-holder in the state was present. The hall was elaborately decorated. At one end hung Pinckney's portrait under which were the words "il faut de l'argent; il faut beaucoup d'argent?—'No, No! not a six-pence.' " In front of the City Hall was a painting of a woman seated on a rock with an American eagle at her side. In the distance a dove was returning with an olive branch she had sent. The woman was about to seize several arrows at her feet, seeming to prepare for combat. Over her head were the stirring words, "millions for defense, not a cent for tribute."

As Pinckney prepared to enter the City Hall, a band struck up a

---

30. Phila. *Gazette of the United States*, Feb. 23, 1799.
31. Eola Willis, *The Charleston Stage in the XVIII Century* (Columbia, S.C., 1924), 421–22.

rousing version of "Hail Columbia," while in the harbor the ship *Amity* fired a salute of sixteen guns. When Pinckney entered the banquet room the citizens arose and the band played "Pinckney's March." After an excellent dinner, toasts were drunk and patriotic verses sung to the accompaniment of field pieces discharged by the "Ancient Battalion of Artillery."[32]

Pinckney's popularity in South Carolina, however, did not shield him from mounting Republican criticism as a military posturer and an eager tool of Hamilton. An opportunity to smear Pinckney came early in 1799 when Timothy Pickering forwarded information to Governor Edward Rutledge and Pinckney that wicked French plotters were aboard a Danish ship, the *Minerva*, bound for Charleston. One Matthew Salmon, a mulatto and former deputy to the French National Convention, was reportedly carrying documents in the false bottoms of tubs. These documents, Pickering believed, were instructions from the Directory ordering its agents to overthrow the American government. The mulatto's specific task was supposedly to foment a slave insurrection in the south.

When the *Minerva* dropped anchor, officials of South Carolina rushed aboard and found Salmon as well as four other citizens of France. Two of the party were mulatto women. The tubs with the false bottoms were also there, containing documents written in French. All of the Frenchmen were immediately taken to jail where Pinckney interrogated them. Pinckney soon learned that the group was actually hostile to the Directory and was on its way to Santo Domingo to arouse the colored people against the French government.

Not knowing that Pickering's information was erroneous, Federalists rejoiced openly that those firm Federalist patriots, General Pinckney and Governor Rutledge, had saved the nation from a horrible French plot. Republicans, however, insisted that the "tale of the Tubs" was founded upon a "*false bottom*" and pretended to believe that Pinckney's supposed Parisian sins had finally found him out. Was it not interesting, they asked, that a woman was involved in this episode? And was it not correct that Pinckney had been in intimate contact with a "lady" in Paris? The official correspondence

32. Charleston *City Gazette*, Feb. 9, 1799; *Newport [R. I.] Mercury*, Feb. 26, 1799.

of the envoys proved that. A man with sound Republican morals and some imagination could see what had happened: after the "lady" had become pregnant, Pinckney had hastily slipped out of Paris to hide in southern France. In her pitiful condition, the "lady" had followed Pinckney to South Carolina where he repaid her former favors by clapping her into a dungeon. Into jail with her went the helpless infant, the only fruit of the XYZ mission. Governor Rutledge's part in the affair was, to say the least, discreditable, for he assisted Pinckney in smuggling the woman on board a departing ship before she could appeal to the public for aid.[33]

It is doubtful that Pinckney and Rutledge saw the humor in such slanders, convinced as they were of the scurrility and corruptness of the Republican press. Those papers known to be Jeffersonian were exactly the ones which reported on the tub plot with such glee. Could Jefferson himself be countenancing or inciting these filthy reports? they surely asked themselves.

Pinckney busied himself in preparing the defenses of the south[34] and in encouraging a militant spirit among his neighbors. To his fellow Charlestonians Pinckney gave the warning that the French were "a people whom no candid appeal to justice, no claim of ancient friendship, and no humiliation can for one moment divert from their long planned system of general oppression."[35] "If our country has erred," he assured the troops near Savannah, "it has been the error of *friendship* in favor of a nation, who has replied to its effusions with insult and indignity." To the Camden County Battalion of South Carolina, Pinckney mentioned that he had been sent to France to arrange "a speedy accomodation of existing differences." Now, he added ominously, the "objects of my present visit [to you], are of a nature far different indeed."[36]

It is difficult to determine whether Pinckney favored declaring

33. The best account of this episode is found in John C. Miller, *Crisis in Freedom: The Alien and Sedition Acts* (Boston, 1951), 146–50. See also *Newport [R. I.] Mercury*, Mar. 26, 1799.

34. Pinckney's activities in preparing the south for an attack can be followed in these letters: Pinckney to George Washington, Mar. 8, 12, 1799; Pinckney to James McHenry, Apr. 19, 1799, and Pinckney to Washington, Apr. 20, 1799; Pinckney to James McHenry, May 19, 1799; Pinckney to George Washington, June 25, 1799, all letters in the George Washington Papers, Lib. Cong.

35. Phila. *Gazette of the United States*, Mar. 15, 1799.

36. Charleston *City Gazette*, Mar. 29, May 4, 1799.

war upon France or whether he wished to wait, fully prepared, for France to strike the first blow; more likely it was the latter. Believing that France respected nothing but strength, Pinckney argued that America must give tangible evidence of its determination to maintain independence. Only then would France respect American rights and be willing to conclude an accommodation of existing differences.

This was certainly in tune with President Adams' thinking in 1799. Just ten days after Pinckney's rousing homecoming dinner at City Hall, Adams struck militant Federalists temporarily dumb by nominating William Vans Murray as minister plenipotentiary to the French Republic. Adams had good evidence that the Directory's attitude had changed and that a minister from the United States would be received.[37]

Senator Theodore Sedgwick wrote to Hamilton that had "the foulest heart and the ablest head in the world been permitted to select the most embarrassing and ruinous measure," it would have been exactly what Adams had done. Though Adams could not be persuaded to discard the peace mission, discussions by Federalist leaders in Congress induced him to drop Murray and send another three-man commission. Pickering groaned to Washington that the "*honor* of the Country is prostrated in the dust—God grant that its *safety* may not be in jeopardy." Peace seemed dangerously near. Yet Pickering urged Rufus King in mid-March not to despair for all was not lost. The cabinet had persuaded Adams to instruct the envoys not to conclude a treaty until France had met certain American demands. Pickering was "morally sure" that France would not "yield them . . . and this has put us all much at our ease."[38]

37. Richardson, ed., *Messages of the Presidents*, I, 282; Kurtz, *Presidency of John Adams*, 341–42, 348; Smith, *John Adams*, II, 999–1001.

38. Sedgwick to Hamilton, Feb. 19, 1798, in John C. Hamilton, ed., *The Works of Alexander Hamilton*, 7 vols. (N.Y., 1850–51), VI, 397; Pickering to George Washington, Feb. 21, 1799, George Washington Papers, Lib. Cong.; Pickering to King, Mar. 12, 1799, Rufus King Papers, Huntington Lib.; Dauer, *Adams Federalists*, 230–32. Adams' strategy and timing in sending the mission is analyzed by Stephen G. Kurtz, "The French Mission of 1799–1800: Concluding Chapter in the Statecraft of John Adams," *Political Science Quarterly*, 80 (1965), 543–57. For a discussion of William Vans Murray's role in the negotiations with France and the events which led to the Franco-American Convention of 1800, see Alexander DeConde, "William Vans Murray and the Diplomacy of Peace: 1797–1800," *Maryland Historical Magazine*, 48 (Mar., 1953), 1–26; E. Wilson Lyon, "The Franco-American Convention of 1800," *Journal of Modern History*, 12 (1940), 305–33; DeConde, *Quasi-War*, 223–326.

While Pinckney may have wanted war with France, he acted as though he did not expect it. When his wife became seriously ill in the summer of 1799, he suddenly left his command early in September to take her to Newport, Rhode Island, for her health.[39] Either Pinckney considered his wife's health more important than the military safety of the south or he had reliable information that there would be no war with France.

Pinckney was evidently receiving letters from his friends in France assuring him that the Directory did not want war.[40] Yet Pinckney may be criticized for failing to inform Washington that he was leaving his post.[41] Although Secretary of War McHenry granted Pinckney a leave of absence, Washington was obviously annoyed. He complained to Hamilton that Pinckney's part-time service was "not only contrary to my original design, but unpleasant in its nature and operation; inasmuch as it incurs responsibility with out proper means for decision." Against his wishes Washington was compelled to make provision for quartering certain regiments which were Pinckney's responsibility. Washington was not relieved of his unwanted duties until Pinckney returned to headquarters at Shepherdstown, Virginia, early in December.[42]

While Washington struggled with what should have been Pinckney's problems, Pinckney and his entire family were enjoying the salubrious climate of Newport. Arriving there September 13 on the brig *Hermes*,[43] the Pinckneys found the company entertaining and

39. Pinckney had written to George Washington early in June: "On my return [from Georgia] I found Mrs. Pinckney very ill; she was then better but has had two relapses since I arrived, and to day has been attacked with a vomiting of green black bile," June 4, 1799, Misc. Mss., Huntington Lib. Bishop Robert Smith of Charleston told John Rutledge, Jr., late in August that Mrs. Pinckney "has long been despaired of—I this morning hear, that the only hope is a removal," Aug. 31, 1799, John Rutledge Papers, Southern Hist. Coll., U. of N.C.

40. Pinckney was in contact with his trusted friend, Major James Mountflorence, an American consular official in Paris. Pinckney to George Washington, June 25, 1799, George Washington Papers, Lib. Cong.

41. Pinckney, probably embarrassed, had his military aide in Virginia write Washington that he had left for Rhode Island. Presley Thornton to Washington, Sept. 16, 1799, *ibid*.

42. Washington to Hamilton, Oct. 27, 1799, Washington to Secretary of War, Nov. 5, 1799, in Fitzpatrick, ed., *Writings of Washington*, XXXVII, 409, 419–21; Pinckney to Henry Rutledge, Dec. 12, 1799, Rutledge Papers, Dreer Coll., Hist. Soc. of Pa.

43. *Newport [R. I.] Mercury*, Sept. 17, 1799.

their duties light. General Pinckney did take time to inspect Forts Adams and Wolcott and to visit the frigate *United States* to the accompaniment of cheers and a "federal salute." After a month's rest, the Pinckneys left Newport for Trenton and Philadelphia. The *Newport Mercury* did comment graciously that during his "short stay in this Town" General Pinckney "inspired a very general Respect and Veneration for his Talents and Virtues. . . ."[44]

Pinckney had hardly arrived at Shepherdstown when Washington died from a severe throat infection at his Mount Vernon estate. Washington's unexpected death caused mourning throughout the nation. Even many who had bitterly attacked him during his days as president now admitted his courage and devotion to duty. Pinckney learned of Washington's death from the personal servant of Tobias Lear, Washington's private secretary.[45] There was no man in public life that Pinckney revered more than Washington. The convivial air of the Christmas season was undoubtedly dampened in the Pinckney home, for Washington's death came as a personal blow.

Pinckney was also saddened when he learned of the serious illness of Edward Rutledge. In mid-January 1800, Rutledge was struck down by an "apoplectic fit" soon after returning from a difficult legislative session in Columbia. When his senses returned the doctors discovered that his right arm and leg were paralyzed and his speech blurred. Rutledge believed that he would not recover, and the doctors could give him little encouragement. During the night of January 21, 1800, Rutledge died quietly.[46]

Charles Cotesworth Pinckney had been closer to Rutledge than to any other man except his own brother Thomas. There was an implicit confidence between them, a respect of each for the ability and

44. Oct. 29, 1799. The Pinckneys left Newport on Oct. 22. The Phila. *Gazette of the United States*, Nov. 14, 1799, reported that Pinckney was to leave Philadelphia the next day for headquarters in Virginia.
45. Carroll and Ashworth, *George Washington*, VII, 626, 646.
46. Pinckney to Jacob Read, Feb. 7, 1800, Emmet Coll., N.Y. Pub. Lib. Ill, Edward Rutledge had requested the legislature to permit him to return home during its session. The legislature believed the request could not be granted, that it was unconstitutional for the governor to be absent when it was in session. Rutledge's friends indignantly withdrew the motion. After the session was over, Rutledge was caught in a storm on his way to Charleston and thoroughly chilled. As soon as he reached Charleston he went to bed and there suffered his stroke. See Sanderson, *Biography of the Signers*, V, 178–79.

integrity of the other that cemented the bonds of family ties and political interest. Rutledge's letter to his son Henry in 1796 urging him to accept an appointment as Pinckney's secretary clearly showed the close relationship between himself and Pinckney. Their business partnership was another indication of this intimate relationship. The fact that Rutledge altered his political views in 1797 and 1798, becoming one of the most active enemies of France in the south, is evidence of his confidence in Pinckney's judgment. Pinckney's regular correspondence with Rutledge throughout the mission to France likewise shows that the confidence was reciprocal. When Pinckney was appointed major general in 1798 he chose Henry Rutledge to be his military aide, a compliment to Henry but a bow to his father Edward as well.

Rutledge's death was bound to affect Pinckney's political career. Together they formed a colossus of political power in South Carolina. With the death of Rutledge, who was perhaps better able than any other man to compromise the differences between the emerging political parties in South Carolina, the political influence of Charles Cotesworth Pinckney was significantly diminished. Rutledge was at the height of his political power and had drawn increasingly closer to the positions taken by John Adams. Staunch Federalist Theodore Sedgwick of Massachusetts believed that the "renovated [i.e. Federalist] character of S. Carolina seemed to have been created by, and its continuance to depend upon" Edward Rutledge.[47] As governor of the state, Rutledge would have played an important part in determining the political fortunes of the South Carolina Federalists in 1800. Surely Rutledge, who was instrumental in South Carolina's casting its presidential electoral votes equally for Jefferson and Thomas Pinckney in 1796, would have tried to secure no less for his "dear Friend" Charles Cotesworth in 1800.

When Rutledge died, it was not entirely clear who would be placed upon the Federalist presidential ticket. The clash of policies and personalities within the party prevented it from concentrating on its true enemy, the Republican party. President Adams was

47. Sedgwick to Henry Van Schaack, Feb. 9, 1800, Papers of Theodore Sedgwick, Mass. Hist. Soc. Sedgwick undoubtedly got his information from Thomas Pinckney and John Rutledge, Jr.

forced to fight a vigorous rearguard action against the supporters of Hamilton and the friends of Pickering throughout most of his administration. Since Adams was not enough of a party man for his enemies, their fury mounted as he shaped administration policies without consulting them. Adams, they complained, had not used federal patronage to strengthen the Federalist party, had ostracized Alexander Hamilton politically, and had not directed foreign policy to serve the interests of federalism.[48]

Pinckney's role in the widening split between the Hamiltonian and Adams Federalists is often obscure. Although Pinckney favored enlarging the army and assuming a militant posture toward France, there seems to be little convincing evidence that he favored war as a step toward obliterating the Republican party. His opposition to the Alien and Sedition Acts makes this clear.[49] Rather, as has been said, he was convinced from his firsthand observations that France respected nothing but power; therefore he urged that a large American army was a necessary first step to successful negotiations with France. Pinckney was one founding father who believed that an energetic foreign policy is possible only when supported by a substantial military force.

Pickering's friends despaired when Adams appointed the second diplomatic mission to France in 1799, but Pinckney said very little. He did not want to offend his high Federalist friends or to align himself with the war-at-any-price faction. When it was finally settled that the envoys were to sail, Pinckney wrote guardedly to Hamilton: "I presume this must be a very deep measure—much too profound for my penetration."[50]

High Federalists nevertheless seemed to believe that Pinckney

48. For an analysis of the factors which led to a virtual civil war within the Federalist party, see Kurtz, *Presidency of John Adams*; Dauer, *Adams Federalists*; Mitchell, *Hamilton*, II, 454–87; Schachner, *Founding Fathers*; and Miller, *Federalist Era*, 210–64 and *passim*.

49. William Vans Murray to John Quincy Adams, Mar. 22, 1799, in Ford, ed., "Letters of William Vans Murray," Amer. Hist. Assoc., *Annual Report* (1912), 530. Murray was puzzled because both Pinckney and Marshall opposed the Alien and Sedition Acts, despite their harrowing experiences in France. It evidently did not occur to Murray that their experiences in France made both generals more determined than ever to preserve free men's rights in the United States.

50. Pinckney to Hamilton, Oct. 25, 1799, in Steiner, *Life of James McHenry*, 419.

was one of their circle, and they leaned heavily upon his popularity and great political influence in the south. There was a national political campaign approaching, and Federalists were aware that fear of the standing army and the genuine public indignation against the Alien and Sedition Acts had offended many former friends of the Federalist party.[51] All Federalist politicians were aware as well that candidates must be run who would be politically attractive and likely to draw support from without as well as within their own geographical sections.

Influential Federalists at first favored dropping Adams as a candidate because of Adams' studied independence of them. Timothy Pickering believed that a ticket of Chief Justice Oliver Ellsworth and Charles Cotesworth Pinckney would be popular and would receive strong support in all sections. Robert Troup of New York, another high Federalist, urged that the *decided and deep rooted disgust*" with Adams among even his oldest friends dictated dropping Adams from the ticket. But Stephen Higginson, a great merchant of Boston, saw that Adams could not be discarded without disrupting and possibly destroying the Federalist party. While Higginson liked Adams no better than Pickering and Troup did, he realized that to drop an eager and still popular incumbent such as Adams would be political suicide.[52]

Hamilton was distressed to find strong support for Adams in the north throughout all levels of the party. Adams was most popular, Hamilton found, among what he called the "leaders of the second class." They positively refused to consider discarding Adams for any other man.[53] But Hamilton and his most intimate associates still could not bring themselves to support Adams for another term as president. Hamilton decided that the mischievous and reprehensible policy of 1796 was worth another gamble. If the Federalists nominated a "discreet" man for the vice-presidency, Hamilton reasoned, some

51. Miller, *Crisis in Freedom*, 182–83, 192–93, 224–25; Kurtz, *Presidency of John Adams*, 308, 323–24.

52. Higginson to Pickering, Jan. 12, 1800, in J. Franklin Jameson, ed., "Letters of Stephen Higginson, 1783–1804," Amer. Hist. Assoc., *Annual Report* (1896), I, 835; Hamilton to Charles Carroll, July 1, 1800, in Lodge, ed., *Works of Hamilton*, X, 379; Robert Troup to Rufus King, Mar. 9, 1800, in King, *Life of Rufus King*, III, 208.

53. Hamilton to Charles Carroll, July 1, 1800, Lodge, ed., *Works of Hamilton*, X, 379.

skillful intrigue and a little luck might possibly place him in the presidential chair. He had almost succeeded with Thomas Pinckney in 1796, a fact that argued for another such try. Because the Federalists had already lost the election in New York, it was mandatory that this man have strong support in the south; without electoral votes from the south the Federalist ticket would certainly be defeated.[54] The vice-presidential candidate must also be popular outside the south and presumably amenable to the wishes of Alexander Hamilton.

Hamilton believed that Charles Cotesworth Pinckney met all of the necessary qualifications. Yet there were many obstacles to overcome before Pinckney could be named president. Hamilton's first step was to urge the Federalist caucus that met in Philadelphia early in May to pledge that every presidential elector would support Adams and Pinckney equally for the presidency. This was the only policy, Hamilton warned, "that can possibly save us from the fangs of *Jefferson*." By committing all Federalists to equal support of the two candidates, Adams and Pinckney, Hamilton hoped to keep the votes for Pinckney and Adams even in those states where Federalists were predominant. In the south where Pinckney was popular and Adams was weak, Pinckney's electoral vote would then sweep him into the presidency ahead of an infuriated but helpless Adams.[55]

The Federalist caucus nominated Adams and Pinckney with the understanding that Adams was the party's candidate for president. Of course many members of the caucus made the pledge with tongue in cheek and fingers crossed. They agreed with Hamilton that if "we must have an *enemy* at the head of the government" it should be one "who will not involve our party in the disgrace of his foolish and bad measures." Dissatisfied Federalists knew, however, that Adams could be displaced only if his followers would abandon, as Pickering said, the "miserable policy of regarding men, not measures. . . ."[56]

54. Kurtz, *Presidency of John Adams*, 394; Miller, *Hamilton*, 515.
55. Hamilton to Theodore Sedgwick, May 4, 10, 1800, in Lodge, ed., *Works of Hamilton*, X, 371, 375–76; Timothy Pickering to Rufus King, May 7, 1800, Rufus King Papers, Lib. Cong.
56. Hamilton to Sedgwick, May 10, 1800, in Lodge, ed., *Works of Hamilton*, X, 375; Pickering to King, May 7, 1800, Rufus King Papers, Lib. Cong.; Oliver Wolcott to James McHenry, July 18, 1800, in Steiner, *Life of James McHenry*, 462.

Adams was aware of the plot to unseat him. Shortly after the Federalist caucus met, Adams publicized his defiance of the Hamiltonians by forcing James McHenry and Timothy Pickering out of the cabinet. Adams' Federalist enemies retaliated by spreading rumors that Adams was secretly holding friendly meetings with Jefferson. Pickering and his friends pretended to believe that Adams and Jefferson had concocted a plot to retain themselves in office for another four years.[57]

When Pinckney learned of McHenry's and Pickering's dismissal, he immediately wrote to them from Shepherdstown asking why they had been treated so shabbily. McHenry replied noncommittally, but Pickering sent a long letter describing his "indignation and disgust" with Adams, "disgust at his intolerable vanity; indignation for the disgrace and mischief which his conduct has brought on the cause of Federalism and the country. . . ." Pickering assured Pinckney that Adams was guided by "selfishness, ambition and revenge," his heart "cankered with envy, and deficient in sincerity" and that he was "blind, stone blind, to his own faults and failings. . . ."[58]

Pinckney evidently accepted Pickering's critical estimate of Adams' abilities and motives and began to believe that Adams should be replaced as the presidential candidate of the Federalists. Pinckney knew of Hamilton's plan to bring him to the presidency,[59] but he was unwilling to be elected on the basis of deceit in the north and broken promises in the south. Pinckney explained his position in detail to James McHenry:

With regard to the conduct of the Southern States at the ensuing Election, I think they are bound fairly and candidly to act up to their agreement entered into by the federal party at Philadelphia, with out [unless] the Eastern States should be convinced of Mr. A's abandonment of federal

57. Steiner, *Life of James McHenry*, 453–54; Kurtz, *Presidency of John Adams*, 393; Smith, *John Adams*, II, 1028–31; James Gunn to John Rutledge, Jr., May 12, 1800, John Rutledge Papers, Southern Hist. Coll., U. of N.C. Gunn reported that "Mr. *Adams* and his dear friend Mr. *Jefferson* have been *twice closeted* together since Saturday last. . . ."

58. Pinckney to Pickering, May 19, 1800, Pickering Papers, Mass. Hist. Soc.; Pinckney to McHenry, May 20, 1800, C. C. Pinckney Papers, S. Caroliniana Lib.; Pickering to Pinckney, May 25, 1800, in Henry Adams, ed., *Documents Relating to New England Federalism, 1800–1815* (Boston, 1877), 332.

59. William O. Heth to Charles Cotesworth Pinckney, June 1, 1800, Thomas Pinckney Letters, Duke Univ. Lib.

principles, his attempt to form a party with Jefferson, and his unfitness to be President, and on these accounts or some of them, should consent to substitute another Candidate in his stead. This Event I do not think impossible, and his conduct and the critical situation of our Country may require it. But to preserve the Union, this must originate to the Eastward —The Middle States can then take it up, and the Southern ones with propriety may follow.[60]

Pinckney's insistence that Adams be dropped first in the area where his political strength was greatest was precisely what could not be done, as Hamilton had already discovered.

When Adams Federalists in New England learned positively of the plan to discard Adams, they began to take steps to lessen Pinckney's electoral vote in their section. Hamiltonians were alarmed by this movement and tried to assure the New Engand non-cooperators that there was no plot to diminish Adams' vote in the south. Robert Goodloe Harper of South Carolina, for example, untruthfully reported to Harrison Gray Otis, a Massachusetts Adams Federalist, that he had reliable information from South Carolina that Adams was running stronger there than Pinckney! No "people in the Union would more decidedly reject any attempt to supersede" Adams, Harper stated, than those of South Carolina.[61]

In the midst of this intrigue, described by Fisher Ames, the Massachusetts Federalist, as "more complicated with underplot" than "an old Spanish play," the Republicans gleefully published a letter of President Adams which they hoped would further divide the Federalists. Adams had written to his friend Tench Coxe in 1792 accusing the Pinckney family of having plotted in the 1780's to replace him as American minister to Great Britain with Thomas Pinckney. Dis-

60. Pinckney to McHenry, June 10, 1800, in Steiner, *Life of James McHenry*, 459–60. Thomas Pinckney concurred in his brother's opinion to remain faithful to the Philadelphia agreement "unless we should receive undeniable proofs of an intention of foul play, as will render our change not only just but necessary." Thomas Pinckney to John Rutledge, Jr., Sept. 23, 1800, John Rutledge Papers, Southern Hist. Coll., U. of N.C.

61. Steiner, *Life of James McHenry*, 463n; Ebenezer Huntington to Oliver Wolcott, Aug. 6, 1800, in Gibbs, *Administrations of Washington and Adams*, II, 398; Harper to Otis, June 25, 1800, in Morison, *Life of Otis*, I, 192. Harper confessed to John Rutledge, Jr., that he supported Adams "as a mean[s] of getting Pinckney. In no other view would I turn a th[umb?] to ensure his election. This again is mum." Harper to Rutledge, Sept. 4, 1800, John Rutledge Papers, Southern Hist. Coll., U. of N.C.

missed from his position as Commissioner of the Revenue in December 1797, Coxe decided to have his revenge and to help his new friend Jefferson into the presidency.[62] He therefore forwarded the old letter to William Duane, editor of the Republican *Aurora*. Duane was only too happy to give Adams' indiscreet letter a public review.[63] In the letter Adams said:

The Duke of Leeds once inquired of me very kindly after his classmates at Westminster school, the two Mr. Pinckneys, which induces me to conclude that our new ambassador [Thomas Pinckney] has many powerful old friends in England. Whether this is a recommendation of him for the office or not, I have other reasons to believe that his family have had their eyes fixed on the embassy to St. James for many years, even before I was sent there; and that they contributed to limit the duration of my commission to three years, in order to make way for themselves to succeed me. I wish they may find as much honor and pleasure in it as they expected, and that the public may derive from it dignity and ability. But knowing as I do the long intrigue, and suspecting as I do much British influence in the appointment, were I in any executive department I should take the liberty to keep a vigilant eye upon them.[64]

This letter put both Adams and the Pinckney brothers in an unfavorable light.

The Pinckney brothers had every right to be indignant with Adams although they controlled their anger publicly. They had never intrigued for positions in the federal administration and were certainly not Anglophiles as Adams had insinuated. In his published reply to Adams' letter, Thomas Pinckney did not berate Adams but instead tried to throw the Republicans off balance. Thomas argued that the letter was either a vicious forgery intended to influence the election, or *"if genuine, must have been founded on a misapprehension of persons."* This was a rather shrewd attempt to pin the dishonorable label of "office seeker" upon his Republican cousin, Senator Charles Pinckney.[65]

62. Theodore Sedgwick to [Ephraim Williams?], Dec. 26, 1797, Papers of Theodore Sedgwick, Mass. Hist. Soc. Sedgwick gave a short yet complete explanation for the dismissal of Coxe: "He was a Jacobin."
63. Harold Hutcheson, *Tench Coxe; A Study in American Economic Development* (Baltimore, 1938), 39–40.
64. Quoted in Pinckney, *Life of Thomas Pinckney*, 158–59.
65. In writing to Adams for an explanation of the letter, Thomas Pinckney enclosed a copy of his letter to the Charleston *City Gazette*, published on Sept.

Few people were deceived by Thomas' ruse, however. Republicans were not disappointed in the effect of the Adams letter, for it undoubtedly helped to kill any remaining sentiment for Adams in South Carolina and further convinced Hamiltonians that the President's poor judgment was only exceeded by his pettiness and envy.

While Federalists were trying to heal the wounds opened by this blow, Hamilton committed a *faux pas* that exposed himself and the Federalist party to further Republican ridicule. Hamilton had become increasingly depressed by the iron determination of many Federalists not to abandon Adams in favor of Pinckney. In order to convince these Federalists that Adams was unfit for the presidency, Hamilton assiduously collected information that he considered damaging to Adams and forwarded it in a letter to the party faithful.[66] A copy fell into the hands of Aaron Burr, who immediately rushed it into print.

Hamilton described the "Vanity without bounds," the "jealousy capable of discoloring every object," and the "paroxysm of anger" and "outrageous behavior" which characterized the conduct and personality of Adams. John Adams' patriotism was not questioned, Hamilton emphasized, only his intelligence, judgment, and administrative ability. The greatest surprise for the reader came at the end of the letter; after pronouncing Adams unfit for high public office, Hamilton announced that he had "resolved not to advise withholding from him a single vote." This was not because it was the wisest course, Hamilton continued, but because the "body of [less prominent] Federalists, for want of sufficient knowledge of facts, are not convinced of the expedience of relinquishing" Adams.[67]

Hamilton's campaign gift to the Republicans dissolved any remaining doubt among Adams Federalists that there was a nefarious

---

16, 1800. At the end of the published copy, Thomas Pinckney penciled in: "With the view of counteracting the immediate effect which the publication of this letter [Adams'] was obviously intended to produce on our State elections I have inserted in the Charleston Gazette a letter of which the inclosed is a copy." Pinckney's letter to Adams, dated Sept. 16, 1800, is in the Pinckney Family Papers, Lib. Cong.

66. Hamilton to McHenry, Aug. 27, 1800, Hamilton to Oliver Wolcott, Sept. 26, 1800, in Lodge, ed., *Works of Hamilton*, X, 388–89.

67. Alexander Hamilton, *Letter from Alexander Hamilton concerning the Public Conduct and Character of John Adams* . . . (N.Y., 1800), 51.

Hamiltonian plot to unseat Adams. This policy of undermining the agreement made in good faith at the Federalist caucus to support Adams and Pinckney for different offices aroused the indignation of the Adams Federalists. Many Adams Federalists believed correctly that if the party split over the candidate it should support for president, it would mean not only defeat at the coming election but also ruin for the party itself. A defeated party, they argued, could not be rebuilt on a foundation of mistrust, intrigue, and broken pledges. Foreseeing defeat by late August, Fisher Ames advised Hamilton that the "question is not . . . how we shall fight, but how we and all federalists shall fall, that we may fall, like Antaeus, the stronger for our fall."[68]

Charles Cotesworth Pinckney saw that unless he made a personal pledge not to seek southern votes independently of Adams, the Federalist party could destroy itself in the election. He therefore wrote a letter to a New England Federalist promising to forbid any persons to vote for him who were not also pledged to Adams. Secretary of the Navy Benjamin Stoddert saw the letter and reported its contents to John Rutledge, Jr. Pinckney frankly stated that although he had personal reasons to be unhappy with Adams, "his efforts would be directed to obtain for [Adams] . . . in So Carolina, as many votes as should be given to himself." Stoddert predicted that if Pinckney "should defeat himself he will gain by the defeat. . . . It will be the noblest revenge for the imprudent letter of Mr. A."[69]

Pinckney certainly did not believe that he would lose his own state, but with the pledge he made to the Adams Federalists, the prospects for a Federalist electoral victory dimmed. Hamiltonian Federalists had wanted Pinckney on the party ticket precisely because South Carolinians in Congress had vowed that Pinckney would receive half of their state's electoral votes whether South Carolina was Republican or Federalist in 1800. Pinckney's popularity apparently transcended hardening party lines in South Carolina. There-

68. The wrath of the Adams Federalists with Hamilton is seen in [Noah Webster], *A Letter to General Hamilton, Occasioned by his letter to President Adams* (N.Y., 1800). See also Fisher Ames to Hamilton, Aug. 26, 1800, in Ames, ed., *Works of Fisher Ames*, I, 281.

69. Stoddert to Rutledge, Oct. 2, 1800, John Rutledge Papers, Southern Hist. Coll., U. of N.C.

fore, if all other Federalist states voted equally for Adams and Pinckney, even a Republican-inclined South Carolina would put Pinckney into the presidential chair.[70] But by pledging to accept no votes from electors not committed to Adams, Pinckney negated the plans of the Hamiltonians who had secured his nomination.

The crucial election campaign in South Carolina opened weeks before Pinckney was able to leave camp at Shepherdstown. The general of the Republican forces in South Carolina was Charles Pinckney, the former governor and present senator. Charles Pinckney, a perplexing person to historians, had been consistent in his Republican politics since the middle 1790's, refusing to alter his political allegiance in light of his cousin's unfortunate experiences in France. It seems likely that Charles Pinckney was more acutely aware of the development of national political parties than were his relatives in Charleston, and that he had established his loyalties to the Republican party while the party system was still embryonic in South Carolina. Politics in the state remained relatively unaffected by national party issues until late in the 1790's. It was the old political system, based on wealth, social connections, friendships, and sectionalism that continued to operate in South Carolina for some time after other states were torn by party issues. National party politics in South Carolina was a phenomenon of the very late 1790's, not reaching maturity until 1799 or the election of 1800.[71]

Electioneering strategy itself revealed the old and the new in the state's political structure. Charles Pinckney and the Republicans urged the voters to choose candidates for the legislature who were avowedly Republican and who would cast their votes, on principle, only for

70. Theodore Sedgwick to Rufus King, Sept. 26, 1800, in King, *Life of Rufus King*, III, 309.

71. John Rutledge, Jr., to Bishop Robert Smith, Aug. 14, 1798, Thomas Pinckney to John Rutledge, Jr., Sept. 23, 1800, John Rutledge Papers, Southern Hist. Coll., U. of N.C. Thomas Pinckney reported to Rutledge why it was impossible to decide how strong his brother and Jefferson were in South Carolina: ". . . you know we can form no certain estimates [of numerical strength] from the persons returned [to the state legislature], because hitherto the distinctions of political parties has been marked by a very faint line." One can argue that national party labels, when adopted in South Carolina, were really the old sectionalism writ large, at least in the 1790's. This might help to explain why party identification, Federalist or Republican, initially had so little significance for South Carolinians; what was "new" on the political scene was in practice very old.

nominees of the Republican party. Although Charles Cotesworth Pinckney was supported by Federalists, his friends did not present him to the electorate as the candidate of that party alone. Instead they concentrated on rallying support for him by making his character and personal worth the major issues. This type of appeal to the electorate had been standard practice before the establishment of political parties within the state.

Republicans at first hesitated to attack Charles Cotesworth Pinckney openly, but when his friends maintained that he himself was the single issue, Republicans were forced to challenge Pinckney's qualifications for high civil office. Whatever Pinckney's good personal qualities, "A Republican" stated, no man who loved military honors as Pinckney did and who had held high military office should be transferred to a high civil office. If nothing else it would be a dangerous precedent.[72]

Another objection to Pinckney raised by "Republican" was that his belligerent attitude toward France would injure Franco-American relations. "A late Officer in the American Army" retorted that Pinckney did not consider the insults he received in France personal ones but ones offered to his country. "Literatus," who claimed that Pinckney was "as dear to me as *my own blood*," quickly answered that "the strength of passion is prone to confound the nice distinction between a personal insult and an insult to a nation through one's person."[73] Pinckney was also accused of religious neglect, no doubt as an antidote to the Federalist charge that Jefferson was a religious heretic. One South Carolinian wrote to a friend in Philadelphia that "such a length of time has elapsed, since [Pinckney] has honored a sermon with his presence, that he must almost forget the common forms of divine worship—His friends have been remarkably silent on this subject, although they have made it such a clamourous objection to his opponent."[74]

72. Charleston *City Gazette*, Aug. 11, 1800. Charles Pinckney was the author of at least 24 numbers of the "Republican." See Charles Pinckney to Thomas Jefferson, Oct. 12, 1800, in [J. Franklin Jameson, ed.], "South Carolina in the Presidential Election of 1800," *Amer. Hist. Rev.*, 4 (1898–99), 114.

73. Charleston *City Gazette*, Aug. 16, 19, 27, 1800.

74. This letter was printed in the Phila. *Aurora*, Oct. 27, 1800. The letter was dated Sept. 10, 1800. This marked it as a fraud, for Pinckney did not arrive in Charleston from Virginia until Oct. 29, 1800! Charleston *City Gazette*, Oct. 30, 1800.

In the midst of the opening exchanges in the press, South Carolina held its biennial elections for the state legislature. In order to capitalize upon Pinckney's personal popularity within that body, his friends decided to run him for one of Charleston's two seats in the senate. When Charles Pinckney confidently predicted that his cousin would be defeated by Thomas Lee, Charles Cotesworth's friends redoubled their efforts. "All the elderly men, of high character, whose health will allow them . . . will come out efficiently at the elections," Henry William De Saussure asserted, and the Republicans would quickly learn that they had overrated "their strength prodigiously."[75]

The campaign for the election tickets in Charleston was strenuous; while the Federalists appeared confident at the outset, they wished to take no chances. On election day, to the consternation of Charles Pinckney and the other Republicans, it was discovered that the election tickets had been printed in different colors, and Federalists were stationed at the polls evidently to record the names of those who took a Republican ticket. It is doubtful that Charles Cotesworth needed help of this kind, but the rest of the Federalist ticket may have profited by the tactic. Charles Pinckney, who was not a gracious loser, also complained that the *"lame, crippled, diseased and blind were either led, lifted or brought in Carriages to the Poll."*[76]

An analysis of the fifteen representatives elected from Charleston to the legislature reveals that South Carolina was in a twilight era of mixed political systems. The representatives receiving the six highest votes were run on both the Federalist and Republican tickets. These were men who were popular but who were not aligned politically. Only one of the fifteen was an avowed Republican, Lieutenant-Governor John Drayton. The other eight run on the ticket with

75. Henry William De Saussure to John Rutledge, Jr., Aug. 14, 1800, John Rutledge Papers, Southern Hist. Coll., U. of N.C. This was the first time Charles Cotesworth Pinckney had been opposed in a Charleston election.

76. Charles Pinckney to Thomas Jefferson, Oct. 12, 16, 1800, in [Jameson, ed.], "South Carolina in the Presidential Election of 1800," *Amer. Hist. Rev.*, 4 (1898–99), 115. Charles Cotesworth Pinckney received 623 votes and Colonel Thomas Lee received 387, according to the Charleston *City Gazette*, Oct. 15, 1800. Charles Cotesworth was also returned as a representative from St. Thomas' and St. Dennis' parishes, a complimentary gesture, or as insurance if he were defeated in Charleston. Charleston *City Gazette*, Oct. 16, 1800.

Charles Cotesworth Pinckney were known to be exclusively his friends.[77] It is little wonder that Thomas Pinckney found it difficult to estimate the strength of the Federalist and Republican parties throughout the state.[78] Party lines were being forged in the heat of the present contest, and many men were still without a party label.

After the legislature elections and shortly after the appearance of Hamilton's letter, the anti-Charles Cotesworth Pinckney articles became more frequent and raised more sensitive issues. Charles Pinckney repeated the embarrassing point that his cousin had become the candidate of those Federalists who wished for war with France. Was Charles Cotesworth Pinckney merely the engine of Hamilton's ambition? "Republican" asked. It was well known that Hamilton had threatened military violence if Charles Cotesworth were not elected. "Does General Pinckney know this," "Republican" queried, "and yet stand a candidate for the presidency on such terms? Or does he patiently bear the dishonor of being brought forward by a man who . . . would put himself at the head of an army, to inflict on the people . . . all the terrors of military violence?"[79]

"A Rice Planter" charged that Pinckney had been placed on the Federalist ticket to confuse the political situation in South Carolina. It was nothing but a Federalist trick to make an essentially Republican state vote the Federalist ticket, he asserted. "Rice Planter" had heard it urged that Jefferson and Pinckney jointly should be South Carolina's electoral choice, for in this way the factious "spirit of party" would be ameliorated. This would be worse than useless, "Rice Planter" argued, as Pinckney was not a candidate for the vice-presidency but for the presidency itself. Hamilton's notorious letter was proof of this. Since Pinckney and Jefferson were in fact candidates for the same office, to give them an equal vote would "entirely destroy the political weight of Carolina in the national scene; it is . . . precisely the same as not voting at all."[80]

This argument was almost unanswerable. The Hamiltonians as well as many of Pinckney's supporters in South Carolina wished him to

77. Charleston *City Gazette*, Oct. 18, 1800.
78. See n. 71.
79. Charleston *City Gazette*, Nov. 14, 21, 1800.
80. *Ibid.*, Nov. 19, 1800.

be president. Pinckney was depressed, however, by the tone of the campaign and by the attacks launched against his candidacy within his own state. He was accused of being a potential military despot, an ill-tempered diplomat, the puppet of Hamilton and the war faction. It was no comfort either that these attacks were directed by his ambitious cousin.

Charles Cotesworth Pinckney's friends were indignant, and they rightly put the blame for the shrewd attacks against him on Charles Pinckney. His friends were also angry with Charles Pinckney because he had read Adams' now famous letter to Tench Coxe, probably in 1799, and had not told his cousins of its existence. It is possible that the Pinckney brothers thought their cousin had advised Coxe to publish the letter, not a difficult charge to believe. When Thomas Pinckney later asked Charles why he had not mentioned the letter, Charles replied that he thought probably Thomas already knew about it, and "as the subject was not an agreeable one You would consider it as rather officious in me or dislike it's being mentioned; and therefore from motives of Delicacy I did not shew it to you."[81]

The Pinckney brothers and their friends were convinced that "Delicacy" had nothing to do with Charles's action. A friend, and a relative even more, should have told them about this letter. By actions such as these, Charles Pinckney brought upon himself the nickname of "Blackguard Charley." Charles Pinckney did not seem especially disturbed by the social and political separation from his kinsmen, however, and prepared to exert all his influence at Columbia, the state capital, for the Republican electoral ticket.

At Columbia the legislators first met to honor the deceased Edward Rutledge. Charles Cotesworth Pinckney was in his Senate seat when Lieutenant-Governor Drayton gave the official eulogy on Governor Rutledge. As was the custom, Drayton's message to the legislature was referred to a committee on which Pinckney, appropriately, was placed.[82]

The pressure of political maneuvering left little time for melancholy reflection, for party leaders in South Carolina and throughout

81. Charles Pinckney to Thomas Pinckney, Nov. 10, 1800, Pinckney Family Papers, Lib. Cong.
82. Nov. 20, 1800, Senate Jour., S.C. Archives.

the nation believed that South Carolina's electoral vote would decide the outcome of the national election.[83]

The political situation at Columbia was highly confusing. The personal popularity of Charles Cotesworth Pinckney, the essentially Republican character of the state by election time, and the political nonalignment of many representatives within the legislature made the outcome of the electoral vote for president uncertain. What actually happened at Columbia during those hectic November days has been difficult to determine because of the flatly contradictory statements made by informed participants. Some swore that Charles Cotesworth Pinckney could have been placed on a compromise electoral ticket with Jefferson, but Charles Pinckney vehemently denied this to Thomas Jefferson.[84]

One might question the reliability of Charles Pinckney's accounts to Jefferson. His letters to Jefferson during these days reveal that he was trying desperately to ingratiate himself with Jefferson and to impress Jefferson that the national Republican victory was due to his own heroic exertions in Columbia.[85] An ambitious Charles Pinckney had much to lose if Jefferson believed that some Republicans would have risked Jefferson's election in order to avoid injuring Charles Cotesworth Pinckney's feelings.

Two other witnesses and participants are more reliable than Charles Pinckney. One, Peter Freneau, was co-editor of the Charleston *City Gazette*, a Republican, and a friend of Charles Pinckney. Freneau followed the meetings at Columbia closely and wrote as many as two or three letters a day to his partner in Charleston, Seth Paine, describing the struggle to gain votes. Another reliable witness was Henry William De Saussure, a confidant of Charles Cotesworth Pinckney.

83. John Marshall to Charles Cotesworth Pinckney, Nov. 20, 1800, Pinckney Family Papers, Lib. Cong.; Thomas Jefferson to Thomas Mann Randolph, Nov. 30, 1800, *Jefferson Papers* (Mass. Hist. Soc. *Collections*, 7th Ser., 1 [1900]), 78.

84. Charles Pinckney to Thomas Jefferson, Jan. 24, 1801, in [Jameson, ed.], "South Carolina in the Presidential Election of 1800," *Amer. Hist. Rev.*, 4 (1898–99), 127–28.

85. For example, Pinckney wrote to Jefferson just after the election was over: "We have Had a hard and arduous struggle and I found that as there Were no hopes from Philadelphia and it depended upon our State entirely to secure Your Election and that it would be almost death to our hopes for me to quit Columbia I have remained until it is over and now permit me to congratulate You my dear sir. . . ." Dec. 2, 1800, in *ibid.*, 119. Jefferson was duly impressed and appointed Charles Pinckney minister to Spain in 1801.

One historian has discounted De Saussure as a witness, arguing that he was an excited young man who had no feel for the political situation at Columbia.[86] But De Saussure had been a member of the bar since 1784, and was known for his unimpeachable integrity. He became director of the mint in 1794 and was elected a judge of the Court of Equity in 1808 and chancellor of South Carolina in 1824. There is every reason to believe that De Saussure would not—did not —falsify the events that transpired at Columbia in November 1800.[87] There were other witnesses whose statements have helped to fill out the history of those frantic twelve days, but their accounts do not add substantially to the stories told by Charles Pinckney, Peter Freneau, and Henry W. De Saussure.

There were 161 members elected to the state legislature, but 10 were absent. Therefore, if either side could win the support of 76 votes for all its presidential electors, the election would be decided. In the final count the Jeffersonian electors polled between 82 and 87 votes. The highest vote for a Federalist elector was 69, the lowest 63. If only 7 votes had been switched at the right time, at least 2 Federalists would have become electors. As this calculation is carried out, it becomes apparent that had 13 members of the legislature decided to throw their support consistently to the Federalist ticket, the South Carolina electoral vote would have been reversed completely.[88]

The following then becomes the crucial question: were there thirteen additional votes available to the Federalist ticket, and if so, on what terms were they available? Charles Pinckney admitted that there were almost seventy persons who were absolutely pledged to Jefferson. Peter Freneau stated that there were between fourteen and sixteen members of the legislature who were "trimming" and who "required all our Labor to keep right. . . ." Freneau mentioned that "on the first and second day of the Session, an offer of accommodation was

86. Wolfe, *Jeffersonian Democracy*, 159n.
87. See John B. O'Neall, *Biographical Sketches of the Bench and Bar of South Carolina . . .*, 2 vols. (Charleston, 1859), I, 243–52, for an appraisal of De Saussure.
88. Wolfe, *Jeffersonian Democracy*, 158n. An analysis of the vote reveals that one member of the legislature cast only seven votes. See also Charles Pinckney to Thomas Jefferson, Jan. 24, 1801, in [Jameson, ed.], "South Carolina in the Presidential Election of 1800," *Amer. Hist. Rev.*, 4 (1898–99), 128.

made, but the answer was, _____ [Charles Cotesworth Pinckney] disdained to be run on a ticket with Mr. J _____. This settled the business."[89] Freneau informed Seth Paine immediately after the balloting that if Charles Pinckney had not cancelled a last minute meeting of Republicans when he learned that Federalists planned to attend and plead for Charles Cotesworth, a compromise would "in all probability" have taken place.[90]

A long letter from De Saussure written just two days after the balloting for electors substantiates the accounts sent by Freneau to Paine:

When we arrived here [Columbia], we found the anti-federalists assembled in great numbers on the spot, and they immediately had a meeting [November 25], at which it was moved and carried, (about 60 members present) to support electors, who would vote for Mr. Jefferson and Mr. Burr. This joint mode they fastened upon every one who arrived, and who was known or supposed to be attached to Mr. J. and notwithstanding many of them revolted at the idea of abandoning General Pinckney, they by degrees won them over. As the election approached, the houses filled to the unprecedented number of 115 in the house of representatives, and to the number of 36 in the senate. The nine seats unfilled in the house of representatives, were all from the *lower country*. On examining of the members, we discovered that we could rely on about 68 or 70. The opinion of about a dozen members were not known, and on sounding them, it appeared reasonable to expect 6 or 7 of them to be with us. This would give us a bare majority. In this dilemma, the Federalists had a very serious discussion of the proper measures to be pursued. On the one hand, we had a doubtful chance of carrying a ticket of electors who would vote for Mr. Adams and General Pinckney. On the other hand, it was certain, that if we would give up Mr. Adams, and consent to vote for electors who would vote for Mr. Jefferson and Mr. Pinckney, we could easily secure the election of Gen. Pinckney; for about 30 of the Jeffersonians were extremely reluctant to give up Gen. Pinckney; and many of them requested us privately to agree to the arrangement. We should then have been certain of at least 95 or 96 votes for electors, who would unite in Mr.

89. [Jameson, ed.], "South Carolina in the Presidential Election of 1800," *Amer. Hist. Rev.*, 4 (1898–99), 128; Peter Freneau to [Seth Paine], Dec. 4, 1800, Miscellaneous Papers, S. Caroliniana Lib.

90. Freneau to Paine, [Dec. 2], 1800, Freneau Papers, Lib. Cong. Earlier, Wade Hampton, a Republican, wrote to Colonel Holmes in Virginia: "I think there will be a want of nerve to resist the pretensions of Gen. Pinckney. Mr. Jefferson will have every vote here, but there is a great danger that General Pinckney will also." Nov. 11, 1800, printed in the Phila. *Aurora*, Dec. 2, 1800.

Jefferson and General Pinckney. After mature deliberation, we resolved to venture all on the election of Mr. Adams and Gen. Pinckney, doubtful as it was, rather than abandon the ground deliberately agreed on by the Federalists all over the continent to support Mr. Adams and Gen Pinckney equally.[91]

De Saussure then claimed that the compromise proposal came from Jeffersonians, that it was informal in nature, and that it was by a sufficient number to make a Jefferson-Pinckney ticket overwhelmingly certain of election. Each was to receive an equal number of electoral votes.

In comparing this with the account of Charles Pinckney, there is one similarity to be found: both De Saussure and Pinckney agreed that the Republican caucus did not make the offer to Charles Cotesworth. But Charles Pinckney differs widely from De Saussure and Freneau on the size of the trimming squad of Republicans who hated to vote against Charles Cotesworth. "I do positively deny," Charles Pinckney wrote to Jefferson, "that any . . . compromise was offered by the body of the republican interest. . . . If any thing was ever said on that subject it must have been by some one or two [!] of our friends who might have been very anxious to secure Your Election and would rather compromise than risque it, but if even one did whisper such a thing it was *wholly unknown* to me. . . ."[92] Charles Pinckney's account is obviously quite different from the ones given both by his friend Freneau and by De Saussure. It is difficult to believe that Charles Pinckney was not aware of the compromising efforts; as a party leader he would probably have been the first to

91. De Saussure to ?, Dec. 4, 1800, printed in *Newport* [R. I.] *Mercury*, Dec. 30, 1800. "Pyrrhus," writing in the Charleston *City Gazette*, July 23, 1802, gives essentially the same account as De Saussure's. There is the possibility that "Pyrrhus" and De Saussure were one and the same person. A little over a month after the election, De Saussure wrote to John Rutledge, Jr.: "On reflection I am satisfied we did right in refusing a compromise, and I rejoice that you and our federal friends concur so freely in the propriety of it. I am now more compleatly satisfied, as I find that the Rhode Island Electors threw away one vote from Genl: P. so that he would have had but 72 votes if we had compromised; and Mr. Jefferson would have had 73. Genl: P. could have been V.P. only, which was not worth a compromise. . . ." Jan. 12, 1800, John Rutledge Papers, Southern Hist. Coll., U. of N.C.

92. Charles Pinckney to Jefferson, Jan. 24, 1801, in [Jameson, ed.], "South Carolina in the Presidential Election of 1800," *Amer. Hist. Rev.*, 4 (1898–99), 127–28.

know. The historian is reduced to concluding one of three things: Freneau and De Saussure imagined the distinct possibility of a compromise being arranged; Charles Pinckney actually did not know that many Republicans were wavering (Why did he call off the Republican caucus?); or Charles Pinckney misled Jefferson.

Twenty-five years later De Saussure claimed that two proposals had been made to Charles Cotesworth by a committee representing the legislature. It is certain that the committee did not represent the legislature but probably the "trimming" group mentioned in Freneau's letter of December 4. In any case, De Saussure asserted that the committee first offered to cast enough votes for Federalist electors to give Charles Cotesworth the vice-presidency. Pinckney responded that in all fairness he could not accept votes only for himself when Adams men in the eastern states had cast their votes evenly for both of the Federalist nominees. After considering his answer the committee returned, according to De Saussure, offering Pinckney enough electoral votes to give him the presidency. Pinckney replied that he did not want the presidency as a result of intrigue. If the gentlemen were unable to vote jointly for him and Adams as Federalists, then they should vote according to their political convictions.[93] While De Saussure's later account may be questioned because of the time lapse, he agreed essentially with Freneau that there were two attempts to win Pinckney's approval of a compromise ticket, but that both were unsuccessful because of Pinckney's refusal to cooperate.[94]

In sifting the testimony of the participants, their statements at the time, and their recollections years later, several facts seem to stand out as undeniable. A majority of the legislature in varying degrees identified themselves with the Republican party. The hard core Republicans, about seventy in number, were determined to vote only for electors pledged to Jefferson. Between ten and fifteen, perhaps more, vaguely considered themselves party Republicans, but because

93. Pinckney, *Life of Thomas Pinckney*, 156–57. Reverend Pinckney asserts that part of his information was derived from conversations with De Saussure.

94. Freneau to Seth Paine, [Dec. 2], 1800, Freneau Papers, Lib. Cong. Charles Cotesworth Pinckney wrote a letter from Columbia to John Marshall on Nov. 29 advising him that the Republicans would be able to carry the election. Pinckney made no mention of the compromise proposals. The letter was printed in the Phila. *Aurora*, Dec. 15, 1800.

of their friendly feeling toward Charles Cotesworth Pinckney they wavered in their loyalty to Jefferson. If Charles Cotesworth had encouraged them to link his name with Jefferson on the ticket, it is probable that South Carolina would have split its electoral ticket and Pinckney would have been elected vice-president.[95] De Saussure's later statement that Pinckney might have received more votes than Jefferson if he had asked for them is not corroborated by any other account; it is more likely that Pinckney was approached twice and urged to accept an equal number of votes with Jefferson.

It is not difficult to understand why Pinckney refused the support of the trimming group. He had given his word that he would accept no votes from electors not also pledged to Adams, and Pinckney was not a man to go back on his promises. A little foresight would have indicated that his term as president (for this was the office which many of his friends in South Carolina hoped he would get) would have been a trying four years. Despised by the Jeffersonians and mistrusted by the Adams Federalists, Pinckney would have had support only from the Hamiltonian Federalists. His good name would have been besmirched and he would have been denounced in the press as a modern Catiline, a lackey of Hamilton. Only an inordinately ambitious man would have wished for the presidency under these conditions.

Pinckney had made it clear to James McHenry that he would actively seek the presidency only if the northern states first dropped Adams and indicated that they wished to elect Pinckney. When this was not done, insofar as Pinckney was concerned his hands were tied.

While he abhorred the development of parties early in the 1790's, once he entered the national political scene Pinckney was unable to maintain the neutrality he had cultivated as a state politician. Circumstances had led him to identify himself with the Federalist

95. Professor Wolfe, in his *Jeffersonian Democracy*, 158–61, says that though a compromise was discussed it was never probable. Wolfe proceeds in his analysis on the basis that party lines were rigid by 1800, with every person identifying himself with one of the national political parties. There is too much contradictory evidence to accept this generalization. I think also that Professor Wolfe underestimated the immense personal popularity of Charles Cotesworth Pinckney. Pinckney had many fast friends throughout the state who were identified with the Republican party. One can easily imagine these Republican friends wishing to resolve their personal dilemma by voting a compromise ticket.

party. As a Federalist he then found himself unable to accept the divided electoral vote of his own state. Yet the blow of losing his state's votes was probably softened by the knowledge that many of his Republican friends would have cast their votes for him if he had consented. By his refusal to accept those votes, Pinckney had lost the vice-presidency but had preserved his reputation. He was no longer in Hamilton's shadow.

IX

THE POLITICS OF DEFEAT

—————— ⬥●⬥ ——————

*What will be the vote of So. Car.? Will she always turn her back
upon her distinguished citizen [Pinckney] and be the bar to his elevation to the first Dignity of the republic, which is the first in the
world? Will S: Car: still be beguiled into the error that he is unfriendly to . . . republican constitutions and Institutions, tho' for 30
Years he has been either fighting for them, or counselling the wisest
measures for their support? I hope not.*

—Henry William De Saussure, 1808.

—————— ⬥●⬥ ——————

REPUBLICANS WERE ALARMED AND FEDERALISTS OVERJOYED WHEN AN
unexpected tie in the electoral vote between Jefferson and Aaron
Burr threw the election of the president into the House of Representatives. Some Federalists saw delightful possibilities for mischief.
If Burr were elected with Federalist help, the Republican party might
split and the way be prepared for a Federalist return to power in 1804.

When Theodore Sedgwick informed Pinckney of the proposed
Federalist strategy, he evidently described Burr as a man of some
character, much less likely than Jefferson to destroy all the virtues
of the Federalist system. Pinckney replied that, like Sedgwick, he
was convinced that "attempts are making to construe away the energy
of our constitution, to unnerve our Government, and to over throw
that system by which we have risen to our present prosperity. . . ."
Pinckney added that while he had no "personal acquaintance with
either of the successful candidates," he was convinced that Burr was
the better man. Therefore, Pinckney concluded, he believed "the

[234]

meditated arrangement of the Federalists with respect to the election, [to be] politic and judicious."[1]

Pinckney thus approved the course of the South Carolina lame duck delegation to Congress, among whom were his brother and John Rutledge, Jr., when it voted for Burr.[2] As one scholar has noted, it is easy to understand the vote of arch-Federalist Robert Goodloe Harper of South Carolina against Jefferson. But how can one explain the position of the Pinckneys and Rutledges, families that had considered themselves Jeffersonians in 1795 and 1796.[3] The process of disillusionment had begun when Jefferson refused to support the administration's preparedness measures after Charles Cotesworth Pinckney's mission to France; this much is clear. The belief that Jefferson was a demagogue and unfit to be the chief executive probably took root during the presidential campaign when Charles Cotesworth was smeared by the Republican press as an adulterer and a sycophant of Hamilton. Could Jefferson, with such friends, be worthy of any office, much less the presidency? No doubt the Pinckneys and the Rutledges also blamed Jefferson for fastening the party system on South Carolina, a system which the Pinckneys considered wicked and factious.

Charles Cotesworth Pinckney's sympathy with the Federalist intrigue reveals the excited state of his mind in 1801. He had become a victim of Federalist propaganda and had temporarily lost his political grip. It is difficult to imagine that Pinckney would have supported the election of Burr if Edward Rutledge had lived. Rutledge, who had corresponded with Jefferson for many years, would likely have encouraged his "dear Friend Pinckney" to see Jefferson in a more realistic light. As a result of backing Burr, the Pinckneys and Rutledges lost any future political support they might have received from the Jeffersonians in South Carolina. Ironically, the very families that deprecated most the development of party politics in South Carolina helped to fasten it firmly upon the state by defying the

1. Pinckney to Sedgwick, Feb. 12, 1801, Sedgwick Papers, Mass. Hist. Soc. Sedgwick's part in the Burr intrigue is discussed in Richard E. Welch, Jr., *Theodore Sedgwick, Federalist: A Political Portrait* (Middletown, Conn., 1965), ch. 15.

2. *Annals*, 6th Congress, Feb. 17, 1801, 1029–34; Washington, D.C. *National Intelligencer*, Feb. 16, 18, 1801.

3. Rogers, *Evolution of a Federalist*, 353–54.

wishes of the state's legislature. No longer could the Pinckneys claim to stand above petty party intrigue, bound to no interest but the national good. And Burr's later notoriety seemingly proved that party regularity was just as reliable a guide to political wisdom as the collective insight of Charleston's self-anointed aristocracy.

Pinckney may have been calmed by a letter from his friend John Marshall, written on Jefferson's inauguration day. Marshall admitted that he was "not disposed to class Mr. Jefferson" with the "absolute terrorists" in Republican ranks but rather with the "speculative theorists." Jefferson's inauguration speech, Marshall added, was "well judged and conciliatory, . . . giving the lie to the violent party declamation which has elected him. . . ."[4] Pinckney could also take some comfort that John Marshall was now the Supreme Court chief justice. A man of such "correct" views would serve as a brake on Jeffersonian plans "to construe away the energy" of the constitution "and to over throw that system" established by Washington and Hamilton.

Perhaps to his surprise, Pinckney soon found that political life in South Carolina continued much as before despite the election of Jefferson. The party system, to be sure, complicated the politics of the state, but to Henry William De Saussure the cloak of parties merely disguised the continuing struggle for power between the various geographical sections of the state. Low-country Federalists were encouraged when they discovered that "in all questions not violently party questions" they had "great, not to say, preponderating weight" within the legislature.[5]

Electing public officials was of course one of the "violently party questions" that revealed the political divisions within the legislature. When Pinckney was asked by Federalists to become a candidate for

4. Marshall to Pinckney, Mar. 4, 1801, Misc. Mss., Charleston Lib. Soc.
5. Henry William De Saussure to John Rutledge, Jr., Jan. 13, 1802, John Rutledge Papers, Southern Hist. Coll., U. of N.C. De Saussure was encouraged because up-country plans to reduce the legislative representation of Charleston and to run congressional candidates on a single state-wide ticket were defeated. Same to same, Dec. 19, 1801, *ibid*. Robert Anderson explained to John E. Colhoun that the Republicans in the state legislature could put the Federalists "compleatly in our power" but the "moderate part of us" declined to do so because the "Federal interest . . . have compleatly struck their Colours and conceive themselves compleatly in our power, as to principle. In addition to that, on a view of the late Census they are struck with the great and growing inequality; and I expect will agree to a Compromise. . . ." Dec. 3, 1801, Colhoun Papers, S. Caroliniana Lib.

the vacated seat of his cousin Charles Pinckney in the United States Senate,[6] he replied that the cause was hopeless. Charles Cotesworth assured his friends that he would draw no more votes in the legislature than any other candidate the Federalists might propose. Party, not ability, now determined the outcome of all elections.[7] John Rutledge, Jr., disagreed with Pinckney. He was positive that Pinckney would best either Aedanus Burke or General Thomas Sumter, the possible Republican candidates, for many of the Republican "Vagabonds who were counted upon at the Presidential election, would rejoice in an occasion of making the *amende honorable* by supporting him as senator."[8] Nevertheless, Pinckney refused to be considered and the Federalists therefore ran Rutledge, Jr., who was decisively beaten.

Pinckney found it difficult to adjust to the new facts of political life. It was bewildering to him that men of "virtue," education, and experience—the Charleston oligarchy—were no longer considered competent to govern the affairs of South Carolina largely by themselves. Pinckney withdrew in disgust at the thought that men's actions were now to be determined according to what the party considered wisest. While he was acknowledged to be the leading Federalist in South Carolina, Pinckney refused to assume leadership of the state's Federalists. By default, his nephew John Rutledge, Jr., became the party leader.[9]

The animus of the party and sectional struggle after 1800 convinced many leaders of the low country that they must take measures to ameliorate the hostility of the up-country Republicans. While the gradual spread of slavery was helping to bind South Carolina together economically, many believed that the sectional strife would continue until the future leaders of the state—from every section—established personal rapport and common points of view. A college, it was suggested, would serve these purposes. Besides, South Carolinians were not pleased when their young men were compelled to leave the state

6. Charles Pinckney was promptly rewarded by Jefferson for his electoral services by an appointment as minister to Spain.

7. Henry William De Saussure to [John Rutledge, Jr.], Aug. 25, [1801], John Rutledge Papers, Southern Hist. Coll., U. of N.C.

8. John Rutledge, Jr., to Harrison G. Otis, Sept. 15, 1801, Otis Papers, Mass. Hist. Soc.

9. Elizabeth Cometti, "John Rutledge, Jr., Federalist," *Jour. of Southern Hist.*, 13 (1947), 186–87.

to obtain advanced training, especially since the economic resources of the state were more than sufficient to finance a state college system. The time now seemed ripe to take constructive action.

Pinckney had enthusiastically supported the idea of founding a state college for many years. He had been sharply disappointed in 1770 when a bill recommending the establishment of a college became a casualty of the struggle between the Crown and the legislature. Now, after thirty-one years, Pinckney had the privilege of guiding a bill through the Senate that authorized the establishment of a state-supported college. His former law student and intimate friend, Henry William De Saussure, was active in writing the bill and steering it through the House of Representatives.[10]

Pinckney's great interest in the college was recognized when he was elected to its first board of trustees. Although he was nominated for the position of chairman, he obtained only five votes to his opponent's nine votes. John Drayton, the Republican governor, had little academic training but was thought by a majority of the trustees to be better qualified for the position than the highly trained and cultured Pinckney.[11] Pinckney at least was able to assist in the early formulation of educational policies for the state college he had so long desired.

As senator for Charleston, Pinckney continued to have considerable influence in the state Senate. A perusal of his legislative activities makes that clear. He was pleased when the Senate approved his bill to establish a court of inferior jurisdiction in Charleston.[12] Pinckney was complimented by being made chairman of the military committee and chairman of a committee to revise and amend the state's gambling laws.[13] But while the Senate was ready to benefit from his

10. Hollis, *University of South Carolina*, I, 10, 15–18; Nov. 27, Dec. 14, 1800, Jan. 19, 1801, Senate Jour., S.C. Archives. Pinckney shared the honor of having helped to shape both education bills with Thomas Smith.

11. Professor Hollis does not believe it likely that the political alignment within the state affected the vote, but given the educational qualifications of Pinckney and Drayton and the political atmosphere of South Carolina, this conclusion might be disputed. See Hollis, *University of South Carolina*, I, 25. John Rutledge, Jr., not known for judicious evaluations of his political enemies, wrote Harrison G. Otis that Governor Drayton "has not Brains enough to fill your Daughters thimble," Sept. 15, 1801, Otis Papers, Mass. Hist. Soc.

12. Dec. 2, 13, 17, 1801, Senate Jour., S.C. Archives.

13. Nov. 28, 1801, *ibid*.

experience or interest in the areas of his special knowledge, there were signs that Pinckney no longer had the complete confidence of his Senate colleagues. No more was he automatically made chairman of committees to consider petitions he brought before the Senate. He found himself excluded from the important taxation committee as well as from the committee which replied to the governor's opening message to the legislature. Each session Pinckney was given less responsibility, no doubt a humiliating circumstance to him. His attendance became sporadic; he was usually late to the sessions, or did not attend them at all. Republicans seized upon his late attendance at the November 1803 session to jockey Pinckney out of his chairmanship of the military committee, replacing him with Colonel Robert Barnwell.[14] The up country was now clearly in the saddle with Pinckney's influence visibly shrinking.

Concrete evidence of the shift of political power to the up country came in 1803 when the legislature redistricted the state, as Pinckney said, "to stifle the voice of federalism." Pinckney complained to John Rutledge, Jr., of this "iniquitous arrangement of districts. . . ." Beaufort, Barnwell, and Edgefield districts were "thrown together; Colleton, Orangeburgh and Richland form another election district; and that there may be a better chance to throw Huger out at the ensuing election, Chesterfield is taken from Cheraw and Georgetown Districts and joined with Camden."[15] It never occurred to Pinckney, apparently, that this "iniquitous arrangement" was completely justified in the eyes of the up country which had long been denied political power commensurate with its wealth and population.

The redistricting law was a sign that the long day of predominantly low-country rule had passed. With it went the base of Charles Cotesworth Pinckney's political power. When his Senate term expired in October 1804, Pinckney's public career was ended.

While Pinckney was sinking beneath the political horizon within his own state, he was far from being forgotten in other parts of the Union, either by his friends or by his enemies. A Republican with a

14. Nov. 24, Dec. 7, 1803, *ibid.*
15. Pinckney to Rutledge, Jan. 17, 1803, John Rutledge, Jr., Papers, Duke Univ. Lib. Rogers discusses this situation more fully in his *Evolution of a Federalist,* 354–55.

scurrilous pen, John Wood, published a book in 1802 purporting to be a history of the Adams administration. Wood gleefully recounted the "tale of the tubs," stating as bald fact that Pinckney and John Marshall had seduced a Paris "female of a respectable family. . . ." Once the woman was pregnant, Pinckney had manfully offered to bring her with him to America, but at the last moment he had changed his mind, leaving Paris for southern France "without either giving her notice, or a compensation for the loss of her virtue." When the poor soul finally made her way to Charleston to ask mercy from Pinckney, a "few tender and affectionate cards, which had been addressed to her by her lovers, and which she carried along with her as passports, were twisted into bills of treason." The "lady" had disappeared, Wood snickered, but shrewd men were making two guesses about her circumstances; either she was being supported by Pinckney and Marshall, or she had been driven off with her infant, "the only known benefit procured to the United States from the embassy of Pinckney, Marshall, and Gerry."[16]

The attack upon Pinckney's character was also carried on in the Republican press. One paper printed a poem supposedly written by Timothy Dwight in 1788, based upon Pinckney's profligate character. Entitled "The Triumph of Infidelity," it gave Pinckney the lines:

> I am the first of men in the ways of evil,
> The truest, thriftiest servant of the Devil;
> Born, educated, glory to engross
> And shine confess'd the Devil's Man of Ross.
> Here's three to one I beat even him in pride;
> Two whores already in my chariot ride.

Editors of the Federalist *Connecticut Courant* protested this slander against Pinckney, pointing out that if any Pinckney was the subject of such a poem, it was more properly the minister to Spain, Charles Pinckney. "That the character is perfectly just, as applicable to the latter *gentleman*," the *Courant* added, "is well known to be true, by all who were acquainted with him at the date of the poem."[17]

16. John Wood, *The Suppressed History of the Administration of John Adams (from 1797 to 1801) as Printed and Suppressed in 1802*, ed. John Henry Sherburne (Phila., 1846), 186–87.

17. Feb. 2, 1803. The poem had been printed in the Hartford *American Mercury*, date unknown.

Charles Cotesworth Pinckney could at least be consoled that his Federalist friends had not forgotten him. He was regularly toasted at Federalist dinners as a man of sterling character, one who would rather be honorable than president. Pinckney maintained intermittent contact with his Federalist friends outside South Carolina, particularly with Alexander Hamilton and John Marshall. Pinckney's letter to Hamilton upon learning that Hamilton's son had been killed in a duel is an indication of the affection that he felt for Hamilton. Calling him "my dear friend," Pinckney tried to solace Hamilton on his "irreparable loss," a loss "which only religion and time can alleviate. . . . The tears of friendship," he assured Hamilton, "will flow with your own."[18]

Hamilton was depressed not only by his son's death but by the continuing political triumphs of his Republican enemies. Hamilton wrote to Pinckney that he had discovered a "garden . . . is a very useful refuge of a disappointed politician," but he made it quite clear that distributing political plums was more to his liking. "Amidst the triumphant reign of democracy, do you retain sufficient interest in public affairs to feel any curiosity about what is going on?" he asked Pinckney.[19]

Though Pinckney did retain some "curiosity" about public affairs, like Hamilton he sought comfort in agricultural pursuits. He dropped his law practice completely and retreated to the isolation of Pinckney Island near Port Royal harbor. There, nearly one hundred miles from Charleston, Pinckney, his wife, and Eliza passed most of the year in isolation together with the plantation slaves. Politics distinctly took a second place to agriculture in Pinckney's life. One reason for this perhaps was that Pinckney, unlike Hamilton, did not feel that the Republican party had deliberately set out to undermine the Constitution and the nation's institutions. Life, after all, continued much as it had before the Republican victory. His friends before the election were still his friends, property appeared secure, and there was prosperity despite the uncertain situation in Europe. There seemed

18. Pinckney to Hamilton, Dec. 24, 1801, Charles Cotesworth Pinckney Miscellaneous Papers, N.Y. Pub. Lib. Marshall and Pinckney corresponded on Marshall's forthcoming biography of George Washington. Marshall asked Pinckney's help in recalling events of the Revolutionary War in the south. See Marshall to Pinckney, Nov. 21, 1802, Pinckney Family Papers, Lib. Cong.

19. Hamilton to Pinckney, Dec. 29, 1802, in Lodge, ed., *Works of Hamilton*, X, 444–45.

to be no great cause for alarm, no condition that called for his strenuous political activity.

Perhaps Pinckney was shaken in his complacency during his five-month tour of New England in 1803. Mrs. Pinckney's usual delicate health seemed to call for a journey to the more bracing climate of New England for the summer months. The Pinckneys left Charleston in May, not returning until late October or early November.[20] While in New England, Pinckney visited his political friends in Massachusetts and Connecticut. They graciously arranged for Pinckney to be granted an honorary Doctor of Laws degree by Harvard College, a sign of his reputation as a lawyer but also an indication that the trustees of Harvard College shared in the Federalist sentiment of New England.[21] Old friends showered the Pinckneys with kindness. On "our whole rout," Pinckney wrote John Rutledge, Jr., they had received "every possible mark of attention and politeness."[22]

The Pinckney tour doubtless had political overtones. There was an election to be held within a year and the Federalists were badly in need of a candidate. Pinckney could hardly have been unaware that he was being considered as a presidential possibility by the Federalist party, for there were actually very few candidates to whom Federalist leaders could turn.

The victory of the Republicans in 1800 and the ways in which the Federalists had contributed to their own defeat had left party members bitter and disunited. Although younger members of the party strove valiantly to organize at all levels, the Federalist party suffered acutely from a lack of popular national leaders. Former president John Adams was detested by the arch-Federalists. Hamilton was not proving himself a constructive party leader in defeat, and Pinckney was not even the chief of the Federalist party in South Carolina. The only geographical area in which Federalism retained an element of vitality was in New England.[23]

20. Charles Cotesworth Pinckney to John Rutledge, Jr., Apr. 30, 1803, John Rutledge, Jr., Papers, Duke Univ. Lib.; Hartford *Connecticut Courant*, Oct. 12, 1803.

21. *Charleston Courier*, Sept. 21, 1803. The degree was bestowed during commencement services on Aug. 31.

22. Pinckney to Rutledge, Sept. 27, 1803, John Rutledge Papers, Southern Hist. Coll., U. of N.C.

23. John Rutledge, Jr., had written Harrison G. Otis in 1801: "That there is this disposition among many of our folks not only to compromise, but to sub-

High Federalists in New England were aware that even within their hallowed bastion the ruinous ferment of Jeffersonian Republicanism was having its effect. If the walls of Federalism fell in New England, they believed, all public virtue, all right principles would be lost. Men like Timothy Pickering did not think it was justifiable to sit calmly by while Jeffersonian trumpeteers marched around Jericho's wall. Yet there appeared to be no possibility of winning the election of 1804 against the Jacobin Jefferson. The administration's "attack" upon the Federalist judiciary and the expense of purchasing the vast Louisiana territory seemed to alarm only the diminishing body of Federalists. Over a period of months, therefore, Pickering and a few of his friends began to consider a plan to take the New England states out of the Union.[24]

The success of their plan depended upon New York's joining the conspiracy. Secessionist Federalists looked to Vice-President Aaron Burr, a candidate for governor, for assistance in their plot.[25] Federalists hoped that as governor of New York, Burr would take the lead in the secession movement; therefore they played upon his dissatisfaction with the way Jefferson had isolated him politically in Washington. Divided counsels as usual plagued Federalists, for while Pickering and his conspirators were cheering Burr on from the sidelines of Massachusetts and Connecticut, Alexander Hamilton was working furiously to defeat him. Though admitting that Federalist

---

mission is I believe true in some degree everywhere. I know that in the south it is preeminently so." Sept. 15, 1801, Otis Papers, Mass. Hist. Soc. An enlightening book on developments within the Federalist party between 1800 and 1816 is David H. Fischer's *The Revolution of American Conservatism: The Federalist Party in the Era of Jeffersonian Democracy* (N.Y., 1965). Fischer shows the differing reactions within the party to the defeat of 1800. While the younger and relatively obscure members of the party attempted to combat the Republican party through organization and propaganda, older Federalists such as Pinckney largely retired from the public eye. Inhibited by a fear that social conflict would become institutionalized through parties, the gentlemen of the "old school" generally refused to participate in organizational efforts sponsored by younger Federalists.

24. Pickering to Judge Richard Peters, Dec. 24, 1803, Pickering to George Cabot, Jan. 29, 1804, Pickering Papers, Mass. Hist. Soc.; Pickering to Theodore Lyman, Feb. 11, 1804, in Lodge, *Life of George Cabot*, 445.

25. Robert E. Reeser, Rufus King and the Federalist Party (unpubl. Ph.D. diss., University of California, Los Angeles, 1947), 213; Pickering to Rufus King, Mar. 4, 1804, in Lodge, *Life of George Cabot*, 448; Roger Griswold to Oliver Wolcott, Mar. 11, 1804, in Adams, ed., *Documents Relating to New England Federalism*, 354.

fortunes were at a new low point, Hamilton saw no reason to compound this unfortunate condition by clasping a Republican tiger to the Federalist bosom. Hamilton assured his excited friends that their strategy was as faulty as their evaluation of Burr and that to separate from the Union would only hasten the spread of Republican poison, not retard it.[26]

It is not certain that Pinckney learned of the New England secession plan in his visit there during the summer of 1803. Probably he did not. Even so, he must have realized that many New England Federalists were feeling much as Satan had upon being cast from Heaven:

> But his doom
> Reserv'd him to more wrath; for now the thought
> Both of lost happiness and lashing pain
> Torments him; round he throws his baleful eyes
> That witness'd huge affliction and dismay
> Mixt with obdurate pride and stedfast hate.[27]

Federalists in other parts of the Union were even less hopeful of an electoral victory in 1804. The south was completely Republican and there were few encouraging signs in the middle states. It was obvious to the most sanguine Federalist that the election of 1804 would be a rout rather than a contest. Divided, discouraged, and with one wing ready for disunion, the Federalist party was more nearly ready to be interred than to provide constructive national leadership.

Nevertheless, Federalists went through the motions of naming candidates. At a public dinner in Washington late in February 1804, Pinckney and Rufus King of New York were nominated by congressional Federalists for the presidency and vice-presidency. At a later meeting it was specifically agreed to support Pinckney for the first office.[28]

By nominating Pinckney the Federalists publicly admitted that the election was lost. In 1800 he had been placed on the electoral ticket to seduce South Carolina from its Jeffersonian predisposition, but now Pinckney had absolutely no hope of carrying that state or any

26. Miller, *Hamilton*, 567–68; Reeser, Rufus King (U. C. L. A.), 212–14.
27. John Milton, *Paradise Lost*, Book I, 53–58.
28. King, *Life of Rufus King*, IV, 350. The meeting, held in Washington on Feb. 22, was reported in the *Charleston Courier*, Mar. 10, 1804.

other section of the Union. Why, then, was he nominated? No doubt because he was the perfect caretaker candidate. No one would be angered by his nomination, neither Adams Federalists nor the friends of Hamilton and Pickering. By nominating a southerner, the Federalists could keep up the appearance of being a national party. Finally, Pinckney's sterling patriotism might help to throw dust into the eyes of prying Republicans intent on proving that influential New England Federalists were involved in disunionist plots.

Pinckney had the dubious honor of being the least publicized candidate in the brief history of American presidential party elections. There is every probability that most Americans were completely unaware that he had been nominated by the Federalist party. Pinckney accepted this circumstance and quietly watched as the Republicans rolled to a sweeping electoral victory, 162 to 14. Only Connecticut and Delaware cast all their votes for Pinckney, with Maryland adding two stray votes. In Congress Timothy Pickering lamented that "162 votes [were cast] for the worst man in the nation,—and 14 for two of the best." Even fortress Charleston fell to the Republicans, a sign that the body of southern Federalism had not only seemingly died but was becoming offensive to its oldest friends as well.[29]

Pinckney disturbed himself very little about the election. During the election period, in fact, he was busy leading a crusade against the custom of dueling. The news that Alexander Hamilton had been mortally wounded by Aaron Burr shocked the nation and motivated Pinckney to wage his only campaign to reform public morals. Pinckney was knowledgeable on dueling customs, not only from observation and word of mouth, but also from firsthand experience. He had been wounded in 1785 in a duel with Daniel Huger and had served as second in the Howe-Gadsden duel in 1778 and in Judge John F. Grimké's encounter with Pierce Butler in 1799.[30]

It is likely that Pinckney's disgust with this practice had been

29. Eugene H. Roseboom, *A History of Presidential Elections* (N.Y., 1957), 55–56; Stanwood, *History of the Presidency*, I, 64; Pickering to Fisher Ames, Feb. 14, 1805, Pickering Papers, Mass. Hist. Soc.; *Charleston Courier*, Nov. 8, 1804.

30. Charleston *State Gazette of South-Carolina*, June 23, 1785; *Newport* [R. I.] *Mercury*, Mar. 26, 1799. Pierce Butler demanded the duel because of an election pamphlet Grimké had written to the electors of Orangeburgh and Beaufort, recommending that John Rutledge, Jr., be preferred to Butler. On the Howe-Gadsden duel, see above, ch. 3, n. 22.

developing over a period of years. Hamilton's death gave him an opportunity to denounce dueling at a dramatic moment. In the summer of 1804 Pinckney began his crusade by urging members of the Society of the Cincinnati, of which he was soon to be president-general, "to declare their abhorrence of this practice. . . ." "Dueling is no criterion of bravery," he assured them, for he had "seen cowards fight duels," and was "convinced real courage may often be better shown in the refusal than in the acceptance of a challenge." Let the members of the Society begin to discourage the custom by neither accepting nor giving challenges, Pinckney urged, as a "tribute of respect to the sentiments and memory of our late illustrious chief."[31]

In South Carolina, Pinckney received the backing of the state Society of the Cincinnati and the American Revolution Society. A committee from each organization sent a joint circular letter to clergymen within the state asking them to preach a "sermon on the sin and folly of *duelling*."[32] Both committees then gathered signatures for a memorial to the legislature asking that the legislature make illegal "this custom [which] originated in dark and barbarous ages, when a regular and impartial administration of justice was unknown and unpractised."[33] Pinckney's good friend, Baptist minister Richard Furman, set the example for other ministers by holding a public memorial in the Baptist Church for Hamilton. During the sermon Furman made it quite clear that no man who participated in the willful taking of life should claim the name of "Christian."[34]

Pinckney's efforts to have dueling outlawed were unsuccessful. but he never abandoned the idea that the practice was un-Christian and therefore ought to be abolished. Perhaps he had waited too long to take his stand; fiery young men could argue that General Pinckney had been a brave man in his day but that he was no longer as sensitive about questions of honor or as likely to be challenged. Or perhaps dueling was by now too firmly rooted in custom and in the

31. Pinckney to the New York State Society of the Cincinnati, Aug. 18, 1804, in Lorenzo Sabine, *Notes on Duels and Duelling* . . . (Boston, 1855), 322–23.

32. *Ibid.*, 324. The letter was signed by Pinckney, James Kennedy, and William Read, representing the Society of the Cincinnati. David Ramsay, Henry William De Saussure, William Allen Deas, James Lowndes, and Richard Furman were those who signed representing the American Revolution Society.

33. Printed in the Washington *National Intelligencer*, Oct. 10, 1804.

34. *Charleston Courier*, Aug. 16, 1804.

frontier temperament to be shaken by condemnations from old generals and well-meaning preachers.

As far as Pinckney was concerned, the great issue of 1804 was not whether he would be elected president but whether dueling would be banished by law and a hostile public opinion. He was unsuccessful both in the election and in his anti-dueling crusade.

Pinckney largely vanished from public view for over two years after the election of 1804, as did the Federalist party. His political career and the hopes of the Federalist party began to rise once the Jefferson administration started to founder in the troubled waters of international relations. The continuing warfare between France and Great Britain created problems for Jefferson that seemed almost insurmountable. Although American trade expanded at a remarkable rate between 1803 and 1806,[35] Jefferson and Secretary of State James Madison realized that the increasingly rigid restrictions placed upon American commerce by Britain and France and the British practice of impressing American sailors might lead to an incident which would trigger a war.[36]

This incident that Jefferson feared came in June of 1807. When a virtually defenseless American frigate, the *Chesapeake*, refused to allow itself to be searched for British deserters, the guns of *HMS Leopard* poured repeated broadsides into her, killing three men and wounding eighteen. After firing only one shot, the *Chesapeake* struck its colors. A British boarding party then lined up the American crew, seizing four who were supposedly deserters. Commodore James Barron brought the smashed and bloody *Chesapeake* back to Norfolk only hours after it had sailed.[37]

Americans were outraged when they learned of the *Chesapeake-*

35. Anna C. Clauder, American Commerce as Affected by the Wars of the French Revolution and Napoleon, 1793–1812 (unpubl. Ph.D. diss., University of Pennsylvania, 1930), 25.

36. The development of British policy toward American commerce and commercial carriers is analyzed in Bradford Perkins, *Prologue to War: England and the United States, 1805–1812* (Berkeley, 1961); Reginald Horsman, *The Causes of the War of 1812* (Phila., 1962); Harry L. Coles, *The War of 1812* (Chicago, 1965).

37. An old but still useful account of the *Chesapeake-Leopard* affair is in Henry Adams, *History of the United States During the Administrations of Jefferson and Madison*, 9 vols. (N.Y., 1891–98), II, 1–26.

Leopard encounter—or rather, slaughter. Never "have I seen this country in such a state of exasperation as at present," Jefferson reported to one correspondent.[38] If Jefferson had wanted war with England, he probably could have had it.

Together with their fellow Americans, the citizens of Charleston raised an indignant cry of protest. The town's most prominent citizens promptly gathered to consider what action might be necessary. Pinckney met with the group that assembled in the Exchange Building on July 3 and was placed upon the committee to report a plan of action.[39]

Six days later the town leaders met at the Circular Church to consider the committee's recommendations. After a lengthy and heated discussion, it was resolved to give no British man-of-war "any succor or comfort." Furthermore, anyone who supplied a British vessel in the harbor of Charleston would be considered a public enemy. Black crepe bands were to be worn on the left arm for ten days to honor those men killed on the *Chesapeake*. Pinckney and his brother were placed on a committee of twenty-one to enforce these regulations.[40]

Charlestonians were not content to entrust the safety of their town to a Republican president, particularly one who chose to believe that only gunboats and not men-of-war were necessary to protect the nation's commerce and coastal cities. Evidently on their own initiative, Charlestonians hired an engineer, Colonel Macomb, to put Forts Johnson, Moultrie and Pinckney into a state of war readiness. Charles Cotesworth Pinckney quickly offered to assist the engineer, an offer that was gratefully accepted. Though growing corpulent and slightly deaf, the old warrior was still ready to answer the call of the military, particularly against his old enemy of '76. Charlestonians showed their appreciation of Pinckney's service by marching in a crowd to his home and giving him nine rousing cheers.[41]

While Pinckney was reliving his military experiences of past years, Jefferson was grappling with the increasingly knotty problems of

38. Jefferson to Du Pont de Nemours, July 14, 1807, in Andrew A. Lipscomb, ed., *The Writings of Thomas Jefferson*, 20 vols. (Washington, D.C., 1904), XI, 274.
39. *Charleston Courier*, July 4, 1807.
40. *Ibid.*, July 9, 1807; Wolfe, *Jeffersonian Democracy*, 215.
41. *Charleston Courier*, Aug. 26, 1807, Aug. 19, 1808.

neutral rights. France, as well as Great Britain, gradually enlarged her list of restrictions upon American trade.[42] Jefferson became desperate. Hoping to force one or both belligerents to accept the American position on neutral rights, Jefferson persuaded the Congress to vote an embargo in December 1807. Under its terms no American ships were to leave for foreign ports.[43]

Although the embargo was ruinous to many shippers and economic interests within the United States, it was a godsend to the Federalist party. As in 1798, the fortunes of the party rose in proportion to the disasters that were plaguing the country. Pinckney and his Federalist friends were encouraged by divisions within the Republican party, one led by the volatile and unstable John Randolph of Virginia, others guided by state politicians within Pennsylvania and New York. Randolph and other party dissidents were proving a greater vexation to Jefferson than the emasculated body of Federalists. As the election of 1808 approached, Randolph threw his support behind James Monroe for president. Jefferson, while professing to be neutral in the contest between his friends Monroe and Madison, actually favored the latter and worked to secure his nomination by the Republican party.[44]

With the Republicans divided and the nation economically distressed by the embargo, Federalists hoped to reverse the electoral decisions of 1800 and 1804. But while Federalists rejoiced at Republican divisions, they were vexed by their own differences on possible electoral strategy. Some Federalists were doubtful that their party should seek power. The nation was obviously entering upon a difficult period internationally and the Federalists might take office just in time to face the disastrous results of Jefferson's policies. Perhaps, some said, it would be wise to throw Federalist votes to a Republican. If misfortune struck, the Republican party might be destroyed, paving the way for an easy Federalist return to power in 1812. At

42. For a complete list of French and British restrictions on American foreign trade between 1793 and 1810, see Clauder, American Commerce (U. of Pa.), 9–14.

43. Perkins, *Prologue to War*, 153–56; Nathan Schachner, *Thomas Jefferson, a Biography*, 2 vols. (N.Y., 1951), II, 860.

44. Schachner, *Jefferson*, II, 863–64; Cresson, *James Monroe*, 223–24; Irving Brant, *James Madison*, 6 vols. (Indianapolis, 1941–61), IV, 419; Jefferson to Monroe, Feb. 18, 1808, in Washington, ed., *Writings of Jefferson*, V, 247–48; Noble E. Cunningham, Jr., "Who Were the Quids?" *Miss. Val. Hist. Rev.*, 50 (1963), 252–63.

least the favored Republican, elected in part by Federalist votes, would feel obliged to follow a course not overtly hostile to commerce and right principles.

Early in 1808 many congressional Federalists seemed to favor supporting James Monroe for the presidency.[45] Other Federalists felt that the aging George Clinton of New York seemed most likely to play the Federalist game. Christopher Gore of Boston was certain that Clinton "would support and cherish Commerce, and further that they could make a Bargain, with which he would comply, as to the principal measures and offices of Government."[46] When Federalists such as Theodore Sedgwick and John Rutledge, Jr., reacted with disgust to these flirtations with Republicans, Harrison Gray Otis reminded them that it was "by no means our policy to effect the election of a Federal president, if by any other means the Virginia snake can be scotch'd." While Otis admitted that "honorable men on the first impression will shrink with disgust from this sort of compromise," he felt that honor and principle were meaningless words when the stakes were so high.[47]

To be sure, Federalists did not forget to consider men within their own party who would be suitable presidential and vice-presidential candidates. Pinckney, Rufus King, and John Marshall were thought to be the party's most promising candidates. Pinckney was aware that his nomination was being discussed by party leaders and that John Rutledge, Jr., was his chief sponsor for that office within the party. There were, in fact, suggestions in the Charleston press that Pinckney would be the Federalist nominee even before the Federalist party leaders had decided whether to support a Republican or to nominate a Federalist electoral ticket.

45. Barent Gardenier to Rufus King, Jan. 16, 1808, in King, *Life of Rufus King*, V, 58; Timothy Pickering to Charles W. Hare, Jan. 16, 1808, Pickering Papers, Mass. Hist. Soc. Pickering thought Monroe a "practical man, and we think more upright than either of the candidates [Madison and George Clinton]." Also, "being ... thoroughly cured of his French attachment, we greatly prefer him to the other candidates for the office of President."

46. Samuel E. Morison, "The First National Nominating Convention, 1808," *Amer. Hist. Rev.*, 17 (1911–12), 746; Christopher Gore to Rufus King, June 16, 1808, in King, *Life of Rufus King*, V, 101–02; George Cabot to H. G. Otis, Aug. 14, 1808, Otis Papers, Mass. Hist. Soc.

47. Theodore Sedgwick to Harrison G. Otis, June 6, 1808, Otis Papers, Mass. Hist. Soc.; Otis to John Rutledge, Jr., July 3, 1808, John Rutledge Papers, Southern Hist. Coll., U. of N.C.

"Sons of Carolina!" one writer queried, "is there one of you who would prefer a stranger [for president] to this illustrious citizen, a native of your own State?" To reject Pinckney, a man of "strict honour and incorruptible integrity, of talents and energy" would be an "insult" to the "judgment and patriotism" of South Carolinians.[48] The seeming assurance of this anonymous writer that Pinckney would be the Federalist nominee suggests that the article was inspired or written by John Rutledge, Jr.

Federalists in other states were not at all certain that Pinckney should be their candidate again. Twice a loser, a resident of a Republican state, and a slaveholder, Pinckney was not an attractive candidate to many northern Federalists. With Rufus King and George Clinton supported by powerful factions within the party, it seemed necessary for party leaders to meet and to choose candidates. No one wanted a repetition of the disastrous campaign of 1800.

Only the scent of victory could have brought the scattered Federalist pack together. Christopher Gore explained the Federalist mood in New England and the reason for the party's rising hopes: "I think the Federalists were never more united or more encouraged than at present. The Embargo is producing real and extensive distress. . . ."[49] The idea of a nominating convention evidently developed while Harrison Gray Otis was visiting party leaders in New York and Philadelphia in May of 1808. Shortly after Otis' exploratory visit, a committee of correspondence was appointed to sound out party leaders on the wisdom of holding a convention. Since the reaction to the committee's overtures was favorable, the leaders decided to hold the convention secretly in New York City during the latter part of August. Many New England Federalists hoped that in a general meeting they could convince Pinckney men to support either Rufus King or, if a Federalist victory seemed unlikely, the Republican George Clinton.[50]

By the time party leaders had assembled, the Clinton faction led by Otis and George Cabot was in retreat. If Clinton had proven

48. "A Voter," Charleston Courier, Aug. 11, 1808.
49. Gore to Rufus King, June 8, 1808, in King, Life of Rufus King, V, 100.
50. Reeser, Rufus King (U. C. L. A.), 238; Christopher Gore to Rufus King, June 8, 1808, in King, Life of Rufus King, V, 100; Harrison G. Otis to John Rutledge, Jr., July 3, 1808, John Rutledge, Jr., Papers, Southern Hist. Coll., U. of N.C.; Morison, "The First National Nominating Convention," Amer. Hist. Rev., 17 (1911–12), 748–53.

that he could carry Pennsylvania against the opposition of Madison Republicans, he would have received strong support in the Federalist convention. But a truce had been arranged between the warring factions within the Republican party in Pennsylvania by the time the convention met. It was uncertain, therefore, that Clinton would now be properly pliable or even that his political strength would be sufficient to carry the national election with Federalist support. Leaders of the Federalist party also recognized that a split would develop if Clinton were nominated, for New York Federalists positively refused to support their old enemy. A lost election, they argued, would be better for the party than lost honor.[51]

With Clinton eliminated, Pinckney and King were sure to get the nomination. It is not clear why a majority of the delegates preferred Pinckney to King for the presidential nomination. Perhaps John Rutledge, Jr., assured them that South Carolina would not reject her native son a third time if he were placed first on the ticket. Moreover, Pinckney's honorable conduct in the election of 1800 had been well publicized and he could therefore be supported by the old Adams Federalists as well as the high Federalists. Finally, at a time when the nation was involved in a crisis that could develop into a war, a soldier might have more appeal to the electorate than another member of the Virginia dynasty.

Even before learning of his nomination, Pinckney was enthusiastically working for the Federalist candidates in Charleston. "The spirit of Federalism which is bursting forth to the North and East of the Susquehannah," he wrote to John Rutledge, Jr., "must have an advantageous effect on our public affairs even if a Virginia Candidate should be again chosen to the Presidency." There was a real chance that Thomas Lowndes would be elected to Congress from the Charleston district if only William Loughton Smith would withdraw and thus avoid taking votes away from Lowndes.[52] An indication of the

51. Morison, "The First National Nominating Convention," *Amer. Hist. Rev.,* 17 (1911–12), 755–58; Theodore Sedgwick to Harrison Gray Otis, June 18, 1808, Otis Papers, Mass. Hist. Soc. In a letter to Killian K. Van Rensselaer, Timothy Pickering explained that the decision to support only Federalist candidates was made because it appeared that Clinton could not be elected even with a combination of Federalist and Republican votes, Sept. 26, 1808, Pickering Papers, Mass. Hist. Soc.

52. Smith did eventually withdraw but to the astonishment of his friends threw his support to the successful Democratic candidate, Robert Marion. Rogers, *Evolution of a Federalist,* 380–81.

new spirit in South Carolina, Pinckney continued, was that "our Democratic District of St. Luke sent me word that they understood I would go to the State Legislature if elected, and offered to elect me unanimously to either branch." Pinckney declined this astonishing offer "for many reasons" but "strongly recommended their electing members of staunch Washingtonian principles."[53]

Rutledge's letter of August 20 informing Pinckney that he was the party's presidential nominee reached Pinckney about September 7. Pinckney assured Rutledge that he was "highly flattered by the very great honour conferred on me" but had no hope that Federalist exertions in South Carolina would "be ultimately successful." Yet they would wage a vigorous campaign in South Carolina "to shew that federalism is not extinct, and that there is in the Union a formidable party of the old Washingtonian school, alert to detect and expose any weak or visionary plans which may endanger the prosperity or safety of our Country." For this reason, Pinckney said, "as well as on several others, in which no private or personal feelings enter, I am glad the compromise you mentioned was overruled." To have supported Clinton, he believed, would have "entangled" the party "in a labyrinth from which we could not extricate ourselves without the greatest difficulties, and, what is worse, loss of principle."[54]

Pinckney's political associates in South Carolina energetically participated in the campaign to elect Federalists to the state legislature. They also flooded the newspapers with letters arguing the electoral cause of Pinckney. With South Carolina suffering acutely from the effects of the embargo,[55] many Charlestonians were willing to listen to the siren song of Federalism. And Pinckney, a "Federal Republican" assured the hard-pressed electorate of Charleston, has "ways

53. Pinckney to John Rutledge, Jr., Aug. 24, 1808, John Rutledge Papers, Southern Hist. Coll., U. of N.C.

54. Pinckney to Rutledge, Sept. 8, 1808, *ibid*.

55. Wade Hampton, in a letter to Thomas Sumter, Mar. 15, 1808, complained: "It is difficult to imagine the pecuniary effect and the individual distress, occasioned by the embargo. It pervades all classes, and extends to every corner of the state. The peculiar state of the African [slave] trade had stripped the planting interests, pretty generally, of their resources, and involved many of them in debt. The crop was just coming to their aid, but being cut off from this, there remains nothing between the hammer of the sheriff's auctioneer and their property—and indeed sales of this description have multiplied to an astonishing degree in every part of the state." Quoted in Wolfe, *Jeffersonian Democracy*, 222.

and means to extricate you from your present difficulties, without committing the national honour."[56]

What those "ways and means" were was not stated. At any rate, the Federalists in South Carolina did not choose to conduct the campaign so much on issues as on the personal merit of General Pinckney. GUSTAVUS VASA reminded readers of the Charleston *Courier* that Pinckney was *"personally known to us,"* had defended the honor of his nation while minister to France, and had recently been active in the movement to prepare Charleston against a possible British attack. A man who defended his country against every enemy surely deserved bipartisan support, GUSTAVUS declared, and he called for a meeting of Pinckney's supporters at the Exchange.[57]

James Madison, the Republican candidate, was denounced by "Lucius Junius Brutus" as an "Accomodating trimmer," one known to be "radically and incurably opposed to commerce." Madison's personal courage was questioned and his supposed timidity was compared with Pinckney's sterling soldierly qualities. "Bunker Hill" joined "Brutus" in an appeal to disregard party labels and to vote for the "venerable patriot," Charles Cotesworth Pinckney. State pride alone, "Bunker Hill" urged, should compel South Carolinians to vote for Pinckney.[58]

Pinckney was pleased by the vigorous Federalist campaigning in the state but continued to believe that South Carolina would not be wooed from her Republican allegiance. To John Rutledge, Jr., he wrote that the situation did at least look hopeful for electing Lowndes to Congress since the city's Democrats had fallen out over who should be elected intendant and warden. "The Demos," he confided to Rutledge, ". . . are all by the ears, the most outrageous [outraged?] of them have denounced the Lees, Johnsons, Howards, Major Robertson etc." However, the Federalists were perplexed by William Loughton Smith's continuing "to hold his name up" for election to Congress, a circumstance that would undoubtedly draw votes away from Lowndes.[59]

56. *Charleston Courier*, Aug. 6, 1808.
57. *Ibid.*, Aug. 19, 1808.
58. *Ibid.*, Aug. 22, Sept. 17, 1808.
59. Pinckney to John Rutledge, Jr., Sept. 20, 1808, John Rutledge Papers, Southern Hist. Coll., U. of N.C.

Henry William De Saussure shared Pinckney's opinion that South Carolina would once again reject Federalism and her native son. In despair, De Saussure asked a friend, "Will she [South Carolina] always turn her back upon her distinguished citizen and be the bar to his elevation to the first Dignity of the republic . . . ?"[60]

"A Voter" asked the same question publicly. He also chided Federalists for allowing Pinckney to be beaten in the two previous presidential contests by their lack of conscientious electioneering. Do not "let this disgrace . . . be urged against us again," implored "Voter." Enthusiasm and a heavy voter turnout could yet carry the day.[61] "Pyrrhus" added that South Carolina had disgraced itself in 1800 by voting for the "miscreant" Aaron Burr. She now had an opportunity to redeem herself by voting for a person of honorable character and a native son as well.[62]

Charles Pinckney, who was now completing his fourth term as governor, became alarmed by the extraordinary exertions of the Federalists in Charleston. He reported to Jefferson that Charles Cotesworth's friends had stimulated "the most formidable opposition I have ever seen" to Republican candidates. For the previous month he had "never known so much struggle and animosity. . . ." Federalist literature was being "sent into every part of the country and no exertion left untried that art and rancorous hatred to you and Mr. Madison could devise."[63]

To Governor Pinckney's distress, the Federalists in Charleston seemed to be winning votes every day. It was difficult for Republicans to urge faithfulness to the Republican party nominees, Madison and Clinton, when Charles Cotesworth Pinckney himself was proclaimed by Federalists the sole issue. Governor Pinckney saw that Republicans would have to meet this challenge squarely; Charles Cotesworth's claims to the office of president would have to be discredited in 1808 as they had been once before in 1800.

To discredit Charles Cotesworth, Charles Pinckney collaborated with a supposed friend of Charles Cotesworth who wrote two pieces

60. De Saussure to Ezekiel Pickens, Sept. 12, 1808, Henry William De Saussure Papers, S. Caroliniana Lib.

61. *Charleston Courier*, Sept. 19, 1808.

62. *Ibid.*, Sept. 21, 1808.

63. Charles Pinckney to Thomas Jefferson, n.d. [*ca.* Oct. 12, 1808], Pinckney Papers, S.C. Hist. Soc. (a photostat of the original in Lib. Cong.).

to the papers and signed himself "An Elector of Georgetown." Charles Pinckney explained to Jefferson in some detail, and with obvious relish, how the claims of Charles Cotesworth were crushed:

. . . it was thought adviseable to attack their candidate on the grounds contained in the two pieces enclosed which I beg you to read and give to Mr. Madison. In a future letter I will tell you who is the author unless you guess at once on reading them. For a variety of reasons it was necessary to give them a disguise. These reasons will shake you. They were written by one of the oldest and certainly the most intimate friend and acquaintance he has in Charleston, and one who has long lived with him in the same house, and who thought it his duty on the occasion, when he saw such virulent attacks made on him [Madison] and that doubts existed as to the Election, to come forward in a manner that he knew would be decisive. . . . I do not know [that] they have much merit. You will read them and judge for yourself; but certain it is they had great effect on the Election. Before I send you this letter I shall know the result. The Signature of these pieces, and the *pretended youth* of the writer you and Mr. Madison will well understand, and know where they come from.[64]

The attacks made upon Charles Cotesworth Pinckney by his supposed friend, "An Elector of Georgetown," appeared in the Charleston *City Gazette* between October 4 and 10. In the articles, "Elector" declared that Charles Cotesworth Pinckney was unfit for the presidency for a variety of reasons: his services to the nation during the Revolutionary War were hardly worthy of notice; he was sadly out of touch with national affairs; although he had the qualities which made a good lawyer, those qualities did not prepare one to be a successful statesman; he was now too old to assume the strenuous duties of the chief executive; he was a mediocre orator; as a military man he could not be trusted in a civil office; he knew very little about foreign affairs and still held a lingering resentment against France; southern property in slaves would not be safe under his administration since he was supported by New England abolitionists; and finally, a vote for Pinckney would be wasted since Pinckney had absolutely no chance to win.

Some of "Elector's" charges were obviously false, but others were

64. *Ibid.* It has been impossible to determine who this so-called "intimate friend" of General Pinckney was. It is possible that it was a member of his immediate family although this is almost unthinkable.

true enough to sting Pinckney and his friends. "A Friend to Mechanicks" urged his fellow citizens not to believe "the modest youth of Georgetown" when he belittled Pinckney's Revolutionary services. Go to a "venerable and respectable fellow-craftsman," a "Friend" advised, and "ask of *him*, the impression General Pinckney's services made on his mind, in the *'times which tried men's souls.'* "[65] This letter of "Friend" revealed one reason why Pinckney had little appeal even to the middle-aged voters. Pinckney was now from another generation, a dated hero whose friends in the Revolutionary era were mostly gone. The elderly people remembered General Pinckney and flocked to the polls to support him in substantial numbers,[66] but it was not enough. The Federalist ticket was easily defeated even in Charleston.[67]

Pinckney was not only rejected by his own city in 1808 but by his state and the nation for the third successive time. He did not seem to take his defeats in a bitter spirit. It is likely, in fact, that the honor of the nomination was all he wished. To be admired and respected by men of virtue and talents—Federalists—and to have been their choice for high office three times was honor enough.[68] Henry William De Saussure caught Pinckney's feelings perfectly: "He is contented

---

65. *Charleston Courier*, Oct. 11, 1808. Other defenses of Pinckney were made in the *Courier* by "Coriolanus" (Oct. 7), "Camillus" (Oct. 7), "Examiner" (Oct. 10), and "Elias" (Oct. 12, 1808).

66. *Ibid.*, Oct. 11, 1808. "It was highly gratifying," the editor remarked, "to see so many of our eldest inhabitants, yesterday crowding to the poll to give their suffrages to those who would promote the election of our revered fellow citizen, Gen. PINCKNEY to the Presidential chair."

67. Wolfe, *Jeffersonian Democracy*, 230–31; *Charleston Courier*, Oct. 12, 1808. The vigor with which South Carolina Federalists fought the election supports the thesis of Fischer that Federalists did revive after 1800 and tried, upon occasion, to combat Republicans with their own methods, but were generally beaten back by Republican resourcefulness, *Revolution of American Conservatism*, xviii–xix.

68. Pinckney had also received public support from his Baptist minister friend, Richard Furman. Reminding Charlestonians that Pinckney had been one of the earliest supporters of religious liberty for dissenters, Furman urged his readers to support General Pinckney: "Mr. Madison may be a good and great man; we know that Gen. Pinckney is so. Let not our citizens then under the influence of party spirit again do violence to their friendship and their feelings as well as justice and propriety, by withholding their votes from a man, most worthy of them, and by bestowing them on one who has no claim to their confidence and regard." Furman signed the article "A Carolinian." The entire letter is printed in [Furman], *A Biography of Richard Furman*, ed. Cook, 55–60.

in the shade of privacy which he cultivates, and seeks not public favor or employment; but he cannot resist the call of his Country if it be made."[69]

After 1808 Pinckney participated in no more elections. "With regard to Politics," he wrote his old friend Andrew Pickens, "I have done with them; tho I cannot help deploring the rancour of party. . . ."[70] With scarcely a backward glance Pinckney abandoned the struggle to unseat the Republicans. Ardent New England Federalists did not understand how Pinckney could so easily give up this fight with the political incarnation of evil.

Pinckney and his New England friends did not see the Jeffersonians through the same eyes. Where men of Pickering's stamp saw treachery and depravity in Republicans, Pinckney saw only mistaken or naïve views. Pinckney had long believed the Republicans to be soft on jacobinism and France, but he found little fault with them in their domestic program. When President Jefferson made it clear that he was not a dupe of France by obviously pursuing the self-interest of the United States during his eight years as president, Pinckney found few reasons to continue as an unrelenting antagonist. It was party friendships and the honors which he had received from Federalist administrations in earlier years that kept Pinckney allied to the Federalists.

After 1808 Pinckney served the party only as an adviser. When a Federalist committee of correspondence asked him, for example, if he would consider running on the Federalist electoral ticket in 1812, he urged its members not to think of nominating him "or any southern federalist, . . . for by so doing the federal votes would be absolutely thrown away as the Southern States are at present so thoroughly Democratic we should not obtain a single vote from either of them." Pinckney suggested that John Jay or Rufus King might be promising candidates if there were support for them in New York and the states "Northward of the Powtomac. . . ." If not, Pinckney thought that Federalists should support any "Democratic Candidate" who

69. De Saussure, as quoted in a letter from John Rutledge, Jr., to Harrison Gray Otis, Sept. 18, 1808, Otis Papers, Mass. Hist. Soc.
70. Pinckney to General [Andrew] Pickens, Dec. 1, 1809, Misc. Mss., Charleston Lib. Soc.

would give Federalists assurance that he would "obtain a speedy and honourable peace," unshackle American commerce, "avoid all french influence and alliance," and strengthen the armed forces.[71]

Between 1808 and 1812 Pinckney had been converted to the view of New England Federalists that maintaining the party intact was less important than influencing key policies of the Republicans with the lever of electoral votes. What had been discreditable and dishonorable to him in 1808 had now become sound and judicious policy. There was a good reason for Pinckney's about-face. Since the 1790's Pinckney had repeatedly stressed that a sound foreign policy, one based upon the nation's best interests, could only be successful if pursued with firmness and with armed forces sufficient to realize the national objectives. Jefferson's and Madison's aversion to maintaining armed forces sizable enough to defend the nation at home and commerce abroad struck Pinckney as being reckless and as playing the enemy's game, whether that enemy was France or Great Britain. By 1812, Pinckney was so alarmed by Republican foreign policy that he was ready to abandon the Federalist party in order to support a Republican presidential candidate who would see that the nation's true interest was peace, a peace founded on national strength, not on mean submission either to France or Great Britain.

After extended provocation by Britain, a nettled President Madison asked the Congress for a declaration of war against that power on June 1, 1812. Pinckney immediately offered to do whatever he could to promote the war effort, perhaps hoping to be called back to active service. To Federalist friends who asked him if they should support the Republican administration by enlisting in the armed forces, Pinckney replied that indeed they should.[72] "Unite in crisis" had been one

71. Pinckney to James Milnor, Andrew Bayard, C. W. Hare, Horace Binney, and John B. Wallace, Aug. 24, 1812, Pinckney Family Papers, Lib. Cong. Other Federalists agreed with Pinckney's recommendation, and at a nominating convention, held in New York in Sept. 1812, decided to support a Republican, DeWitt Clinton. Reeser, *Rufus King* (U. C. L. A.), 263–64. Fischer, in his *Revolution of American Conservatism*, 89, points out that Pinckney's letter was used by one faction in the Federalist party to dampen enthusiasm for nominating Chief Justice John Marshall.

72. Garden, *Eulogy on Pinckney*, 12. Pinckney was appointed to a committee of 17 in Charleston in May 1812 to prepare resolutions on the state of the nation. Pinckney took no part in the proceedings, however, for he was at Pinckney Island when the resolutions were written and approved. *Charleston Courier*, May 19, 21, 23, 1812.

theme of his life and the old soldier saw no reason to change that maxim in 1812. One can imagine how Pinckney enjoyed heaping coals of fire on the heads of Republicans; where the Republicans had been factious and uncooperative with the Federalist administration in the crisis with France in 1798–1800, Pinckney could boast that he and his southern Federalist friends put country above both party and ideology in the dispute with England.

His brother Thomas accepted a position as major general and commander of the southern forces, an indication that the Pinckney brothers had made their peace with the administration. From 1812 on, the brothers were sentimental Federalists, recalling the old days and taking pride that they had been friends of George Washington. The days of faction and struggle were over. Charles Cotesworth Pinckney could now devote his life wholly to agriculture and to promoting the welfare of numerous organizations in which he had maintained a deep interest.

X

AN UNBROKEN CAREER OF VIRTUE
AND USEFULNESS

———————◆•◆•◆———————

God has been pleased, dear General to give you Length of Days, with the Power and Disposition to do good. The Voice of the Community declares, that Respectability and Worth are connected in your Character.

—Richard Furman to Pinckney, 1823.

[Pinckney's] was the rare felicity of running an unbroken career of virtue and usefulness—honored and honorable from the bloom of youth to the maturity of manhood and the frosts of old age.

—Resolution, Society of the Cincinnati, 1825.

———————◆•◆•◆———————

IF POLITICS HAD BEEN PINCKNEY'S PASSION AND SUCCESS HIS CENTRAL goal, his closing years would have been marred by frustration and misery. Happily, this was not the case. Pinckney enriched his life with activities that were enjoyable for himself and useful to the community. To chronicle his nonpolitical activities between 1801 and his death in 1825 is to reveal what the planter aristocracy of the Revolutionary era expected of its social leaders: a sensitivity to the state's educational needs, an interest in philanthropy, a concern to promote the state's prosperity, a willingness to maintain the standards of society and its instruments of discipline and exclusion, and a Christian piety, if not deep, at least proper. If these were the standards, then Pinckney was a prototype of the low-country gentry, interested in the right projects, active in the best causes, sociable with the right people, and altogether aware that society's elite should prove its claim to leadership.

For a time after the election of 1800 it almost seemed that Pinckney was trying to withdraw from society. Perhaps his feelings had been wounded more deeply than he cared to admit. Pinckney Island, where he was to spend the greater part of his last twenty-five years, certainly provided him ample solitude to quiet his thoughts. Here he pursued the life of the gentleman planter, supervising his plantation, building his library, reading omnivorously, and entertaining occasional guests. Sharing Pinckney's retreat to isolation were his wife Mary and his youngest daughter Eliza. Mrs. Pinckney was not altogether happy on the island. Her friends and relatives in Charleston noted her reluctance to leave town except when measles and yellow fever were rampant; at these times she nearly panicked in her concern to avoid contamination.[1]

Her friends, Mrs. Ralph Izard and Mrs. Gabriel Manigault (mother and daughter), left interesting descriptions of Mrs. Pinckney. She seems to have been a sickly woman, continually suffering from one complaint or another. Her near death in 1799 forced General Pinckney to leave his military command to take her northward for more healthful air. In May of 1803 Mrs. Izard did not expect Mary Pinckney to live. Mrs. Manigault noted how "dismally disappointed [we were] at finding our poor Mrs. Pinckney in her bed and the children were very much struck and shocked at witnessing her sufferings. You know how little she conceals her emotions."[2] Mrs. Pinckney's delicate health was a constant topic of conversation among her friends.

Though in poor health, Mrs. Pinckney remained intellectually active. She was a sprightly conversationalist, full of charm and wit. Like her husband, she was a systematic reader who was able to discuss the books she read in a lively fashion.[3] She also shared her husband's interest in botany and achieved local recognition for her

1. Alice Izard to Mrs. [Margaret] Manigault, July 27, Sept. 4, 1801; Mrs. M. I. Manigault to Alice Izard, Apr. 23, 1802, Manigault Letters, S.C. Archives.

2. Mrs. R. Izard to Mrs. Manigault, May 5, 1803, Papers of Ralph Izard, Lib. Cong.; Mrs. M. I. Manigault to Mrs. Alice Izard, May 3, 1803, Manigault Letters, S.C. Archives.

3. Mrs. M. I. Manigault to Mrs. Alice Izard, Nov. 25, 1810, Ralph Izard Papers, Lib. Cong.

work in collecting specimens of plant life in South Carolina.[4] In her role as foster mother to the Pinckney girls, especially Eliza, Mrs. Pinckney tried to be more than a stepmother. Her friends commented on her success in winning Eliza's love and devotion. But it was not surprising to them, for as Mrs. Izard noted, Mrs. Pinckney "possesses so fine an understanding, and so many excellent qualities."[5]

Mrs. Pinckney's death in January 1812 was not unexpected, for she had been declining since 1809. Just before the Pinckneys left Charleston for Pinckney Island early in January, Mrs. Manigault lamented that her friend "looks wretchedly—and has continually in her mind the very precarious state of her existence."[6] On January 3 the Pinckney entourage left town on the first leg of the journey, reaching the tavern at Parker's Ferry by evening. It was there that Mrs. Pinckney became violently ill, cried to her servant to help her to bed, and died within a few hours. The grief-stricken party made its way back to Charleston where Mrs. Pinckney was buried five days later.[7]

As Mrs. Manigault observed, General Pinckney was the "picture of woe," refusing to leave his room except for the funeral services.[8] Two days after the funeral he resolutely set out for Pinckney Island again, this time accompanied by all three daughters. When Mrs. Manigault visited General Pinckney several weeks later in Charleston, she noted approvingly that "General P's demeanor is what it ought to be. His grief is thoroughly marked. He seems to take pleasure in speaking of Mrs. Pinckney—not to dwell upon her character—but in the course of conversation to recollect that she said or did this, or that."[9]

But as Mrs. Manigault had somewhat cynically commented earlier, "Genl. P. will grieve and feel—but men do not grieve, and feel long."[10]

4. Ramsay, *History of South-Carolina*, II, 195.

5. Mrs. Alice Izard to Mrs. M. I. Manigault, June 15, 1801, Manigault Letters, S.C. Archives.

6. Mrs. M. I. Manigault to Mrs. Alice Izard, Jan. 2, 1812, *ibid.*

7. A good description of the circumstances of Mrs. Pinckney's death is found in the letter of Mrs. M. I. Manigault to Mrs. Alice Izard, Jan. 5, 1812, *ibid.* See also the *Charleston Courier*, Jan. 9, 1812.

8. Mrs. M. I. Manigault to Mrs. Alice Izard, Jan. 12, 1812, Manigault Letters, S.C. Archives.

9. Mrs. M. I. Manigault to Mrs. Alice Izard, Mar. 5, 1812, *ibid.*

10. Mrs. M. I. Manigault to Mrs. Alice Izard, Jan. 5, 1812, *ibid.*

Perhaps she was right. Mary Stead Pinckney had been an important part of her husband's life, but Pinckney's activities do not appear to have been organized around her nor his happiness dependent upon her. When they came to Charleston, he was always busy and active while his wife rested. He usually gave the appearance of being pressed for time. For a number of years he was involved in the activities of the Jockey Club, two of those years as president. Pinckney in fact had been one of the original proprietors and owners of the Washington Race Course which held its first races in 1791.[11] It might seem strange that a man who did not breed race horses and who, according to Rev. Christopher Gadsden, "neither made bets nor played cards"[12] was so active in promoting a sport which encouraged "the rattling of cash . . . in all directions," a course where "Thousands are lost or won in a moment."[13] But the Jockey Club was more than an organization which promoted horse racing; it was a social club of such pre-eminence that to be admitted was a recognition of pedigree or an indication of acceptance into the social establishment.

Race Week in February was the highlight of Charleston's social season. The city was crowded as planters poured in to carry on business, to exchange gossip, and to see the races. The customary four days of racing were likely to satisfy even the most ardent horsemen. For the ladies, it was the Jockey Club Ball that held first interest. Each wore her most stunning gown to the ball while the gentlemen were on their most courtly behavior for this, the greatest event of the social season. Little wonder that the planning of the week's events was not left to inexperienced hands. During his presidency Pinckney did all in his power to make Race Week once again the usual memorable occasion. Throughout the week itself, Mrs. Manigault noted, Pinckney was "always very much occupied with the Jockey Club . . . and that employs him all day long. . . ."[14]

11. John B. Irving, *The South Carolina Jockey Club* (Charleston, 1857), Part IV, 14. Turf racing began in Charleston in 1734 on "The York Course" and was continued from 1754 to 1792 on "The New Market Course." Pinckney was president of the Jockey Club in 1796 and 1805.

12. Gadsden, *Sermon on the Decease of Pinckney*, 14.

13. Ramsay, *History of South-Carolina*, II, 225.

14. Mrs. M. I. Manigault to Mrs. Alice Izard, Feb. 20, 1805, Ralph Izard Papers, Lib. Cong.

Attending to his duties as a general officer in the Society of the Cincinnati also took a share of Pinckney's time when he was in town. This society, established in May 1783 by officers of the American Revolutionary Army, was intended to fulfill several functions. Through the Society wartime friendships could be renewed and fellow officers could insure one another against the hazards of ill-fortune by establishing loan funds. To its founders the Society appeared perfectly innocent of any attempt to subvert Republican principles. Critics took a different view. The hereditary principle of membership and the restriction of membership to officers in the Continental Army aroused lively fears that a native aristocracy was in the making. Judge Aedanus Burke of South Carolina wrote a powerful tract in which he accused the Cincinnati of a conspiracy to create "a race of hereditary patricians or nobility."[15] Burke was joined in his views by men like Jefferson and John Adams—and many others who did not qualify for membership, including officers of the state militias.

Pinckney never let this charge disturb him. He likely saw no reason to frown upon the formation of local oligarchies composed of the patriotic elite—men such as himself, his brother, and such worthies as General Moultrie and George Washington. When the South Carolina chapter of the Cincinnati was organized in 1783, General Moultrie and Charles Cotesworth Pinckney were elected president and vice-president, and Thomas Pinckney secretary.[16] Charles Cotesworth Pinckney was re-elected to his office each year until 1805.

The death of George Washington, the first president-general of the Society, in 1799, led to Alexander Hamilton's election as president-general in 1800. At the same meeting Charles Cotesworth Pinckney was elected vice-president-general, no doubt due to the sterling reputation he had acquired among Federalists by his missions to France. None other than arch-Federalist Timothy Pickering was in the chair of the general meeting at Philadelphia when Hamilton and Pinckney were unanimously elected, a fact which lent credence to

15. Burke wrote under the pseudonym of "Cassius." See his attacks, printed in the Charleston *Gazette of the State of South Carolina*, Oct. 1, 8, 15, 1783. Edgar E. Hume shows the extent of the "Early Opposition to the Cincinnati," *Americana*, 30 (1936), 597–638.

16. Charleston *South Carolina Gazette and General Advertiser*, Jan. 6, 1784.

266 CHARLES COTESWORTH PINCKNEY

the charge that the Society was essentially an auxiliary arm of the Federalist party.[17]

Full responsibility for the Society's welfare fell on Pinckney in May 1805 when he was elected president-general, replacing Hamilton after his death at the hands of Aaron Burr. It was obvious to contemporaries that the Society declined markedly during the period of Pinckney's leadership from 1805 to 1825. Only two general meetings were held, in 1811 and 1812; state organizations scattered funds intended for the relief of members and their families; and local chapters dissolved.[18] One of the few signs between 1812 and 1825 that the Society had not died was a memorial sent to Congress in 1818 asking that Congress vote half pay for life to qualified Revolutionary Army officers.[19]

It is difficult to say what share of the responsibility for the Society's languishing condition should be placed upon Pinckney's shoulders and what share attributed to circumstances. As original members grew old and died it was natural that the ties of friendship which stimulated local annual meetings should loosen.[20] Also, there was no hard core of self-interest to keep the organization active since the nation had not yet accepted the principle that veterans should receive continuing compensation for their wartime sacrifices. Perhaps in a Republican era the Revolutionary veterans and their sons did not care to tar themselves with the brush of Federalism or participate in a society perpetuated on hereditary lines and guided by old Federalists. Even though the Society nearly expired, Pinckney was naturally proud to be its president-general and to say that he led a group once commanded by Washington and Hamilton, a group which had done so much to win American independence.

17. Charleston *City Gazette*, June 12, 1800; Box 8, Papers of the Society of the Cincinnati, Lib. Cong. Thomas Pinckney was a delegate from South Carolina to the meeting.

18. Alice Izard to Mrs. M. I. Manigault, July 5, 1811, Manigault Letters, S.C. Archives; Charles Cotesworth Pinckney to Rev. [Jedediah Morse], July 30, 1811, Gratz Coll., Hist. Soc. of Pa.; circular letter of Charles Cotesworth Pinckney to the Societies of the Cincinnati, Papers of the Society of the Cincinnati, Lib. Cong. The meeting in 1812 drew representatives from only four states. Memorandum in Box 7, the Society's Papers, Lib. Cong.

19. This memorial is in Box 9, the Society's Papers, Lib. Cong.

20. By 1808, 67 of the 114 original members of the South Carolina chapter had died. *The Original Institution of the General Society of the Cincinnati* . . . (Charleston, 1808), 45–47 (copy in Box 14, Pinckney Family Papers, Lib. Cong.).

Just as close to Pinckney's heart was the welfare of the Charleston Library Society. His connection with this society as a young man just returned from England has already been noted. Pinckney's interest in this society was not for purposes of show. His participation continued because he loved books,[21] because he believed it was the duty of the educated to raise the general educational and cultural level of the less privileged, and because he was convinced that a store of knowledge was useful to the entire community.

From 1786 until 1796 Pinckney served as the Library Society's vice-president and was elected to the office of president in 1796.[22] There was much work to be done in the postwar period, for the Society's collections had gone up in flames in 1778. When the Society found permanent quarters on the third floor of the State House on the corner of Broad and Meeting Streets, the officers assiduously began to rebuild the Library's collection. Pinckney undoubtedly ordered books for the Society while he was in France and the Netherlands. When he returned he resumed his duties as president of the Society, remaining in that office until 1807 when Henry William De Saussure was elected. Pinckney maintained his connection with the Society, however, and was a regular member of the committee on books until the year he died.[23]

The Charleston Museum, an outgrowth of the Library Society's activities, began a quasi-autonomous existence toward the end of the century. Persons with scientific interests were encouraged to contribute items of educational value which might be placed on exhibit. Pinckney, as one writer has said, "seems to have maintained the most steady interest in the Museum," lending his name to the project and encouraging persons with a scientific bent to exhibit their collections in the museum room.[24]

21. Simms, "A Memoir of the Pinckney Family," *Dawson's Hist. Mag.*, 2nd Ser., 1 (1867), 138.

22. Charleston *State Gazette of South-Carolina*, Jan. 16, 1786; Charleston *City Gazette*, Jan. 22, 1796.

23. *Charleston Courier*, Jan. 22, 1807; Jan. 19, 1811; Jan. 20, 1825. A description of the library in 1817 is found in Sidney W. Martin, ed., "Ebenezer Kellogg's Visit to Charleston, 1817," *S. C. Hist. and Gen. Mag.*, 49 (1948), 12–13.

24. Bragg, "Birth of the Museum Idea," *Charleston Museum Qtly.*, 1 (1923), 12. Pinckney's encouragement of the sciences was recognized in 1813 when he was elected a member of the American Antiquarian Society. Pinckney to Samuel M. Burnside, Jan. 31, 1814, Misc. Mss., S.C. Hist. Soc. Pinckney's certificate of membership is in Box 11, Pinckney Family Papers, Lib. Cong.

Another project in which Pinckney took considerable interest was the Agricultural Society's experimental farm located just outside Charleston. The Agricultural Society had been incorporated in 1785, as Pinckney's historian friend David Ramsay said, "to import and circulate foreign articles that were suitable to the climate of Carolina, and to direct the attention of the agriculturalists of the State to useful objects, and to reward such as improved the art."[25] Planters also sought means of escaping the British stranglehold on American commerce, hoping by a diversification of crops to be placed in a better position to enter new markets.[26] Pinckney had joined these early efforts at diversification and had written several times to Thomas Jefferson (then in France) about the practicality of importing olive vines and caper plants.[27]

Although severely crippled by lack of funds, the Agricultural Society continued its experimental work. After 1800 the Society entered a more prosperous period when the state permitted it to run a lottery. The Society purchased a forty-acre farm on which, Ramsay reported, "agricultural experiments are occasionally made." In 1808 the Society had a membership of forty, among whom was Pinckney, each contributing twenty-five dollars annually to support the experimental farm.[28]

Perhaps Pinckney's desire to contribute to the state's general prosperity had its roots partly in his faint but cherished memories of his father. Charles Cotesworth remembered as a boy his father pointing out to him the first wagon arriving in Charleston from the back country. "Charles," his father remarked, "by the time you are a man, I don't doubt there will be at least twenty wagons come to town [in one day]!" And whenever General Pinckney saw a long line of wagons wending their way into Charleston, he was apt to say: "How happy my father would have been in the growth and prosperity of Carolina."[29]

Alexander Garden, Pinckney's eulogist, mentions that it "was late

25. Ramsay, *History of South-Carolina*, II, 126.
26. Rogers, *Evolution of a Federalist*, 137.
27. See ch. 5, n. 28.
28. Ramsay, *History of South-Carolina*, II, 126; [Mrs. M. I. Manigault to Mrs. Alice Izard], Feb. 18, 1805, Ralph Izard Papers, Lib. Cong.
29. As quoted in Simms, "A Memoir of the Pinckney Family," *Dawson's Hist. Mag.*, 2nd Ser., 1 (1867), 137.

in life before General PINCKNEY turned his attention to the sciences, . . . but by unwearied diligence, he speedily acquired very considerable knowledge, in Botany and Chemistry, and, to the end of his life, he went on increasing his stores of information."[30] Perhaps this interest in science was stimulated by his acquaintance with persons like André Michaux, who was sent to the United States by France in 1785 to continue his world-wide research in botany.[31] Pinckney and his wife were helpful to Michaux while he was in South Carolina, and Michaux responded to their friendship by naming what was commonly known as Georgia bark *Pinckneya pubens*.[32]

In his later years Pinckney became an avid student of medicine and medical practices and began to offer medical advice to his friends, not all of whom were inclined to accept his judgment. His lawyer friend Timothy Ford, for example, was using arsenic in his own health prescriptions and enthusiastically recommending the same to his acquaintances. Pinckney protested to Ford that arsenic "is suspected on such strong grounds of undermining the Constitution, and laying the foundation for Mortal diseases, that its general use ought to be discouraged. Surely, my dear Sir, these authorities are sufficient to make you hesitate before you continue the use of this deleterious substance, or recommend it to our friends."[33]

Pinckney's reading in the sciences, like his activity in other fields, usually took a practical turn. It might be reasonable to expect that an immensely learned man such as Pinckney would enjoy theorizing in some field for the pure pleasure and mental stimulation it would afford. But one searches his life in vain for some sign that his mind soared beyond the mundane in any field, for some indication that playing with ideas was itself reward enough for him. Perhaps his educational training had dulled his powers of originality or perhaps a founding father was obliged to distill practical essences from all fields of learning. The frontier society of early America undoubtedly placed a premium upon the practical rather than the theoretical.

30. Garden, *Eulogy on Pinckney*, 32n.
31. Salley, *Washington's Tour Through South Carolina*, 17.
32. Hennig, *Great South Carolinians*, I, 201.
33. Pinckney to Timothy Ford, Oct. 27, 1810, in "Three Letters From Ford and Ravenel Papers," *S. C. Hist. and Gen. Mag.*, 26 (1925), 146–47.

Whatever the reason, Pinckney never exhibited the intuition or the genius that advances the boundaries of knowledge. At the Constitutional Convention of 1787, while Hamilton and Madison expounded political theory, Pinckney was content to ask how their theories would affect southern interests in practice. While André Michaux was classifying plants and questioning their relationships, Pinckney was contributing an Indian hatchet and a clam concretion to the Charleston Museum. Where men of delicate conscience were pointing out the stark contradictions in a political system which acknowledged men equal in the abstract but sanctioned slavery, Pinckney's only answer was that the south needed slaves, contradictions notwithstanding.

With all of his exemplary personal qualities, Pinckney was a man of essentially pedestrian mind, accepting—indeed embracing—the conventions and values of his society. The necessity of slavery, the duty to act honorably in public and private relationships, the obligation of the privileged and virtuous to render service to the community, and the absolute values of the Christian religion were all accepted by Pinckney as guides for his thinking and conduct. This is not to say that these values should be or were rejected by his more individualistic contemporaries, but that a man of Pinckney's stature and training should systematically avoid deviations from the normal, or perhaps more truly never think to challenge the orthodoxies of his day, tells us much about the man and the society that helped to mold him.

"Religion is always venerable, always necessary; and when she is delineated with the beauty and eloquence she was today in the (Baptist) church, we are enraptured with her portrait and sensibly feel that all her ways are ways of pleasantness and all her paths are paths of peace."[34] So Pinckney wrote to Reverend Furman. While Pinckney's religious convictions were his own, one senses the continuing influence of early parental suggestion. Chief Justice Pinckney had directed in his will that ten guineas be charged against his Charleston "mansion house" each year so that a minister could be

34. Pinckney to Rev. Richard Furman [ca. 1790], quoted in Furman, Biography of Richard Furman, ed. Cook, 61.

hired each May and October to preach a sermon on the "Greatness and Goodness of God," a charge that was faithfully observed. Every year either the Pinckney family or a minister friend chose the guest lecturer. On the same day the sermon was delivered, the town clergymen were entertained by the Pinckneys at a traditionally lively dinner.[35]

Like his father before him, Pinckney agonized little over the questions of doctrine which troubled his contemporaries, fixing his gaze instead upon the Christian "ways of pleasantness" and "paths of peace." Throughout his lifetime Pinckney adhered to the practices of the Episcopal Church whose ritual and order suited his temperament well. And as he grew older, he clung increasingly to the ancient practices, to the service and the customs exactly as he had known them from his earliest days.

He became particularly exercised in 1816 at the proposal that the communion service ritual be shortened. It was suggested that the priest administer the elements to the whole table at once and then recite a general prayer, rather than reading an admonition or blessing to each communicant as he administered the elements. To William Doughty, Pinckney wrote that there was no warrant in church precedent for administering the elements to the entire table. "And fatiguing as this most solemn and beautiful service is when there are so many communicants as attended the last celebration, I would rather submit to that than see an unauthorized alteration take place."[36] To the Reverend Christopher Gadsden, Pinckney defended the liturgy, protesting that it was not too long "for those who carry a devout mind to the Church. . . ." Pinckney admitted that he was one who "dread[s] innovation in the service of our Church, and I would much rather hear the sermon confined to 20 or 30 minutes than any part of our Liturgy be destroyed."[37]

His critics might say that General Pinckney was unduly conservative, confusing substance with form. Perhaps for Pinckney form already had become substance, reciting the ritual a redemptive act in itself. The doors of the Protestant Episcopal Church in low-country South Carolina could hardly be thrown open to fresh

35. Ravenel, *Eliza Pinckney*, 184–85.
36. Pinckney to Doughty, Aug. 2, 1816, Pinckney Family Papers, Lib. Cong.
37. Pinckney to Gadsden, Aug. 15, 1816, *ibid*.

theological breezes or to new experiments in religious worship when men such as General Pinckney insisted, "remove not the ancient landmark, which thy fathers have set."[38] And yet there is another, more positive side to the expression of Pinckney's religious sentiments. Like Saint James, he believed that faith without works was dead and that the dedicated Christian was obligated to take the gospel to the unregenerate.

In 1810 Pinckney took the lead in establishing the Bible Society of Charleston, an action revealing that evangelical radical currents had reached South Carolina.[39] The Society's sponsors evidently agreed that Negroes would be evangelized in this way, a resolve that did not meet with universal favor. To his New England friend Reverend Jedediah Morse, Pinckney wrote of those "who are apprehensive, or rather I think, pretend to be apprehensive, that it [distributing Bibles] will have a tendency to excite disturbances among our domestics. I have not the most distant apprehension of the kind."[40]

Under Pinckney's leadership the Charleston Bible Society became an auxiliary of the American Bible Society in 1817. In recognition of this amalgamation, Pinckney was elected one of twenty vice-presidents of the national organization.[41] Reverend Christopher Gadsden mentions that when Pinckney reached the age of seventy he "declared his resolution to withdraw as much as possible from public business, but at the solicitation of this [Charleston Bible] Society he was induced to make an exception in its favor, and continued to discharge to the close of life the duties of his office."[42] Meetings of the Society were held in Pinckney's home, particularly as the old man began to fail.

Even Pinckney's good name and the respectable list of its sponsors and members did not protect the Bible Society against charges that the distribution of Bibles to slaves was undermining their willingness to obey. Slaveowners were alert to the implications of the Biblical teaching that the souls of men were of equal value in God's sight.

---

38. Proverbs 22:28.
39. Constitution of the Charleston Bible Society of Charleston, South Carolina, adopted June 18, 1810, in Letters and Papers Relating to the Charleston Bible Society, S.C. Hist. Soc.
40. Pinckney to Morse, Dec. 1, 1810, Gratz Coll., Hist. Soc. of Pa.
41. *Charleston Courier*, May 21, July 30, 1817.
42. Gadsden, *Sermon on the Decease of Pinckney*, 19–20.

Nor did shrewd Negro preachers miss this point. And if all were to be equal inside the heavenly gates, they asked, why should this present world be such a "valley of sorrows" for the Negro. A favorite sermon text for Negro ministers was: "Masters, give unto your servants that which is just and equal; knowing that ye also have a Master in heaven" (Colossians 4: 1).

Charleston passed through its great alarm in 1822 when Denmark Vesey, a free Negro with all the amenities presumed necessary to keep a Negro happy, and a group of conspirators were arrested (on a tip) and their plot exposed to a horrified public. Vesey had recruited a shadow army of formidable size, hidden weapons in strategic locations, assembled a command staff which included two slaves of the governor, Thomas Bennett, and was quite ready at the appointed hour to massacre the white community in Charleston. Inspired by the Negro uprising that had taken place in Santo Domingo some thirty years previously, Vesey had bolstered his group's morale by exhorting on Biblical texts, assuring the slaves that God smiled on their just cause.[43] And even though most slaves or freed Negroes might not be able to read, Brother Vesey could point to the place where it was printed—perhaps in the Bible given the Negro by the Charleston Bible Society.

It was natural enough that in the aftermath of the Vesey plot frightened men should direct accusing remarks at the Charleston Bible Society. Pinckney and the board members were deeply distressed. All convinced Christians, they saw the inconsistency in trumpeting the civilizing benefits of slavery to doubting northerners while denying the slaves access to God's word. In fear lest the Society's doors be closed by a hostile public, Pinckney and his fellow board members sent a memorial to Governor Bennett in which they asked his help in quieting demands that Bibles no longer be distributed to the Negroes.

The Society wanted it on record that it had "no doubts concerning the moral and Religious Right of holding Slaves, lawfully obtained, when they are treated with justice and humanity."[44] Caught between two orthodoxies of their society—the necessity of slavery and the

43. See John Lofton, *Insurrection in South Carolina: The Turbulent World of Denmark Vesey* (Yellow Springs, Ohio, 1964), ch. 10.
44. This memorial is in the Charleston Bible Society Papers, S.C. Hist. Soc.

Christian's duty to spread the gospel—Pinckney and the board members were unable to discard either. They still hoped for some middle way: slaves that were fully Christianized and yet fully ready to accept the apostle Paul's exhortation that "servants be obedient unto their own masters . . ." (Titus 2:9). The difficulty of reconciling these two objectives is perhaps clearer in retrospect than it was to Pinckney and his contemporaries. The dilemma facing a slaveowner and a Christian was cruel indeed. Rather than being condemned for his acceptance of the institution of slavery, Pinckney may be commended for his determination to let nothing stand in the way of Christianizing the slaves, not even the possibility of Charleston's destruction by gospel-inspired Negroes.[45]

Standing with Pinckney in this fight was Richard Furman, Charleston's Baptist minister and the man for whom Furman University was subsequently named. Ministers were generally fond of Pinckney, for he respected them and always made them welcome in his home.[46] But a special relationship developed between Pinckney and Furman, one that ripened over the years. They had been through the Revolutionary War together and shared those memories. They stood as one for twenty years in counseling on the wickedness of dueling.[47] Furman had argued Pinckney's presidential cause among the non-Episcopal groups in 1808 by reminding them that Pinckney had fought for the disestablishment of his own church in 1777. Pinckney showed his appreciation of Furman by visiting his services from time to time and by making him an annual present of the best Madeira wine, a gift which the good Reverend Furman thoroughly appreciated. In one note Pinckney mentioned that the heat of the summer

45. To an earlier suggestion that the Negro question might be answered by transporting freed Negroes back to Africa, Pinckney responded: "Altho I doubt much the practicality of colonizing part of Africa with free negroes to any beneficial intent as it regards our own People of Colour I yet have put my name to the paper you sent me and have . . . enclosed a Check. . . ." Pinckney to Christopher Gadsden, Sept. 11, 1819, in response to Gadsden's letter to Pinckney, Sept. 8, 1819, asking Pinckney to subscribe to a journal advocating colonization, both, Pinckney Family Papers, Lib. Cong.

46. See the letters of Rev. Sitgreaves who virtually made Pinckney Island his parish headquarters in 1821, in P. J. Staudenraus, ed., "Letters from South Carolina, 1821–1822," *S. C. Hist. Mag.*, 58 (1957), 209–17.

47. Furman to [Charles Cotesworth Pinckney], Oct. 16, 1823, Richard Furman Letters, S. Caroliniana Lib.

had been "more productive of bile than any I have experienced these thirty years; and I have found a few glasses of Madeira Wine the best corrector of it. I therefore take the liberty of recommending the same to you, that I have experienced to be beneficial to myself; and the bearer will deliver to you two dozen of unadulterated Madeira. The dozen marked O.M. is ten years old; that marked M is five years old."[48]

As time passed, the staunch Episcopalian and the fervent Baptist drew close in spirit. It was Richard Furman who pronounced a moving benediction on Pinckney as he saw his friend sinking by degrees:

God has been pleased, dear General to give you Length of Days, with the Power and Disposition to do good. The Voice of the Community declares, that Respectability and Worth are connected in your Character. This is grateful to your Friends. May you continue to live as long as Life, on Earth, is desirable; To be the Supporter of pious and Benevolent Institutions; to exhibit the Excellences of the Christian . . . Character in Acts of private Beneficiance, publick Liberality and all that is amiable and Praiseworthy, and at last obtain Glory in the Heavens. . . .[49]

Religion was a constant comfort to the old general in his later years, as were the good opinions and companionship of his many friends. To his younger companions he was a living legend, the embodiment of ancient and heroic deeds. Many people wanted him to lend his name to their causes. With his basically generous instincts, Pinckney was unable to refuse their requests. It was particularly easy to persuade him to give his public endorsement to forthcoming books.

To the Reverend Mason L. Weems, known to history for his notoriously inaccurate and adulatory biography of George Washington, Pinckney addressed a public letter in 1821. Congratulating him for preparing an American edition of *"LeSage's valuable Atlas . . ."* the General expressed delight that such a work would soon be available to colleges and schools, predicting that it would "form a part of the library of every scholar and gentleman in the country."[50] John Drayton, the son of William Henry Drayton, approached

48. Pinckney to Dr. Richard Furman [*ca.* 1800?], quoted in [Furman], *Biography of Richard Furman*, ed. Cook, 47.

49. Furman to [Pinckney], Oct. 16, 1823, Richard Furman Letters, S. Caroliniana Lib.

50. *Charleston Courier*, Mar. 13, 1821.

Pinckney with his plan to publish his father's memoirs of the American Revolution to 1776. Drayton asked Pinckney, in support of this project, to "be so good as to affix your name, on the [enclosed] upper Ruled line [sheet] for one Copy: as I would be much gratified in having your name at the head of the Subscribers on the paper...."[51] Pinckney happily obliged.

Since Pinckney also made it a point to encourage artists, they naturally turned to him for assistance in obtaining clients. William J. Coffee, a sculptor and portrait artist of some ability, wrote to Pinckney in 1821 asking if enough of Charleston's distinguished citizens would be interested in having themselves immortalized to justify his coming to South Carolina. Pinckney replied that he had approached William Lowndes first but Lowndes refused "tho I assured him that his face was not to be plaistered, but what Beauty was in it would remain uninjured, nay untouched by you." Pinckney believed the general refusal to patronize Coffee was symptomatic of the city's lack of refinement. "The Taste for the fine Arts has not yet made so much progress among us as I could wish; for I have spoken to several of our Men of Influence to set to you for their Busts, but they all refuse...."[52]

Pinckney was able to give more satisfaction to historians, many of whom were eager to tap his knowledge about the Revolutionary days. Alexander Garden, Pinckney's good friend and literary correspondent, drew upon the General's wartime experience in writing his now famous *Anecdotes of the American Revolution*, as did William Johnson who expressed his obligation to Pinckney in the preface of his *Life of Nathanael Greene*.[53] Both seemed to view his collaboration as lending authenticity to their work.

After 1821 it became obvious to Pinckney's friends that his health and vigor were declining. Reverend Samuel Sitgreaves, Pinckney's houseguest, wrote to a friend that the General was "seriously unwell"

51. Drayton to Pinckney, Oct. 18, 1820, Pinckney Family Papers, Lib. Cong.
52. Pinckney to Coffee, Oct. 23, 1821, C. C. Pinckney Papers, S. Caroliniana Lib.
53. Alexander Garden to Pinckney, July 8, 1824; Pinckney to Judge Peters, July 6, 1822, Pinckney Family Papers, Lib. Cong. In this collection, see Pinckney's correspondence with Garden, particularly heavy during the years between 1816 and 1820. Unfortunately, apparently only Garden's letters have been preserved, Box 11. *Charleston Courier*, Feb. 16, 1822.

and that he feared "his irreproachable, his honourable and his useful life is drawing to a close."[54] Yet the old man had a remarkable constitution and appeared in fairly good health the following spring. Pinckney was bothered primarily by his growing deafness and sought eagerly for ways to cure it. To his brother he described a remedy that required him to "sleep half the night without turning" so that a medicinal solution poured into one ear would not drain away.[55]

Pinckney's longevity and general good health did not lull him into the common fantasy that he could wait forever to put his affairs in order. If his business records from 1820 on are an indication, he realized the end was near and fully intended that his estate be left in a prospering condition. He kept receipts meticulously for items down to fifty cents in value.[56] As a lawyer he had seen too many men die leaving their estates exposed to the rapacity of unscrupulous men who demanded payment even on small bills long since honored. Pinckney also became terse in his dealings with debtors. To one person he wrote:

On the 20th. of July . . . your promissory note for $120 was due to me, and still remains unsatisfied, of which I request immediate payment, and you are indebted to me about $1400 for the ground Rent of the Lot you occupy in Market Street between Lotes leased to Mr. Dupont and Mr. Haber which you will please to come and settle immediately.[57]

While Pinckney took this no-nonsense attitude toward delinquent debtors, he was the soul of generosity with his relatives. He patiently guarded his brother-in-law's Georgia land investments, giving Stead a sizable sum in 1821 when poverty threatened to overtake him.[58] General Pinckney was even more generous with his nephews, Charles Cotesworth Pinckney and Thomas Pinckney, both his brother's sons. Perhaps "Cotesworth" in a very real sense took the place of Pinckney's own deceased son of that name. At least General Pinckney could not have been much more liberal with his own children. Ac-

54. Sitgreaves to Rev. Jackson Kemper, Dec. 19, 1821, in Staudenraus, ed., "Letters from South Carolina," *S. C. Hist. Mag.*, 58 (1957), 215.

55. Charles Cotesworth Pinckney to Thomas Pinckney, Feb. 10, 1820, C. C. Pinckney Papers, S. Caroliniana Lib.

56. See the Pinckney Papers in the Duke Univ. Lib. and in Box 13, Lib. Cong.

57. Pinckney to ? , Oct. 28, 1822, C. C. Pinckney Papers, Duke Univ. Lib.

58. Benjamin Stead to Pinckney, May 10, 1821, Sept. 10, 1822, C. C. Pinckney Papers, Duke Univ. Lib.

cording to the draft copy of a sales agreement, General Pinckney "sold" his nephew Cotesworth nearly thirty-five hundred acres in 1810 for one dollar. Fourteen years later, Pinckney sold Pinckney Plains, a five-hundred-acre plantation near Beach Hill, to his nephews for five dollars.[59] With two of his girls unmarried and the third (Eliza) without a male heir, General Pinckney could indulge his nephews in good conscience.[60]

Easy in his pecuniary circumstances and with his family devoted to his comfort, Pinckney remained cheerful, imbued with a sense of gratefulness that his life had been prolonged and that his health was usually good.[61] He seemed to desire the companionship of old friends and new in his last years and therefore spent an increasingly greater share of his time in Charleston. Charles Fraser in his *Reminiscences* mentions that Pinckney met regularly with the "Cossack Club," an association of old Federalists. It was a club, Fraser emphasized, that had no rules, no penalties, and no duties. Rather than indulge in long-faced talk about the past, the group was noted for its light-hearted banter. General Pinckney, Fraser recalls, was particularly happy to regale the younger members with memories of the heroic days, the days when he was in his prime and carrying the burdens of a founding father. Like most old men, Pinckney came increasingly to live in his memories. But he was no bore, for his memories were centered around great men and important events.[62]

Those precious memories must have flooded back when Pinckney learned that the Marquis de Lafayette would shortly return to the United States for a visit. Charleston itself was to be honored by a visit from Lafayette. Pinckney watched with pleasure from his home in Charleston[63] as the citizenry prepared to receive the old Revolu-

59. The draft of the first sales agreement is in Pinckney Family Papers, Lib. Cong. The indenture for the sale of Pinckney Plains is in the Benjamin H. Rutledge Papers, S.C. Hist. Soc.

60. The year of Eliza's marriage to Ralph Izard is uncertain. There is an undated list of 50 Negroes given by General Pinckney to his daughter upon her marriage. The note is in the Benjamin H. Rutledge Papers, S.C. Hist. Soc.

61. Pinckney to Benjamin Stead [*ca.* 1815], Pinckney Family Papers, Lib. Cong.

62. Fraser, *Reminiscences of Charleston*, 50–51.

63. Alice Izard to Mrs. M. I. Manigault, July 13, 1817, Manigault Letters, S. C. Archives. Due to erosion, the house on Pinckney Island was separated from the sea by only three feet of land as early as 1817. In 1824 a severe storm destroyed the house and carried away most of Pinckney's library. Pinckney to Petit de Villers, Oct. 1, 1824, Ford Coll., N.Y. Pub. Lib.

tionary hero with the kind of welcome that romantic and ostentatious Charleston loved so well.

Lafayette badges were sold by the hundreds, the courthouse was cleaned, and an elegant open carriage was readied to carry Lafayette. A troop of cavalry was outfitted in blue uniforms "with white and red facings, of the National Guard of Paris. . . ." A welcoming parade was organized and South Carolina's own Revolutionary heroes, the Pinckney brothers, were asked to ride in one of the carriages. Naturally they agreed and were present as Lafayette entered Charleston to the resounding cries of "Vive Lafayette." When Lafayette learned that his old companions in arms were in the carriage directly behind his, he ordered the steps of his barouche lowered. Alighting from his carriage, Lafayette walked back to greet the Pinckneys, giving them "the accolade in the French fashion, embracing them enthusiastically, and kissing them on both cheeks, while the crowd roared with delight."[64]

Except for a final appearance at the Bible Society, when he was "so feeble that it was necessary to support him to the chair," this was Pinckney's last public appearance.[65] Two months later, on August 16, 1825, at the age of eighty, Pinckney died. It was no shock to his friends for the old General had been sinking noticeably during his last few months.[66] Yet the community was deeply moved. Pinckney was immensely popular. None of Charleston's citizens had been given more honors nor had many borne their honors so modestly.

Praise was given to Pinckney for a life well spent, and his death was mourned as "a public calamity, such as rarely occurs in our community."[67] Orators representing the Society of the Cincinnati, the American Revolution Society, and St. Philip's Church paid their respects to Pinckney and from his life illustrated the beauty and wisdom of spending one's days in service. William Drayton, representing the Society of the Cincinnati, noted Pinckney's "rare felicity of

64. Brand Whitlock, *La Fayette*, 2 vols. (N.Y., 1929), II, 253–54. General Pinckney and Lafayette also dined privately the day after Lafayette arrived in Charleston. Charleston *City Gazette*, Mar. 16, 1825; *Charleston Courier*, Mar. 16, 1825.

65. Garden, *Eulogy on Pinckney*, 43.

66. Henry W. De Saussure to Henry M. Rutledge, Apr. 4, 1825, Rutledge Papers, Dreer Coll., Hist. Soc. of Pa.

67. Resolutions of the vestry of St. Philip's Parish, in *Charleston Courier*, Aug. 25, 1825.

running an unbroken career of virtue and usefulness—honored and honorable from the bloom of youth to the maturity of manhood and the frosts of old age." The American Revolution Society praised Pinckney for his talents as a lawyer, for being "at the head of a party, without being a party-man," and for his "love of honor and the most inflexible honesty."[68]

Pinckney was buried on August 17, 1825, in the churchyard of St. Michael's, Charleston. His tombstone, which rests against the east wall of the church, is still easily read by the visitors who wander through the yard. Inside the lovely white steepled church, on one of the many commemorative plaques that have been hung to honor South Carolina's great and near-great, visitors find this eulogy of Pinckney:

68. *Ibid.*, Aug. 22, 25, 1825; see Aug. 18, 20, 31, 1825, for the resolutions of other organizations on Pinckney's life and character.

TO THE MEMORY OF
GENERAL CHARLES COTESWORTH PINCKNEY
ONE OF THE FOUNDERS OF
THE AMERICAN REPUBLIC.

IN WAR
HE WAS THE COMPANION IN ARMS
AND THE FRIEND OF WASHINGTON.

IN PEACE
HE ENJOYED HIS UNCHANGING CONFIDENCE
AND MAINTAINED WITH ENLIGHTEND ZEAL
THE PRINCIPLES OF HIS ADMINISTRATION
AND OF THE CONSTITUTION.

AS A STATESMAN
HE BEQUEATHED TO HIS COUNTRY THE SENTIMENT,
MILLIONS FOR DEFENCE
NOT A CENT FOR TRIBUTE.

AS A LAWYER,
HIS LEARNING WAS VARIOUS AND PROFOUND
HIS PRINCIPLES PURE HIS PRACTICE LIBERAL.

WITH ALL THE ACCOMPLISHMENTS
OF THE GENTLEMAN
HE COMBINED THE VIRTUES OF THE PATRIOT
AND THE PIETY OF THE CHRISTIAN.

HIS NAME
IS RECORDED IN THE HISTORY OF HIS COUNTRY
INSCRIBED ON THE CHARTER OF HER LIBERTIES,
AND CHERISHED IN THE AFFECTIONS OF HER CITIZENS.

NOTE ON SOURCES

———◆•◆———

STUDENTS OF AMERICAN EARLY NATIONAL HISTORY HAVE GENERALLY been fortunate in the volume of materials available for their study, preserved almost miraculously from floods, fires, or indifferent descendants. Students of the Pinckney family, however, have been circumscribed in their work by the relative scarcity of materials due to fire or British Revolutionary marauders. Consequently, there are gaps in Pinckney primary materials, particularly in the years before 1775. While the record becomes more complete in the Revolutionary War years and in the 1780's, it is not until the early 1790's, when Thomas Pinckney becomes Minister to England, that one can gain direct insight into the thought and activities of Charles Cotesworth Pinckney. It is in these years that General Pinckney's political horizons begin to broaden as he corresponds regularly with his brother and intermittently with national political figures. Fortunately, this habit persisted after his days of holding office ended, so that Pinckney's activities can be chronicled with some fullness in his later years.

The best single collection of Pinckney family papers is in the Manuscripts Division, Library of Congress. Consisting of fourteen boxes of material, the collection contains many important letters of the Pinckneys in the 1780's and the letters between Charles Cotesworth Pinckney and Thomas Pinckney while the latter was in England. Important family business records are also included in these papers. There is no other really substantial collection of Pinckney papers; many libraries throughout the country share the remaining Pinckney materials. The better minor collections, usually miscellaneous in nature, are to be found in the South Carolina Historical Society, the South Caroliniana Library of the University of South Carolina, the Duke University Library, and the New York Public Library.

This lack of concentrated Pinckney material has meant that much research had to be done in the papers of contemporaries who were correspondents of General Pinckney or who had access to information about him. These collections are scattered from the Massachusetts Historical Society in Boston to the Henry Huntington Library in San Marino, California.

Because of the close family and business relationships between the Pinckney and Rutledge brothers, collections with substantial Rutledge materials have been most useful. The best collections of Rutledge materials are found in the Edward Rutledge and John Rutledge, Jr., Papers, Duke University Library; Rutledge Papers in the Ferdinand J. Dreer Collection, Historical Society of Pennsylvania; Edward Rutledge and Henry Middleton Rutledge Papers in the South Caroliniana Library; and the John Rutledge Papers, Southern Historical Collection, University of North Carolina.

Edited letters and papers of Pinckney's contemporaries such as Washington, John Adams, Rufus King and Thomas Jefferson have been of great assistance in reconstructing Pinckney's life, as have been the many biographies of the nation's founding fathers and other lesser but still important men such as William Plumer of New Hampshire or Dr. George Logan of Philadelphia.

Much primary material relating to Pinckney in the Revolutionary Era appears in the *South Carolina Historical Magazine*, a remarkably rewarding tool for students working in South Carolina history. Since its first issue in 1900 the *Magazine*'s editors have placed heavy emphasis upon printing documents of general interest or material relating to prominent state families. Another useful tool is the Charleston *Year Book* in which surprisingly useful miscellany has been printed over the years. The Charleston Library Society is particularly rich in South Carolina newspapers in the Revolutionary and early national periods.

There is much work yet to be done in South Carolina history in the period touched by Pinckney's life. In his recent book on colonial South Carolina, the late M. Eugene Sirmans has given students a fine political history to 1763, but there are many problems of political alliances, motivation, and institutional development still to be explained. The period of South Carolina history from 1763 to the Revolution needs to be reinterpreted and a new synthesis written. Charles G. Singer's work on South Carolina during the Confederation period is now dated, and the historian who attempts to supplant Singer must be prepared to study in detail institutional developments within the state, as Singer did not.

As one approaches the early national years of South Carolina history, the dearth of first-rate studies is striking. George C. Rogers has contributed an outstanding and suggestive work in his biography of William Loughton Smith, one from which I profited greatly, but much remains to be done in the areas of both biography and institutional analysis. John and Edward Rutledge, Thomas Pinckney, Robert Goodloe Harper, Ralph Izard, John Rutledge, Jr., Henry and Arthur Middleton, and many other prominent South Carolinians (including up-country leaders) await good biographies. There is also a genuine need for much research to be done on the development of political, legal, and social institutions within the state, in both the Revolutionary and the early national periods. An analysis of legislative roll-call votes in the 1790's, for example, would be highly useful to the political and social historians of South Carolina. The materials upon which to build these studies are rich and rather easily available, many of them being in the State Archives at Columbia and a few other important centers of South Caroliniana. When these studies have been completed, students will be better able to understand the type of society that was emerging in late eighteenth-century South Carolina and to appreciate more fully the influence of prominent personages such as Pinckney in shaping that society.

INDEX